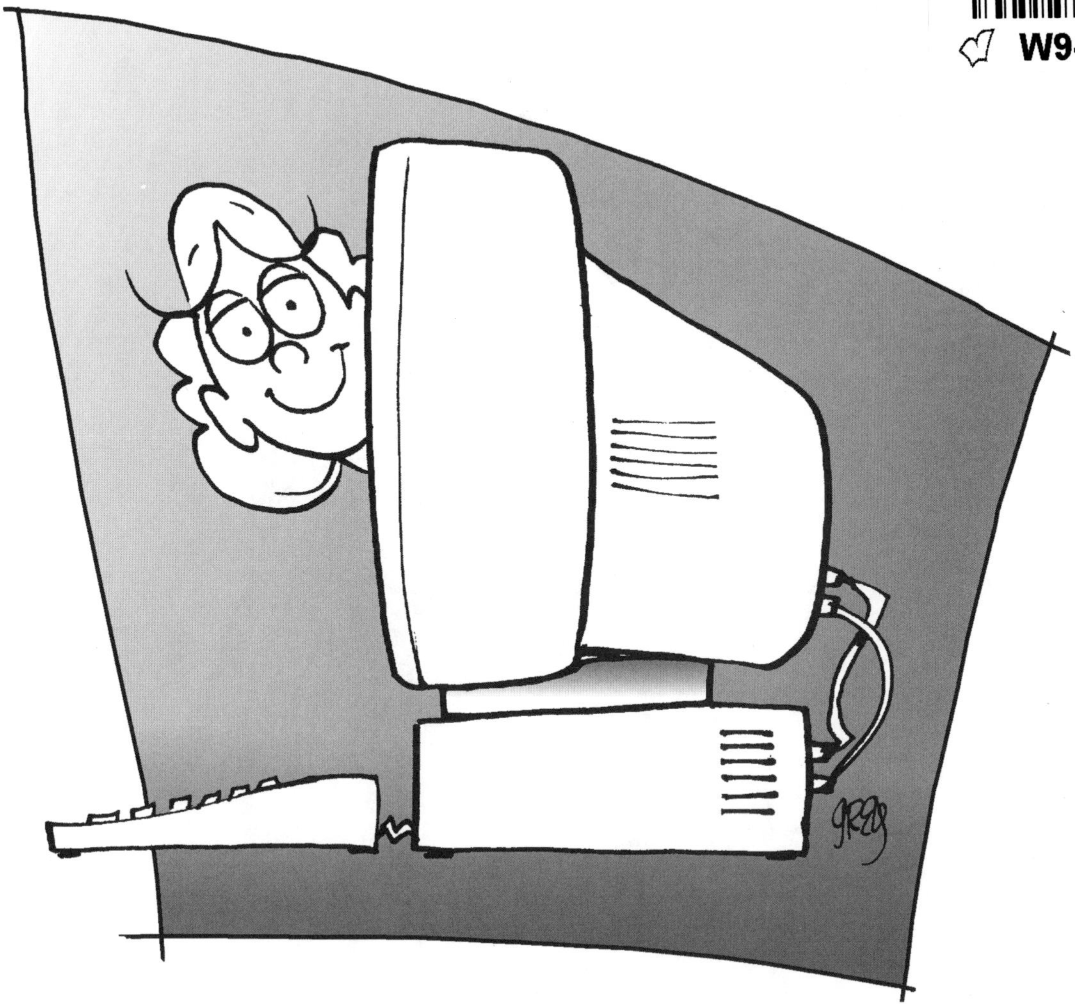
GREG

Find more cool *Luann* stuff and send e-mail to Greg Evans at: www.comiczone.com/comics/luann

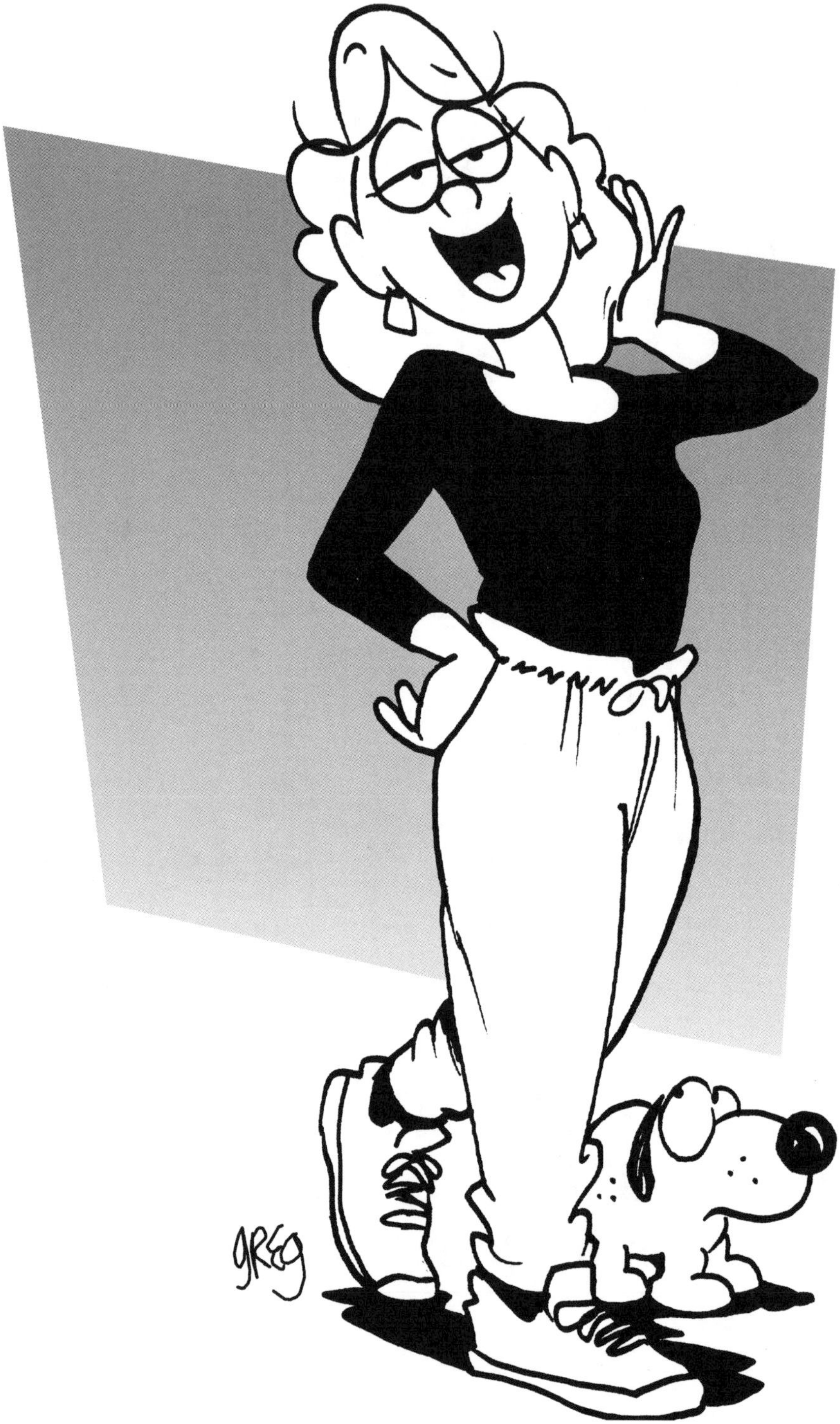
GREG

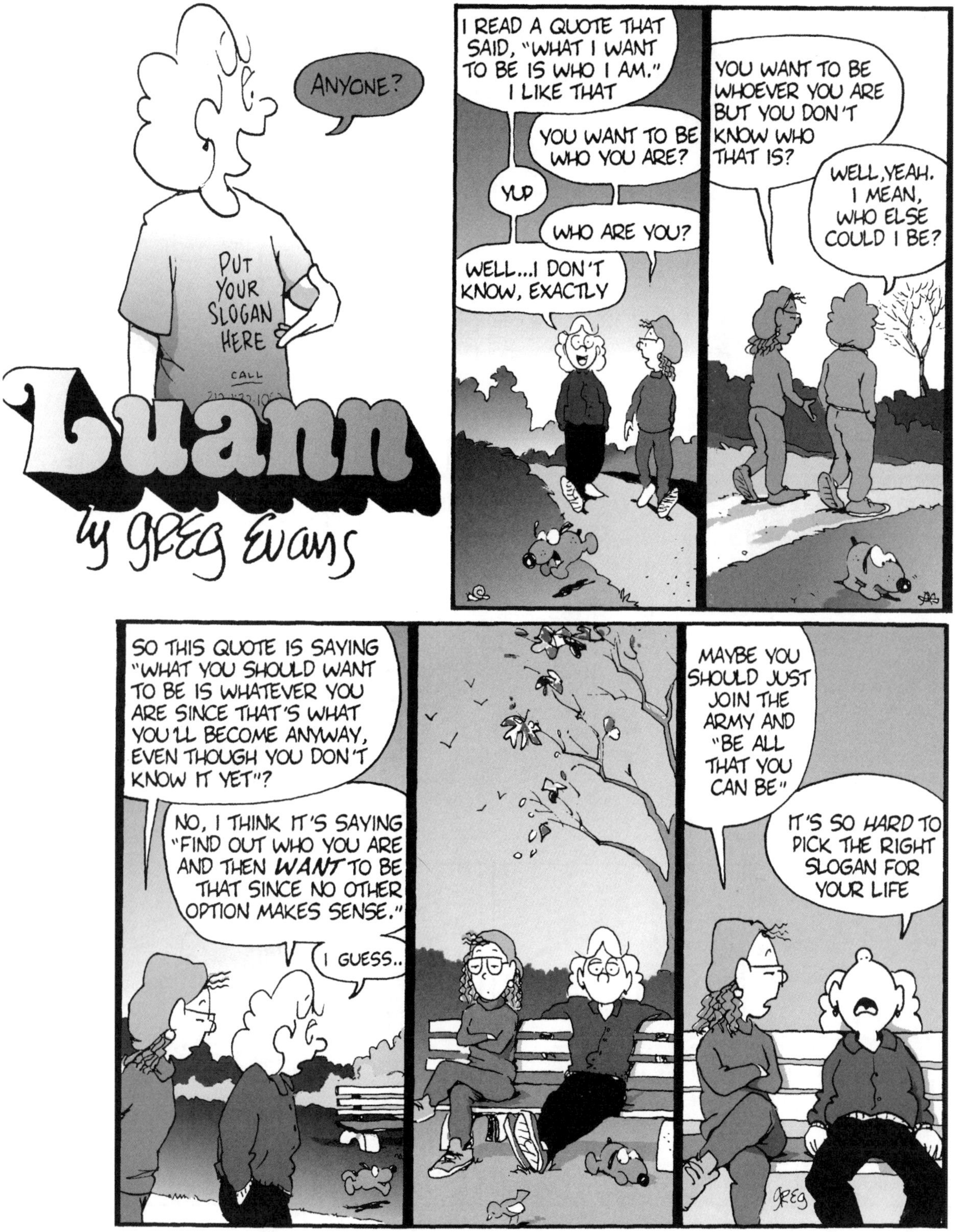
ANYONE?
PUT YOUR SLOGAN HERE
CALL
Luann
by GREG EVANS
I READ A QUOTE THAT SAID, "WHAT I WANT TO BE IS WHO I AM." I LIKE THAT
YOU WANT TO BE WHO YOU ARE?
YUP
WHO ARE YOU?
WELL...I DON'T KNOW, EXACTLY
YOU WANT TO BE WHOEVER YOU ARE BUT YOU DON'T KNOW WHO THAT IS?
WELL, YEAH. I MEAN, WHO ELSE COULD I BE?
SO THIS QUOTE IS SAYING "WHAT YOU SHOULD WANT TO BE IS WHATEVER YOU ARE SINCE THAT'S WHAT YOU'LL BECOME ANYWAY, EVEN THOUGH YOU DON'T KNOW IT YET"?
NO, I THINK IT'S SAYING "FIND OUT WHO YOU ARE AND THEN *WANT* TO BE THAT SINCE NO OTHER OPTION MAKES SENSE."
I GUESS..
MAYBE YOU SHOULD JUST JOIN THE ARMY AND "BE ALL THAT YOU CAN BE"
IT'S SO *HARD* TO PICK THE RIGHT SLOGAN FOR YOUR LIFE
GREG

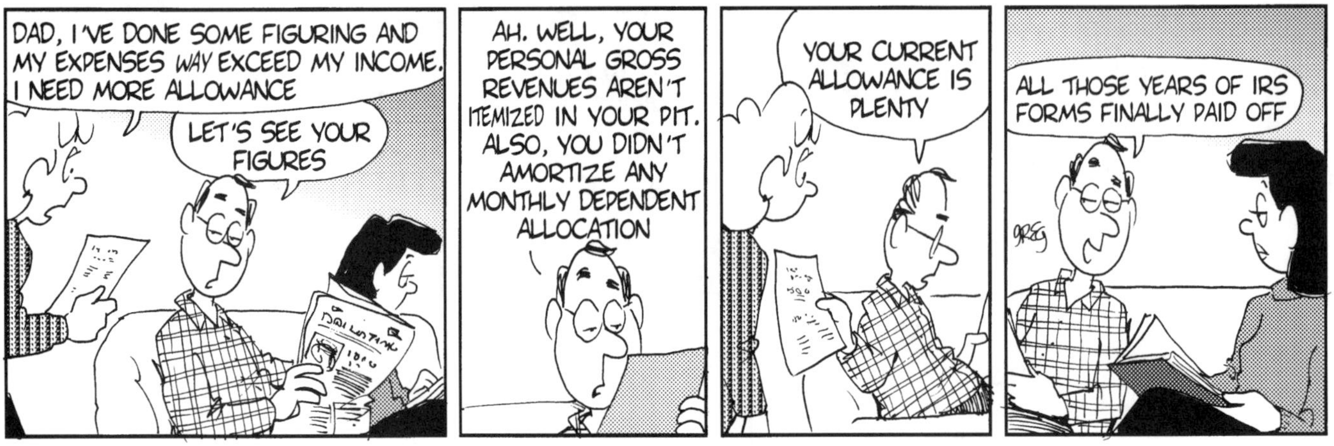
DAD, I'VE DONE SOME FIGURING AND MY EXPENSES WAY EXCEED MY INCOME. I NEED MORE ALLOWANCE
LET'S SEE YOUR FIGURES
AH. WELL, YOUR PERSONAL GROSS REVENUES AREN'T ITEMIZED IN YOUR P/T. ALSO, YOU DIDN'T AMORTIZE ANY MONTHLY DEPENDENT ALLOCATION
YOUR CURRENT ALLOWANCE IS PLENTY
GREG
ALL THOSE YEARS OF IRS FORMS FINALLY PAID OFF

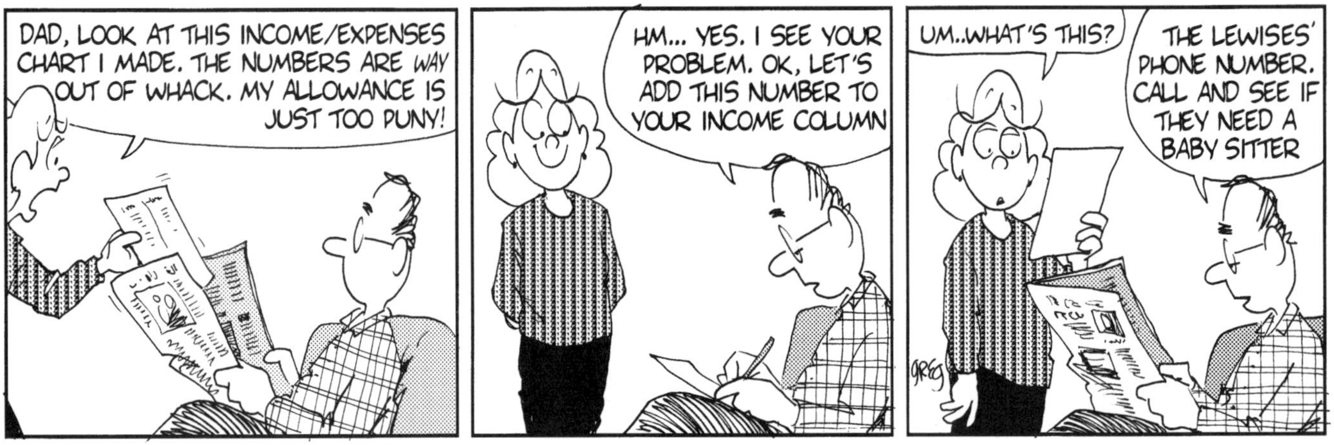
DAD, LOOK AT THIS INCOME/EXPENSES CHART I MADE. THE NUMBERS ARE WAY OUT OF WHACK. MY ALLOWANCE IS JUST TOO PUNY!
HM... YES. I SEE YOUR PROBLEM. OK, LET'S ADD THIS NUMBER TO YOUR INCOME COLUMN
UM..WHAT'S THIS?
THE LEWISES' PHONE NUMBER. CALL AND SEE IF THEY NEED A BABY SITTER
GREG

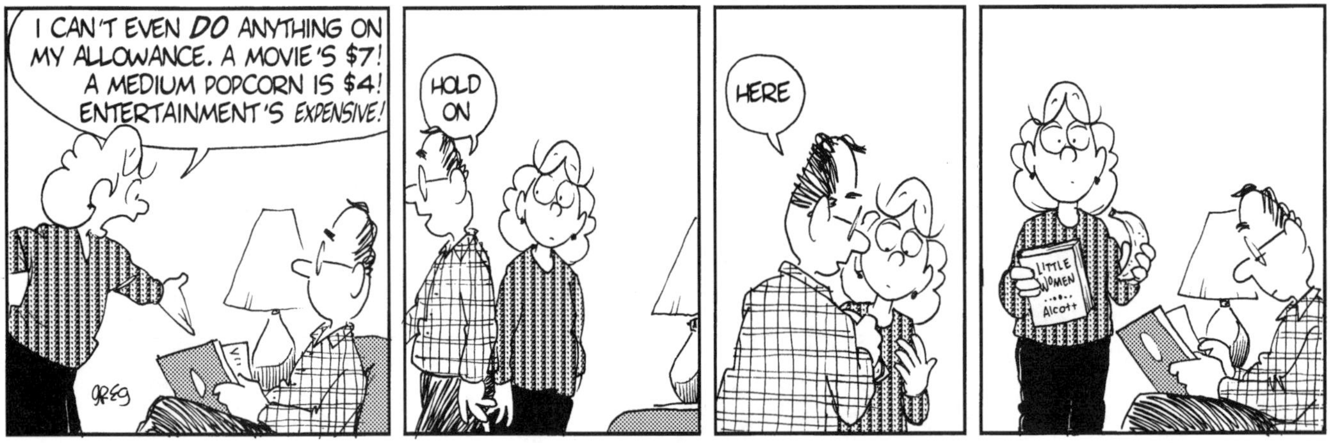
I CAN'T EVEN DO ANYTHING ON MY ALLOWANCE. A MOVIE'S $7! A MEDIUM POPCORN IS $4! ENTERTAINMENT'S EXPENSIVE!
GREG
HOLD ON
HERE
LITTLE WOMEN
Alcott

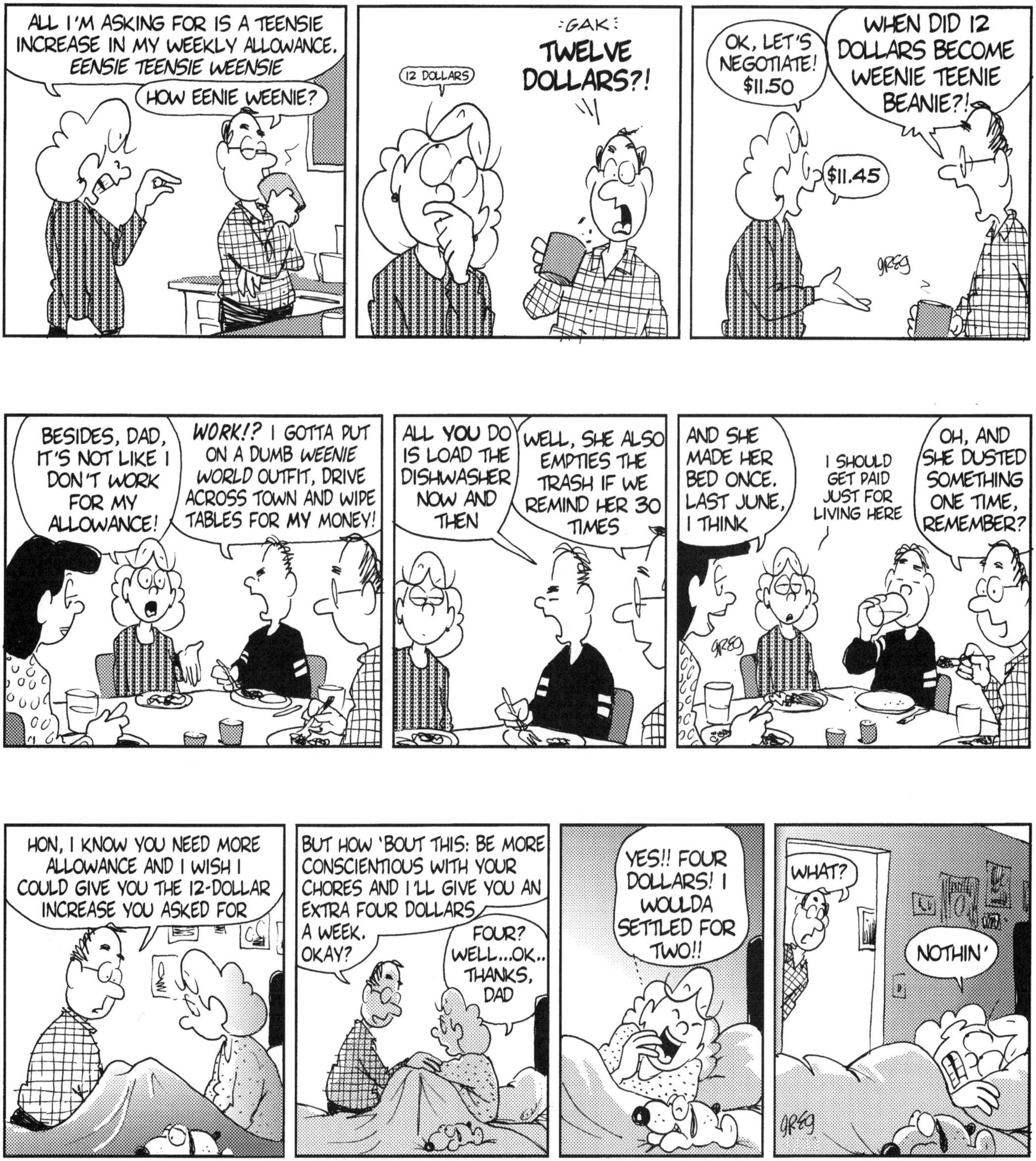
ALL I'M ASKING FOR IS A TEENSIE INCREASE IN MY WEEKLY ALLOWANCE. EENSIE TEENSIE WEENSIE
HOW EENIE WEENIE?
12 DOLLARS
:GAK:
TWELVE DOLLARS?!
OK, LET'S NEGOTIATE! $11.50
WHEN DID 12 DOLLARS BECOME WEENIE TEENIE BEANIE?!
$11.45
BESIDES, DAD, IT'S NOT LIKE I DON'T WORK FOR MY ALLOWANCE!
WORK!? I GOTTA PUT ON A DUMB WEENIE WORLD OUTFIT, DRIVE ACROSS TOWN AND WIPE TABLES FOR MY MONEY!
ALL YOU DO IS LOAD THE DISHWASHER NOW AND THEN
WELL, SHE ALSO EMPTIES THE TRASH IF WE REMIND HER 30 TIMES
AND SHE MADE HER BED ONCE. LAST JUNE, I THINK
I SHOULD GET PAID JUST FOR LIVING HERE
OH, AND SHE DUSTED SOMETHING ONE TIME, REMEMBER?
HON, I KNOW YOU NEED MORE ALLOWANCE AND I WISH I COULD GIVE YOU THE 12-DOLLAR INCREASE YOU ASKED FOR
BUT HOW 'BOUT THIS: BE MORE CONSCIENTIOUS WITH YOUR CHORES AND I'LL GIVE YOU AN EXTRA FOUR DOLLARS A WEEK. OKAY?
FOUR? WELL...OK.. THANKS, DAD
YES!! FOUR DOLLARS! I WOULDA SETTLED FOR TWO!!
WHAT?
NOTHIN'

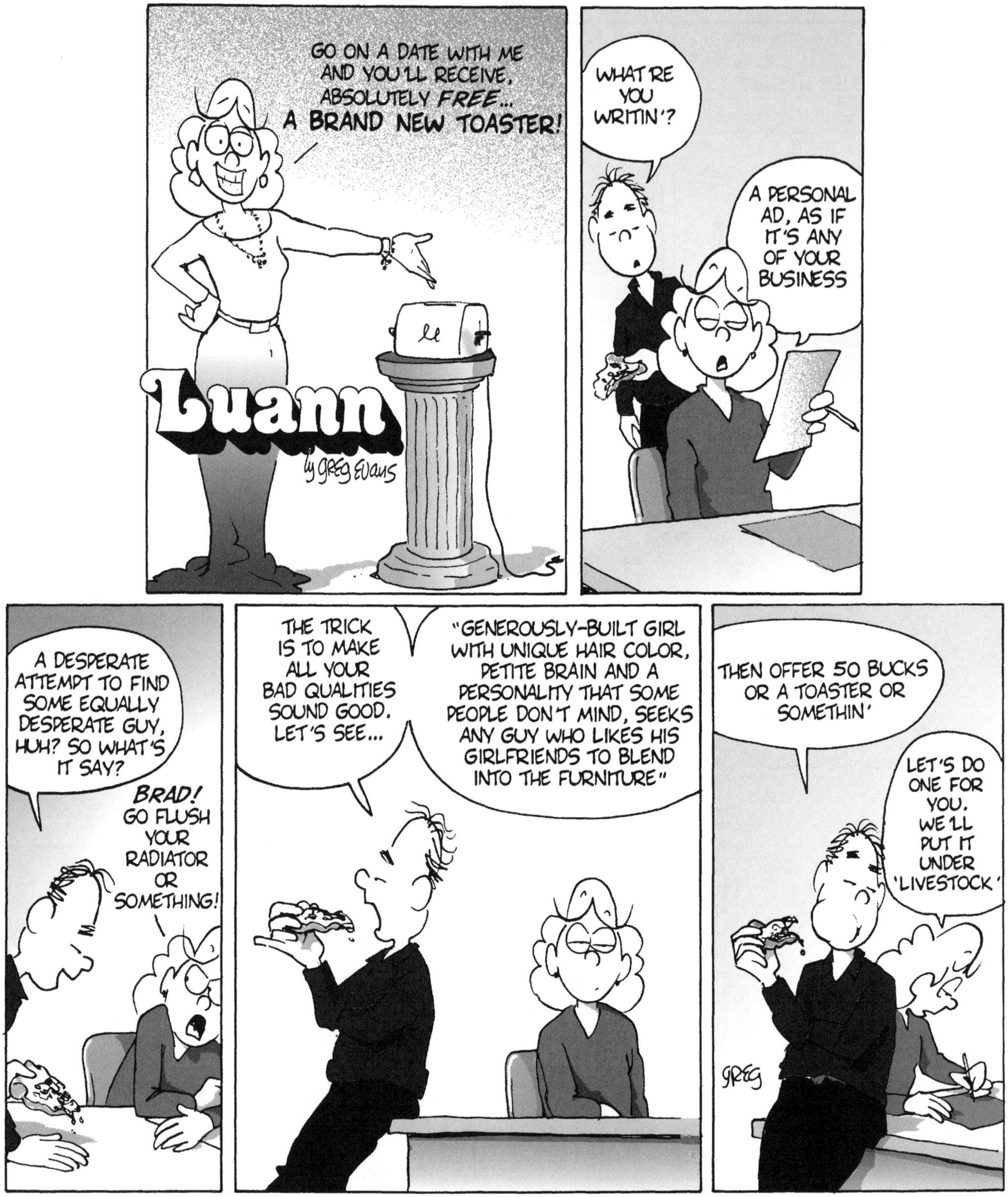
GO ON A DATE WITH ME AND YOU'LL RECEIVE, ABSOLUTELY FREE... A BRAND NEW TOASTER!
Luann
by GREG EVANS
WHAT'RE YOU WRITIN'?
A PERSONAL AD, AS IF IT'S ANY OF YOUR BUSINESS
A DESPERATE ATTEMPT TO FIND SOME EQUALLY DESPERATE GUY, HUH? SO WHAT'S IT SAY?
BRAD! GO FLUSH YOUR RADIATOR OR SOMETHING!
THE TRICK IS TO MAKE ALL YOUR BAD QUALITIES SOUND GOOD. LET'S SEE...
"GENEROUSLY-BUILT GIRL WITH UNIQUE HAIR COLOR, PETITE BRAIN AND A PERSONALITY THAT SOME PEOPLE DON'T MIND, SEEKS ANY GUY WHO LIKES HIS GIRLFRIENDS TO BLEND INTO THE FURNITURE"
THEN OFFER 50 BUCKS OR A TOASTER OR SOMETHIN'
LET'S DO ONE FOR YOU. WE'LL PUT IT UNDER 'LIVESTOCK'
GREG

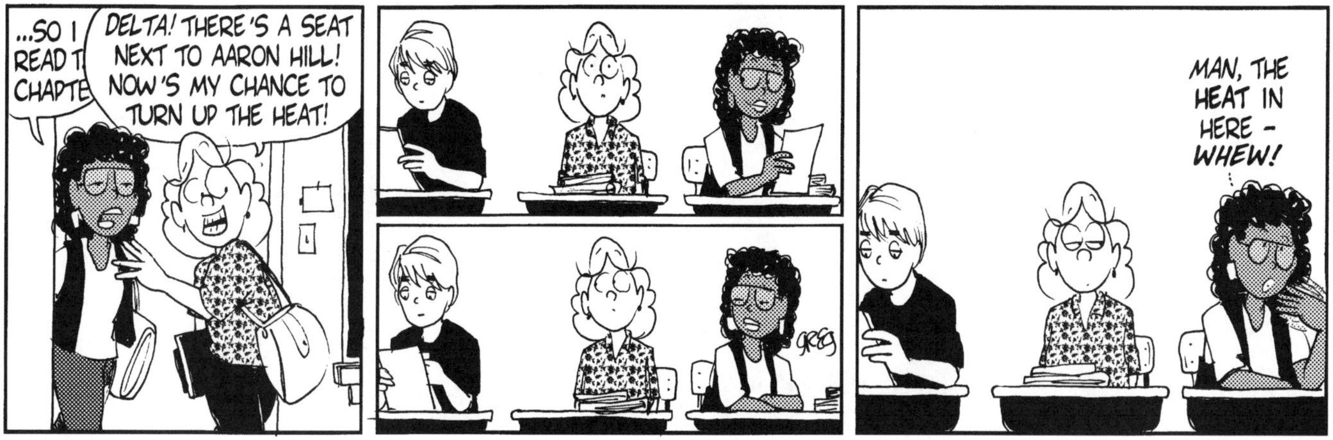
...SO I READ T CHAPTE
DELTA! THERE'S A SEAT NEXT TO AARON HILL! NOW'S MY CHANCE TO TURN UP THE HEAT!
MAN, THE HEAT IN HERE - *WHEW!*

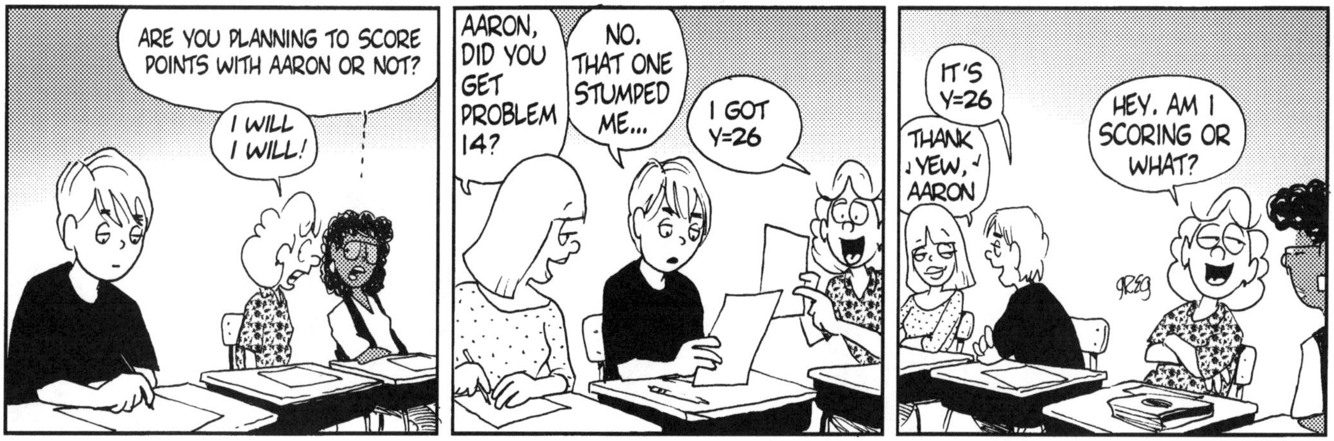
ARE YOU PLANNING TO SCORE POINTS WITH AARON OR NOT?
I WILL I WILL!
AARON, DID YOU GET PROBLEM 14?
NO. THAT ONE STUMPED ME...
I GOT Y=26
IT'S Y=26
THANK YEW, AARON
HEY. AM I SCORING OR WHAT?

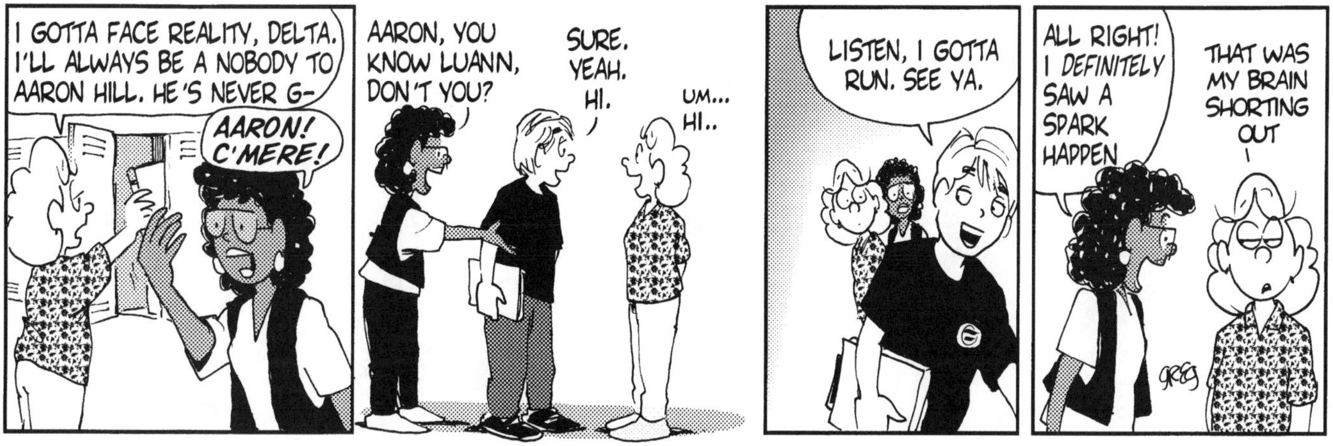
I GOTTA FACE REALITY, DELTA. I'LL ALWAYS BE A NOBODY TO AARON HILL. HE'S NEVER G-
AARON! C'MERE!
AARON, YOU KNOW LUANN, DON'T YOU?
SURE. YEAH. HI.
UM... HI..
LISTEN, I GOTTA RUN. SEE YA.
ALL RIGHT! I *DEFINITELY* SAW A SPARK HAPPEN
THAT WAS MY BRAIN SHORTING OUT

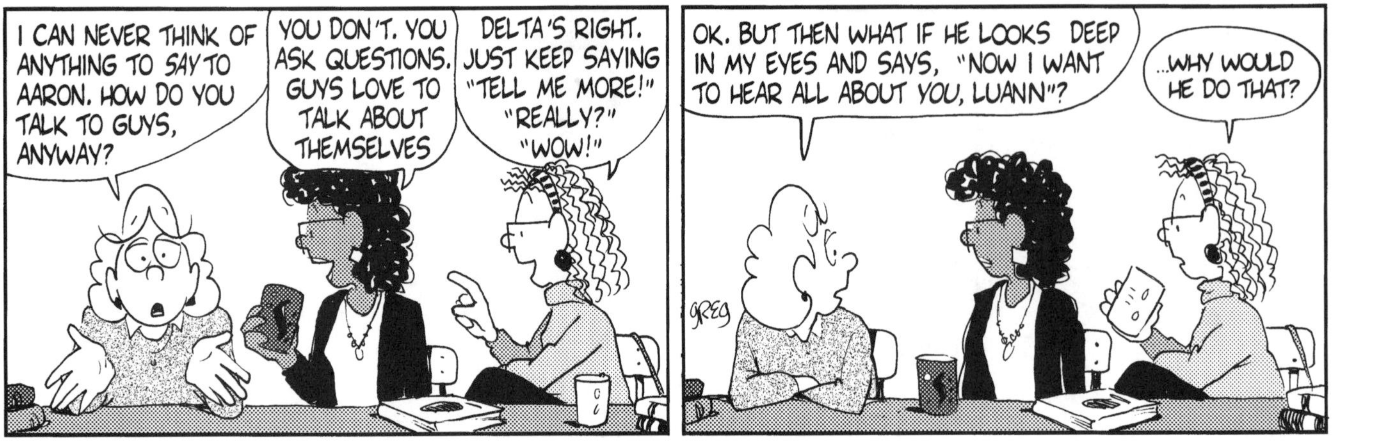
I CAN NEVER THINK OF ANYTHING TO *SAY* TO AARON. HOW DO YOU TALK TO GUYS, ANYWAY?
YOU DON'T. YOU ASK QUESTIONS. GUYS LOVE TO TALK ABOUT THEMSELVES
DELTA'S RIGHT. JUST KEEP SAYING "TELL ME MORE!" "REALLY?" "WOW!"
OK. BUT THEN WHAT IF HE LOOKS DEEP IN MY EYES AND SAYS, "NOW I WANT TO HEAR ALL ABOUT *YOU*, LUANN"?
...WHY WOULD HE DO THAT?
GREG

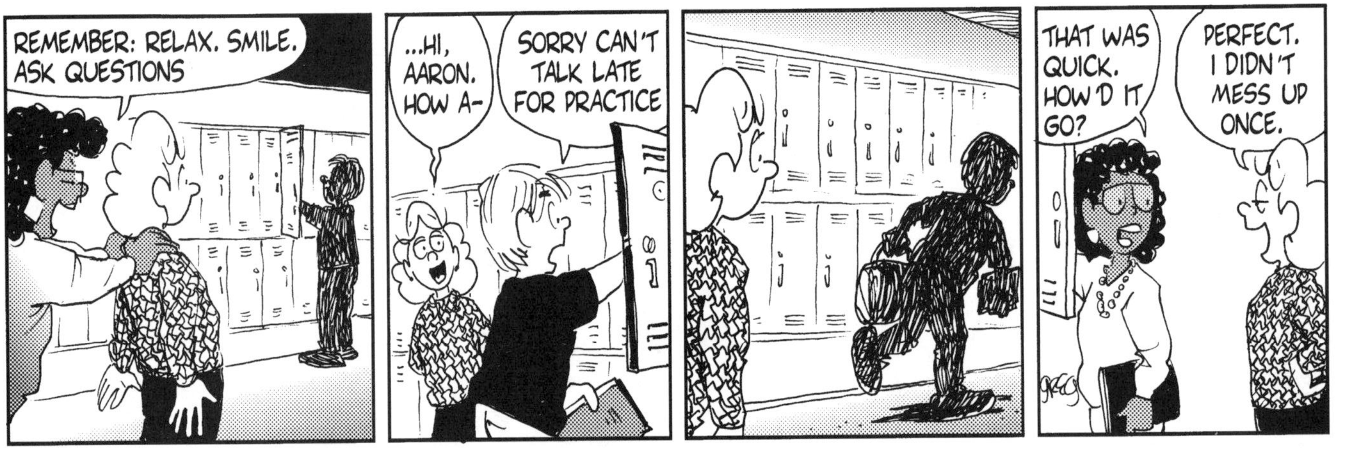
REMEMBER: RELAX. SMILE. ASK QUESTIONS
...HI, AARON. HOW A-
SORRY CAN'T TALK LATE FOR PRACTICE
THAT WAS QUICK. HOW'D IT GO?
PERFECT. I DIDN'T MESS UP ONCE.
GREG

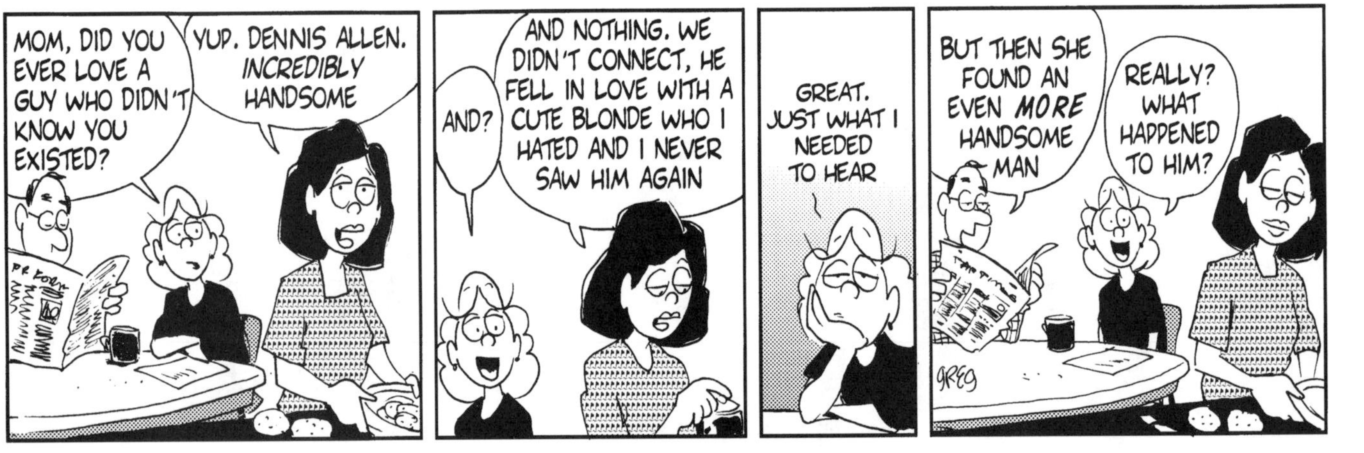
MOM, DID YOU EVER LOVE A GUY WHO DIDN'T KNOW YOU EXISTED?
YUP. DENNIS ALLEN. *INCREDIBLY* HANDSOME
AND?
AND NOTHING. WE DIDN'T CONNECT, HE FELL IN LOVE WITH A CUTE BLONDE WHO I HATED AND I NEVER SAW HIM AGAIN
GREAT. JUST WHAT I NEEDED TO HEAR
BUT THEN SHE FOUND AN EVEN *MORE* HANDSOME MAN
REALLY? WHAT HAPPENED TO HIM?
GREG

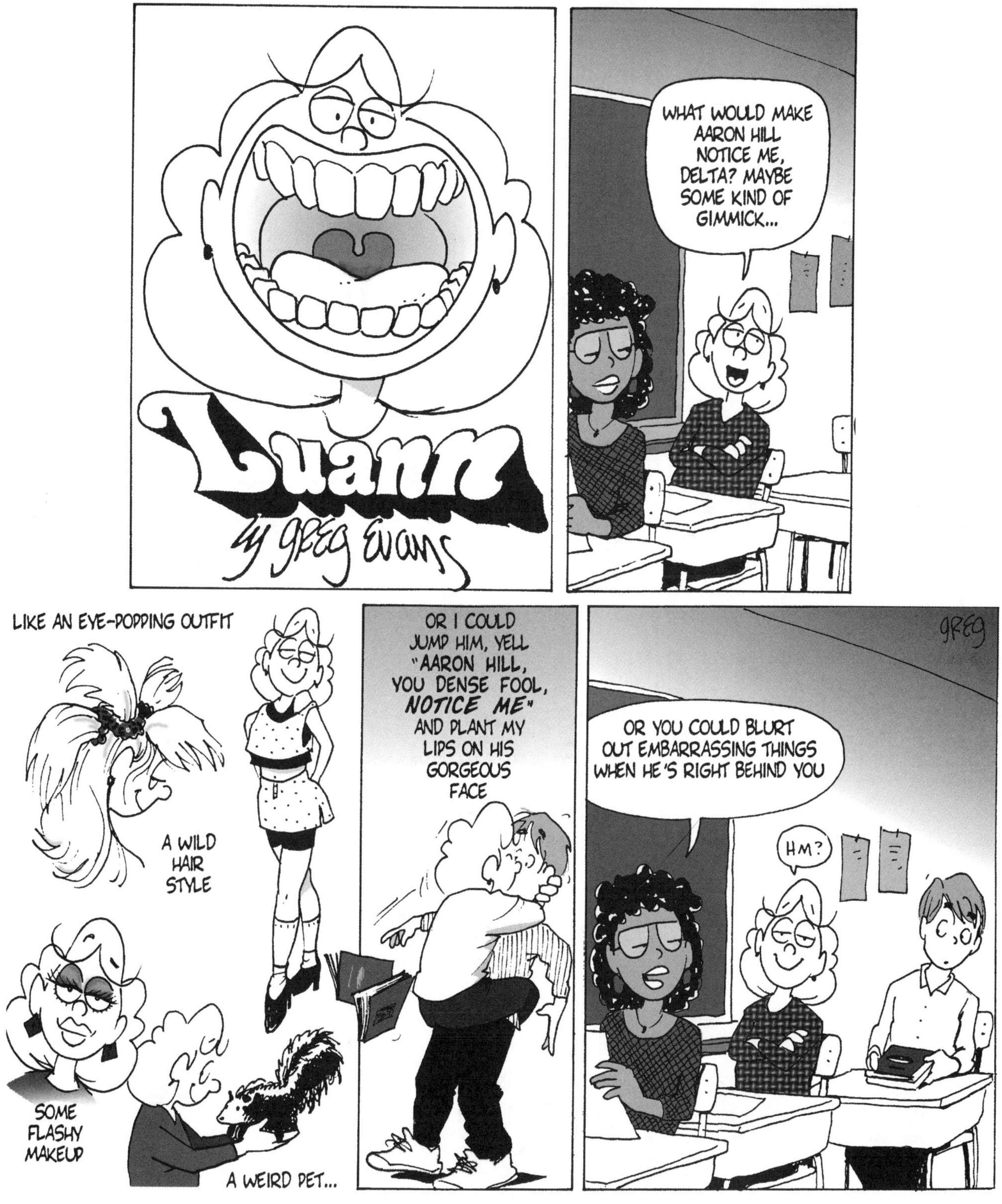
Luann
by Greg Evans
WHAT WOULD MAKE AARON HILL NOTICE ME, DELTA? MAYBE SOME KIND OF GIMMICK...
LIKE AN EYE-POPPING OUTFIT
A WILD HAIR STYLE
SOME FLASHY MAKEUP
A WEIRD PET...
OR I COULD JUMP HIM, YELL "AARON HILL, YOU DENSE FOOL, NOTICE ME" AND PLANT MY LIPS ON HIS GORGEOUS FACE
GREG
OR YOU COULD BLURT OUT EMBARRASSING THINGS WHEN HE'S RIGHT BEHIND YOU
HM?

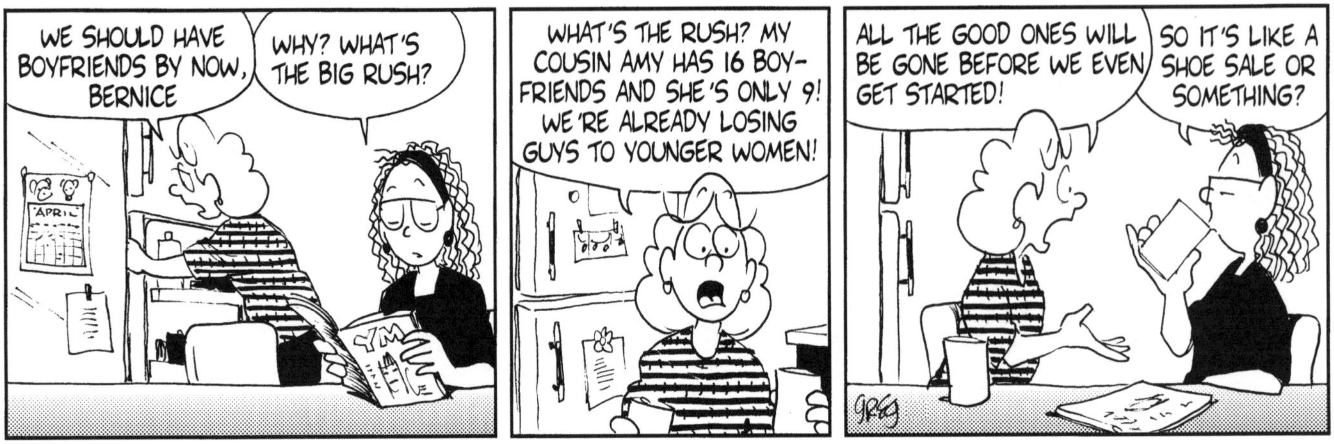
WE SHOULD HAVE BOYFRIENDS BY NOW, BERNICE
WHY? WHAT'S THE BIG RUSH?
YM
WHAT'S THE RUSH? MY COUSIN AMY HAS 16 BOY-FRIENDS AND SHE'S ONLY 9! WE'RE ALREADY LOSING GUYS TO YOUNGER WOMEN!
ALL THE GOOD ONES WILL BE GONE BEFORE WE EVEN GET STARTED!
SO IT'S LIKE A SHOE SALE OR SOMETHING?

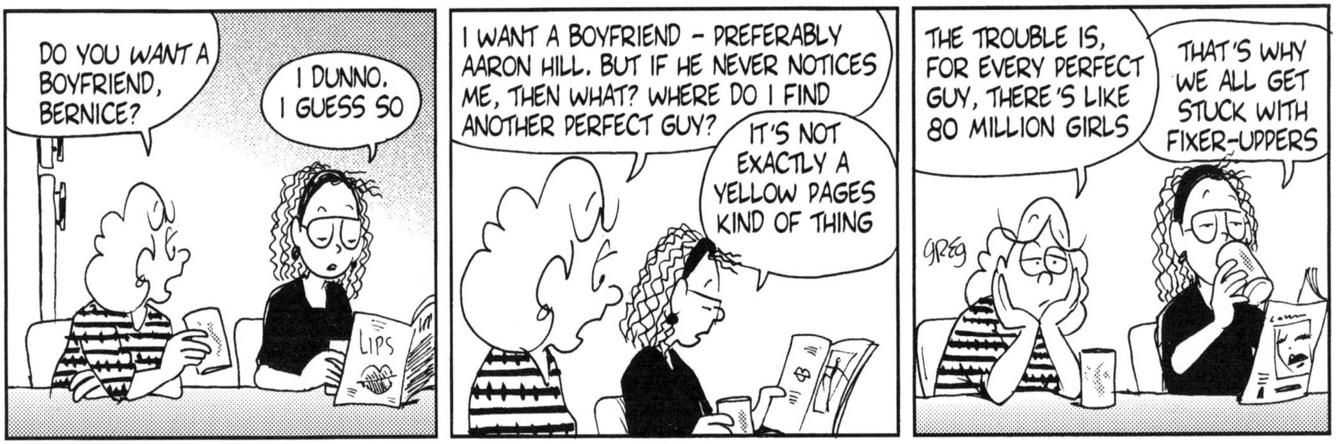
DO YOU *WANT* A BOYFRIEND, BERNICE?
I DUNNO. I GUESS SO
LIPS
I WANT A BOYFRIEND – PREFERABLY AARON HILL. BUT IF HE NEVER NOTICES ME, THEN WHAT? WHERE DO I FIND ANOTHER PERFECT GUY?
IT'S NOT EXACTLY A YELLOW PAGES KIND OF THING
THE TROUBLE IS, FOR EVERY PERFECT GUY, THERE'S LIKE 80 MILLION GIRLS
THAT'S WHY WE ALL GET STUCK WITH FIXER-UPPERS

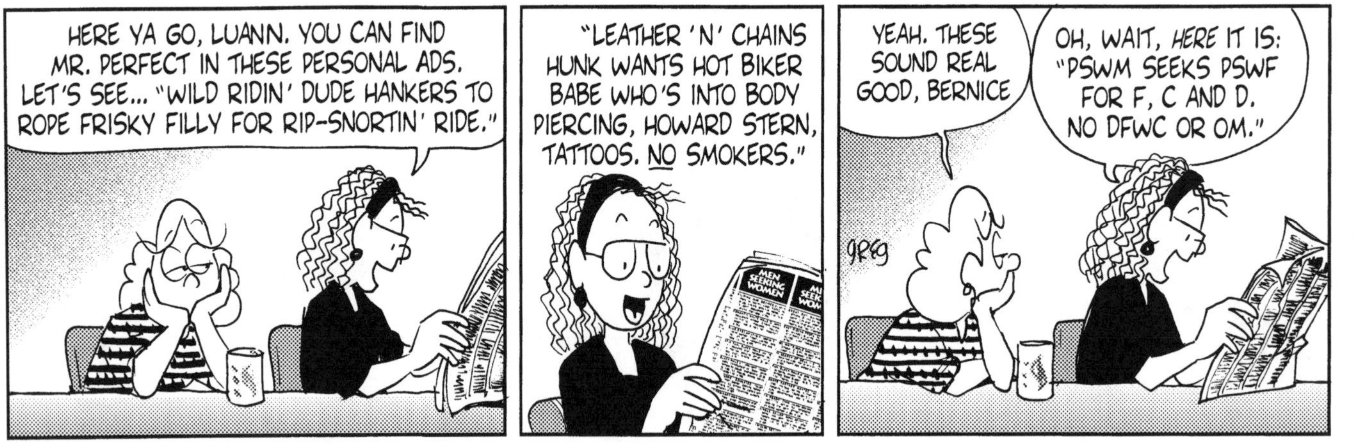
HERE YA GO, LUANN. YOU CAN FIND MR. PERFECT IN THESE PERSONAL ADS. LET'S SEE... "WILD RIDIN' DUDE HANKERS TO ROPE FRISKY FILLY FOR RIP-SNORTIN' RIDE."
"LEATHER 'N' CHAINS HUNK WANTS HOT BIKER BABE WHO'S INTO BODY PIERCING, HOWARD STERN, TATTOOS. NO SMOKERS."
MEN SEEKING WOMEN
YEAH. THESE SOUND REAL GOOD, BERNICE
OH, WAIT, *HERE* IT IS: "PSWM SEEKS PSWF FOR F, C AND D. NO DFWC OR OM."

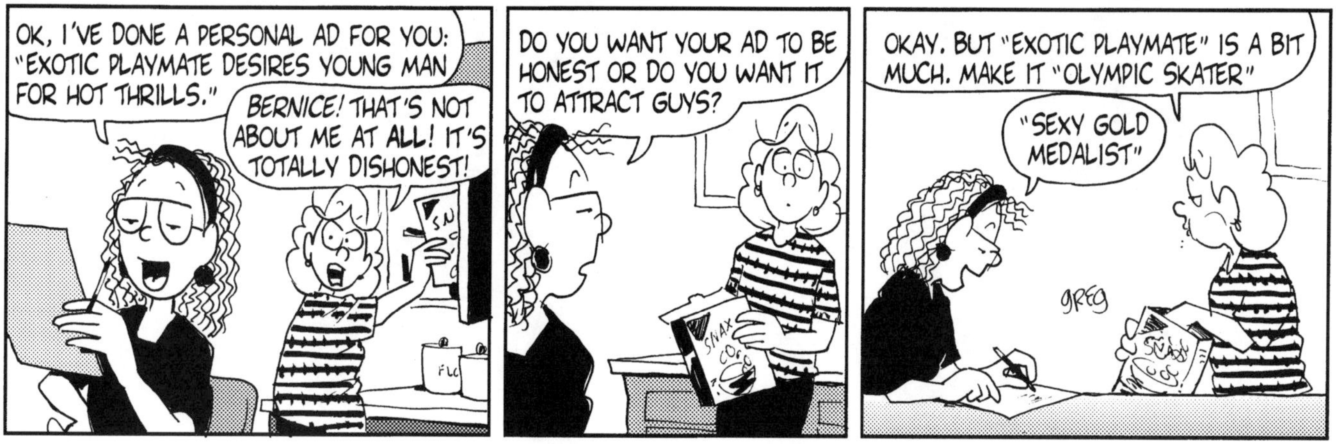
OK, I'VE DONE A PERSONAL AD FOR YOU: "EXOTIC PLAYMATE DESIRES YOUNG MAN FOR HOT THRILLS."
BERNICE! THAT'S NOT ABOUT ME AT ALL! IT'S TOTALLY DISHONEST!
DO YOU WANT YOUR AD TO BE HONEST OR DO YOU WANT IT TO ATTRACT GUYS?
OKAY. BUT "EXOTIC PLAYMATE" IS A BIT MUCH. MAKE IT "OLYMPIC SKATER"
"SEXY GOLD MEDALIST"
GREG

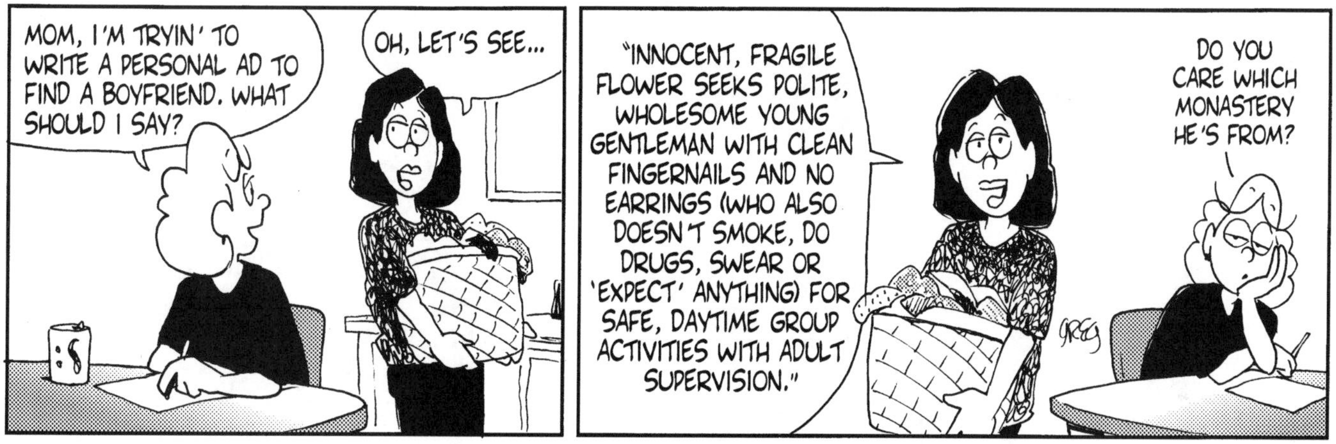
MOM, I'M TRYIN' TO WRITE A PERSONAL AD TO FIND A BOYFRIEND. WHAT SHOULD I SAY?
OH, LET'S SEE...
"INNOCENT, FRAGILE FLOWER SEEKS POLITE, WHOLESOME YOUNG GENTLEMAN WITH CLEAN FINGERNAILS AND NO EARRINGS (WHO ALSO DOESN'T SMOKE, DO DRUGS, SWEAR OR 'EXPECT' ANYTHING) FOR SAFE, DAYTIME GROUP ACTIVITIES WITH ADULT SUPERVISION."
DO YOU CARE WHICH MONASTERY HE'S FROM?
GREG

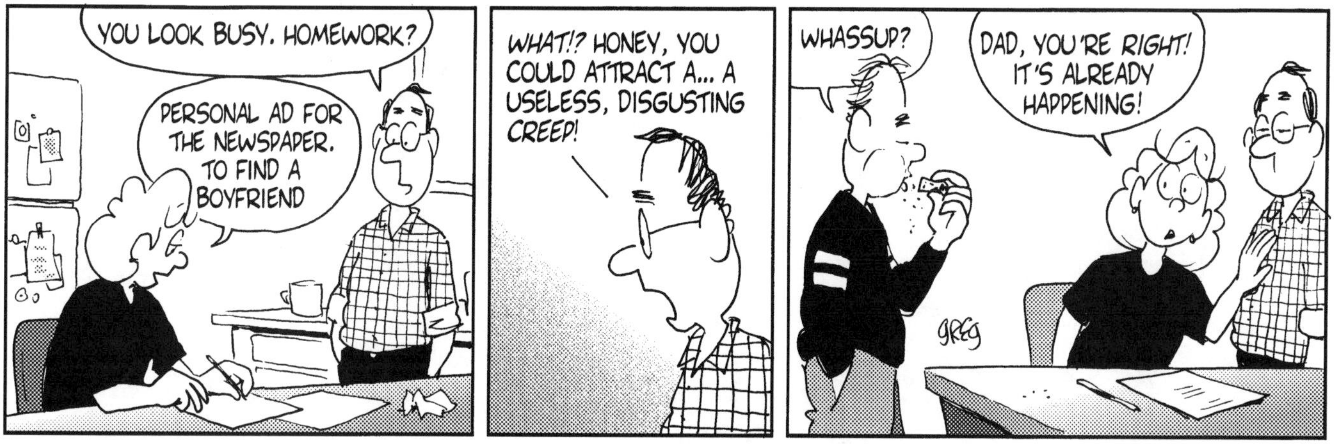
YOU LOOK BUSY. HOMEWORK?
PERSONAL AD FOR THE NEWSPAPER. TO FIND A BOYFRIEND
WHAT!? HONEY, YOU COULD ATTRACT A... A USELESS, DISGUSTING CREEP!
WHASSUP?
DAD, YOU'RE RIGHT! IT'S ALREADY HAPPENING!
GREG

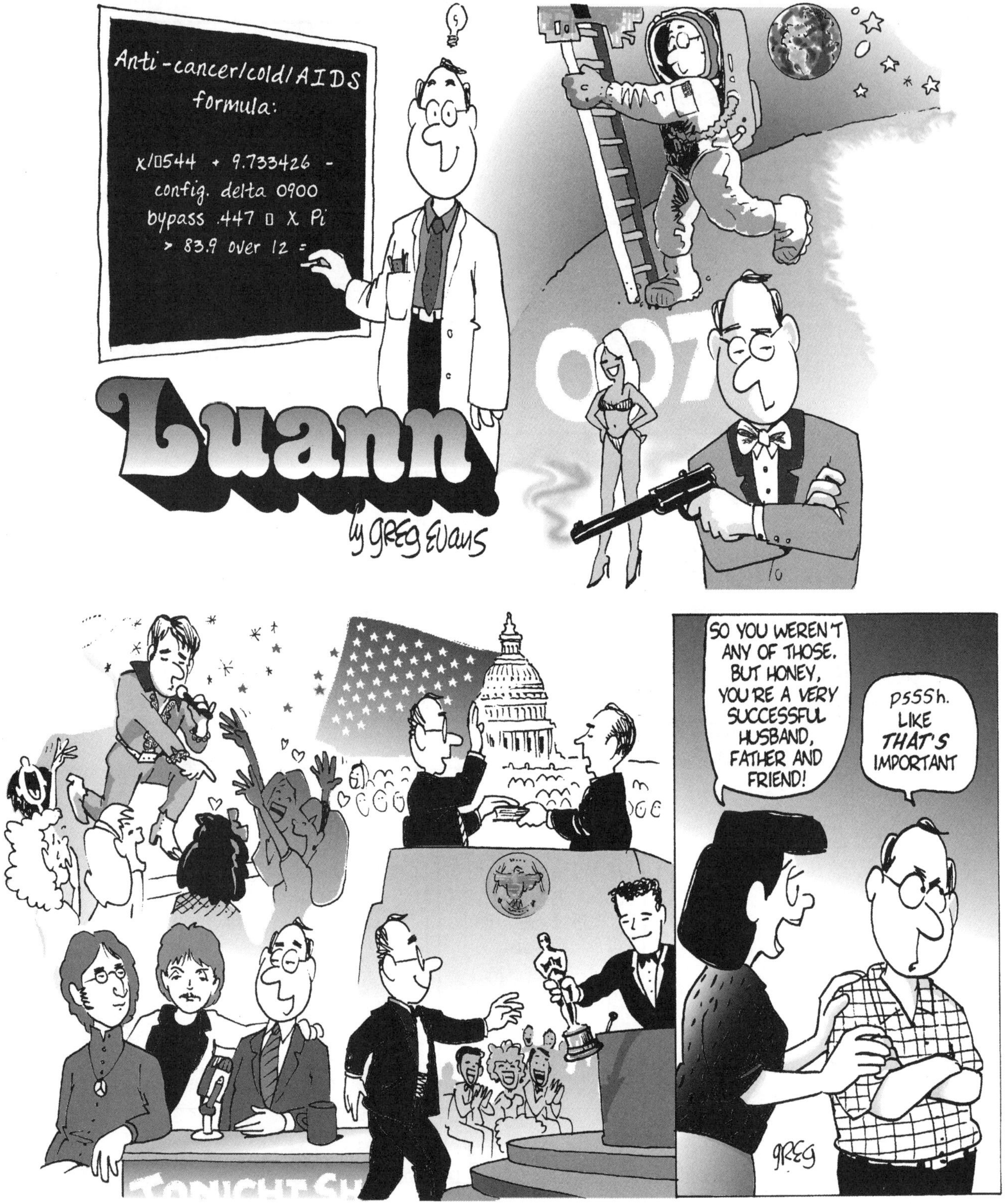
Anti-cancer/cold/AIDS formula:
x/▯544 + 9.733426 - config. delta 0900 bypass .447 ▯ X Pi > 83.9 over 12 =
007
Luann
by GREG EVANS
SO YOU WEREN'T ANY OF THOSE. BUT HONEY, YOU'RE A VERY SUCCESSFUL HUSBAND, FATHER AND FRIEND!
pssSh. LIKE THAT'S IMPORTANT
GREG

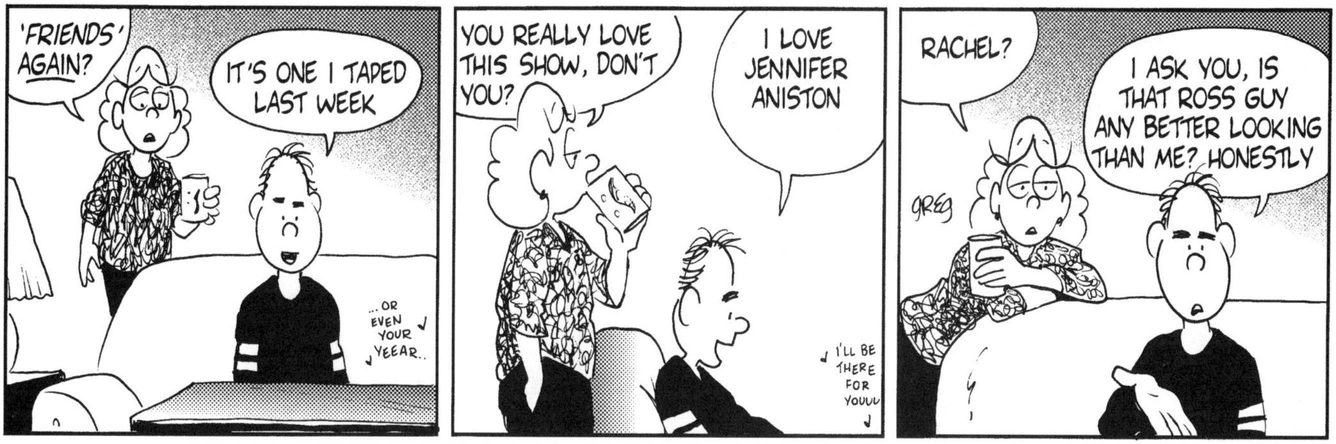
'FRIENDS' AGAIN?
IT'S ONE I TAPED LAST WEEK
...OR EVEN YOUR YEEAR..
YOU REALLY LOVE THIS SHOW, DON'T YOU?
I LOVE JENNIFER ANISTON
I'LL BE THERE FOR YOUUU
RACHEL?
I ASK YOU, IS THAT ROSS GUY ANY BETTER LOOKING THAN ME? HONESTLY
GREG

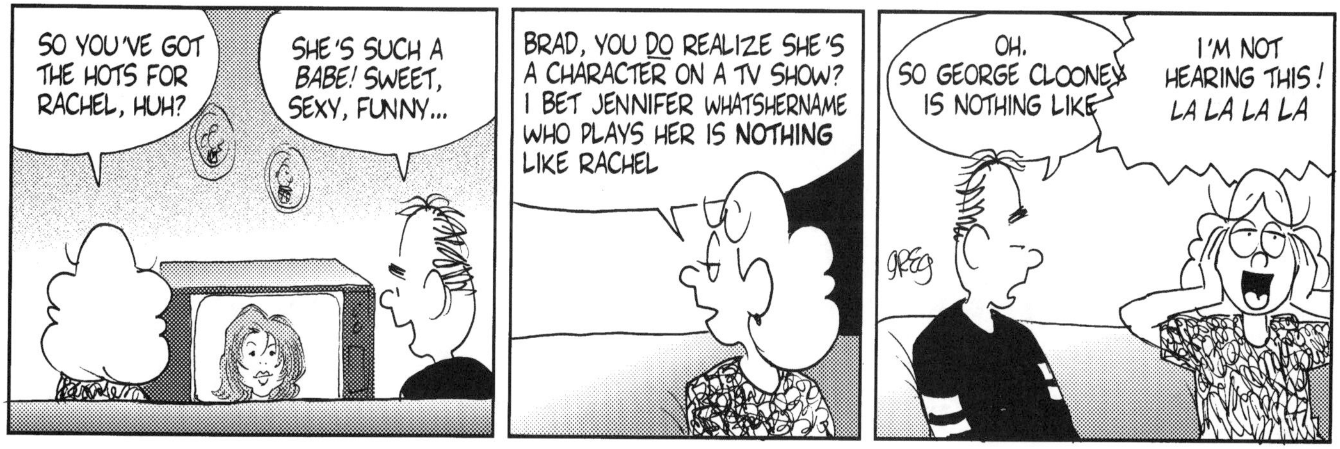
SO YOU'VE GOT THE HOTS FOR RACHEL, HUH?
SHE'S SUCH A BABE! SWEET, SEXY, FUNNY...
BRAD, YOU DO REALIZE SHE'S A CHARACTER ON A TV SHOW? I BET JENNIFER WHATSHERNAME WHO PLAYS HER IS NOTHING LIKE RACHEL
OH. SO GEORGE CLOONEY IS NOTHING LIKE
I'M NOT HEARING THIS! LA LA LA LA
GREG

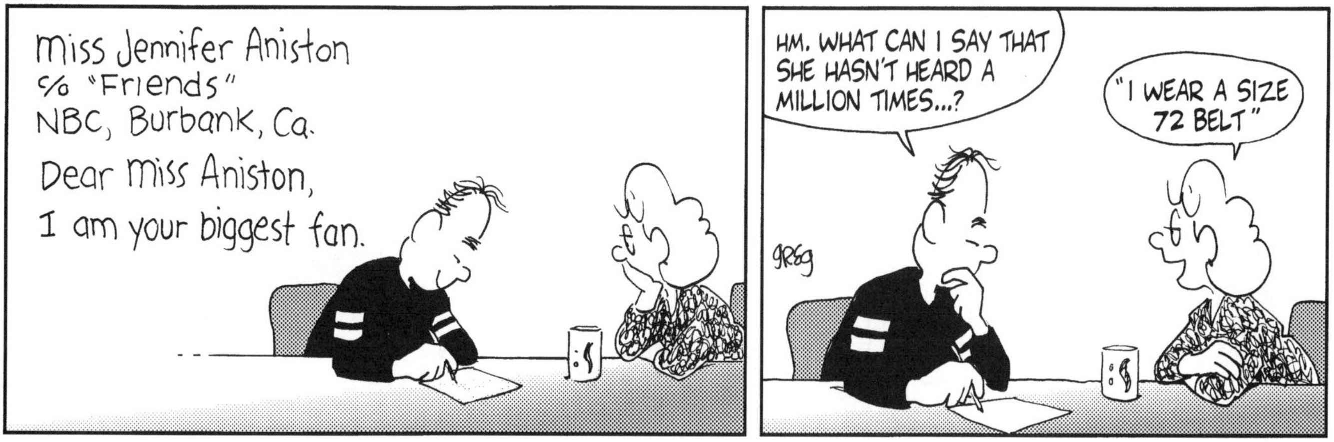
Miss Jennifer Aniston
c/o "Friends"
NBC, Burbank, Ca.
Dear Miss Aniston,
I am your biggest fan.
HM. WHAT CAN I SAY THAT SHE HASN'T HEARD A MILLION TIMES...?
"I WEAR A SIZE 72 BELT"
GREG

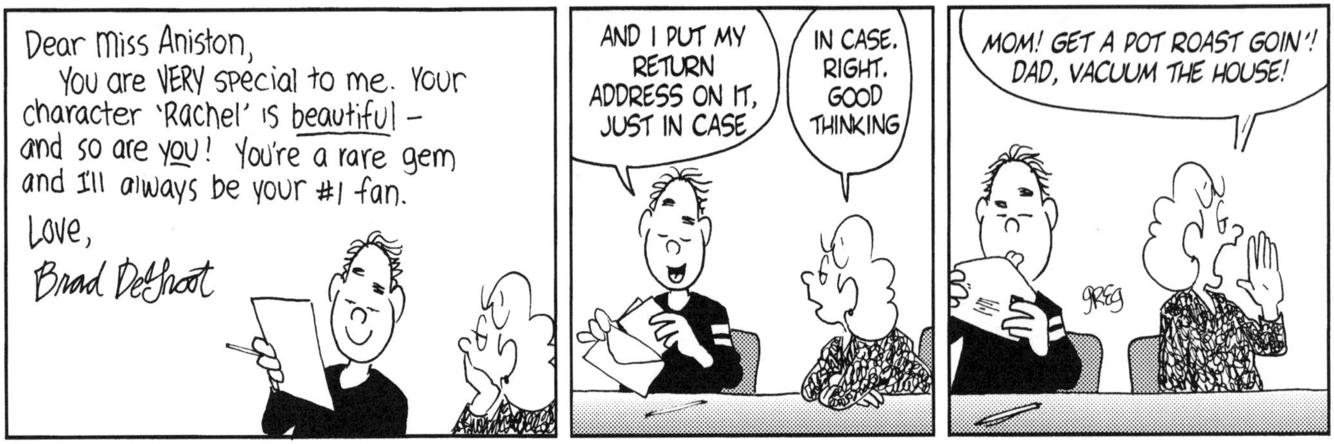
Dear Miss Aniston,
You are VERY special to me. Your character 'Rachel' is beautiful – and so are YOU! You're a rare gem and I'll always be your #1 fan.
Love,
Brad DeGroot
AND I PUT MY RETURN ADDRESS ON IT, JUST IN CASE
IN CASE. RIGHT. GOOD THINKING
MOM! GET A POT ROAST GOIN'! DAD, VACUUM THE HOUSE!
GREG

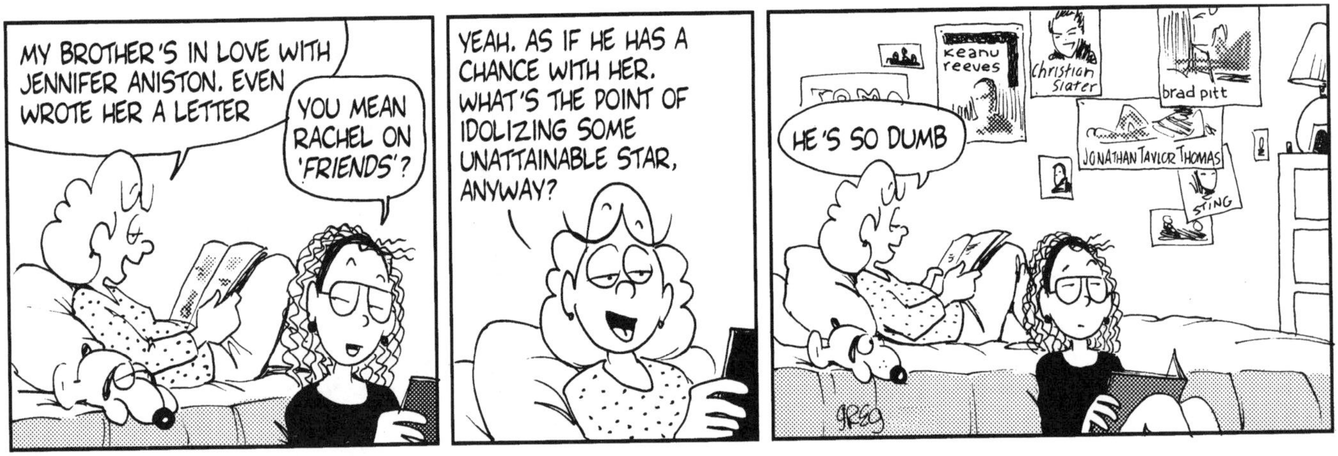
MY BROTHER'S IN LOVE WITH JENNIFER ANISTON. EVEN WROTE HER A LETTER
YOU MEAN RACHEL ON 'FRIENDS'?
YEAH. AS IF HE HAS A CHANCE WITH HER. WHAT'S THE POINT OF IDOLIZING SOME UNATTAINABLE STAR, ANYWAY?
HE'S SO DUMB
Keanu reeves
Christian Slater
brad pitt
JONATHAN TAYLOR THOMAS
STING
GREG

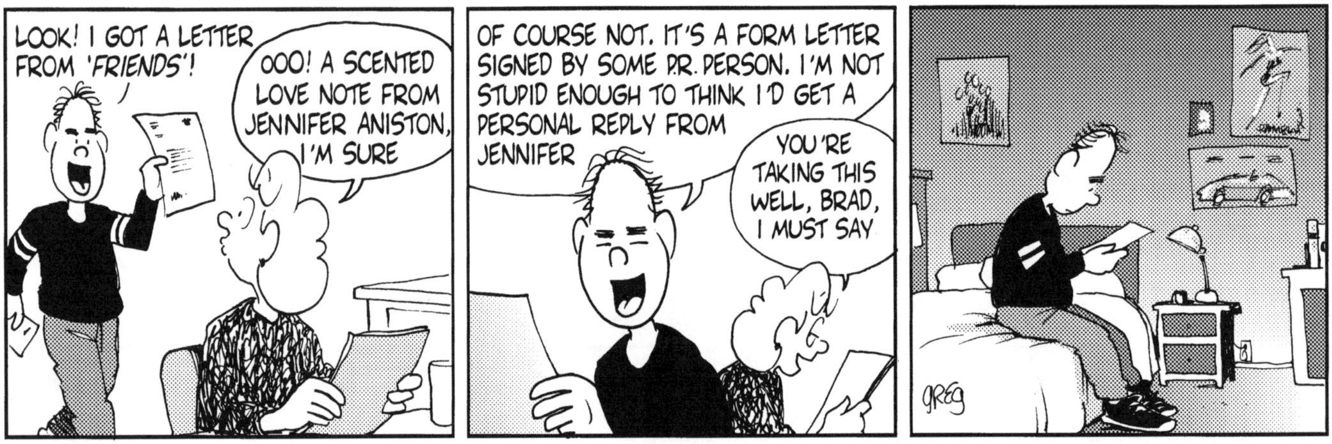
LOOK! I GOT A LETTER FROM 'FRIENDS'!
OOO! A SCENTED LOVE NOTE FROM JENNIFER ANISTON, I'M SURE
OF COURSE NOT. IT'S A FORM LETTER SIGNED BY SOME P.R. PERSON. I'M NOT STUPID ENOUGH TO THINK I'D GET A PERSONAL REPLY FROM JENNIFER
YOU'RE TAKING THIS WELL, BRAD, I MUST SAY
GREG

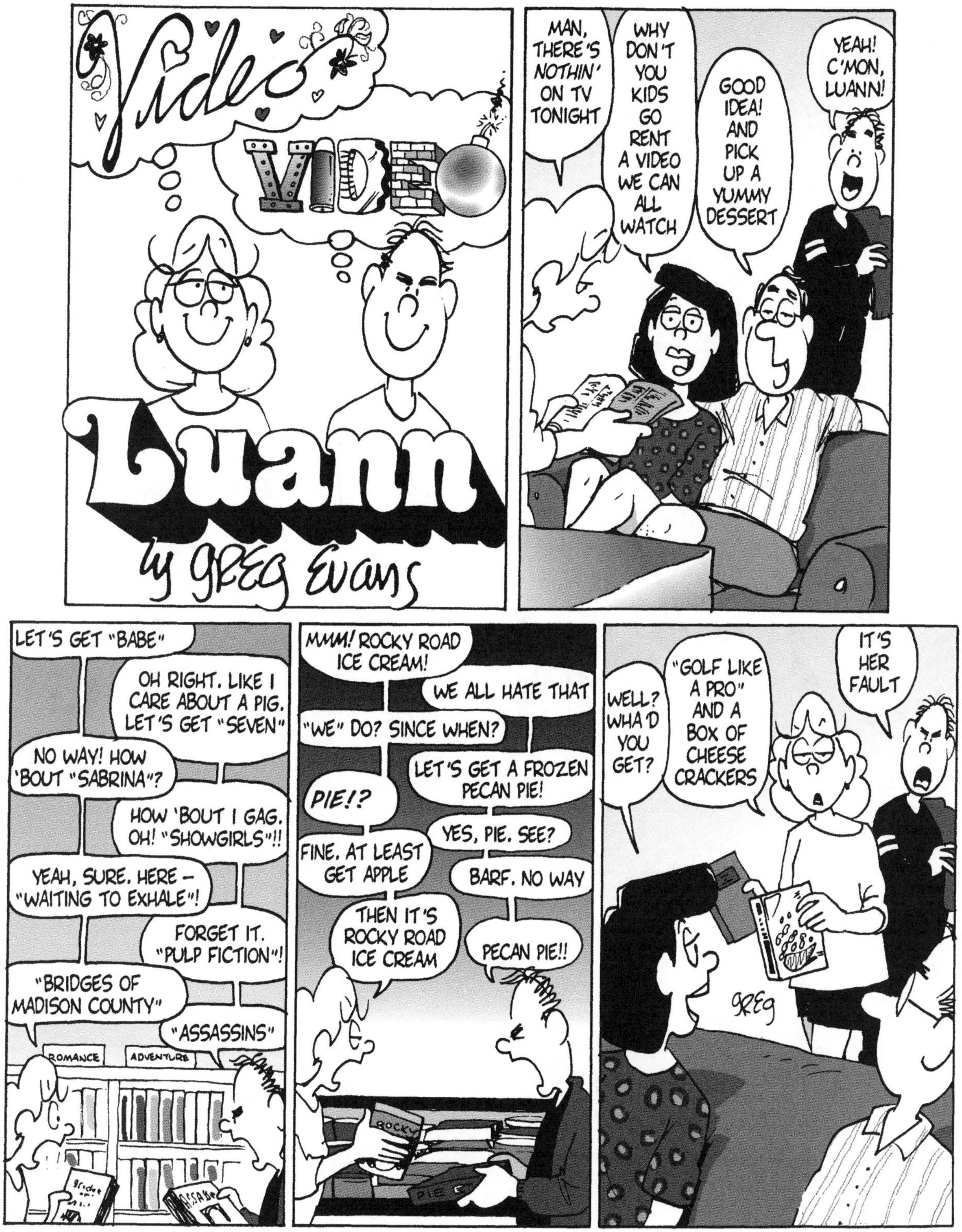
Video
VIDEO
Luann
by GREG Evans
MAN, THERE'S NOTHIN' ON TV TONIGHT
WHY DON'T YOU KIDS GO RENT A VIDEO WE CAN ALL WATCH
GOOD IDEA! AND PICK UP A YUMMY DESSERT
YEAH! C'MON, LUANN!
LET'S GET "BABE"
OH RIGHT. LIKE I CARE ABOUT A PIG. LET'S GET "SEVEN"
NO WAY! HOW 'BOUT "SABRINA"?
HOW 'BOUT I GAG. OH! "SHOWGIRLS"!!
YEAH, SURE. HERE – "WAITING TO EXHALE"!
FORGET IT. "PULP FICTION"!
"BRIDGES OF MADISON COUNTY"
"ASSASSINS"
ROMANCE
ADVENTURE
MMM! ROCKY ROAD ICE CREAM!
WE ALL HATE THAT
"WE" DO? SINCE WHEN?
LET'S GET A FROZEN PECAN PIE!
PIE!?
YES, PIE. SEE?
FINE. AT LEAST GET APPLE
BARF. NO WAY
THEN IT'S ROCKY ROAD ICE CREAM
PECAN PIE!!
ROCKY
PIE
WELL? WHA'D YOU GET?
"GOLF LIKE A PRO" AND A BOX OF CHEESE CRACKERS
IT'S HER FAULT
GREG

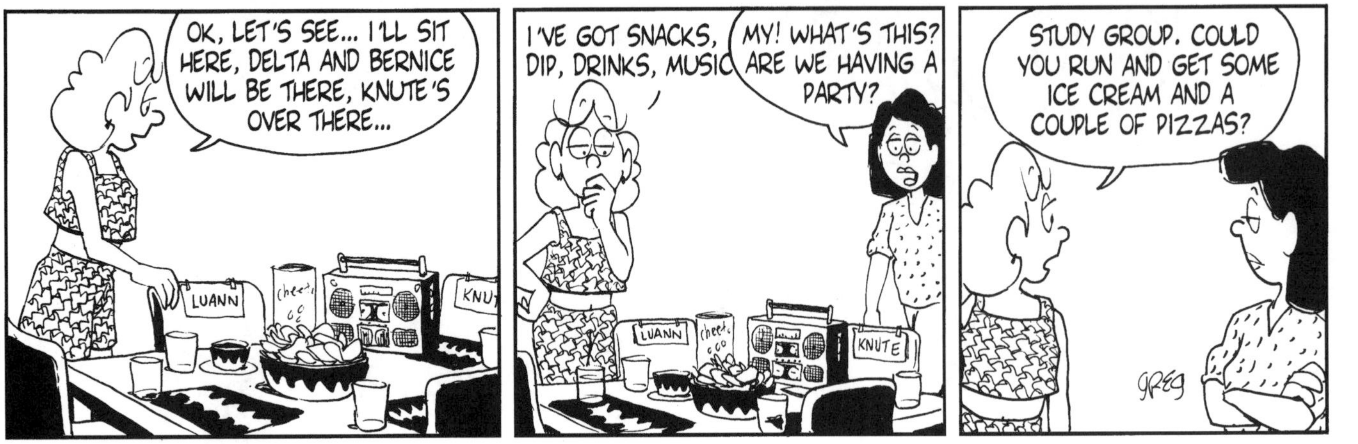
OK, LET'S SEE... I'LL SIT HERE, DELTA AND BERNICE WILL BE THERE, KNUTE'S OVER THERE...
LUANN
KNUTE
I'VE GOT SNACKS, DIP, DRINKS, MUSIC
MY! WHAT'S THIS? ARE WE HAVING A PARTY?
STUDY GROUP. COULD YOU RUN AND GET SOME ICE CREAM AND A COUPLE OF PIZZAS?
GREG

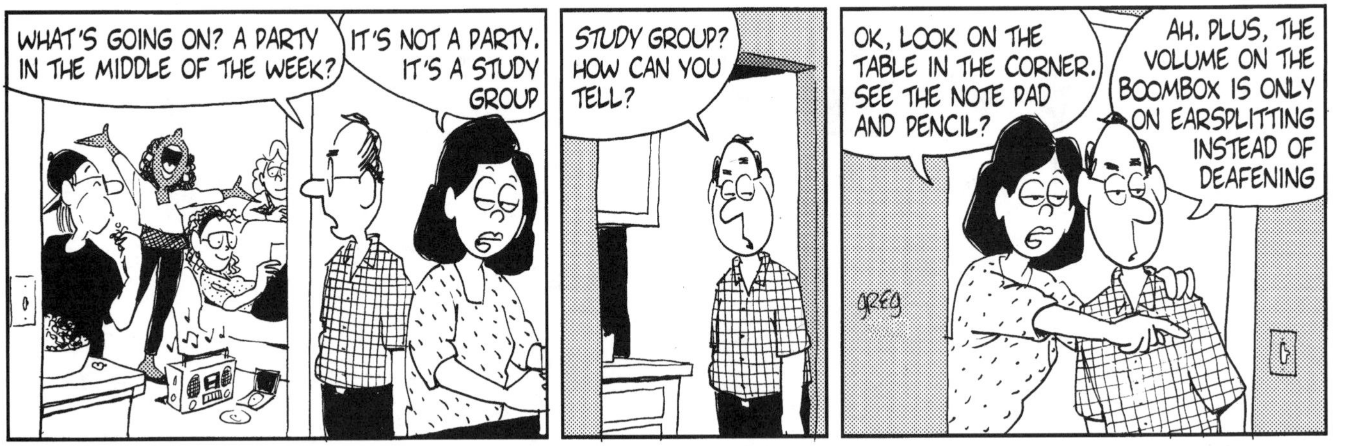
WHAT'S GOING ON? A PARTY IN THE MIDDLE OF THE WEEK?
IT'S NOT A PARTY. IT'S A STUDY GROUP
STUDY GROUP? HOW CAN YOU TELL?
OK, LOOK ON THE TABLE IN THE CORNER. SEE THE NOTE PAD AND PENCIL?
AH. PLUS, THE VOLUME ON THE BOOMBOX IS ONLY ON EARSPLITTING INSTEAD OF DEAFENING
GREG

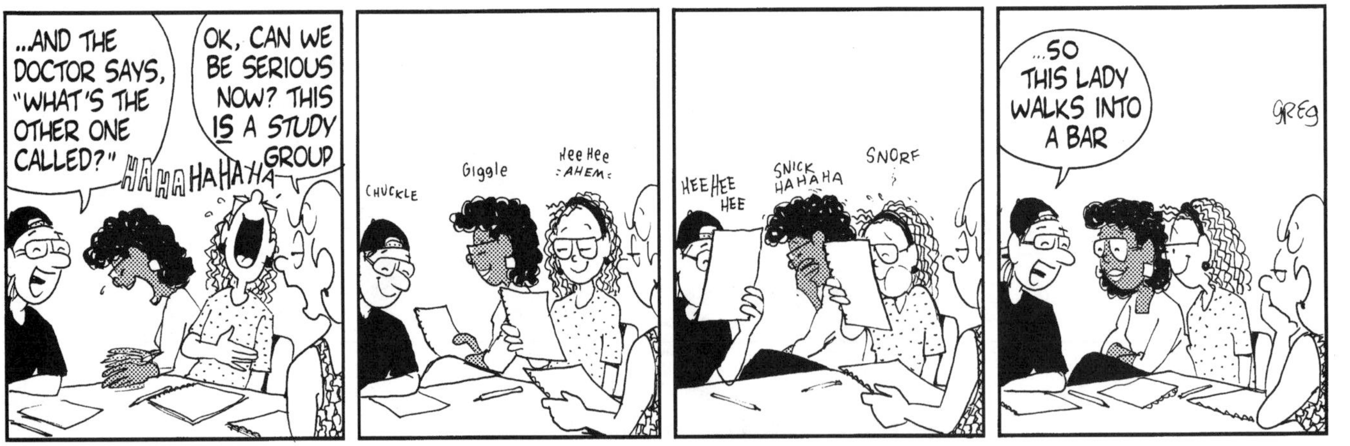
...AND THE DOCTOR SAYS, "WHAT'S THE OTHER ONE CALLED?"
HAHAHAHAHA
OK, CAN WE BE SERIOUS NOW? THIS IS A STUDY GROUP
CHUCKLE
Giggle
Hee Hee :AHEM:
HEE HEE HEE
SNICK HAHAHA
SNORF
...SO THIS LADY WALKS INTO A BAR
GREG

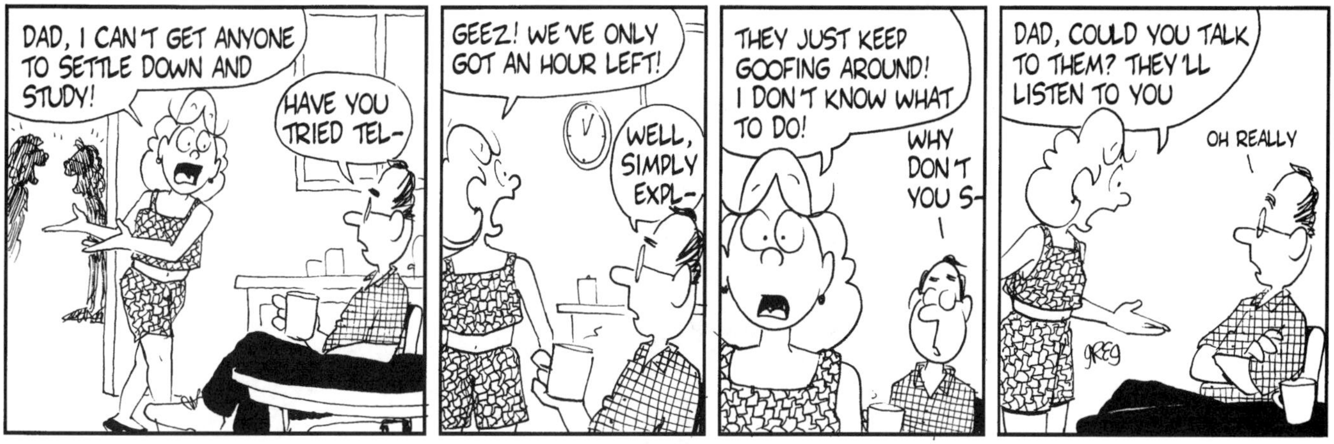
DAD, I CAN'T GET ANYONE TO SETTLE DOWN AND STUDY!
HAVE YOU TRIED TEL-
GEEZ! WE'VE ONLY GOT AN HOUR LEFT!
WELL, SIMPLY EXPL-
THEY JUST KEEP GOOFING AROUND! I DON'T KNOW WHAT TO DO!
WHY DON'T YOU S-
DAD, COULD YOU TALK TO THEM? THEY'LL LISTEN TO YOU
OH REALLY
GREG

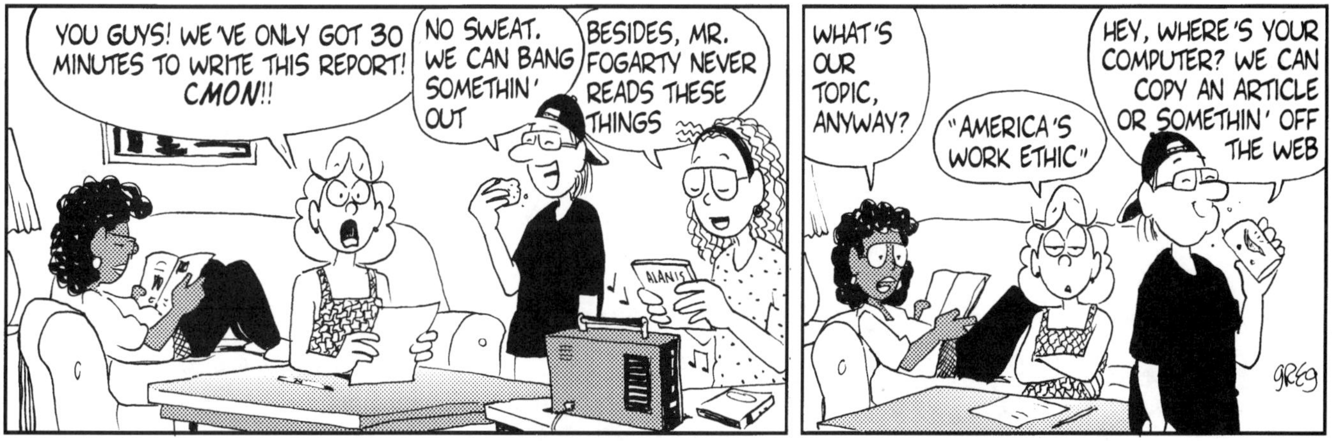
YOU GUYS! WE'VE ONLY GOT 30 MINUTES TO WRITE THIS REPORT! CMON!!
NO SWEAT. WE CAN BANG SOMETHIN' OUT
BESIDES, MR. FOGARTY NEVER READS THESE THINGS
ALANIS
WHAT'S OUR TOPIC, ANYWAY?
"AMERICA'S WORK ETHIC"
HEY, WHERE'S YOUR COMPUTER? WE CAN COPY AN ARTICLE OR SOMETHIN' OFF THE WEB
GREG

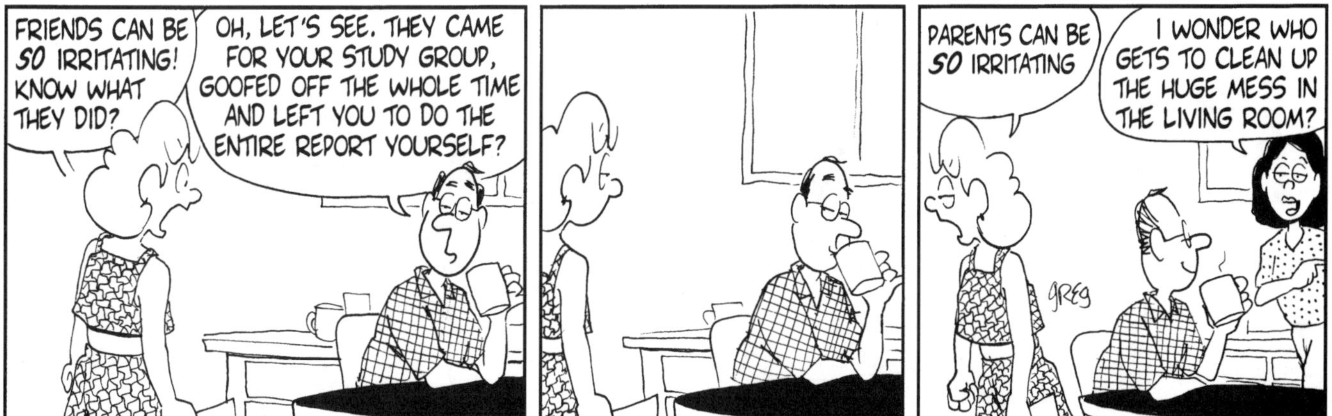
FRIENDS CAN BE SO IRRITATING! KNOW WHAT THEY DID?
OH, LET'S SEE. THEY CAME FOR YOUR STUDY GROUP, GOOFED OFF THE WHOLE TIME AND LEFT YOU TO DO THE ENTIRE REPORT YOURSELF?
PARENTS CAN BE SO IRRITATING
I WONDER WHO GETS TO CLEAN UP THE HUGE MESS IN THE LIVING ROOM?
GREG

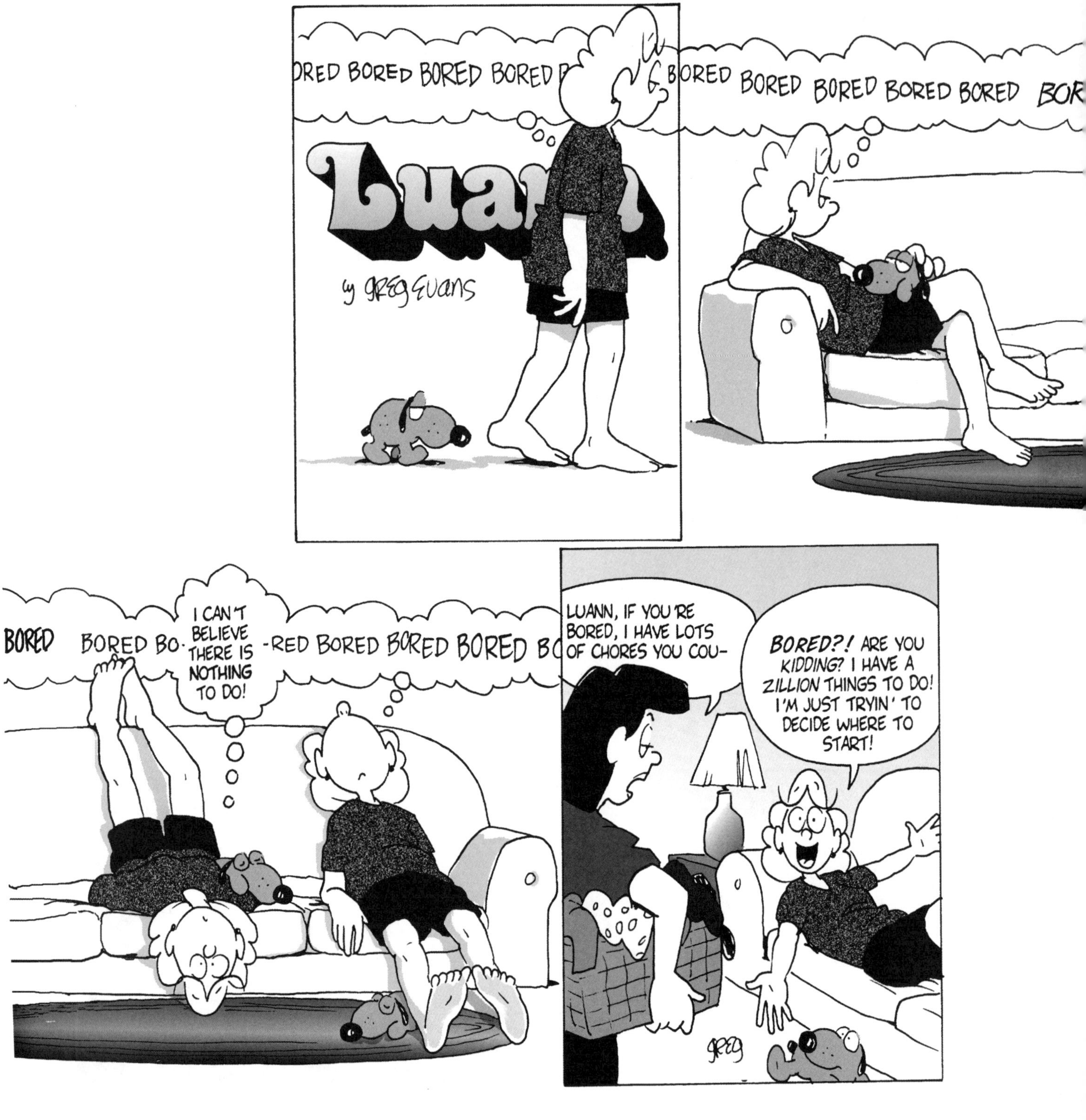

ORED BORED BORED BORED B
BORED BORED BORED BORED BORED BOR
by GREG EVANS
BORED BORED BO-
I CAN'T BELIEVE THERE IS NOTHING TO DO!
-RED BORED BORED BORED B
LUANN, IF YOU'RE BORED, I HAVE LOTS OF CHORES YOU COU-
BORED?! ARE YOU KIDDING? I HAVE A ZILLION THINGS TO DO! I'M JUST TRYIN' TO DECIDE WHERE TO START!
GREG

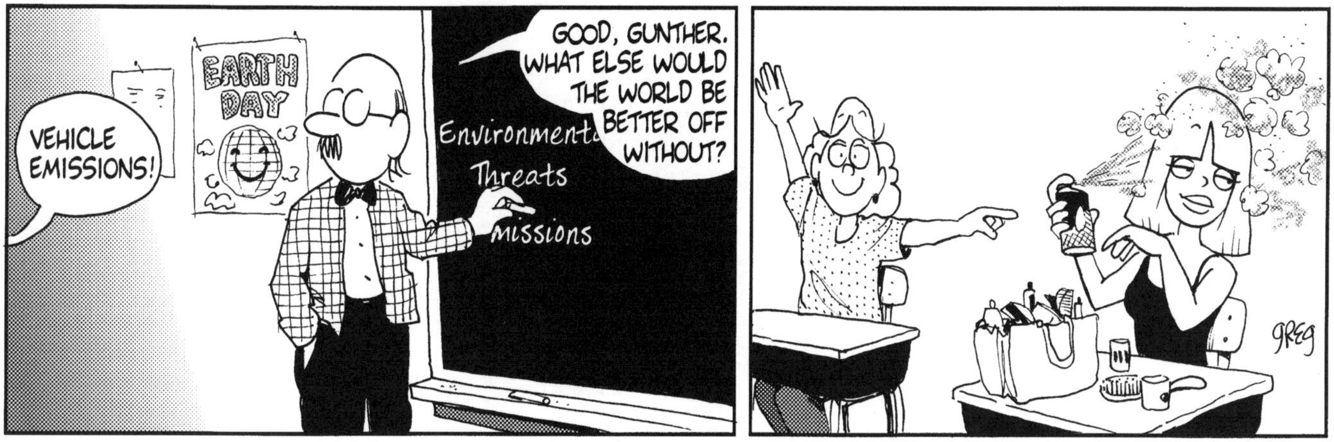
EARTH DAY
VEHICLE EMISSIONS!
GOOD, GUNTHER. WHAT ELSE WOULD THE WORLD BE BETTER OFF WITHOUT?
Threats
GREG

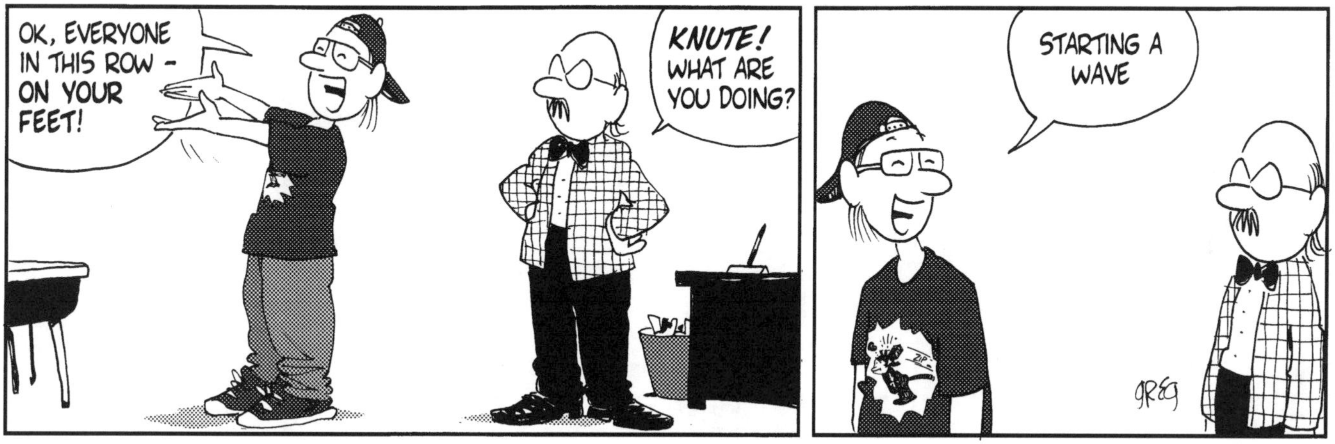
OK, EVERYONE IN THIS ROW - ON YOUR FEET!
KNUTE! WHAT ARE YOU DOING?
STARTING A WAVE
GREG

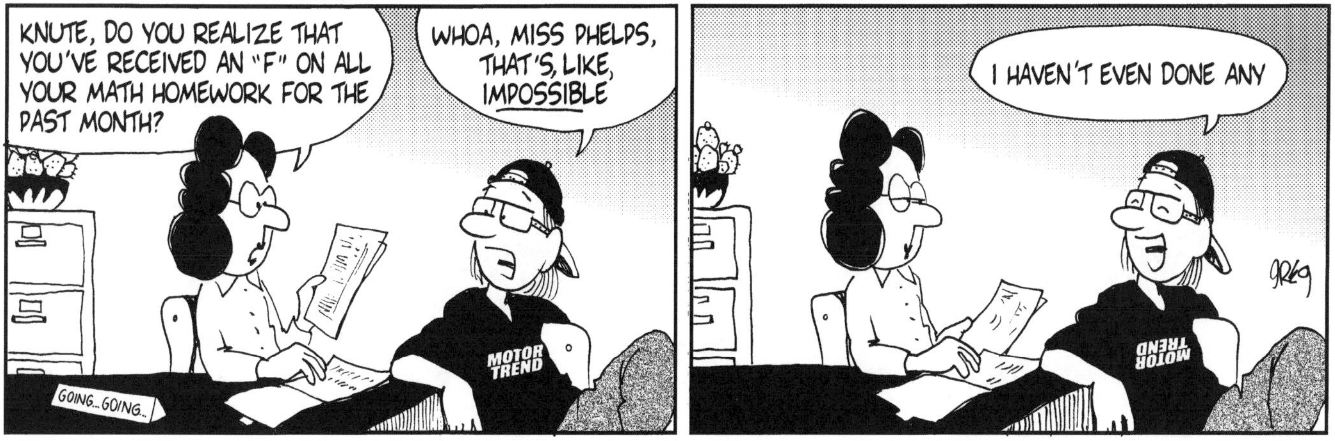
KNUTE, DO YOU REALIZE THAT YOU'VE RECEIVED AN "F" ON ALL YOUR MATH HOMEWORK FOR THE PAST MONTH?
WHOA, MISS PHELPS, THAT'S, LIKE, IMPOSSIBLE
MOTOR TREND
GOING...GOING...
I HAVEN'T EVEN DONE ANY
GREG

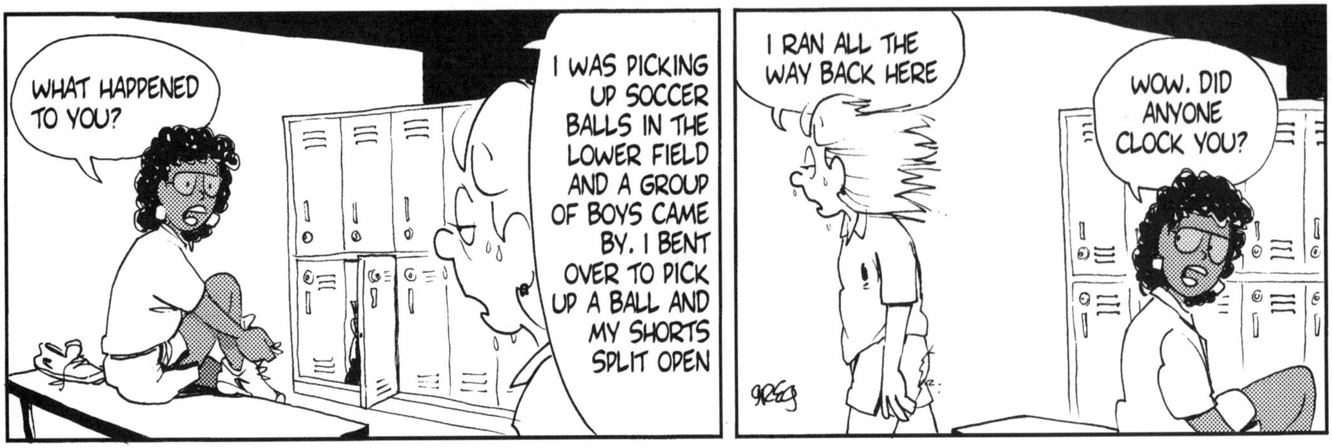
WHAT HAPPENED TO YOU?
I WAS PICKING UP SOCCER BALLS IN THE LOWER FIELD AND A GROUP OF BOYS CAME BY. I BENT OVER TO PICK UP A BALL AND MY SHORTS SPLIT OPEN
I RAN ALL THE WAY BACK HERE
WOW. DID ANYONE CLOCK YOU?

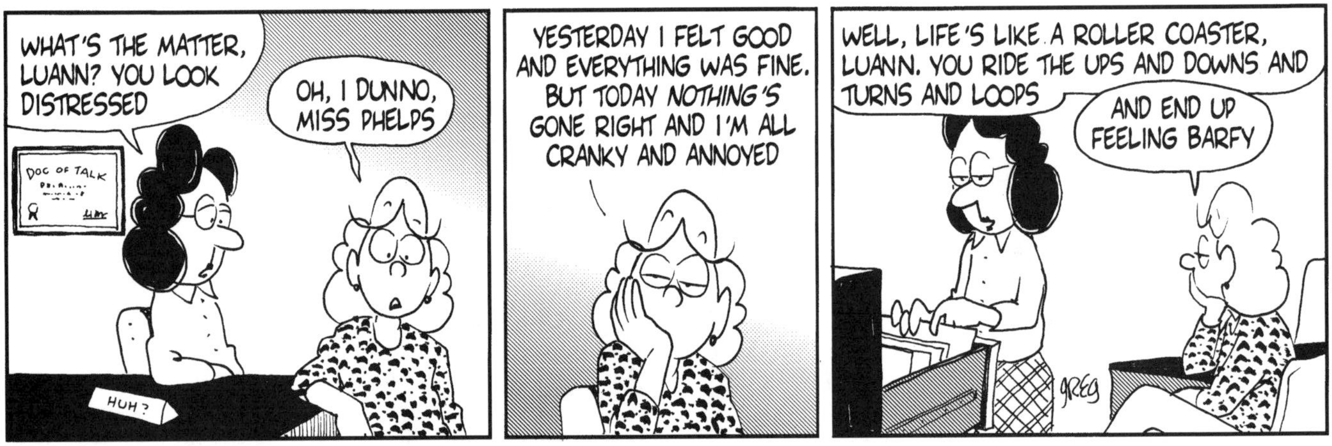
WHAT'S THE MATTER, LUANN? YOU LOOK DISTRESSED
OH, I DUNNO, MISS PHELPS
DOC OF TALK
HUH?
YESTERDAY I FELT GOOD AND EVERYTHING WAS FINE. BUT TODAY *NOTHING'S* GONE RIGHT AND I'M ALL CRANKY AND ANNOYED
WELL, LIFE'S LIKE A ROLLER COASTER, LUANN. YOU RIDE THE UPS AND DOWNS AND TURNS AND LOOPS
AND END UP FEELING BARFY

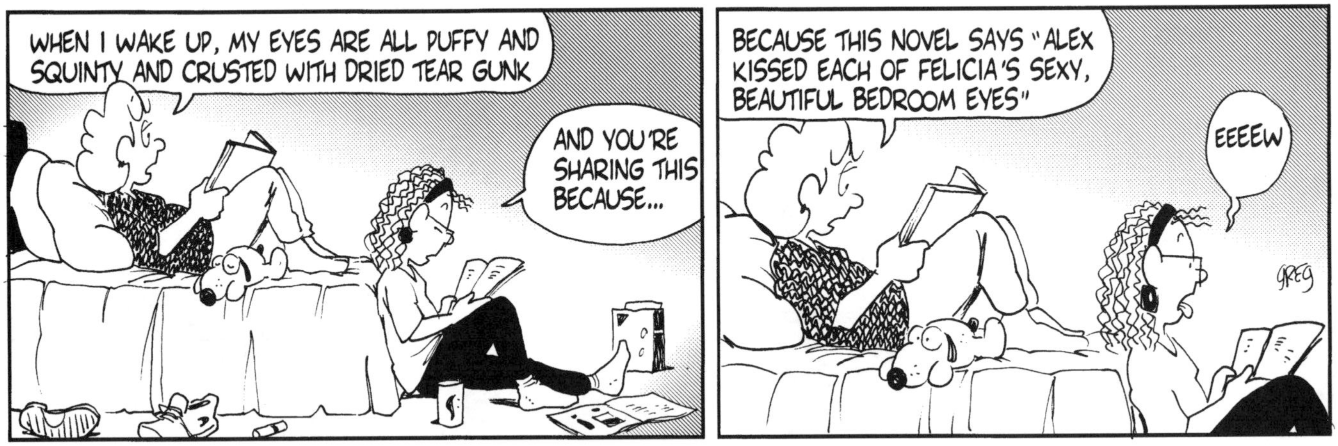
WHEN I WAKE UP, MY EYES ARE ALL PUFFY AND SQUINTY AND CRUSTED WITH DRIED TEAR GUNK
AND YOU'RE SHARING THIS BECAUSE...
BECAUSE THIS NOVEL SAYS "ALEX KISSED EACH OF FELICIA'S SEXY, BEAUTIFUL BEDROOM EYES"
EEEEW

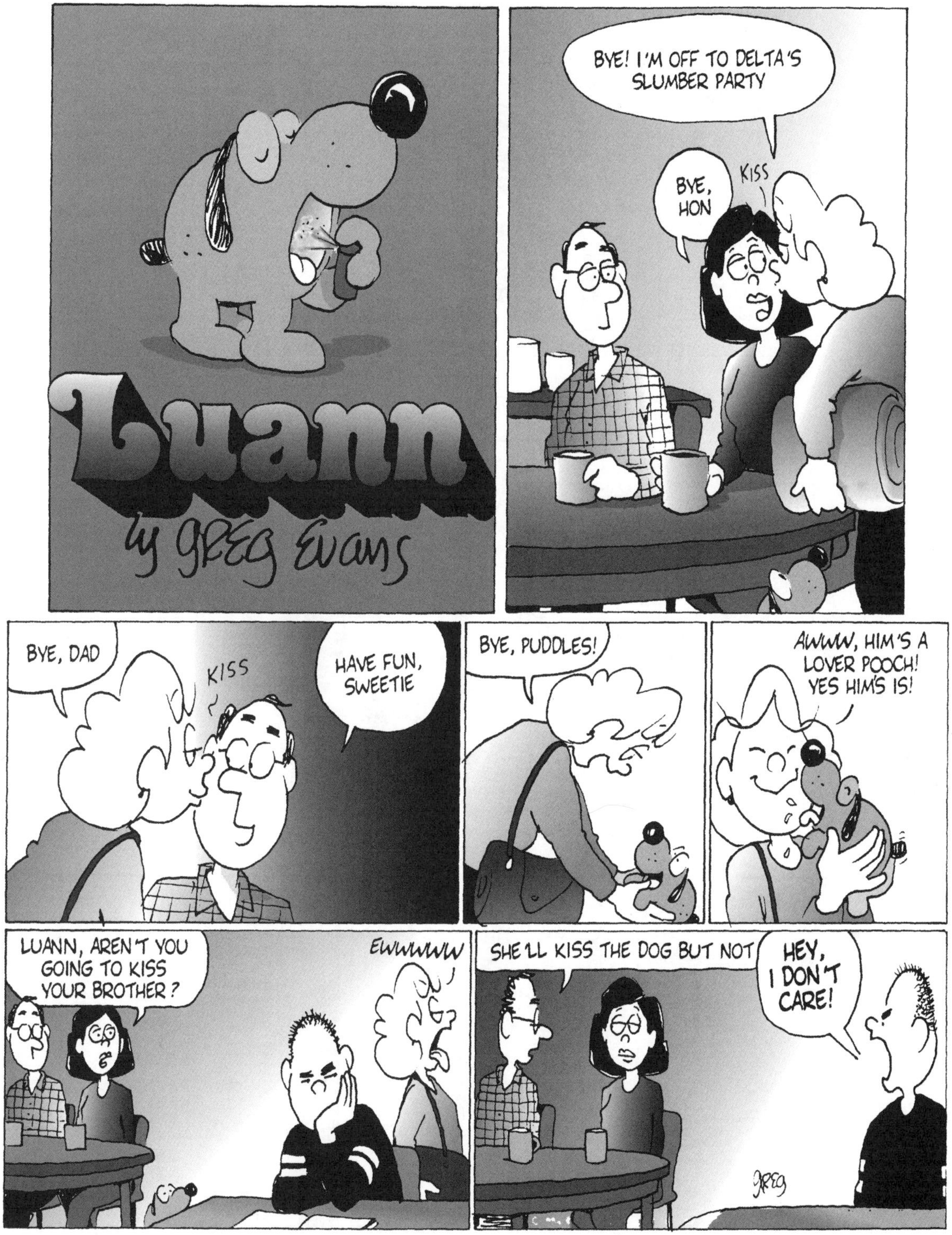
Luann
by GREG EVANS
BYE! I'M OFF TO DELTA'S SLUMBER PARTY
BYE, HON
KISS
BYE, DAD
KISS
HAVE FUN, SWEETIE
BYE, PUDDLES!
AWWW, HIM'S A LOVER POOCH! YES HIM'S IS!
LUANN, AREN'T YOU GOING TO KISS YOUR BROTHER?
EWWWWW
SHE'LL KISS THE DOG BUT NOT
HEY, I DON'T CARE!
GREG

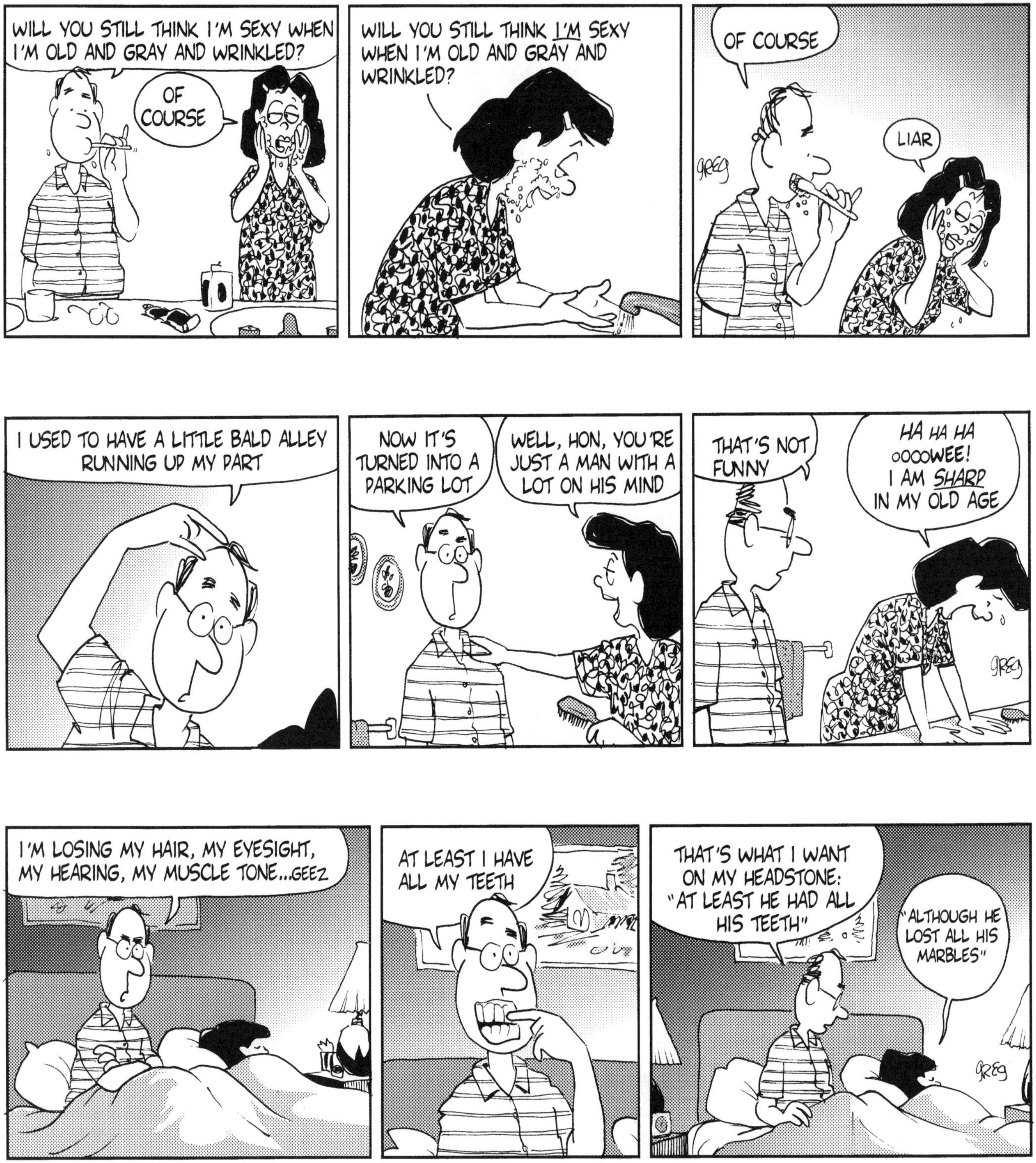
WILL YOU STILL THINK I'M SEXY WHEN I'M OLD AND GRAY AND WRINKLED?
OF COURSE
WILL YOU STILL THINK I'M SEXY WHEN I'M OLD AND GRAY AND WRINKLED?
OF COURSE
LIAR
GREG
I USED TO HAVE A LITTLE BALD ALLEY RUNNING UP MY PART
NOW IT'S TURNED INTO A PARKING LOT
WELL, HON, YOU'RE JUST A MAN WITH A LOT ON HIS MIND
THAT'S NOT FUNNY
HA HA HA OOOOWEE! I AM SHARP IN MY OLD AGE
GREG
I'M LOSING MY HAIR, MY EYESIGHT, MY HEARING, MY MUSCLE TONE...GEEZ
AT LEAST I HAVE ALL MY TEETH
THAT'S WHAT I WANT ON MY HEADSTONE: "AT LEAST HE HAD ALL HIS TEETH"
"ALTHOUGH HE LOST ALL HIS MARBLES"
GREG

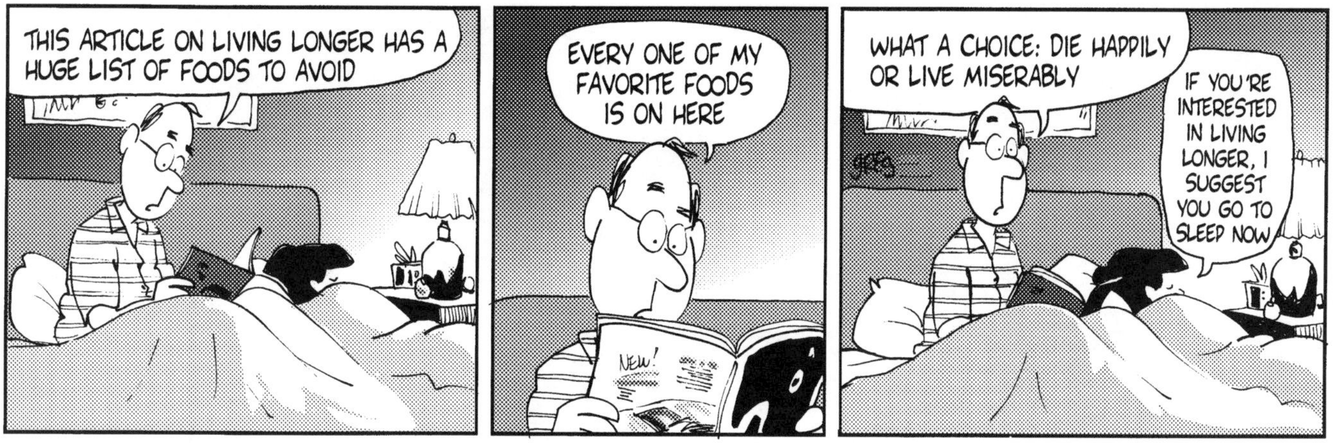
THIS ARTICLE ON LIVING LONGER HAS A HUGE LIST OF FOODS TO AVOID
EVERY ONE OF MY FAVORITE FOODS IS ON HERE
NEW!
WHAT A CHOICE: DIE HAPPILY OR LIVE MISERABLY
IF YOU'RE INTERESTED IN LIVING LONGER, I SUGGEST YOU GO TO SLEEP NOW

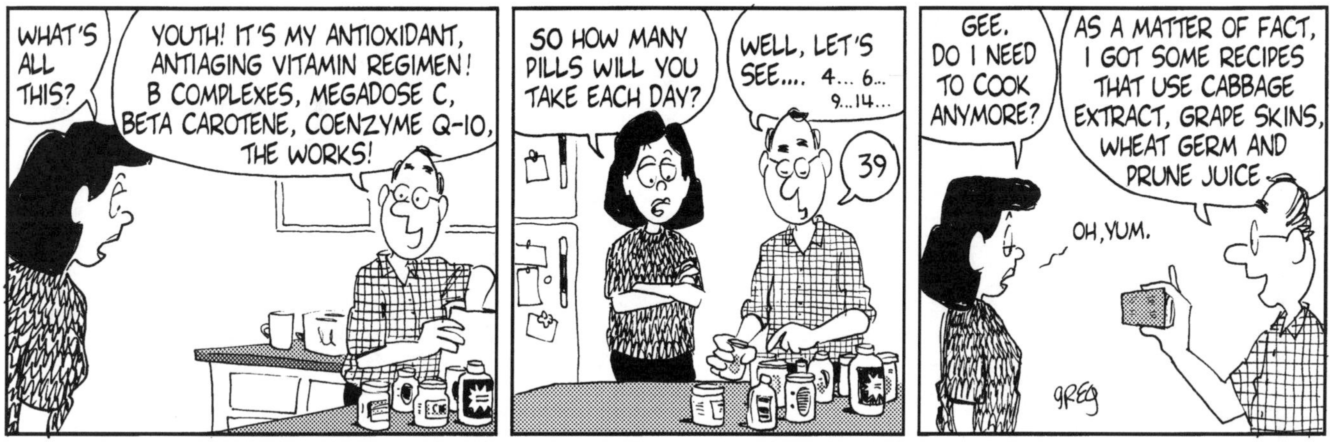
WHAT'S ALL THIS?
YOUTH! IT'S MY ANTIOXIDANT, ANTIAGING VITAMIN REGIMEN! B COMPLEXES, MEGADOSE C, BETA CAROTENE, COENZYME Q-10, THE WORKS!
SO HOW MANY PILLS WILL YOU TAKE EACH DAY?
WELL, LET'S SEE.... 4... 6... 9...14...
39
GEE. DO I NEED TO COOK ANYMORE?
AS A MATTER OF FACT, I GOT SOME RECIPES THAT USE CABBAGE EXTRACT, GRAPE SKINS, WHEAT GERM AND PRUNE JUICE
OH, YUM.

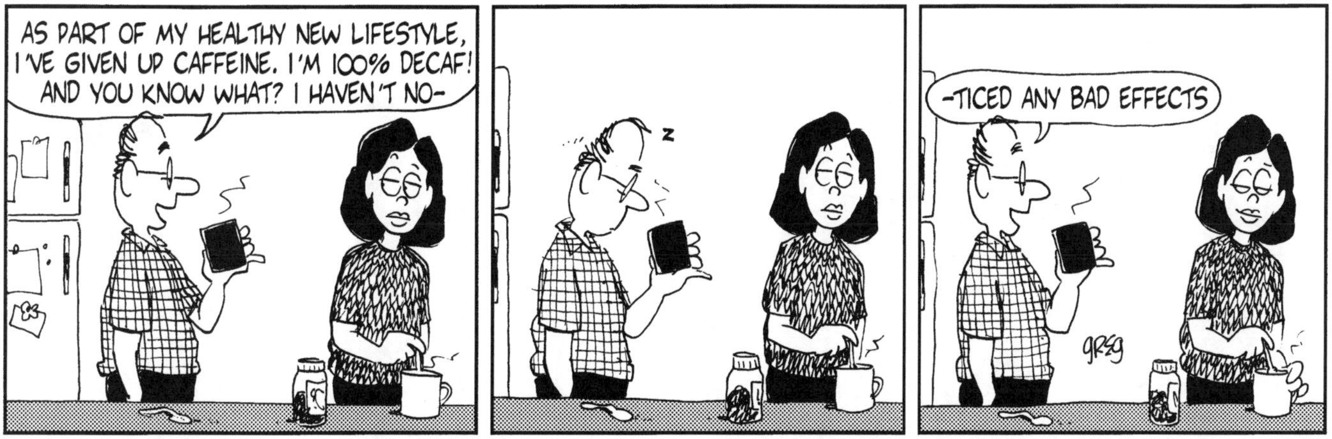
AS PART OF MY HEALTHY NEW LIFESTYLE, I'VE GIVEN UP CAFFEINE. I'M 100% DECAF! AND YOU KNOW WHAT? I HAVEN'T NO-
Z
-TICED ANY BAD EFFECTS

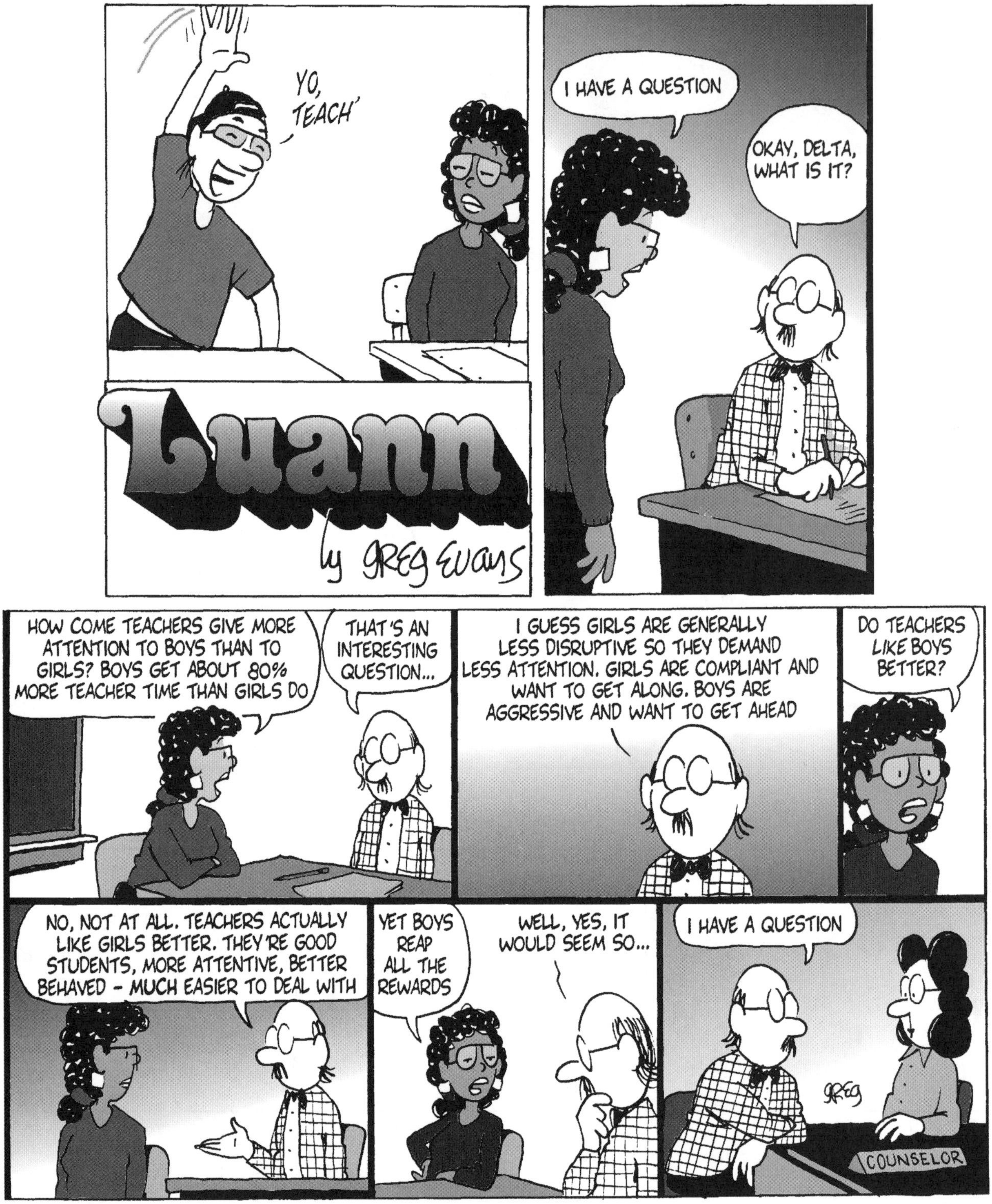
YO, TEACH'
Luann
by GREG EVANS
I HAVE A QUESTION
OKAY, DELTA, WHAT IS IT?
HOW COME TEACHERS GIVE MORE ATTENTION TO BOYS THAN TO GIRLS? BOYS GET ABOUT 80% MORE TEACHER TIME THAN GIRLS DO
THAT'S AN INTERESTING QUESTION...
I GUESS GIRLS ARE GENERALLY LESS DISRUPTIVE SO THEY DEMAND LESS ATTENTION. GIRLS ARE COMPLIANT AND WANT TO GET ALONG. BOYS ARE AGGRESSIVE AND WANT TO GET AHEAD
DO TEACHERS LIKE BOYS BETTER?
NO, NOT AT ALL. TEACHERS ACTUALLY LIKE GIRLS BETTER. THEY'RE GOOD STUDENTS, MORE ATTENTIVE, BETTER BEHAVED - MUCH EASIER TO DEAL WITH
YET BOYS REAP ALL THE REWARDS
WELL, YES, IT WOULD SEEM SO...
I HAVE A QUESTION
GREG
COUNSELOR

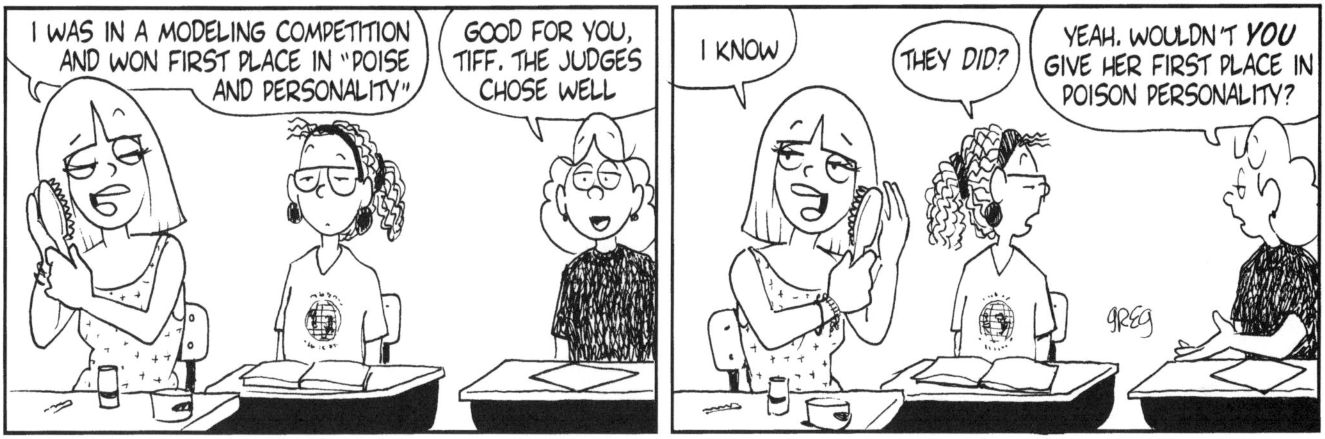
I WAS IN A MODELING COMPETITION AND WON FIRST PLACE IN "POISE AND PERSONALITY"
GOOD FOR YOU, TIFF. THE JUDGES CHOSE WELL
I KNOW
THEY *DID*?
YEAH. WOULDN'T ***YOU*** GIVE HER FIRST PLACE IN POISON PERSONALITY?
GREG

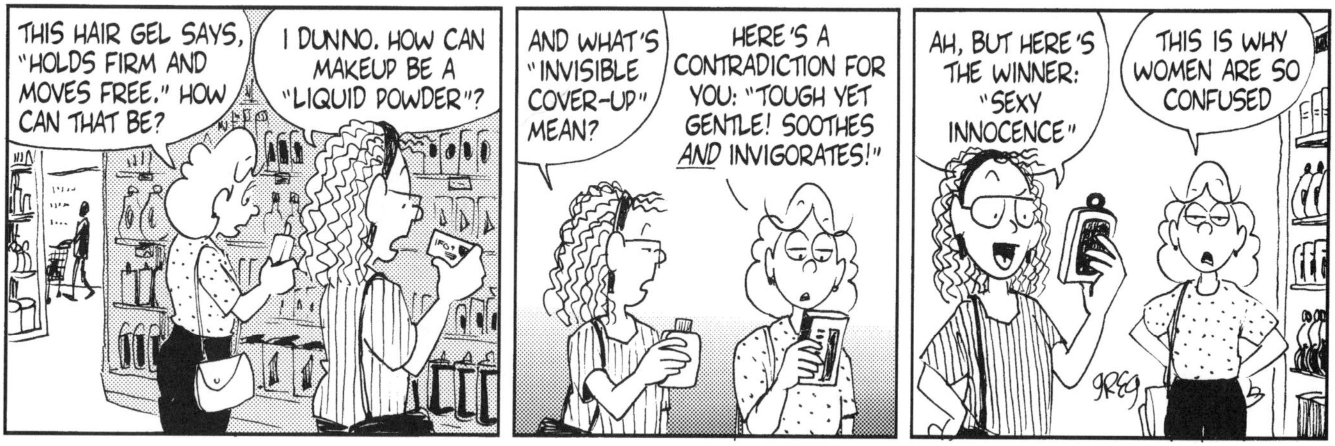
THIS HAIR GEL SAYS, "HOLDS FIRM AND MOVES FREE." HOW CAN THAT BE?
I DUNNO. HOW CAN MAKEUP BE A "LIQUID POWDER"?
AND WHAT'S "INVISIBLE COVER-UP" MEAN?
HERE'S A CONTRADICTION FOR YOU: "TOUGH YET GENTLE! SOOTHES *AND* INVIGORATES!"
AH, BUT HERE'S THE WINNER: "SEXY INNOCENCE"
THIS IS WHY WOMEN ARE SO CONFUSED
GREG

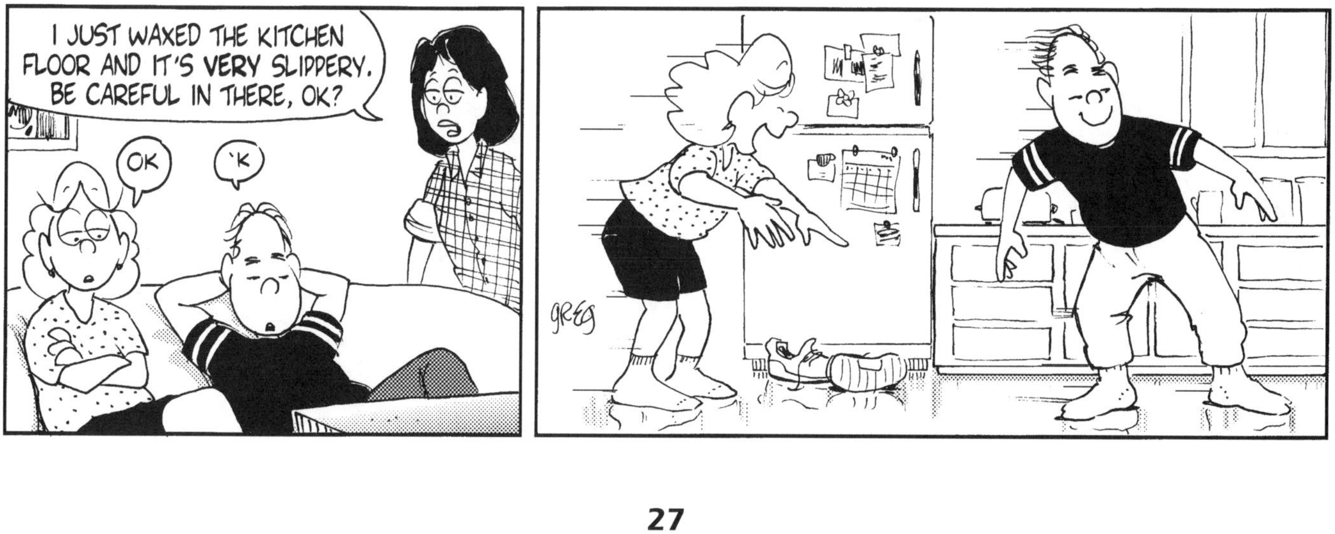
I JUST WAXED THE KITCHEN FLOOR AND IT'S **VERY** SLIPPERY. BE CAREFUL IN THERE, OK?
OK
'K
GREG

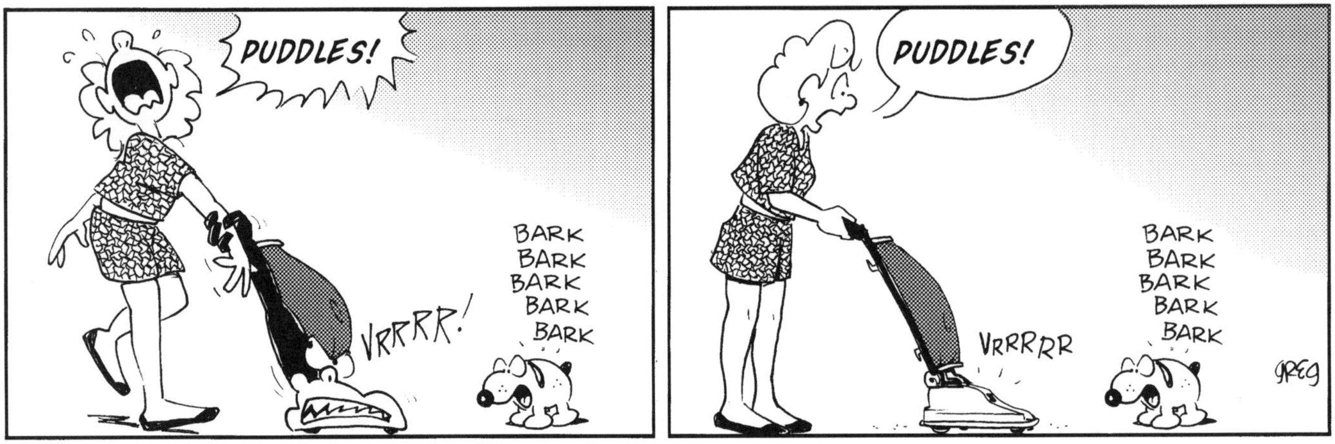
PUDDLES!
VRRRR!
BARK BARK BARK BARK BARK
PUDDLES!
VRRRRR
BARK BARK BARK BARK BARK
GREG

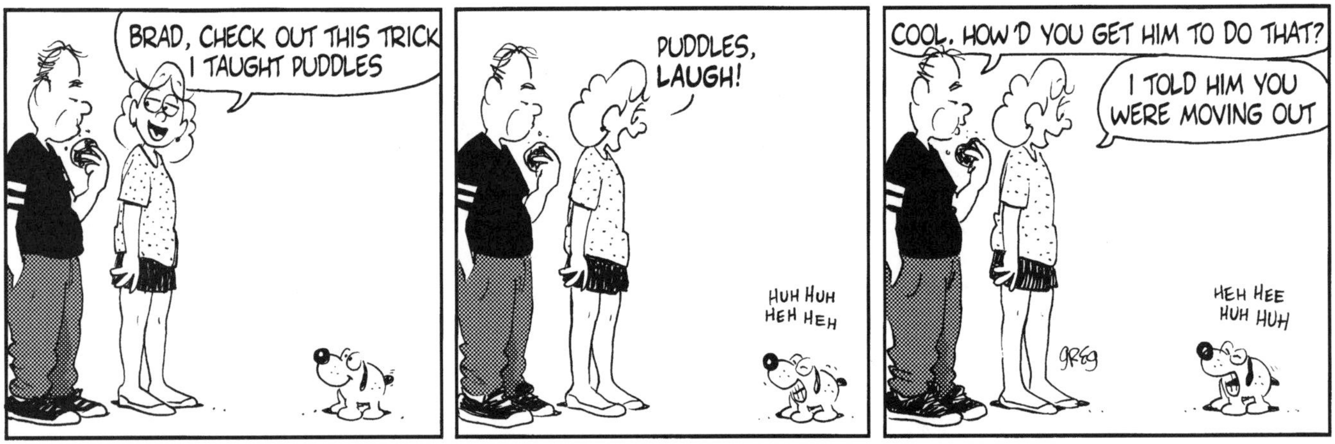
BRAD, CHECK OUT THIS TRICK I TAUGHT PUDDLES
PUDDLES, **LAUGH**!
HUH HUH HEH HEH
COOL. HOW'D YOU GET HIM TO DO THAT?
I TOLD HIM YOU WERE MOVING OUT
HEH HEE HUH HUH
GREG

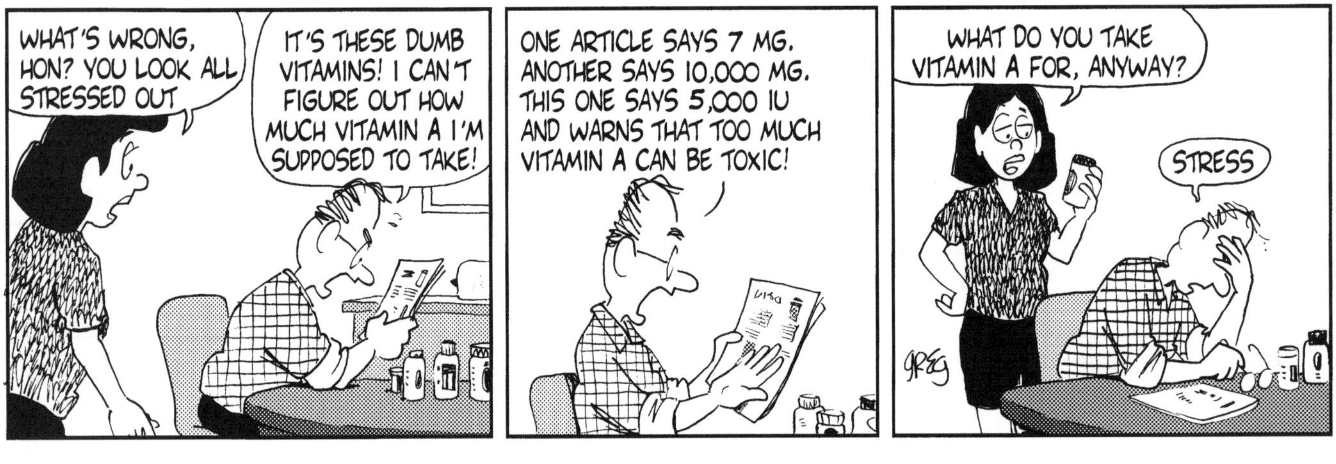
WHAT'S WRONG, HON? YOU LOOK ALL STRESSED OUT
IT'S THESE DUMB VITAMINS! I CAN'T FIGURE OUT HOW MUCH VITAMIN A I'M SUPPOSED TO TAKE!
ONE ARTICLE SAYS 7 MG. ANOTHER SAYS 10,000 MG. THIS ONE SAYS 5,000 IU AND WARNS THAT TOO MUCH VITAMIN A CAN BE TOXIC!
WHAT DO YOU TAKE VITAMIN A FOR, ANYWAY?
STRESS
GREG

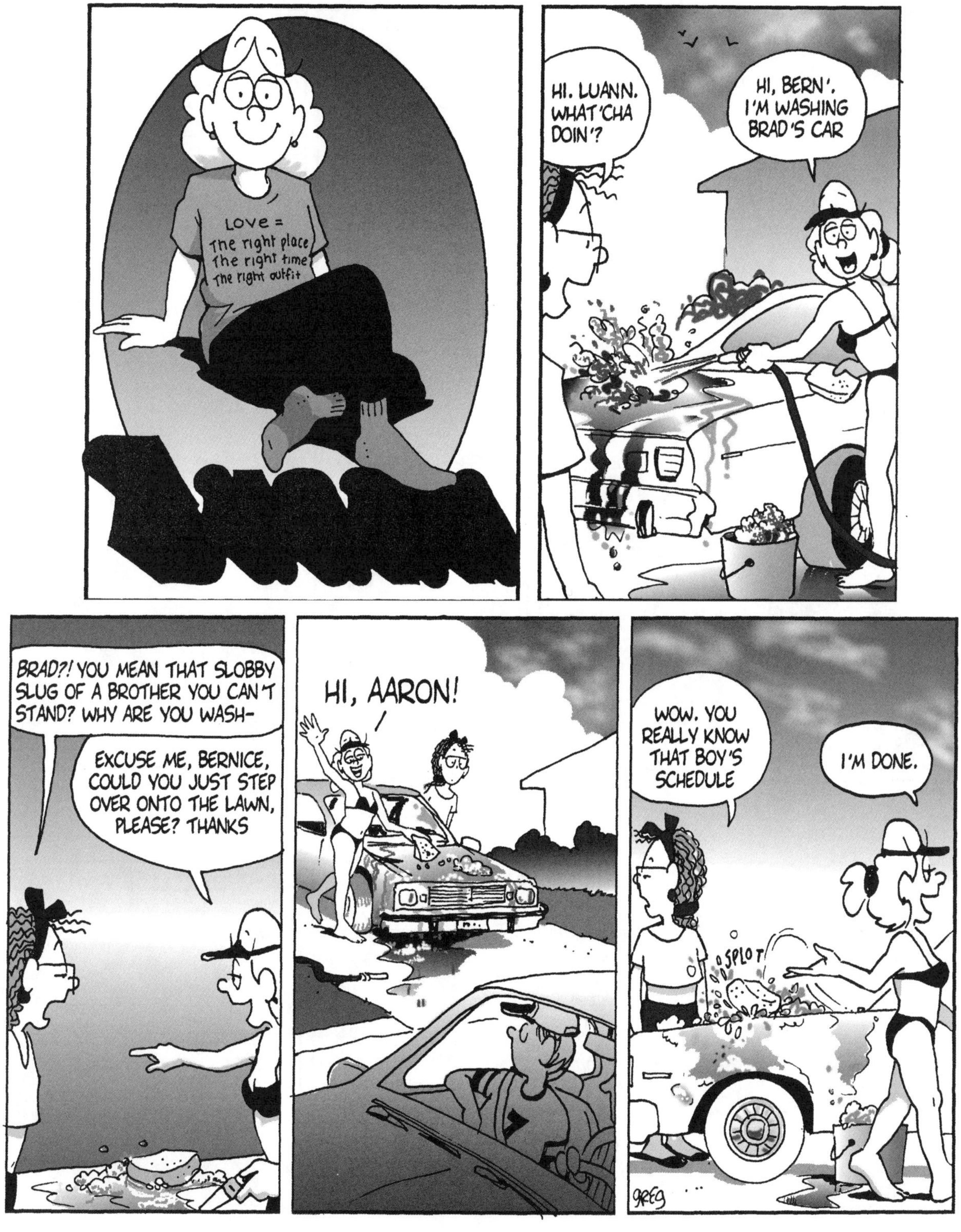
LOVE =
The right place
The right time
The right outfit
HI. LUANN. WHAT'CHA DOIN'?
HI, BERN'. I'M WASHING BRAD'S CAR
BRAD?! YOU MEAN THAT SLOBBY SLUG OF A BROTHER YOU CAN'T STAND? WHY ARE YOU WASH-
EXCUSE ME, BERNICE, COULD YOU JUST STEP OVER ONTO THE LAWN, PLEASE? THANKS
HI, AARON!
WOW. YOU REALLY KNOW THAT BOY'S SCHEDULE
I'M DONE.
SPLOT
GREG

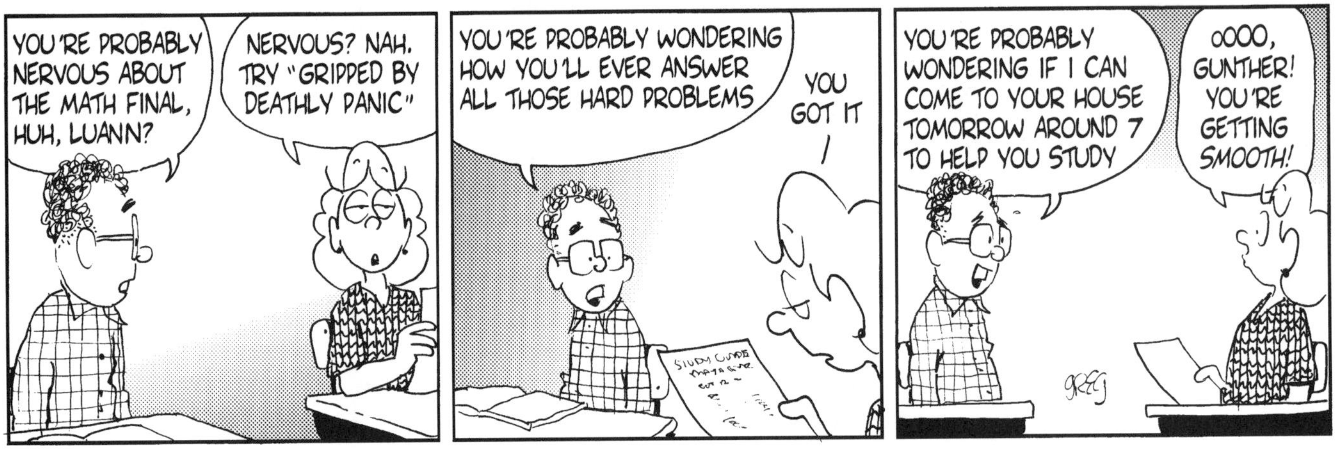
YOU'RE PROBABLY NERVOUS ABOUT THE MATH FINAL, HUH, LUANN?
NERVOUS? NAH. TRY "GRIPPED BY DEATHLY PANIC"
YOU'RE PROBABLY WONDERING HOW YOU'LL EVER ANSWER ALL THOSE HARD PROBLEMS
YOU GOT IT
YOU'RE PROBABLY WONDERING IF I CAN COME TO YOUR HOUSE TOMORROW AROUND 7 TO HELP YOU STUDY
OOOO, GUNTHER! YOU'RE GETTING SMOOTH!

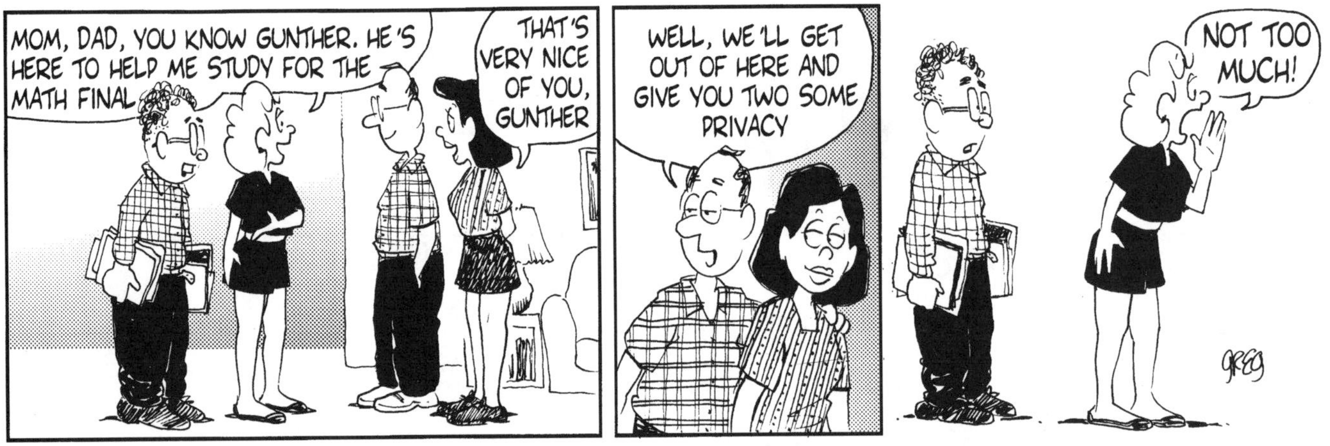
MOM, DAD, YOU KNOW GUNTHER. HE'S HERE TO HELP ME STUDY FOR THE MATH FINAL
THAT'S VERY NICE OF YOU, GUNTHER
WELL, WE'LL GET OUT OF HERE AND GIVE YOU TWO SOME PRIVACY
NOT TOO MUCH!

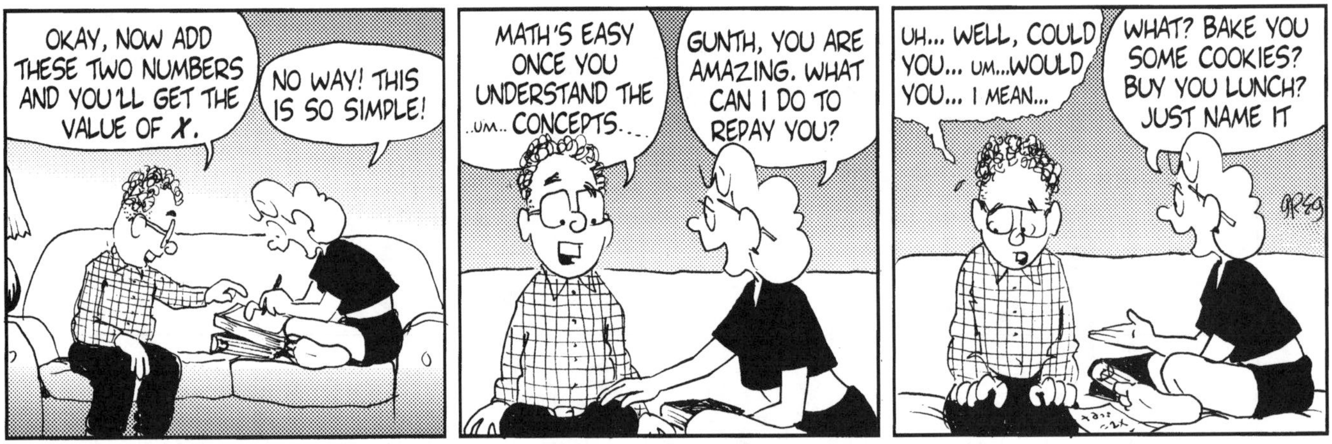
OKAY, NOW ADD THESE TWO NUMBERS AND YOU'LL GET THE VALUE OF X.
NO WAY! THIS IS SO SIMPLE!
MATH'S EASY ONCE YOU UNDERSTAND THE ..UM.. CONCEPTS...
GUNTH, YOU ARE AMAZING. WHAT CAN I DO TO REPAY YOU?
UH... WELL, COULD YOU... UM...WOULD YOU... I MEAN...
WHAT? BAKE YOU SOME COOKIES? BUY YOU LUNCH? JUST NAME IT

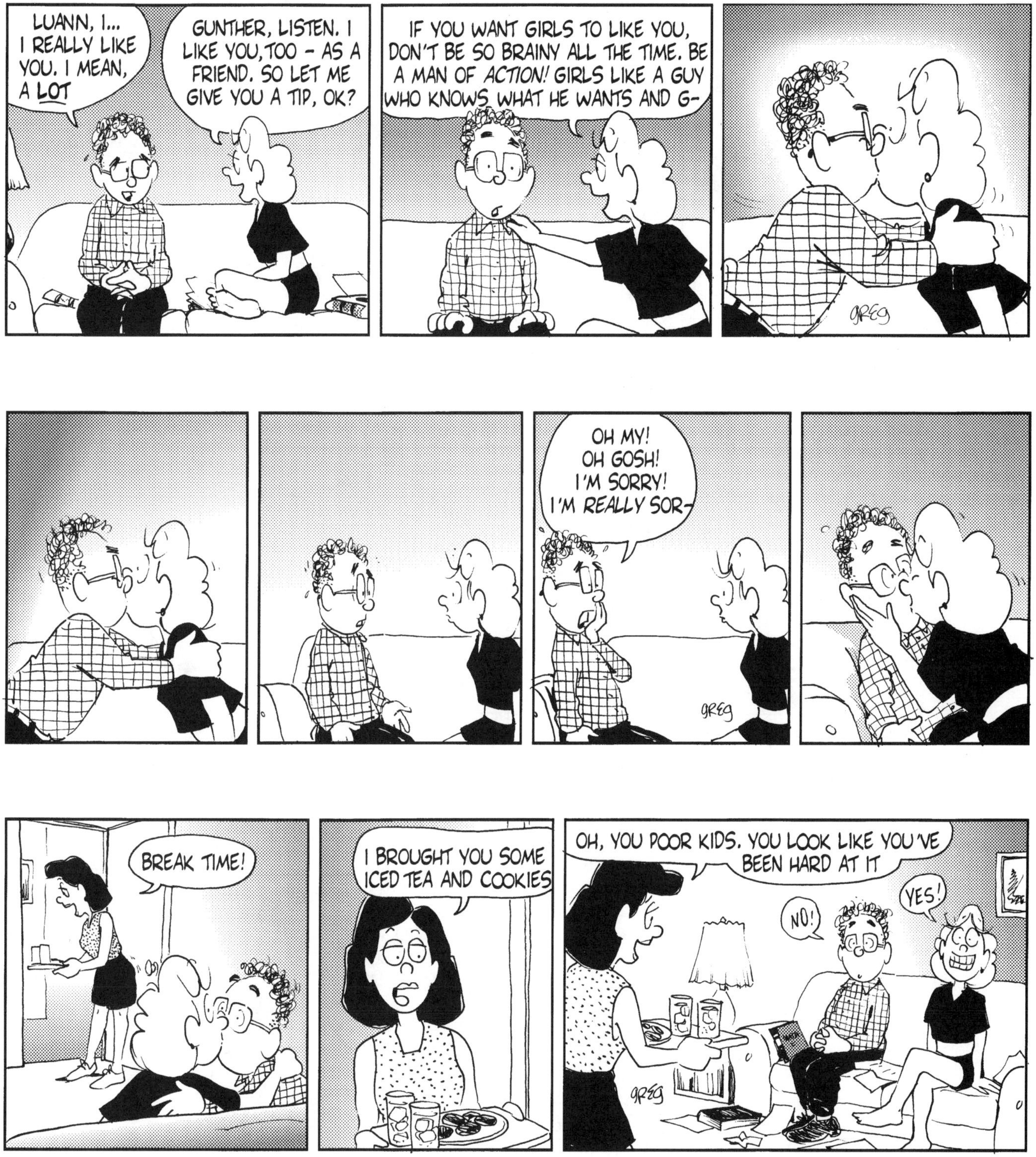
LUANN, I... I REALLY LIKE YOU. I MEAN, A LOT
GUNTHER, LISTEN. I LIKE YOU, TOO - AS A FRIEND. SO LET ME GIVE YOU A TIP, OK?
IF YOU WANT GIRLS TO LIKE YOU, DON'T BE SO BRAINY ALL THE TIME. BE A MAN OF ACTION! GIRLS LIKE A GUY WHO KNOWS WHAT HE WANTS AND G-
GREG
GREG
OH MY! OH GOSH! I'M SORRY! I'M REALLY SOR-
BREAK TIME!
I BROUGHT YOU SOME ICED TEA AND COOKIES
OH, YOU POOR KIDS. YOU LOOK LIKE YOU'VE BEEN HARD AT IT
NO!
YES!
GREG

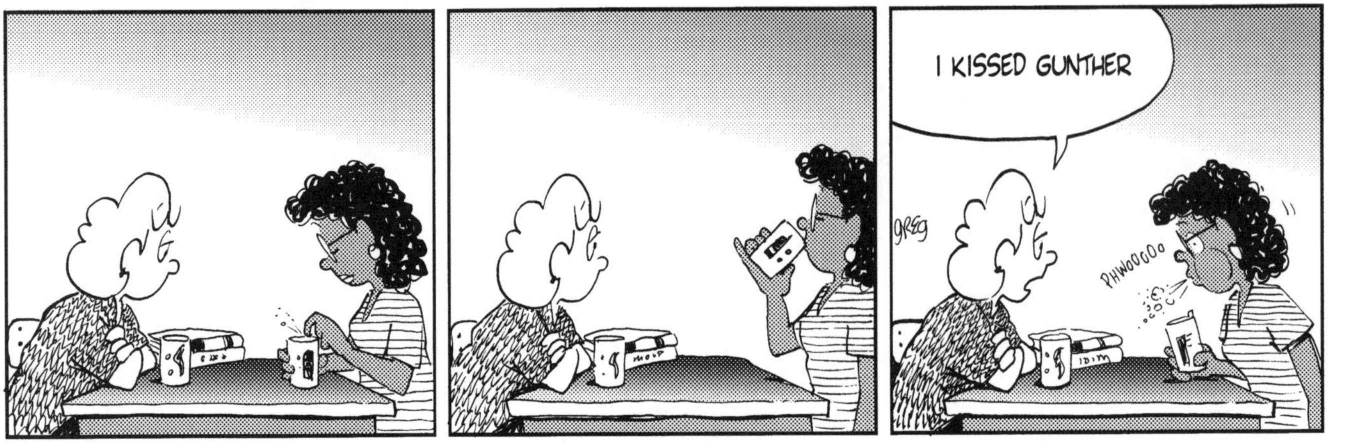
I KISSED GUNTHER
PHWOOOOOo

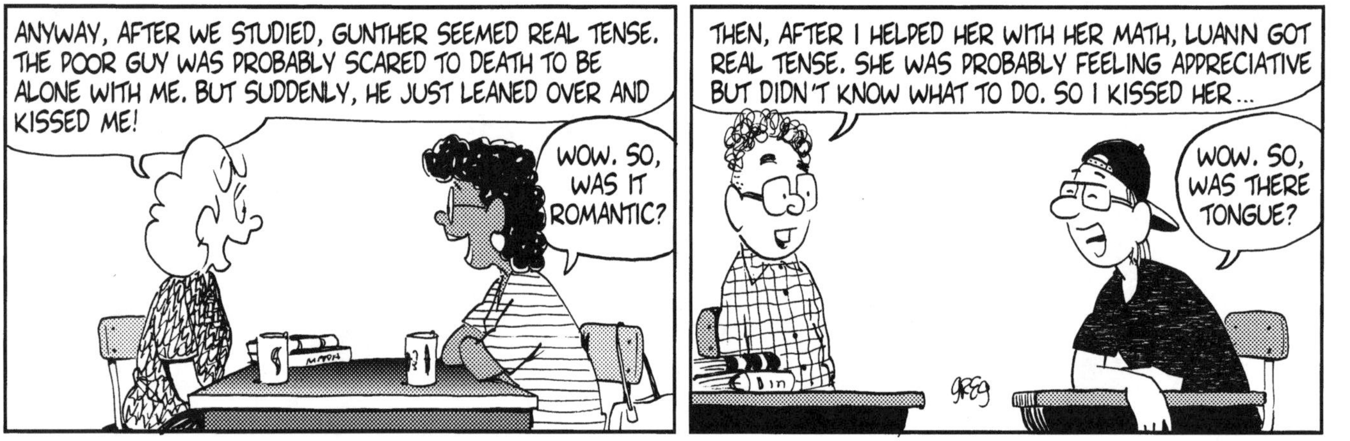
ANYWAY, AFTER WE STUDIED, GUNTHER SEEMED REAL TENSE. THE POOR GUY WAS PROBABLY SCARED TO DEATH TO BE ALONE WITH ME. BUT SUDDENLY, HE JUST LEANED OVER AND KISSED ME!
WOW. SO, WAS IT ROMANTIC?
THEN, AFTER I HELPED HER WITH HER MATH, LUANN GOT REAL TENSE. SHE WAS PROBABLY FEELING APPRECIATIVE BUT DIDN'T KNOW WHAT TO DO. SO I KISSED HER...
WOW. SO, WAS THERE TONGUE?

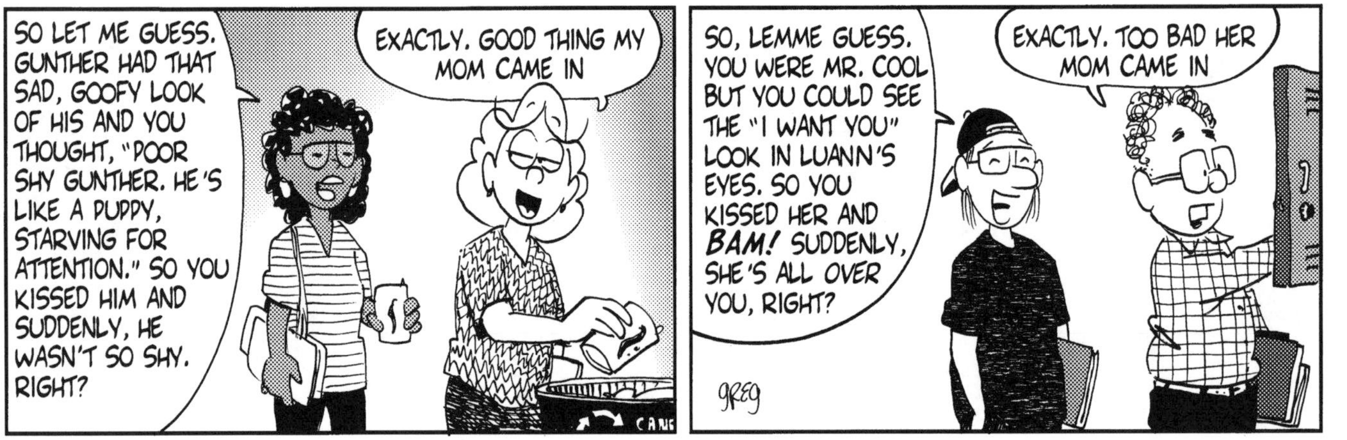
SO LET ME GUESS. GUNTHER HAD THAT SAD, GOOFY LOOK OF HIS AND YOU THOUGHT, "POOR SHY GUNTHER. HE'S LIKE A PUPPY, STARVING FOR ATTENTION." SO YOU KISSED HIM AND SUDDENLY, HE WASN'T SO SHY. RIGHT?
EXACTLY. GOOD THING MY MOM CAME IN
SO, LEMME GUESS. YOU WERE MR. COOL BUT YOU COULD SEE THE "I WANT YOU" LOOK IN LUANN'S EYES. SO YOU KISSED HER AND ***BAM!*** SUDDENLY, SHE'S ALL OVER YOU, RIGHT?
EXACTLY. TOO BAD HER MOM CAME IN

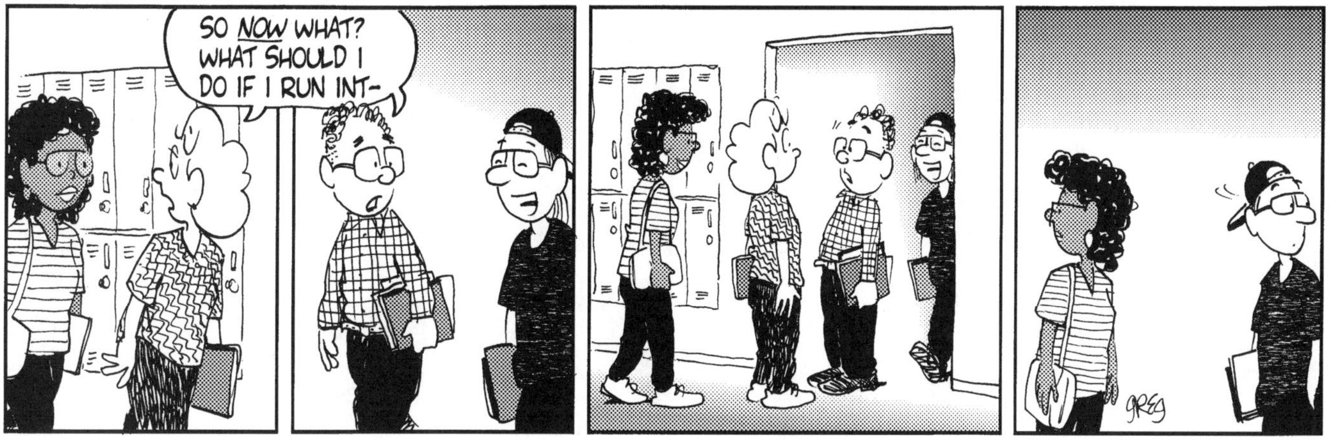
SO NOW WHAT? WHAT SHOULD I DO IF I RUN INT-
GREG

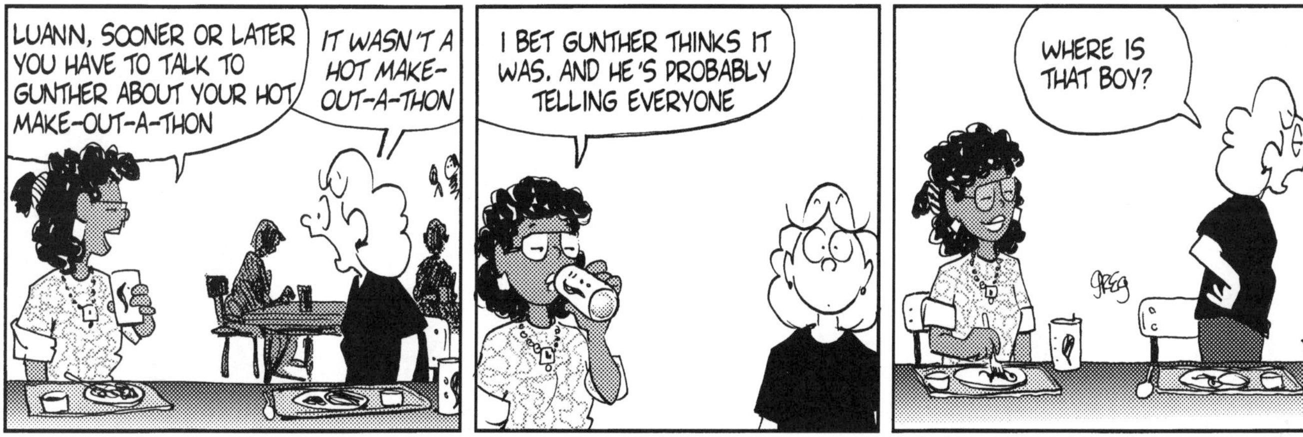
LUANN, SOONER OR LATER YOU HAVE TO TALK TO GUNTHER ABOUT YOUR HOT MAKE-OUT-A-THON
IT WASN'T A HOT MAKE-OUT-A-THON
I BET GUNTHER THINKS IT WAS. AND HE'S PROBABLY TELLING EVERYONE
WHERE IS THAT BOY?
GREG

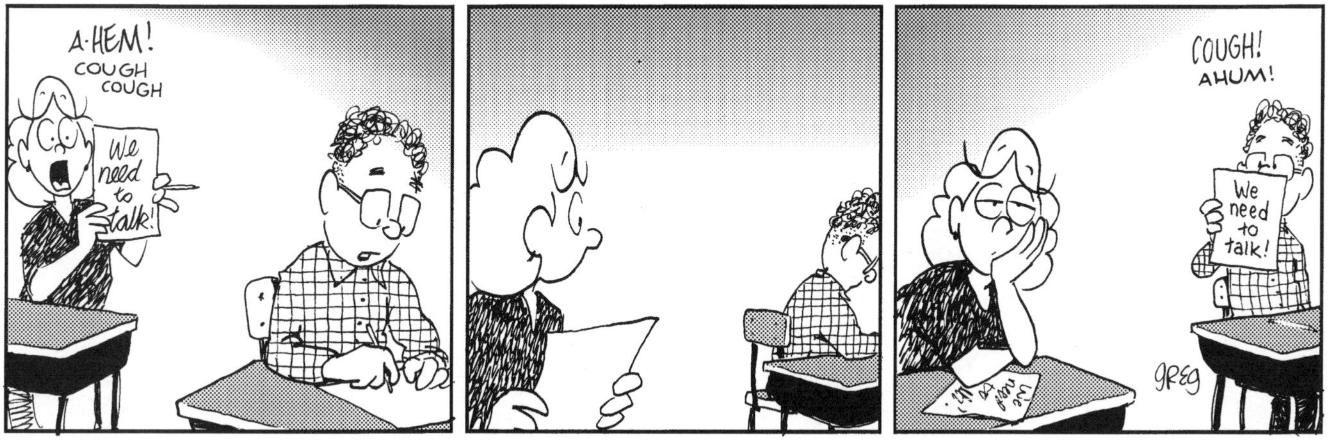
A-HEM! COUGH COUGH
We need to talk!
COUGH! AHUM!
We need to talk!
GREG

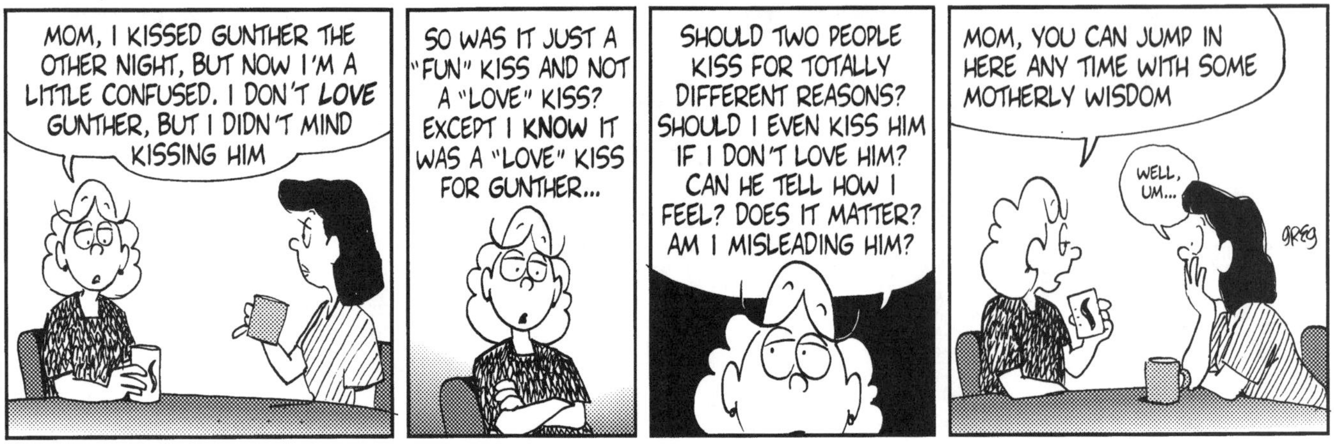
MOM, I KISSED GUNTHER THE OTHER NIGHT, BUT NOW I'M A LITTLE CONFUSED. I DON'T LOVE GUNTHER, BUT I DIDN'T MIND KISSING HIM
SO WAS IT JUST A "FUN" KISS AND NOT A "LOVE" KISS? EXCEPT I KNOW IT WAS A "LOVE" KISS FOR GUNTHER...
SHOULD TWO PEOPLE KISS FOR TOTALLY DIFFERENT REASONS? SHOULD I EVEN KISS HIM IF I DON'T LOVE HIM? CAN HE TELL HOW I FEEL? DOES IT MATTER? AM I MISLEADING HIM?
MOM, YOU CAN JUMP IN HERE ANY TIME WITH SOME MOTHERLY WISDOM
WELL, UM...
GREG

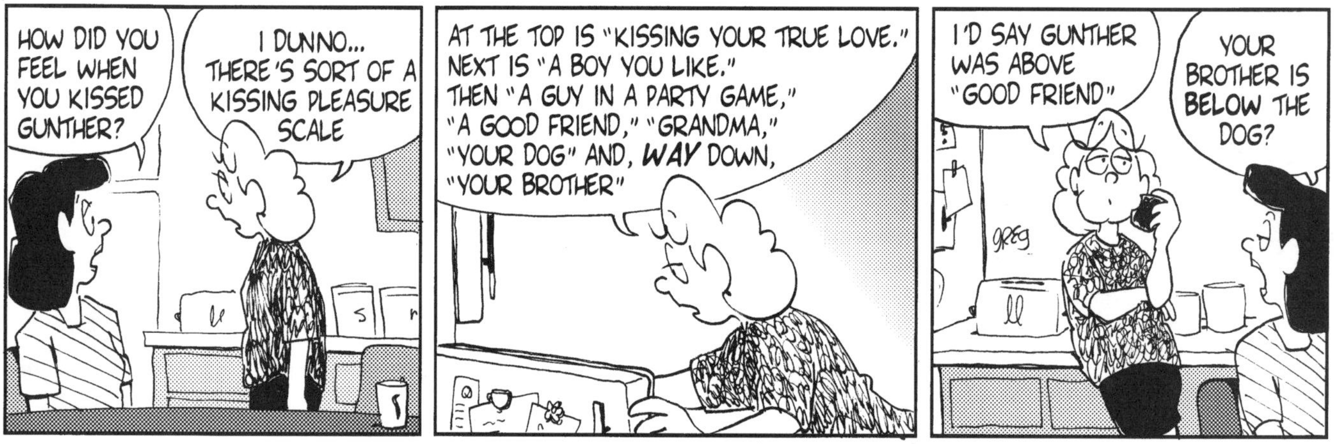
HOW DID YOU FEEL WHEN YOU KISSED GUNTHER?
I DUNNO... THERE'S SORT OF A KISSING PLEASURE SCALE
AT THE TOP IS "KISSING YOUR TRUE LOVE." NEXT IS "A BOY YOU LIKE." THEN "A GUY IN A PARTY GAME," "A GOOD FRIEND," "GRANDMA," "YOUR DOG" AND, WAY DOWN, "YOUR BROTHER"
I'D SAY GUNTHER WAS ABOVE "GOOD FRIEND"
YOUR BROTHER IS BELOW THE DOG?
GREG

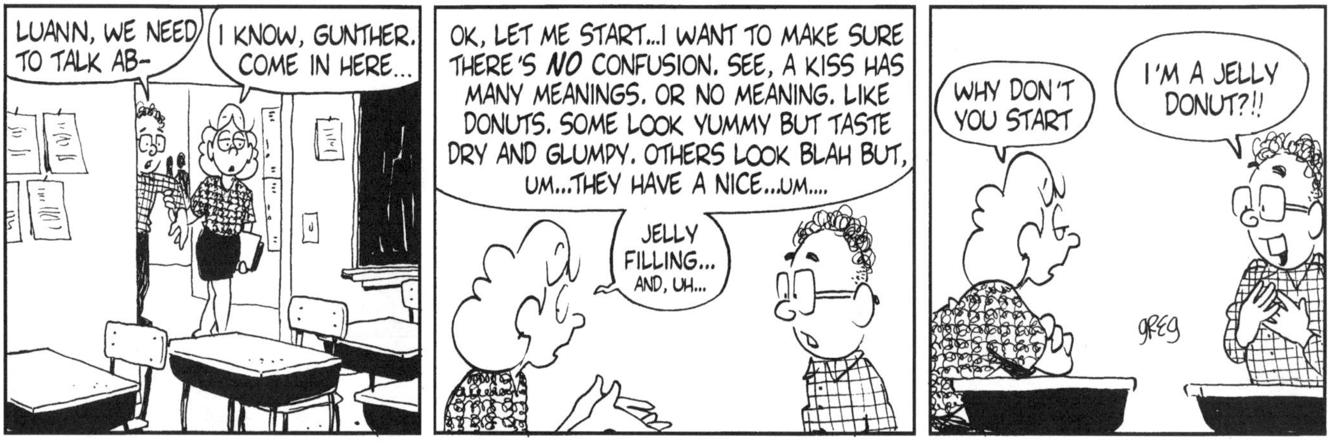
LUANN, WE NEED TO TALK AB-
I KNOW, GUNTHER. COME IN HERE...
OK, LET ME START...I WANT TO MAKE SURE THERE'S NO CONFUSION. SEE, A KISS HAS MANY MEANINGS. OR NO MEANING. LIKE DONUTS. SOME LOOK YUMMY BUT TASTE DRY AND GLUMPY. OTHERS LOOK BLAH BUT, UM...THEY HAVE A NICE...UM....
JELLY FILLING... AND, UH...
WHY DON'T YOU START
I'M A JELLY DONUT?!!
GREG

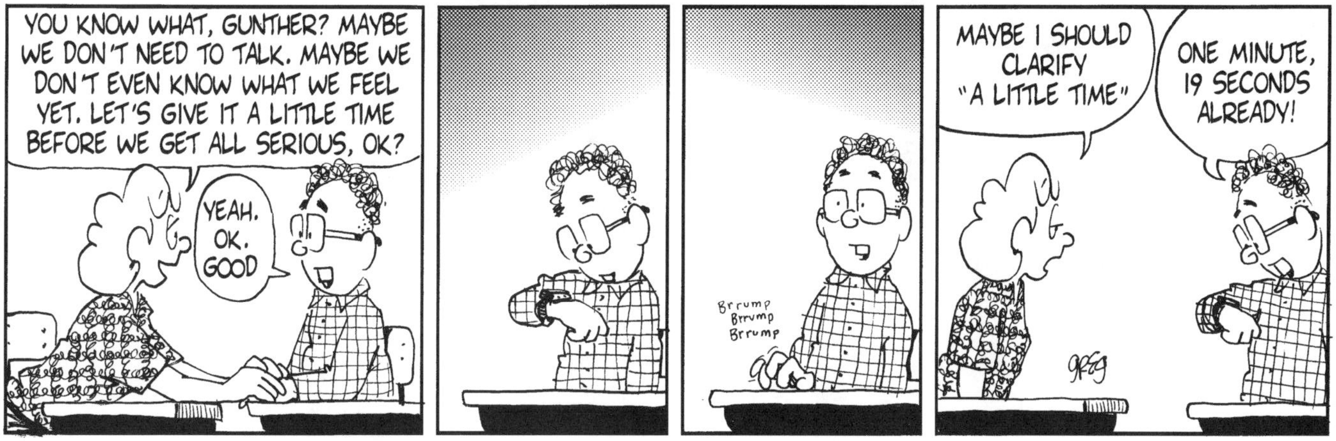
YOU KNOW WHAT, GUNTHER? MAYBE WE DON'T NEED TO TALK. MAYBE WE DON'T EVEN KNOW WHAT WE FEEL YET. LET'S GIVE IT A LITTLE TIME BEFORE WE GET ALL SERIOUS, OK?
YEAH. OK. GOOD
Brrump Brrump Brrump
MAYBE I SHOULD CLARIFY "A LITTLE TIME"
ONE MINUTE, 19 SECONDS ALREADY!
GREG

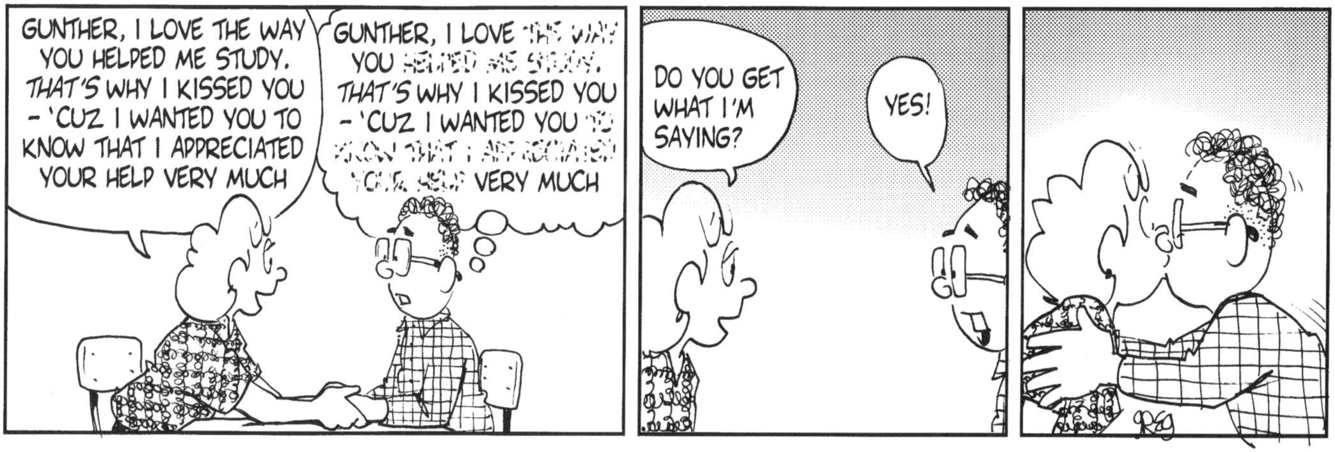
GUNTHER, I LOVE THE WAY YOU HELPED ME STUDY. *THAT'S* WHY I KISSED YOU – 'CUZ I WANTED YOU TO KNOW THAT I APPRECIATED YOUR HELP VERY MUCH
GUNTHER, I LOVE
YOU
THAT'S WHY I KISSED YOU
– 'CUZ I WANTED YOU
VERY MUCH
DO YOU GET WHAT I'M SAYING?
YES!
GREG

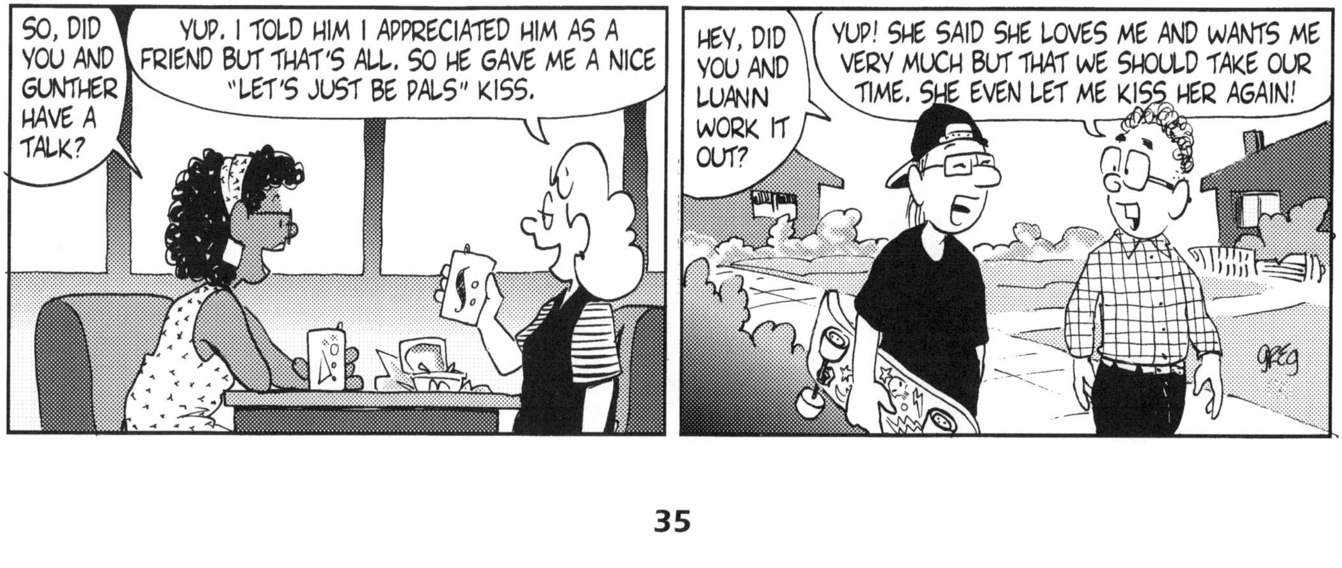
SO, DID YOU AND GUNTHER HAVE A TALK?
YUP. I TOLD HIM I APPRECIATED HIM AS A FRIEND BUT THAT'S ALL. SO HE GAVE ME A NICE "LET'S JUST BE PALS" KISS.
HEY, DID YOU AND LUANN WORK IT OUT?
YUP! SHE SAID SHE LOVES ME AND WANTS ME VERY MUCH BUT THAT WE SHOULD TAKE OUR TIME. SHE EVEN LET ME KISS HER AGAIN!
GREG

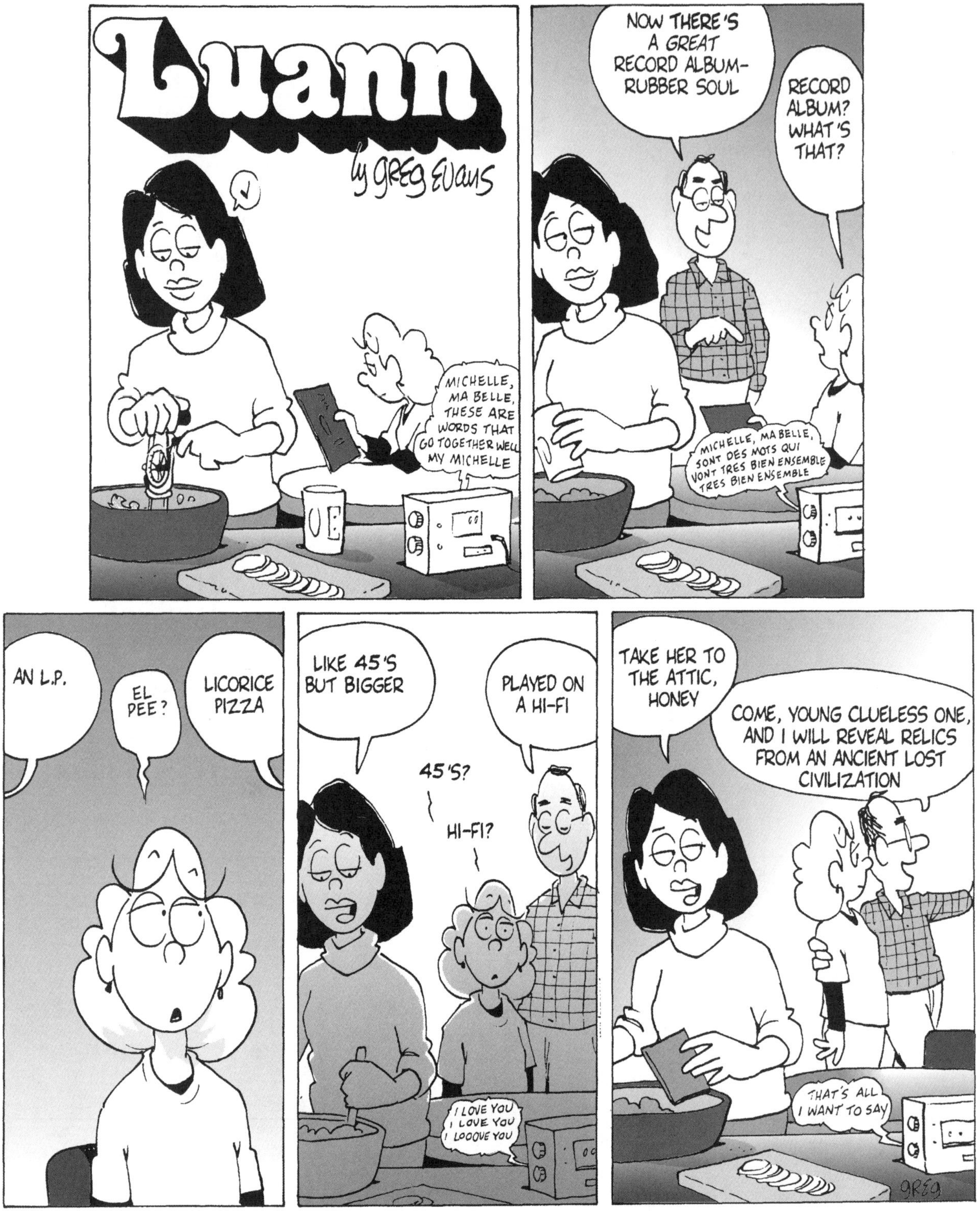
Luann
by GREG EVANS
MICHELLE, MA BELLE, THESE ARE WORDS THAT GO TOGETHER WELL MY MICHELLE
NOW THERE'S A GREAT RECORD ALBUM- RUBBER SOUL
RECORD ALBUM? WHAT'S THAT?
MICHELLE, MA BELLE, SONT DES MOTS QUI VONT TRES BIEN ENSEMBLE TRES BIEN ENSEMBLE
AN L.P.
EL PEE?
LICORICE PIZZA
LIKE 45'S BUT BIGGER
PLAYED ON A HI-FI
45'S?
HI-FI?
I LOVE YOU I LOVE YOU I LOOOVE YOU
TAKE HER TO THE ATTIC, HONEY
COME, YOUNG CLUELESS ONE, AND I WILL REVEAL RELICS FROM AN ANCIENT LOST CIVILIZATION
THAT'S ALL I WANT TO SAY
GREG

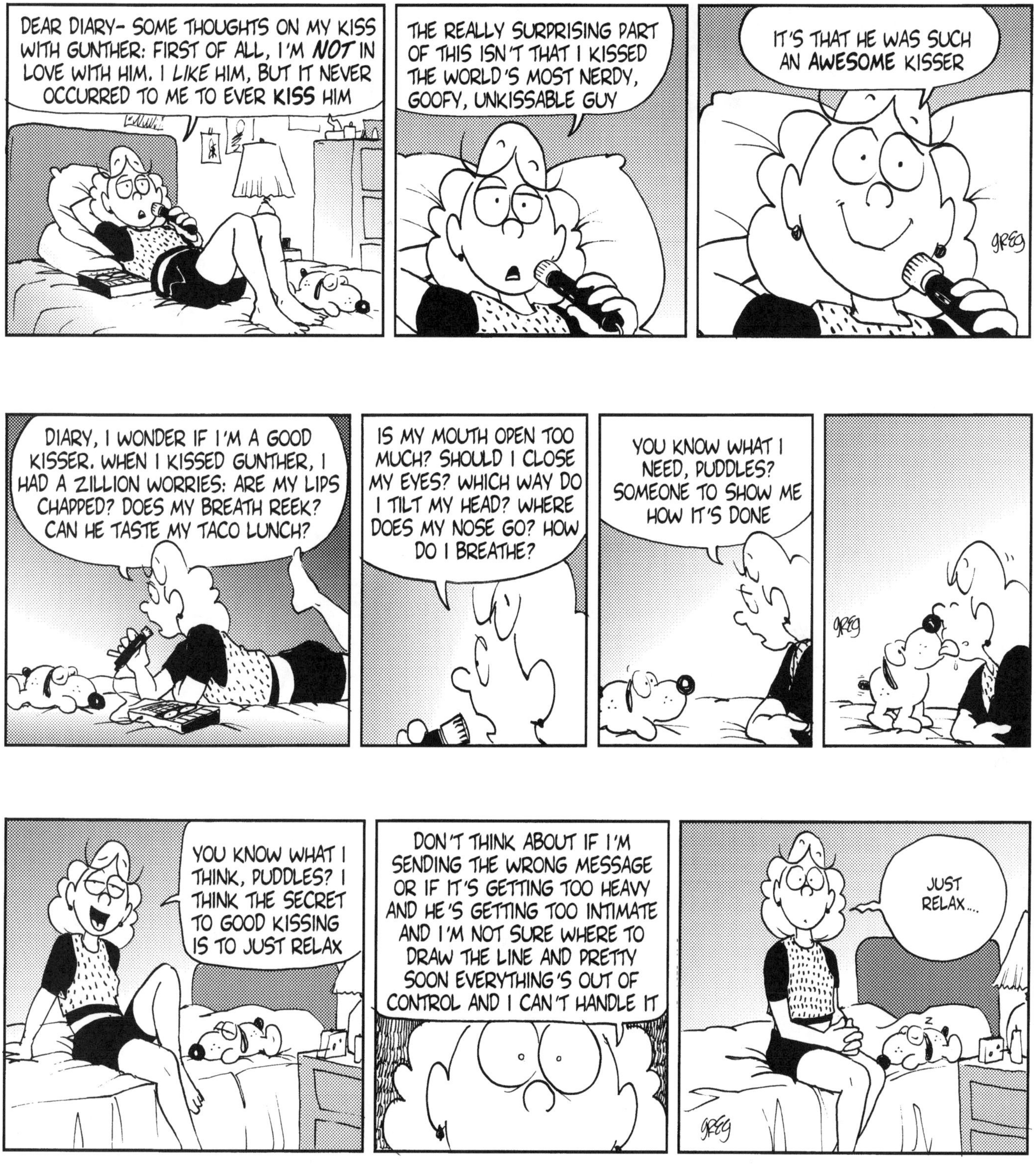
DEAR DIARY- SOME THOUGHTS ON MY KISS WITH GUNTHER: FIRST OF ALL, I'M *NOT* IN LOVE WITH HIM. I *LIKE* HIM, BUT IT NEVER OCCURRED TO ME TO EVER **KISS** HIM
THE REALLY SURPRISING PART OF THIS ISN'T THAT I KISSED THE WORLD'S MOST NERDY, GOOFY, UNKISSABLE GUY
IT'S THAT HE WAS SUCH AN **AWESOME** KISSER
GREG
DIARY, I WONDER IF I'M A GOOD KISSER. WHEN I KISSED GUNTHER, I HAD A ZILLION WORRIES: ARE MY LIPS CHAPPED? DOES MY BREATH REEK? CAN HE TASTE MY TACO LUNCH?
IS MY MOUTH OPEN TOO MUCH? SHOULD I CLOSE MY EYES? WHICH WAY DO I TILT MY HEAD? WHERE DOES MY NOSE GO? HOW DO I BREATHE?
YOU KNOW WHAT I NEED, PUDDLES? SOMEONE TO SHOW ME HOW IT'S DONE
GREG
YOU KNOW WHAT I THINK, PUDDLES? I THINK THE SECRET TO GOOD KISSING IS TO JUST RELAX
DON'T THINK ABOUT IF I'M SENDING THE WRONG MESSAGE OR IF IT'S GETTING TOO HEAVY AND HE'S GETTING TOO INTIMATE AND I'M NOT SURE WHERE TO DRAW THE LINE AND PRETTY SOON EVERYTHING'S OUT OF CONTROL AND I CAN'T HANDLE IT
JUST RELAX....
GREG

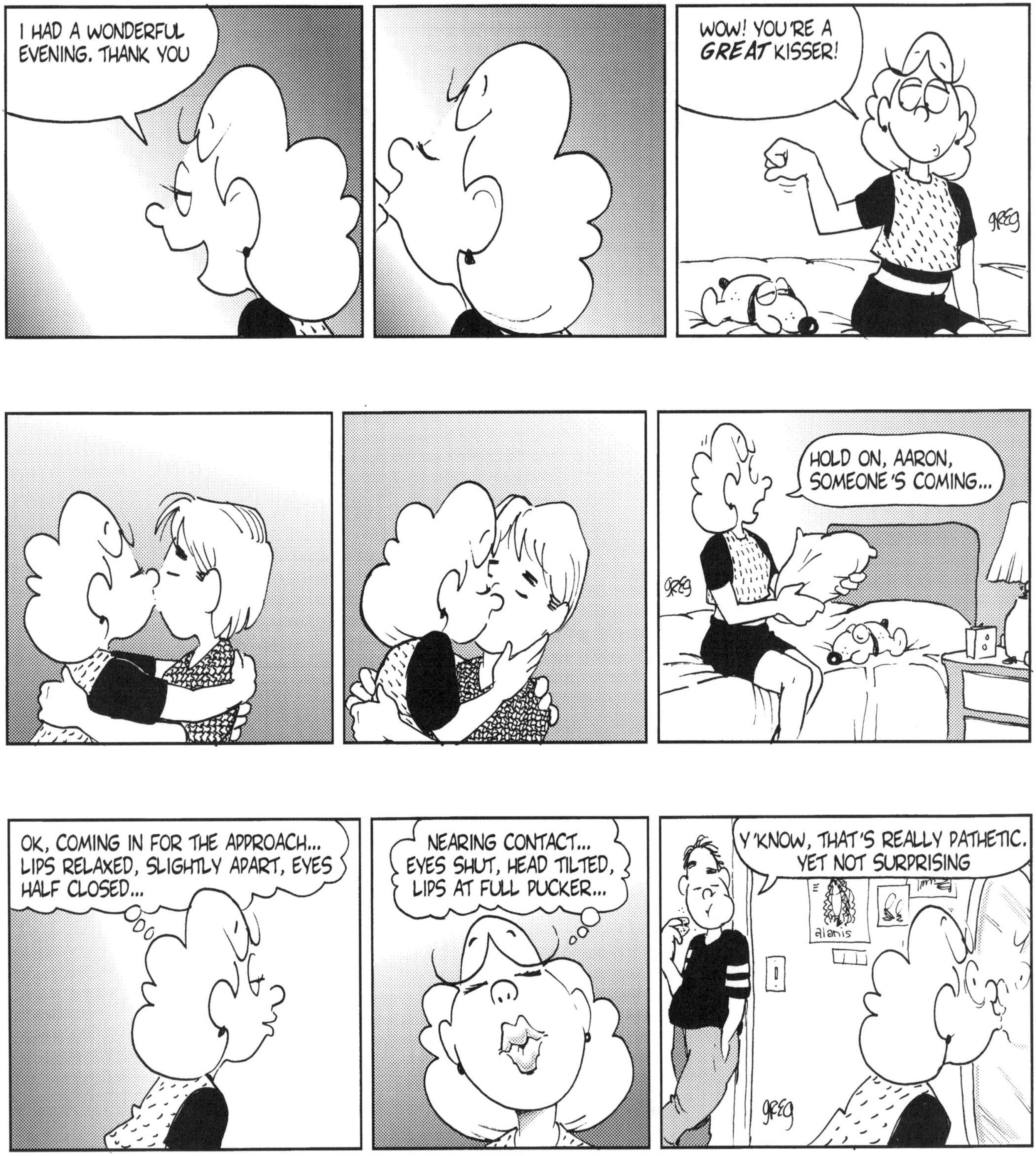
I HAD A WONDERFUL EVENING. THANK YOU
WOW! YOU'RE A GREAT KISSER!
GREG
GREG
HOLD ON, AARON, SOMEONE'S COMING...
OK, COMING IN FOR THE APPROACH... LIPS RELAXED, SLIGHTLY APART, EYES HALF CLOSED...
NEARING CONTACT... EYES SHUT, HEAD TILTED, LIPS AT FULL PUCKER...
Y'KNOW, THAT'S REALLY PATHETIC. YET NOT SURPRISING
alanis
GREG

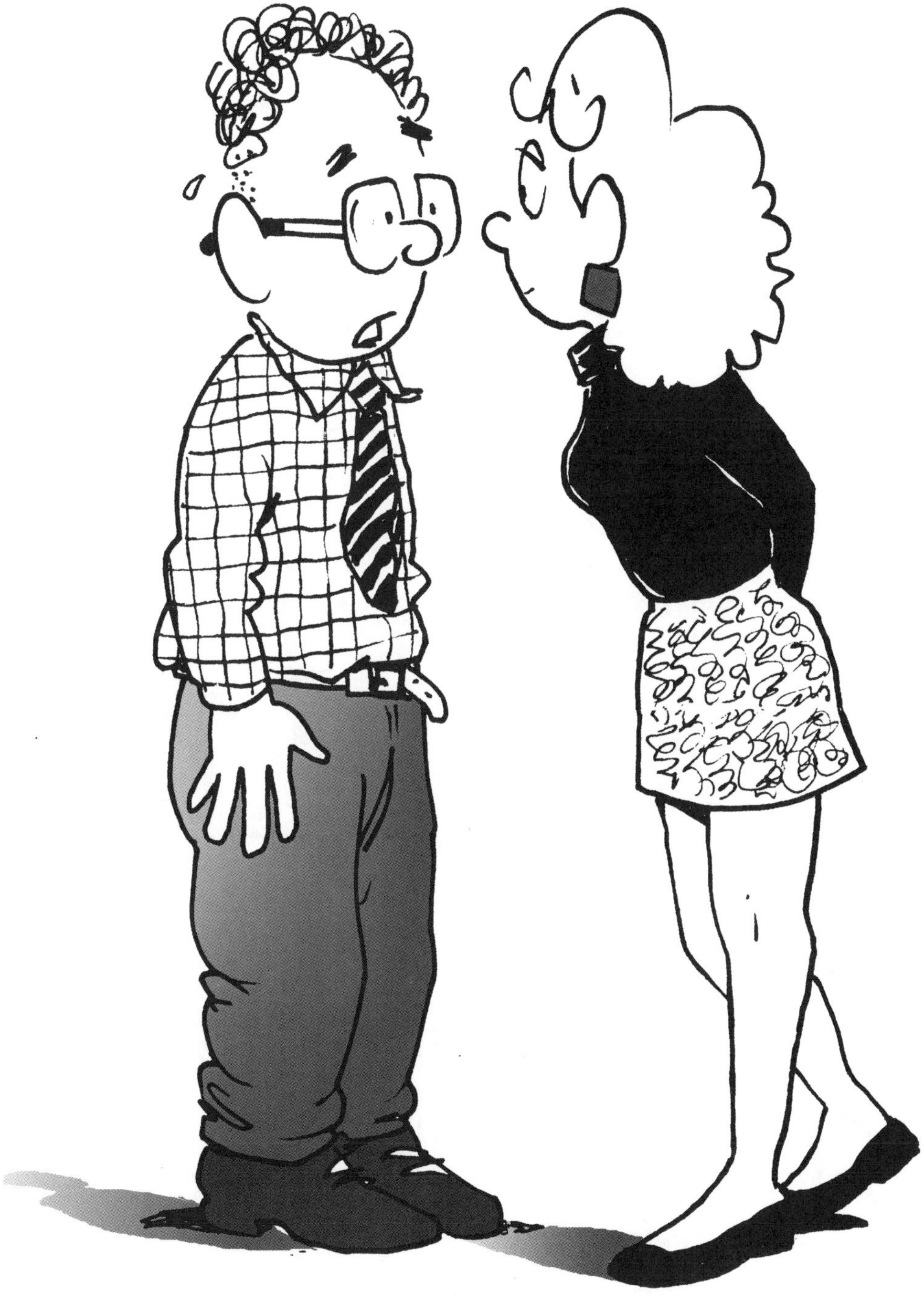

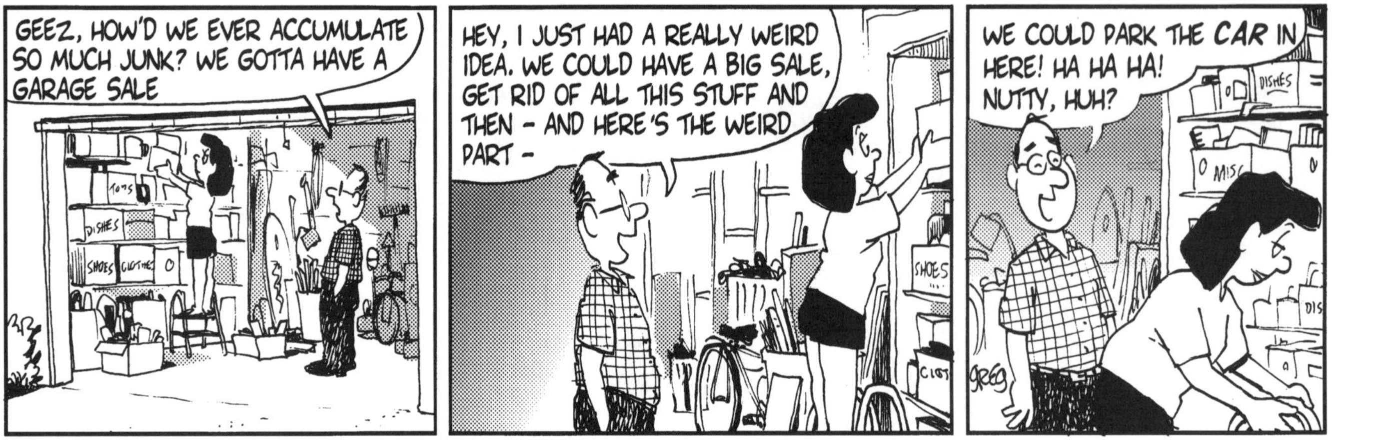
GEEZ, HOW'D WE EVER ACCUMULATE SO MUCH JUNK? WE GOTTA HAVE A GARAGE SALE
HEY, I JUST HAD A REALLY WEIRD IDEA. WE COULD HAVE A BIG SALE, GET RID OF ALL THIS STUFF AND THEN – AND HERE'S THE WEIRD PART –
WE COULD PARK THE *CAR* IN HERE! HA HA HA! NUTTY, HUH?

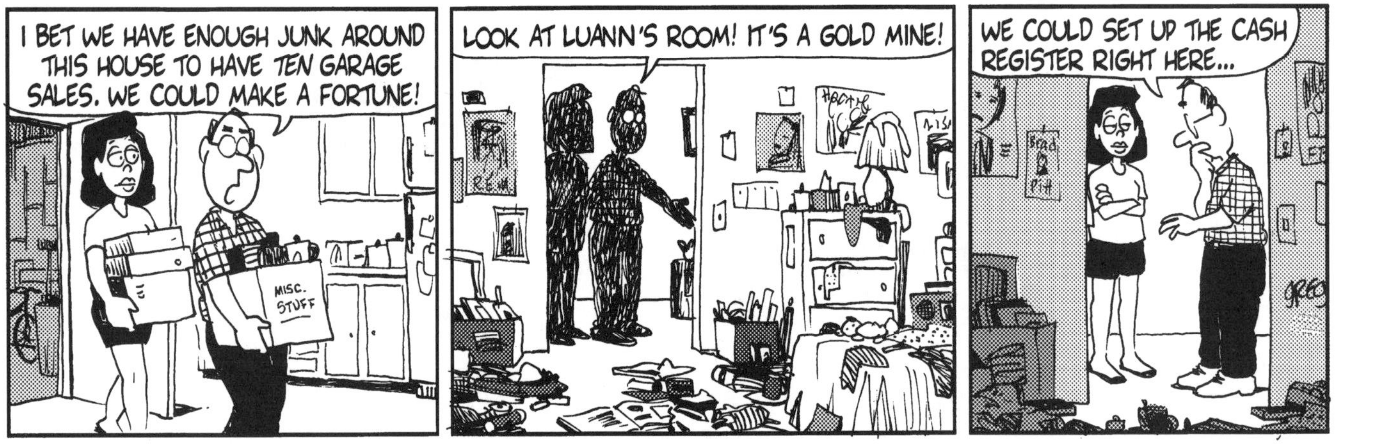
I BET WE HAVE ENOUGH JUNK AROUND THIS HOUSE TO HAVE *TEN* GARAGE SALES. WE COULD MAKE A FORTUNE!
LOOK AT LUANN'S ROOM! IT'S A GOLD MINE!
WE COULD SET UP THE CASH REGISTER RIGHT HERE...

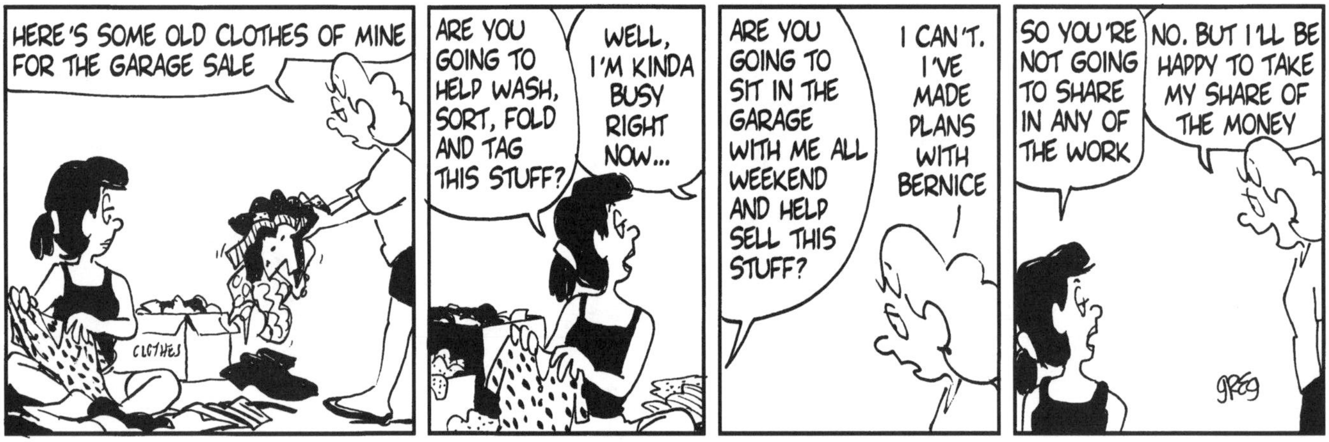
HERE'S SOME OLD CLOTHES OF MINE FOR THE GARAGE SALE
ARE YOU GOING TO HELP WASH, SORT, FOLD AND TAG THIS STUFF?
WELL, I'M KINDA BUSY RIGHT NOW...
ARE YOU GOING TO SIT IN THE GARAGE WITH ME ALL WEEKEND AND HELP SELL THIS STUFF?
I CAN'T. I'VE MADE PLANS WITH BERNICE
SO YOU'RE NOT GOING TO SHARE IN ANY OF THE WORK
NO. BUT I'LL BE HAPPY TO TAKE MY SHARE OF THE MONEY

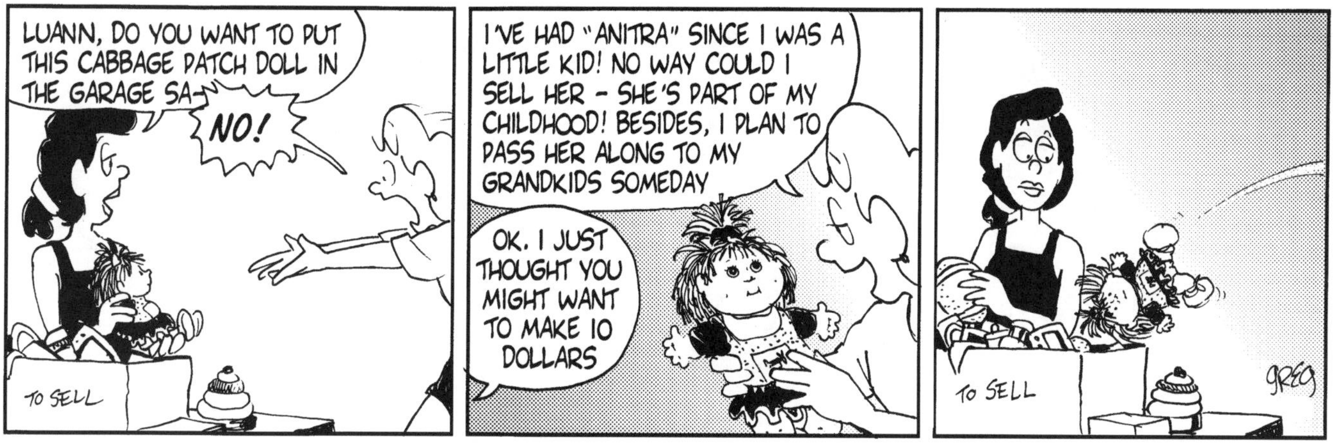
LUANN, DO YOU WANT TO PUT THIS CABBAGE PATCH DOLL IN THE GARAGE SA-
NO!
I'VE HAD "ANITRA" SINCE I WAS A LITTLE KID! NO WAY COULD I SELL HER - SHE'S PART OF MY CHILDHOOD! BESIDES, I PLAN TO PASS HER ALONG TO MY GRANDKIDS SOMEDAY
OK. I JUST THOUGHT YOU MIGHT WANT TO MAKE 10 DOLLARS
TO SELL
TO SELL
GREG

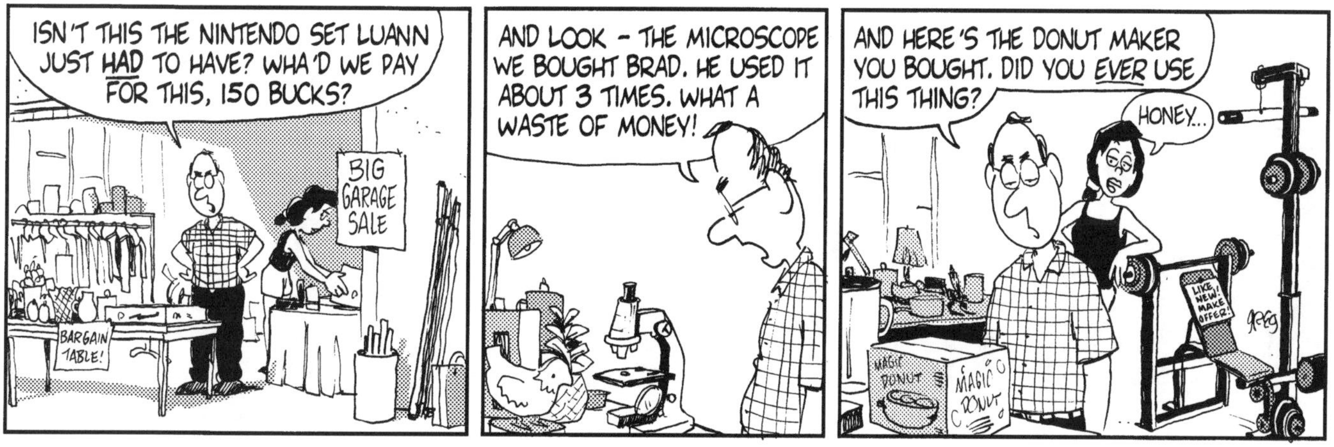
ISN'T THIS THE NINTENDO SET LUANN JUST HAD TO HAVE? WHA'D WE PAY FOR THIS, 150 BUCKS?
BIG GARAGE SALE
BARGAIN TABLE!
AND LOOK - THE MICROSCOPE WE BOUGHT BRAD. HE USED IT ABOUT 3 TIMES. WHAT A WASTE OF MONEY!
AND HERE'S THE DONUT MAKER YOU BOUGHT. DID YOU EVER USE THIS THING?
HONEY...
MAGIC DONUT
MAGIC DONUT
LIKE NEW! MAKE OFFER!
GREG

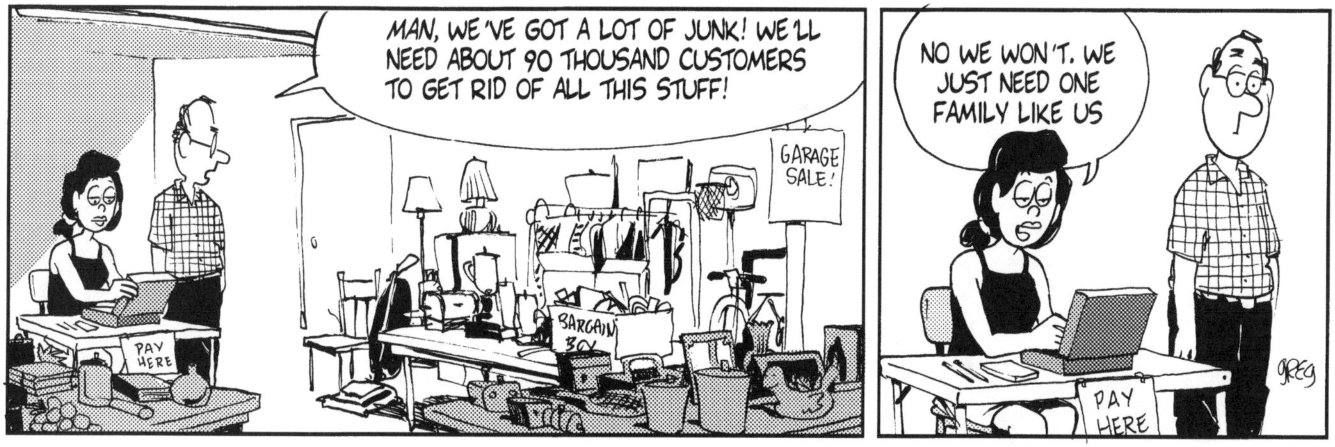
MAN, WE'VE GOT A LOT OF JUNK! WE'LL NEED ABOUT 90 THOUSAND CUSTOMERS TO GET RID OF ALL THIS STUFF!
GARAGE SALE!
BARGAIN BOX
PAY HERE
NO WE WON'T. WE JUST NEED ONE FAMILY LIKE US
PAY HERE
GREG

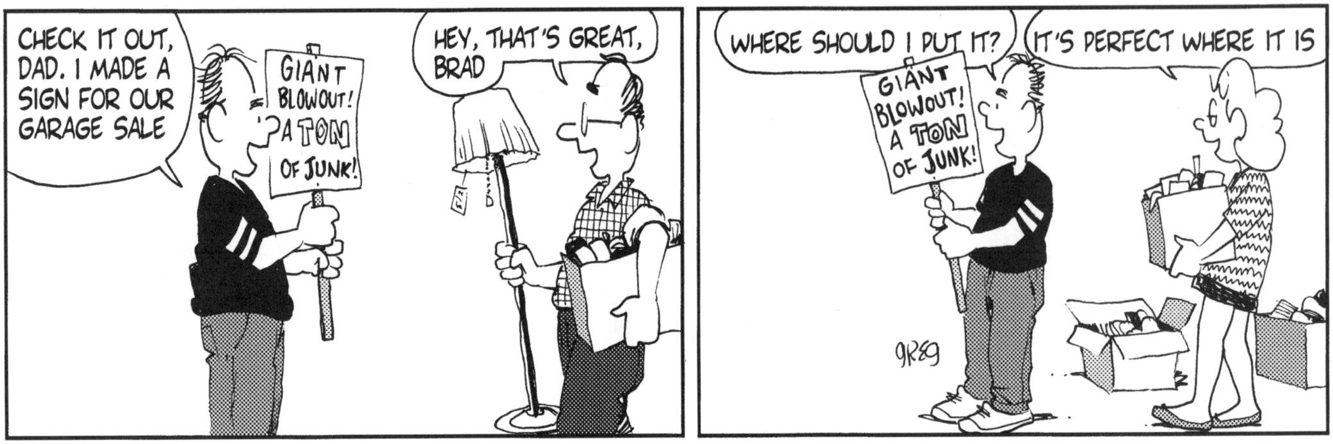
CHECK IT OUT, DAD. I MADE A SIGN FOR OUR GARAGE SALE
GIANT BLOWOUT! A TON OF JUNK!
HEY, THAT'S GREAT, BRAD
WHERE SHOULD I PUT IT?
GIANT BLOWOUT! A TON OF JUNK!
IT'S PERFECT WHERE IT IS

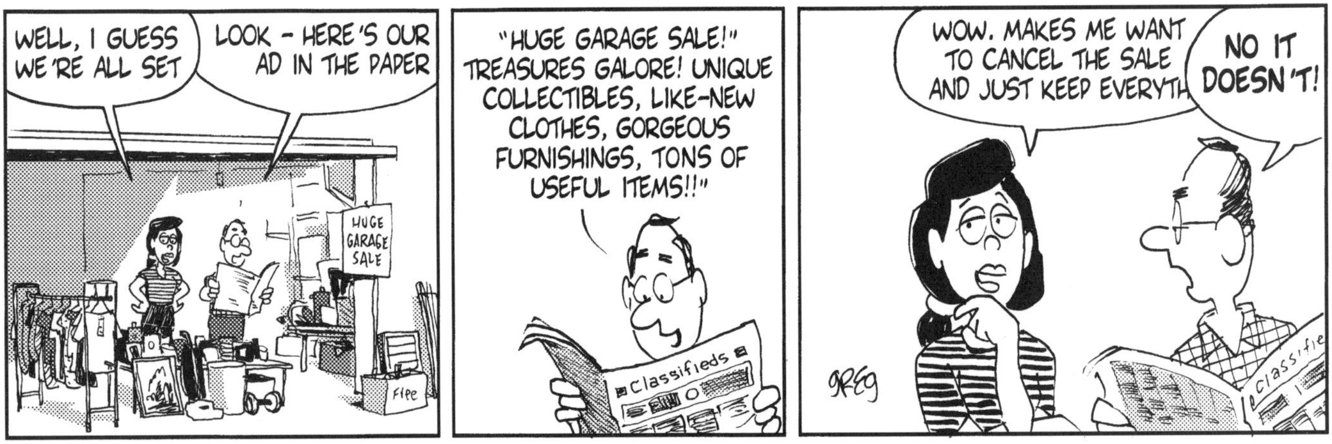
WELL, I GUESS WE'RE ALL SET
LOOK – HERE'S OUR AD IN THE PAPER
HUGE GARAGE SALE
Free
"HUGE GARAGE SALE!" TREASURES GALORE! UNIQUE COLLECTIBLES, LIKE-NEW CLOTHES, GORGEOUS FURNISHINGS, TONS OF USEFUL ITEMS!!"
Classifieds
WOW. MAKES ME WANT TO CANCEL THE SALE AND JUST KEEP EVERYTH
NO IT DOESN'T!

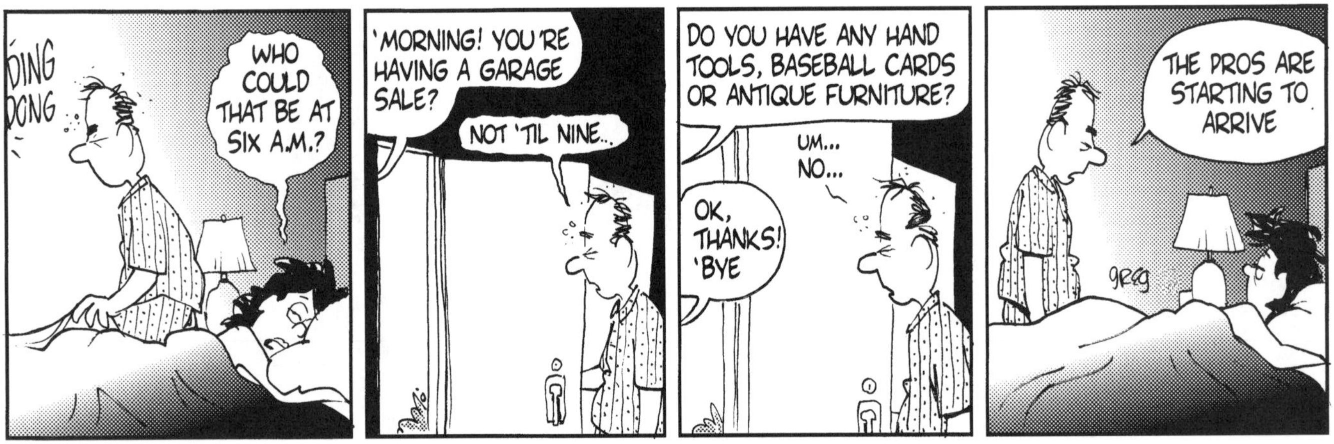
DING DONG
WHO COULD THAT BE AT SIX A.M.?
'MORNING! YOU'RE HAVING A GARAGE SALE?
NOT 'TIL NINE...
DO YOU HAVE ANY HAND TOOLS, BASEBALL CARDS OR ANTIQUE FURNITURE?
UM... NO...
OK, THANKS! 'BYE
THE PROS ARE STARTING TO ARRIVE

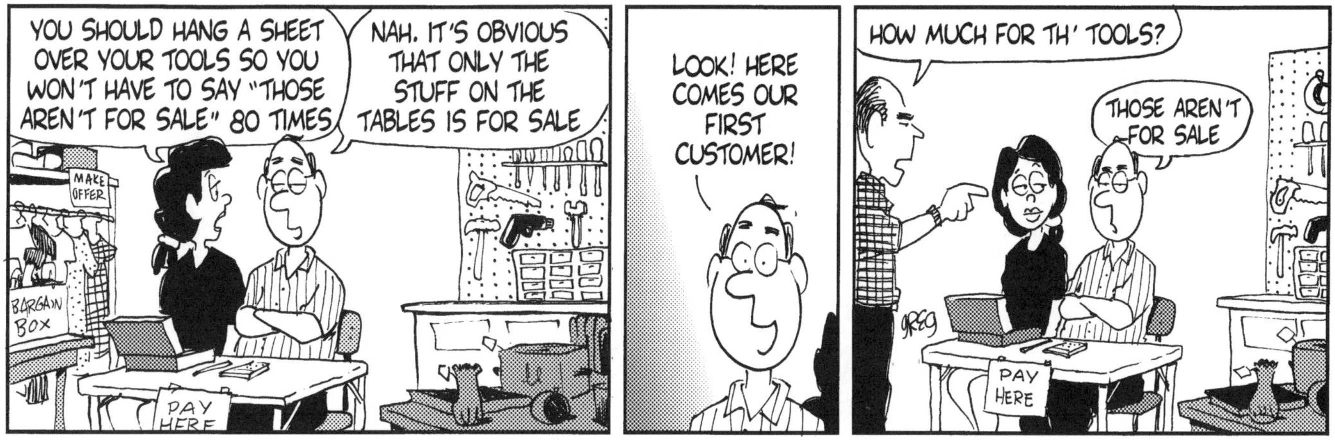
YOU SHOULD HANG A SHEET OVER YOUR TOOLS SO YOU WON'T HAVE TO SAY "THOSE AREN'T FOR SALE" 80 TIMES
NAH. IT'S OBVIOUS THAT ONLY THE STUFF ON THE TABLES IS FOR SALE
MAKE OFFER
BARGAIN BOX
LOOK! HERE COMES OUR FIRST CUSTOMER!
HOW MUCH FOR TH' TOOLS?
THOSE AREN'T FOR SALE
PAY HERE

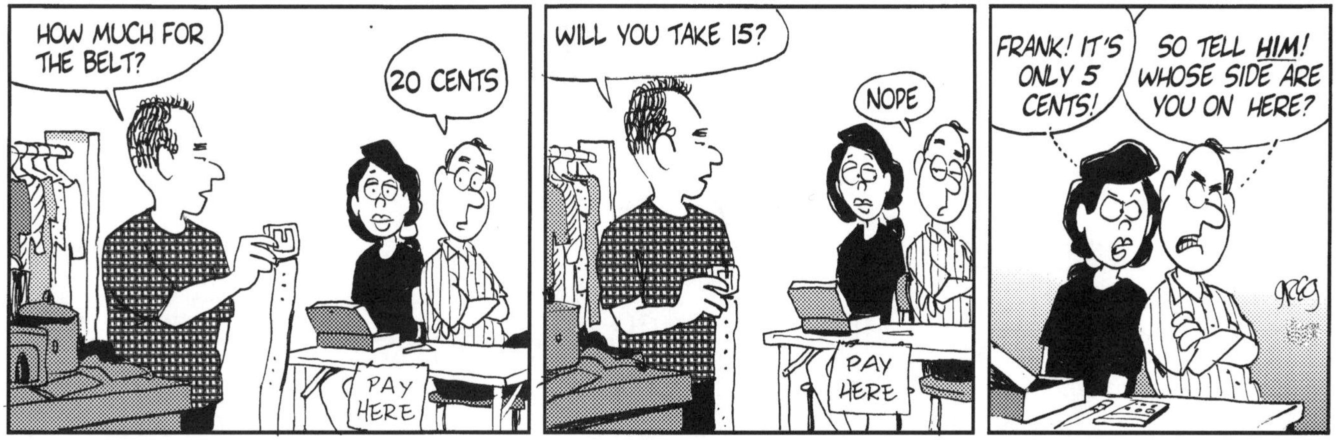
HOW MUCH FOR THE BELT?
20 CENTS
PAY HERE
WILL YOU TAKE 15?
NOPE
PAY HERE
FRANK! IT'S ONLY 5 CENTS!
SO TELL HIM! WHOSE SIDE ARE YOU ON HERE?

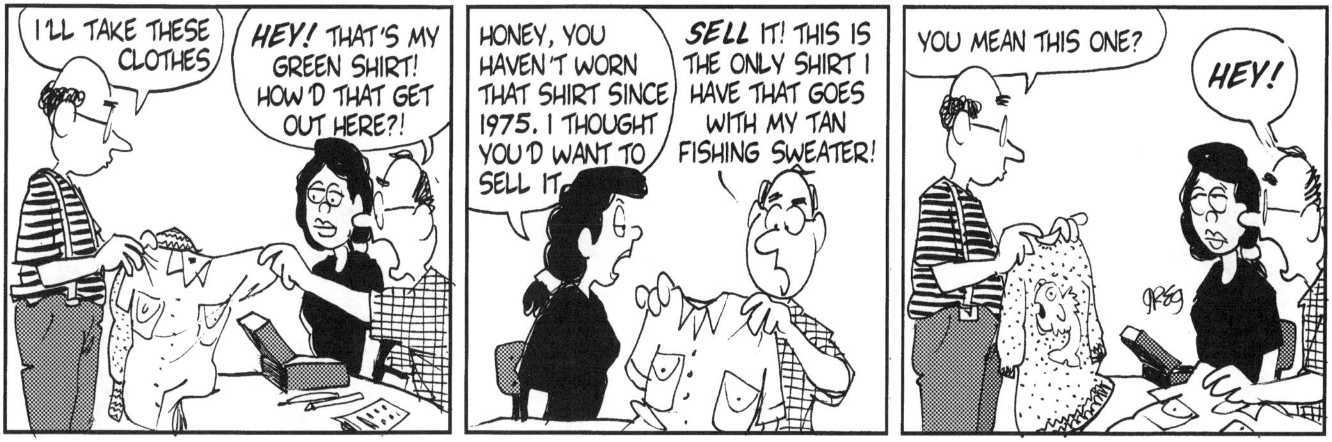
I'LL TAKE THESE CLOTHES
HEY! THAT'S MY GREEN SHIRT! HOW'D THAT GET OUT HERE?!
HONEY, YOU HAVEN'T WORN THAT SHIRT SINCE 1975. I THOUGHT YOU'D WANT TO SELL IT
SELL IT! THIS IS THE ONLY SHIRT I HAVE THAT GOES WITH MY TAN FISHING SWEATER!
YOU MEAN THIS ONE?
HEY!

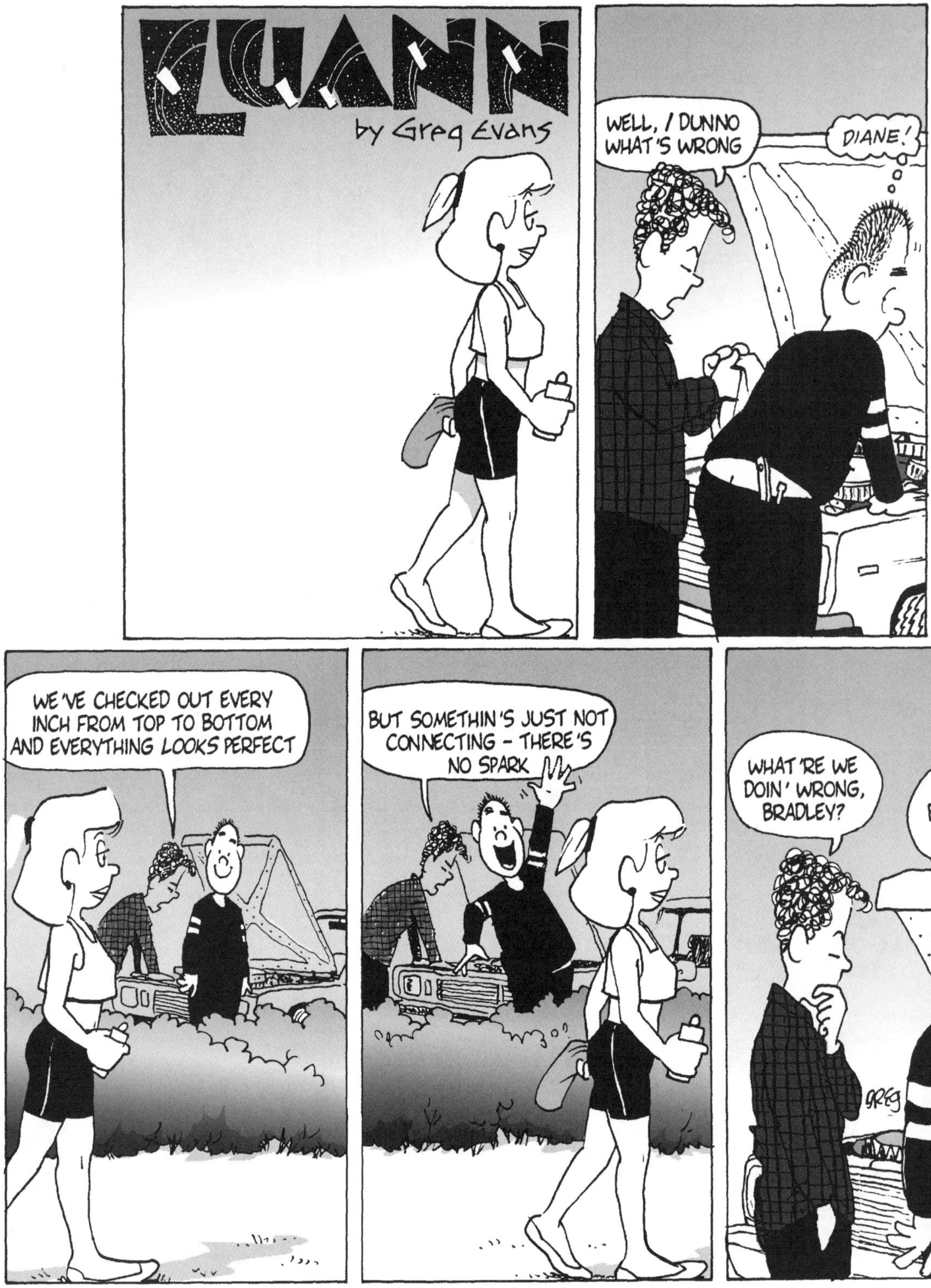
LUANN
by Greg Evans
WELL, I DUNNO WHAT'S WRONG
DIANE!
WE'VE CHECKED OUT EVERY INCH FROM TOP TO BOTTOM AND EVERYTHING LOOKS PERFECT
BUT SOMETHIN'S JUST NOT CONNECTING - THERE'S NO SPARK
WHAT'RE WE DOIN' WRONG, BRADLEY?
BEATS ME...
GREG

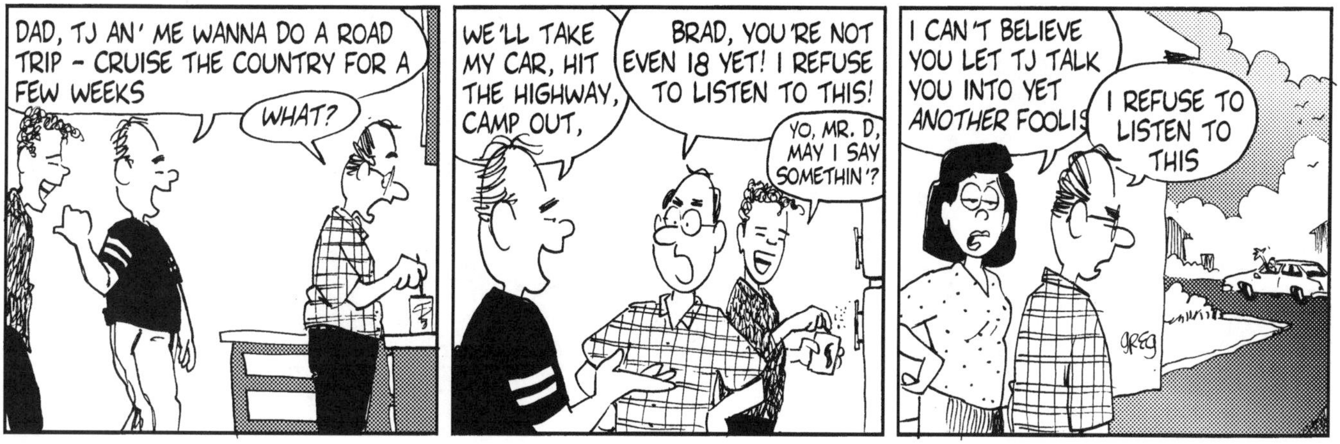
DAD, TJ AN' ME WANNA DO A ROAD TRIP - CRUISE THE COUNTRY FOR A FEW WEEKS
WHAT?
WE'LL TAKE MY CAR, HIT THE HIGHWAY, CAMP OUT,
BRAD, YOU'RE NOT EVEN 18 YET! I REFUSE TO LISTEN TO THIS!
YO, MR. D, MAY I SAY SOMETHIN'?
I CAN'T BELIEVE YOU LET TJ TALK YOU INTO YET ANOTHER FOOLIS
I REFUSE TO LISTEN TO THIS
GREG

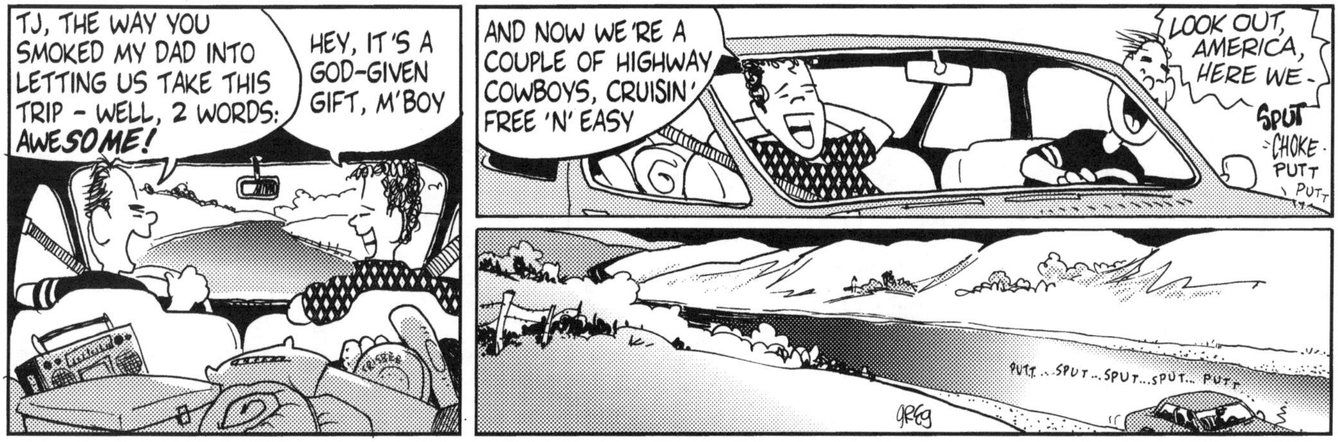
TJ, THE WAY YOU SMOKED MY DAD INTO LETTING US TAKE THIS TRIP - WELL, 2 WORDS: AWESOME!
HEY, IT'S A GOD-GIVEN GIFT, M'BOY
AND NOW WE'RE A COUPLE OF HIGHWAY COWBOYS, CRUISIN' FREE 'N' EASY
LOOK OUT, AMERICA, HERE WE-
SPUT
CHOKE
PUTT
PUTT
PUTT...SPUT...SPUT...SPUT...PUTT
GREG

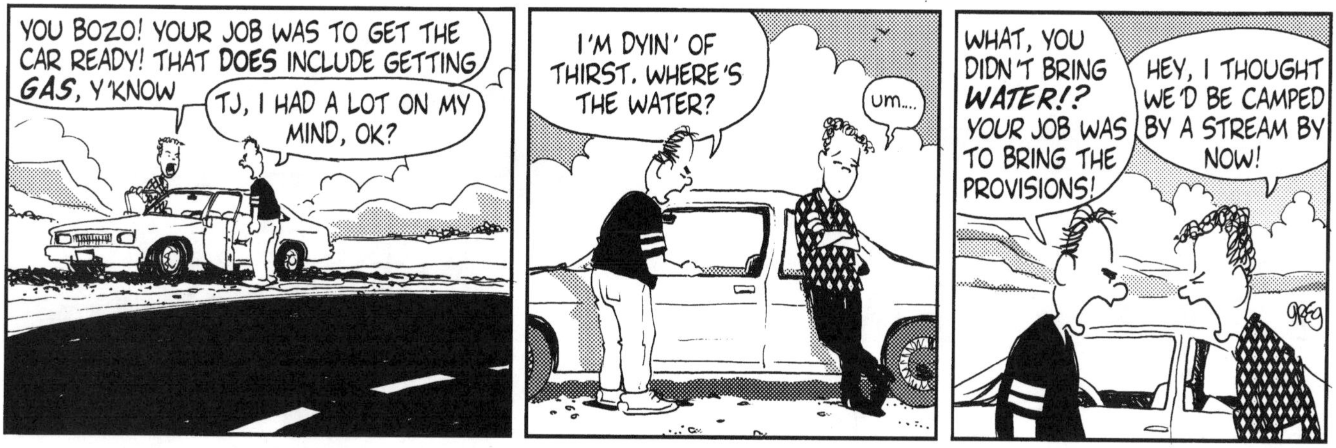
YOU BOZO! YOUR JOB WAS TO GET THE CAR READY! THAT DOES INCLUDE GETTING GAS, Y'KNOW
TJ, I HAD A LOT ON MY MIND, OK?
I'M DYIN' OF THIRST. WHERE'S THE WATER?
um...
WHAT, YOU DIDN'T BRING WATER!? YOUR JOB WAS TO BRING THE PROVISIONS!
HEY, I THOUGHT WE'D BE CAMPED BY A STREAM BY NOW!
GREG

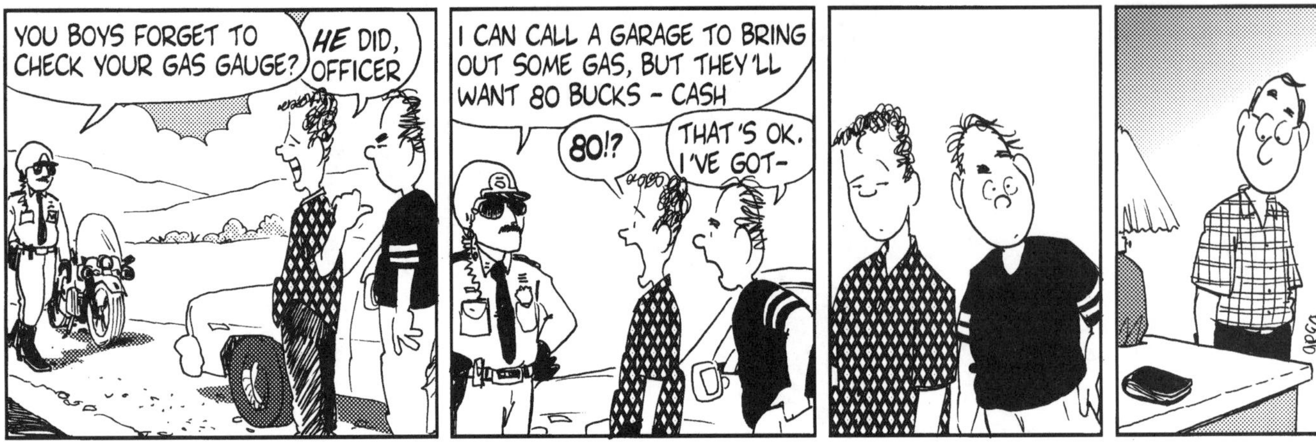
YOU BOYS FORGET TO CHECK YOUR GAS GAUGE?
HE DID, OFFICER
I CAN CALL A GARAGE TO BRING OUT SOME GAS, BUT THEY'LL WANT 80 BUCKS - CASH
80!?
THAT'S OK. I'VE GOT-

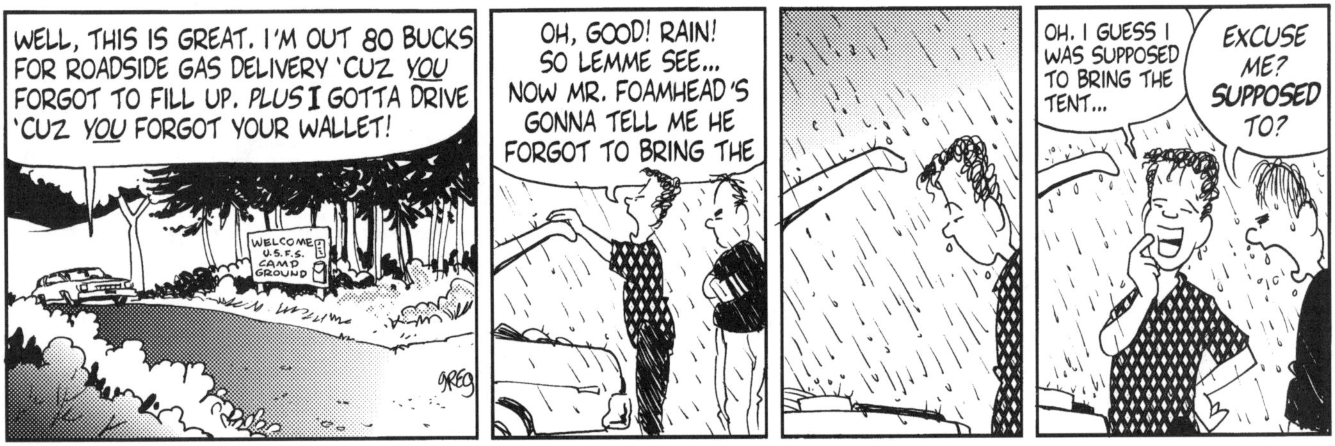
WELL, THIS IS GREAT. I'M OUT 80 BUCKS FOR ROADSIDE GAS DELIVERY 'CUZ YOU FORGOT TO FILL UP. PLUS I GOTTA DRIVE 'CUZ YOU FORGOT YOUR WALLET!
WELCOME U.S.F.S. CAMP GROUND
OH, GOOD! RAIN! SO LEMME SEE... NOW MR. FOAMHEAD'S GONNA TELL ME HE FORGOT TO BRING THE
OH. I GUESS I WAS SUPPOSED TO BRING THE TENT...
EXCUSE ME? **SUPPOSED** TO?

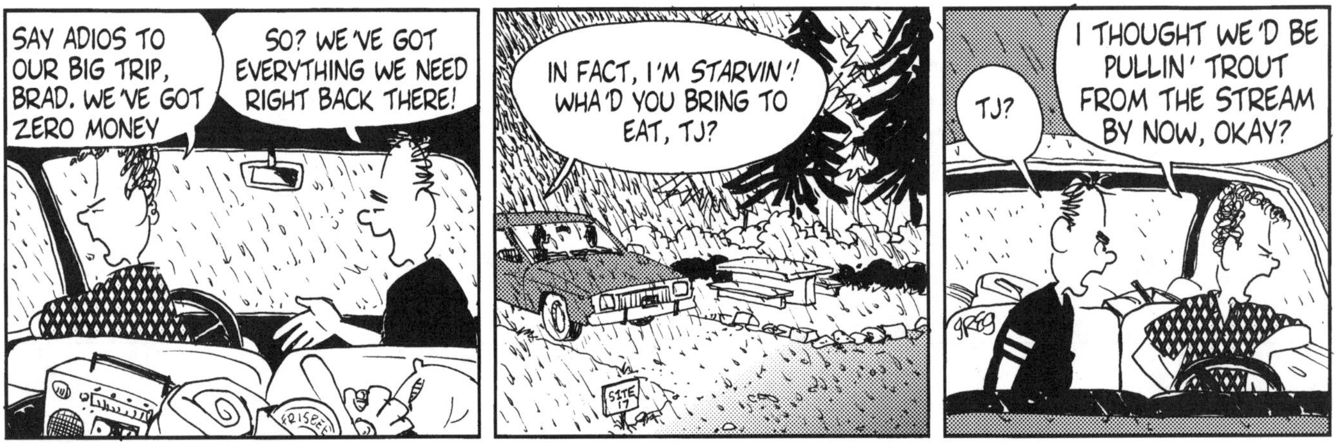
SAY ADIOS TO OUR BIG TRIP, BRAD. WE'VE GOT ZERO MONEY
SO? WE'VE GOT EVERYTHING WE NEED RIGHT BACK THERE!
IN FACT, I'M *STARVIN'*! WHA'D YOU BRING TO EAT, TJ?
SITE 17
TJ?
I THOUGHT WE'D BE PULLIN' TROUT FROM THE STREAM BY NOW, OKAY?

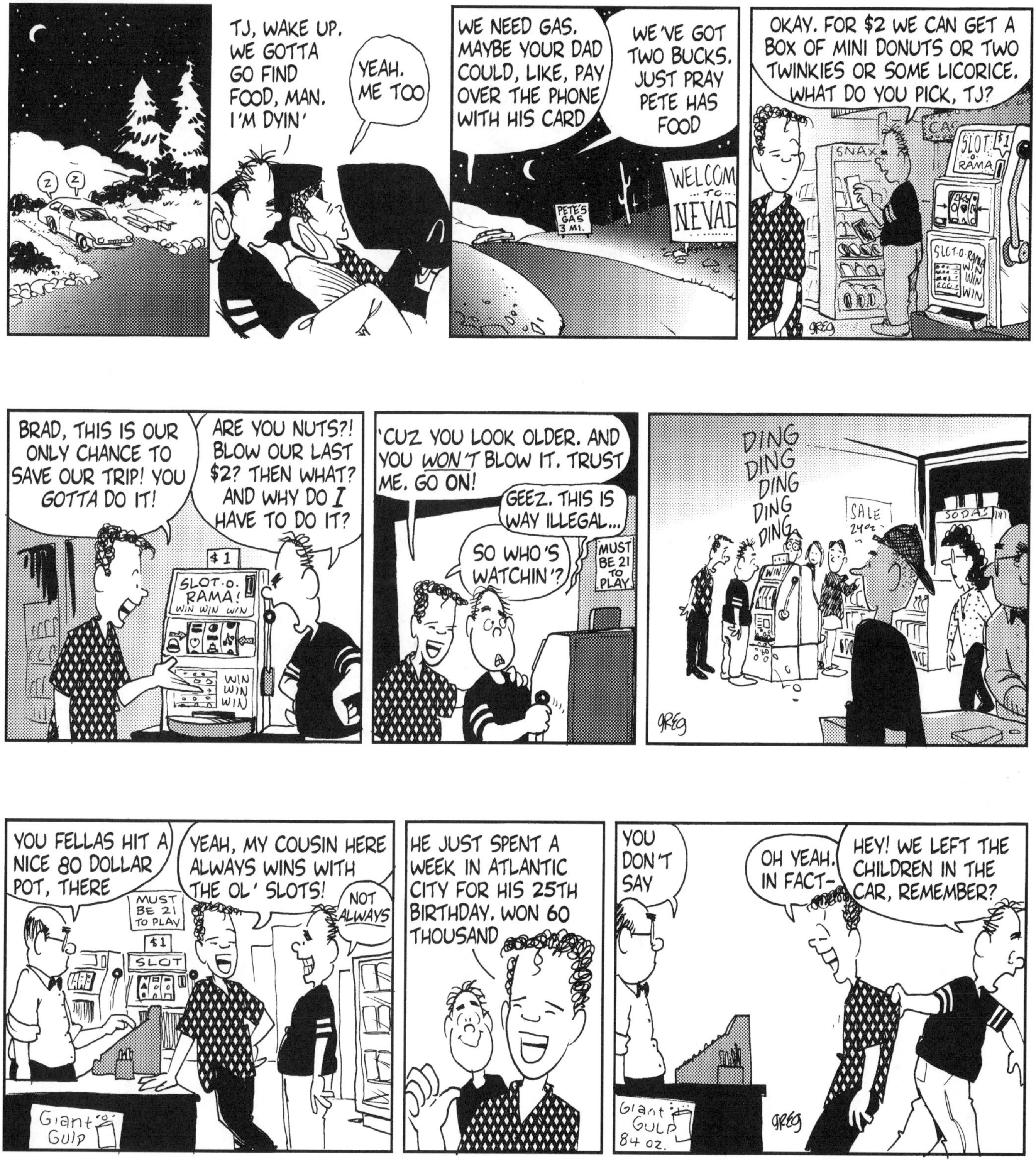
TJ, WAKE UP. WE GOTTA GO FIND FOOD, MAN. I'M DYIN'
YEAH. ME TOO
WE NEED GAS. MAYBE YOUR DAD COULD, LIKE, PAY OVER THE PHONE WITH HIS CARD
WE'VE GOT TWO BUCKS. JUST PRAY PETE HAS FOOD
PETE'S GAS 3 MI.
WELCOM ...TO... NEVAD
OKAY. FOR $2 WE CAN GET A BOX OF MINI DONUTS OR TWO TWINKIES OR SOME LICORICE. WHAT DO YOU PICK, TJ?
SNAX
SLOT-O-RAMA $1
SLOT-O-RAMA WIN WIN WIN
BRAD, THIS IS OUR ONLY CHANCE TO SAVE OUR TRIP! YOU GOTTA DO IT!
ARE YOU NUTS?! BLOW OUR LAST $2? THEN WHAT? AND WHY DO I HAVE TO DO IT?
$1
SLOT-O-RAMA! WIN WIN WIN
WIN WIN WIN
'CUZ YOU LOOK OLDER. AND YOU WON'T BLOW IT. TRUST ME. GO ON!
GEEZ. THIS IS WAY ILLEGAL...
SO WHO'S WATCHIN'?
MUST BE 21 TO PLAY
DING DING DING DING DING
WIN
SALE 24 oz.
SODA
YOU FELLAS HIT A NICE 80 DOLLAR POT, THERE
YEAH, MY COUSIN HERE ALWAYS WINS WITH THE OL' SLOTS!
NOT ALWAYS
MUST BE 21 TO PLAY
$1
SLOT
Giant Gulp
HE JUST SPENT A WEEK IN ATLANTIC CITY FOR HIS 25TH BIRTHDAY. WON 60 THOUSAND
YOU DON'T SAY
OH YEAH. IN FACT-
HEY! WE LEFT THE CHILDREN IN THE CAR, REMEMBER?
Giant GULP 84 oz.

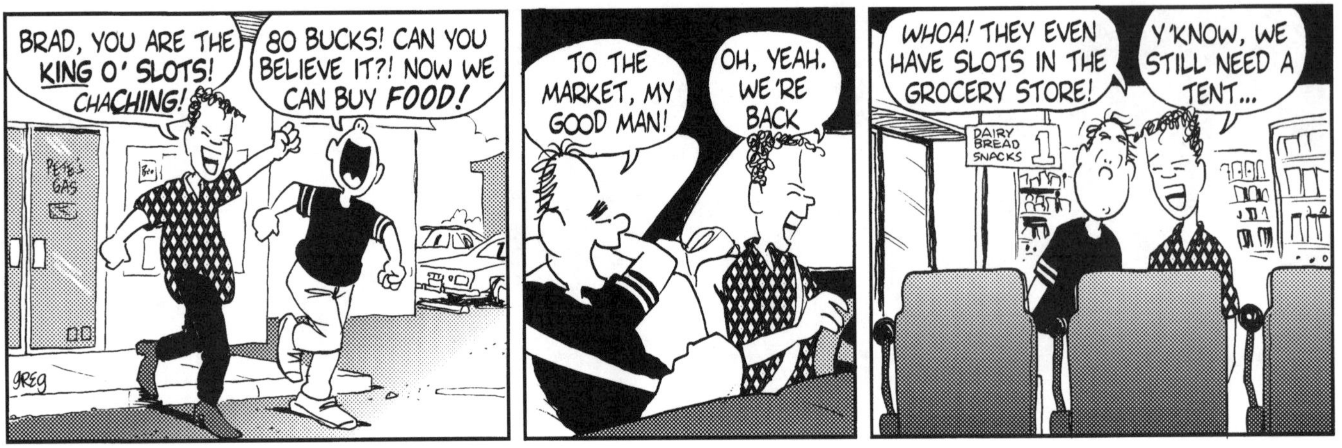
BRAD, YOU ARE THE KING O' SLOTS! CHACHING!
80 BUCKS! CAN YOU BELIEVE IT?! NOW WE CAN BUY FOOD!
PETE'S GAS
GREG
TO THE MARKET, MY GOOD MAN!
OH, YEAH. WE'RE BACK
WHOA! THEY EVEN HAVE SLOTS IN THE GROCERY STORE!
Y'KNOW, WE STILL NEED A TENT...
DAIRY BREAD SNACKS 1

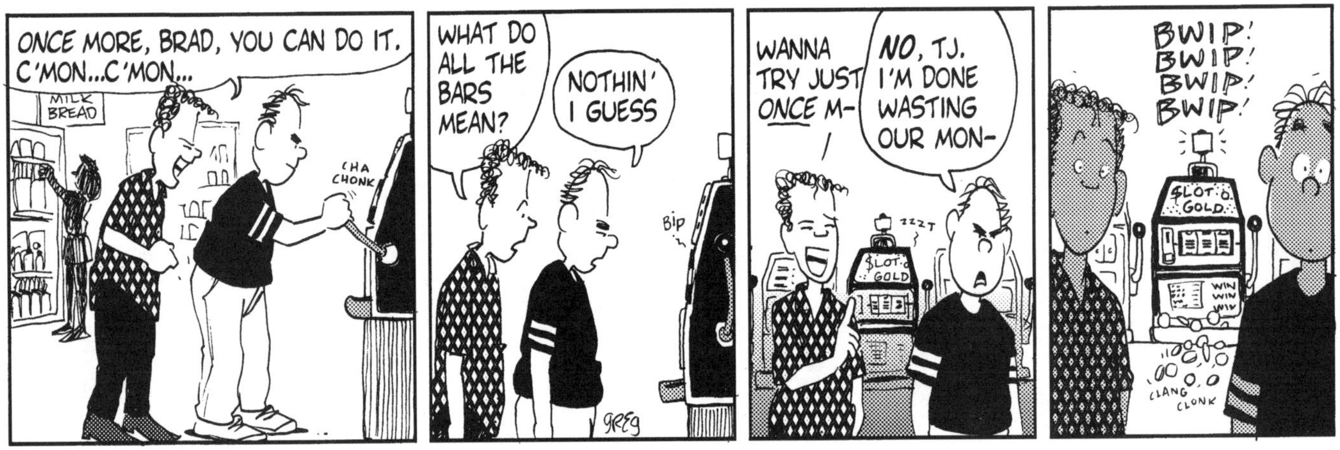
ONCE MORE, BRAD, YOU CAN DO IT. C'MON...C'MON...
MILK BREAD
CHA CHONK
WHAT DO ALL THE BARS MEAN?
NOTHIN' I GUESS
BIP
GREG
WANNA TRY JUST ONCE M–
NO, TJ. I'M DONE WASTING OUR MON–
ZZZT
SLOT O GOLD
BWIP! BWIP! BWIP! BWIP!
SLOT O GOLD
WIN WIN WIN
CLANG CLONK

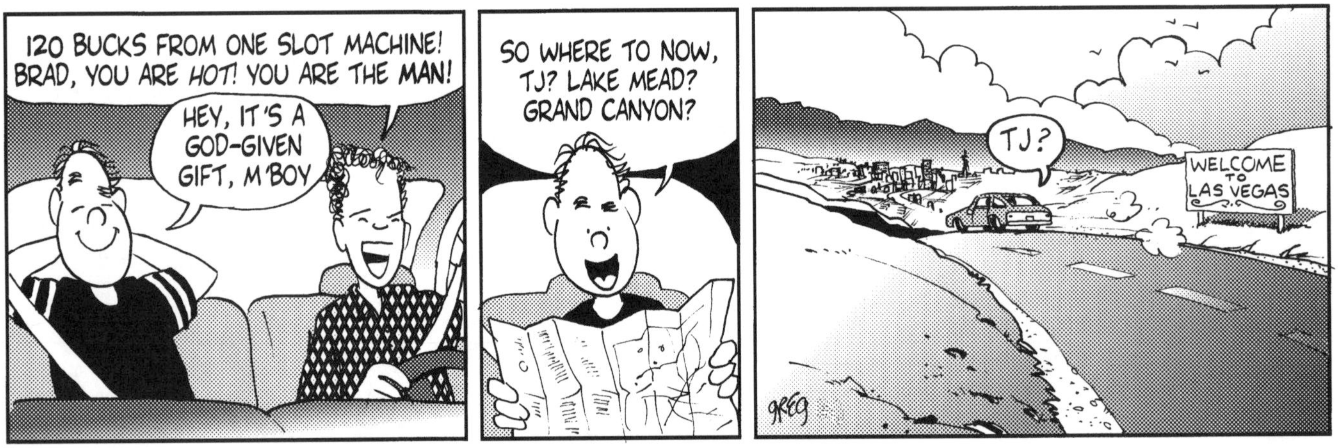
120 BUCKS FROM ONE SLOT MACHINE! BRAD, YOU ARE HOT! YOU ARE THE MAN!
HEY, IT'S A GOD-GIVEN GIFT, M'BOY
SO WHERE TO NOW, TJ? LAKE MEAD? GRAND CANYON?
TJ?
WELCOME TO LAS VEGAS
GREG

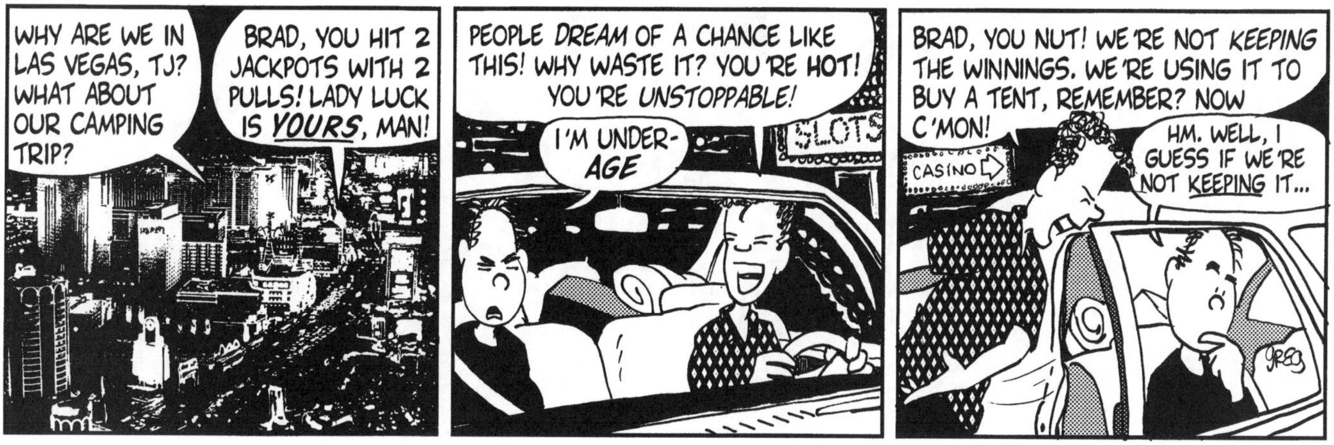
WHY ARE WE IN LAS VEGAS, TJ? WHAT ABOUT OUR CAMPING TRIP?
BRAD, YOU HIT 2 JACKPOTS WITH 2 PULLS! LADY LUCK IS YOURS, MAN!
PEOPLE DREAM OF A CHANCE LIKE THIS! WHY WASTE IT? YOU'RE HOT! YOU'RE UNSTOPPABLE!
I'M UNDER-AGE
SLOTS
BRAD, YOU NUT! WE'RE NOT KEEPING THE WINNINGS. WE'RE USING IT TO BUY A TENT, REMEMBER? NOW C'MON!
CASINO
HM. WELL, I GUESS IF WE'RE NOT KEEPING IT...
GREG

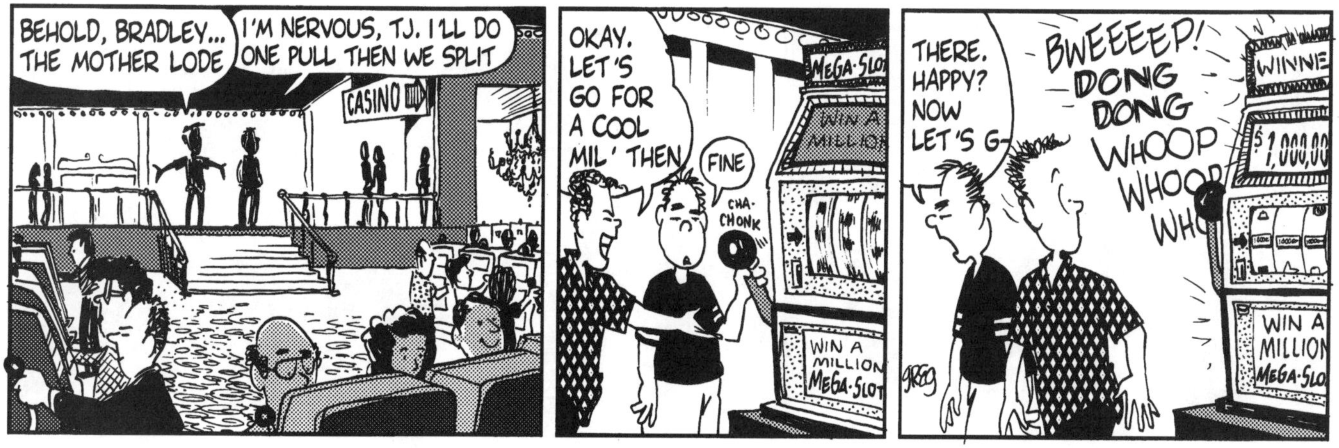
BEHOLD, BRADLEY... THE MOTHER LODE
I'M NERVOUS, TJ. I'LL DO ONE PULL THEN WE SPLIT
CASINO
OKAY. LET'S GO FOR A COOL MIL' THEN
MEGA-SLOT
WIN A MILLION
FINE
CHA-CHONK
WIN A MILLION MEGA-SLOT
GREG
THERE. HAPPY? NOW LET'S G-
BWEEEEP!
DONG DONG
WHOOP WHOOP WHO
WINNE
$1,000,00
WIN A MILLION MEGA-SLO

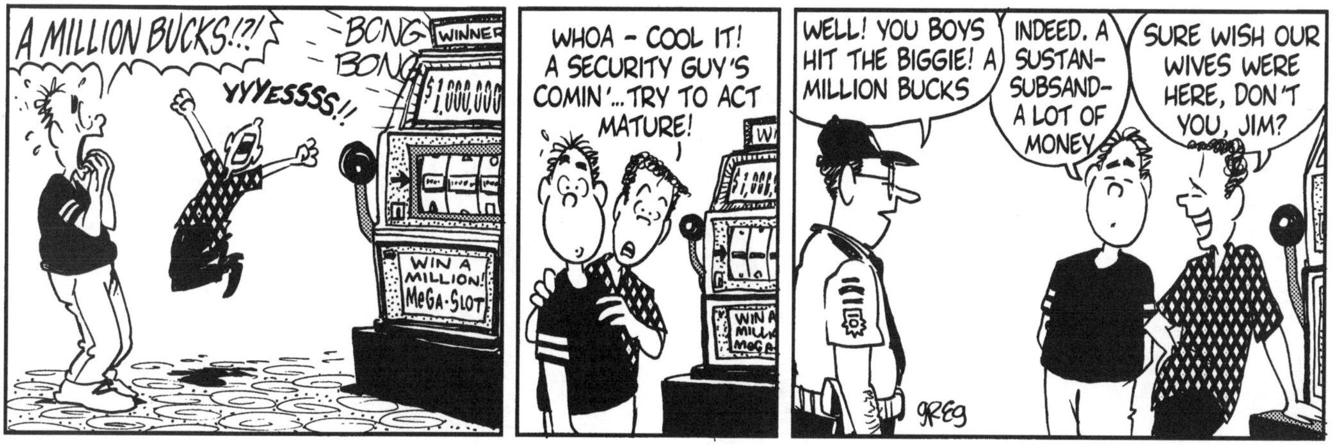
A MILLION BUCKS!?!
BONG BONG
WINNER
$1,000,000
YYYESSSS!!
WIN A MILLION! MEGA-SLOT
WHOA - COOL IT! A SECURITY GUY'S COMIN'...TRY TO ACT MATURE!
WELL! YOU BOYS HIT THE BIGGIE! A MILLION BUCKS
INDEED. A SUSTAN-SUBSAND-A LOT OF MONEY
SURE WISH OUR WIVES WERE HERE, DON'T YOU, JIM?
GREG

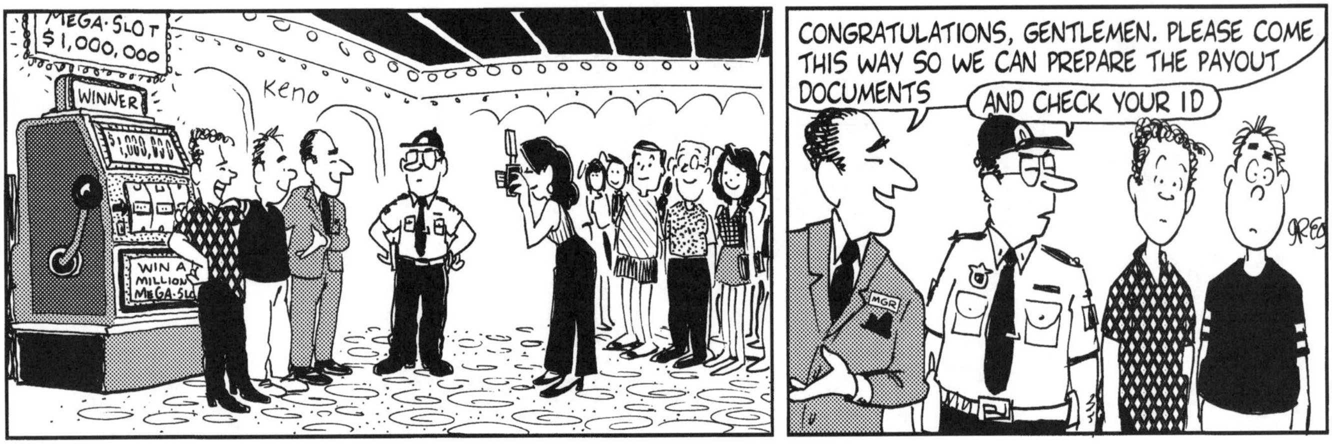
MEGA·SLOT
$1,000,000
WINNER
Keno
$1,000,000
CONGRATULATIONS, GENTLEMEN. PLEASE COME THIS WAY SO WE CAN PREPARE THE PAYOUT DOCUMENTS
AND CHECK YOUR ID
MGR

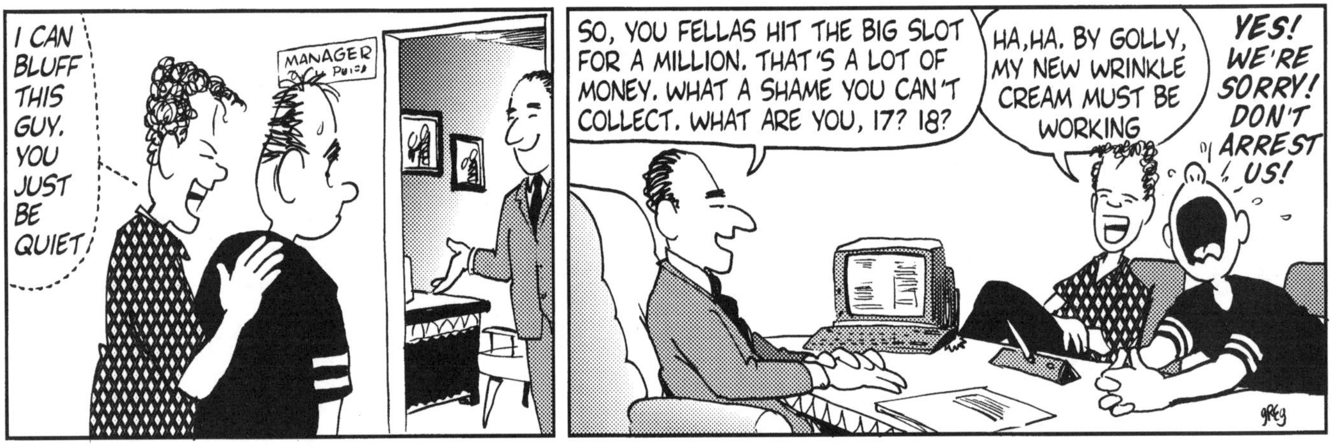
I CAN BLUFF THIS GUY. YOU JUST BE QUIET
MANAGER
SO, YOU FELLAS HIT THE BIG SLOT FOR A MILLION. THAT'S A LOT OF MONEY. WHAT A SHAME YOU CAN'T COLLECT. WHAT ARE YOU, 17? 18?
HA,HA. BY GOLLY, MY NEW WRINKLE CREAM MUST BE WORKING
YES! WE'RE SORRY! DON'T ARREST US!

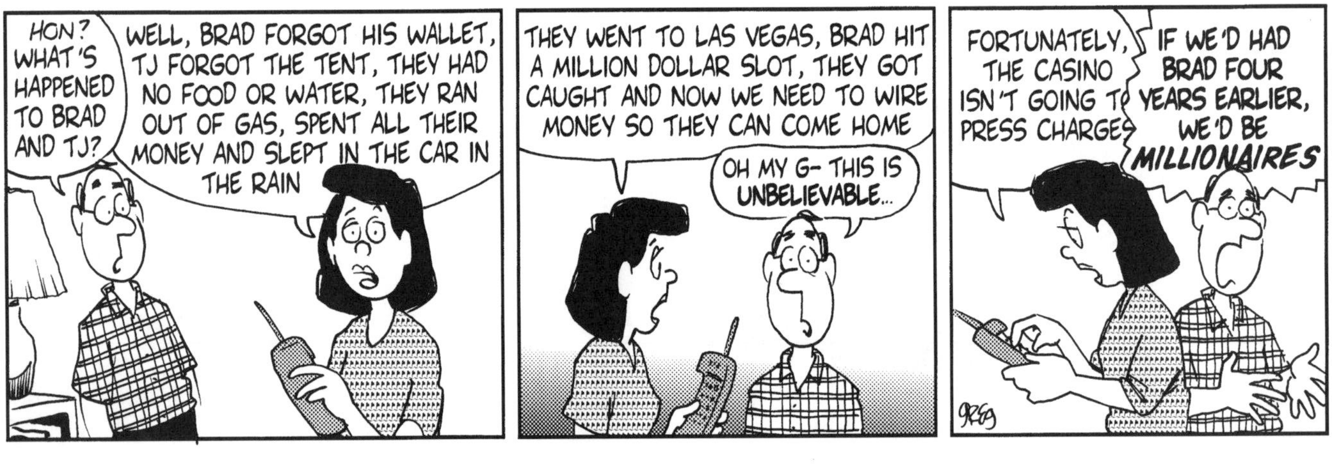
HON? WHAT'S HAPPENED TO BRAD AND TJ?
WELL, BRAD FORGOT HIS WALLET, TJ FORGOT THE TENT, THEY HAD NO FOOD OR WATER, THEY RAN OUT OF GAS, SPENT ALL THEIR MONEY AND SLEPT IN THE CAR IN THE RAIN
THEY WENT TO LAS VEGAS, BRAD HIT A MILLION DOLLAR SLOT, THEY GOT CAUGHT AND NOW WE NEED TO WIRE MONEY SO THEY CAN COME HOME
OH MY G- THIS IS UNBELIEVABLE...
FORTUNATELY, THE CASINO ISN'T GOING TO PRESS CHARGES
IF WE'D HAD BRAD FOUR YEARS EARLIER, WE'D BE MILLIONAIRES

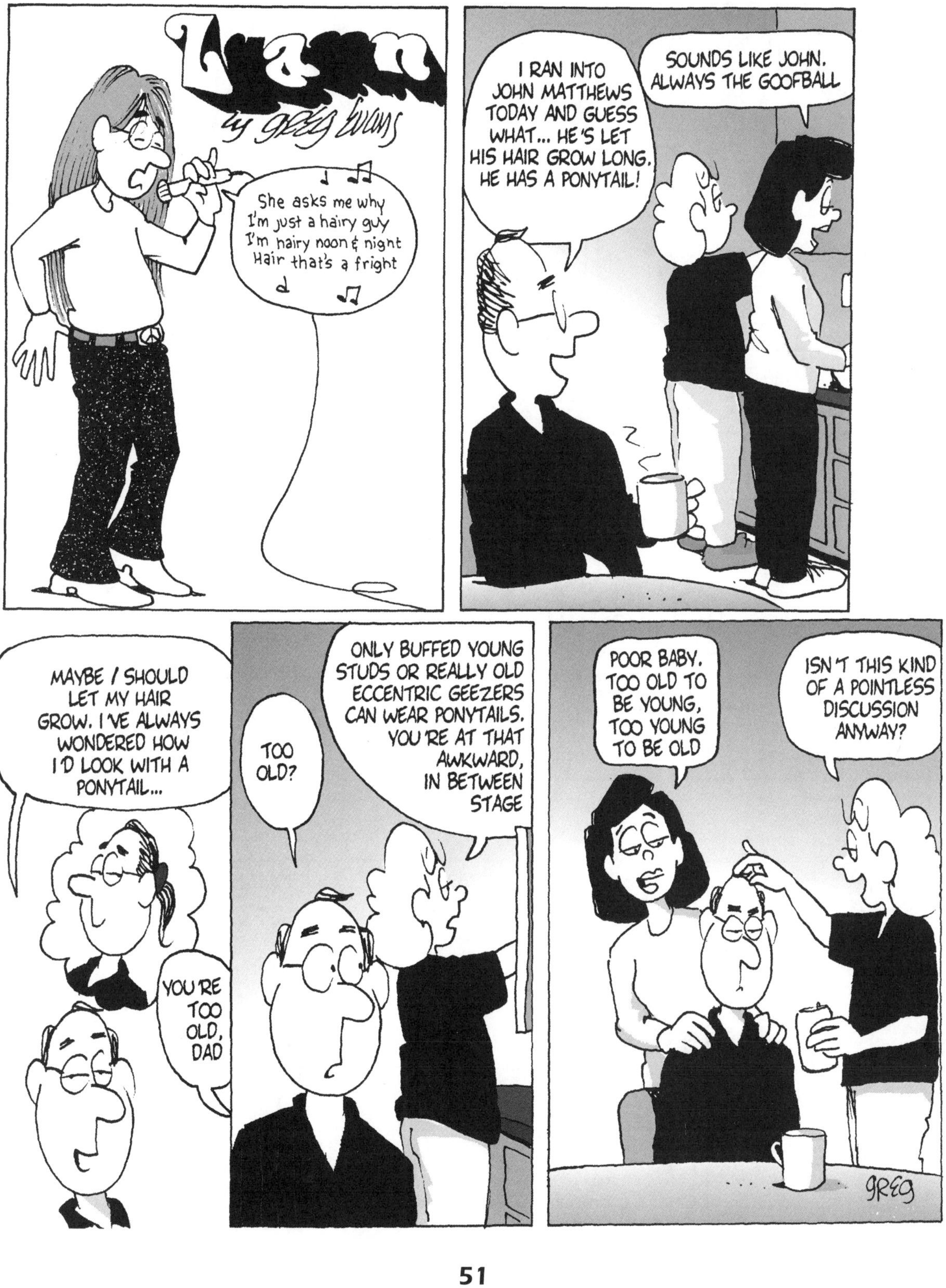
Luann
by Greg Evans
She asks me why I'm just a hairy guy I'm hairy noon & night Hair that's a fright
I RAN INTO JOHN MATTHEWS TODAY AND GUESS WHAT... HE'S LET HIS HAIR GROW LONG. HE HAS A PONYTAIL!
SOUNDS LIKE JOHN. ALWAYS THE GOOFBALL
MAYBE I SHOULD LET MY HAIR GROW. I'VE ALWAYS WONDERED HOW I'D LOOK WITH A PONYTAIL...
YOU'RE TOO OLD, DAD
TOO OLD?
ONLY BUFFED YOUNG STUDS OR REALLY OLD ECCENTRIC GEEZERS CAN WEAR PONYTAILS. YOU'RE AT THAT AWKWARD, IN BETWEEN STAGE
POOR BABY. TOO OLD TO BE YOUNG, TOO YOUNG TO BE OLD
ISN'T THIS KIND OF A POINTLESS DISCUSSION ANYWAY?
GREG

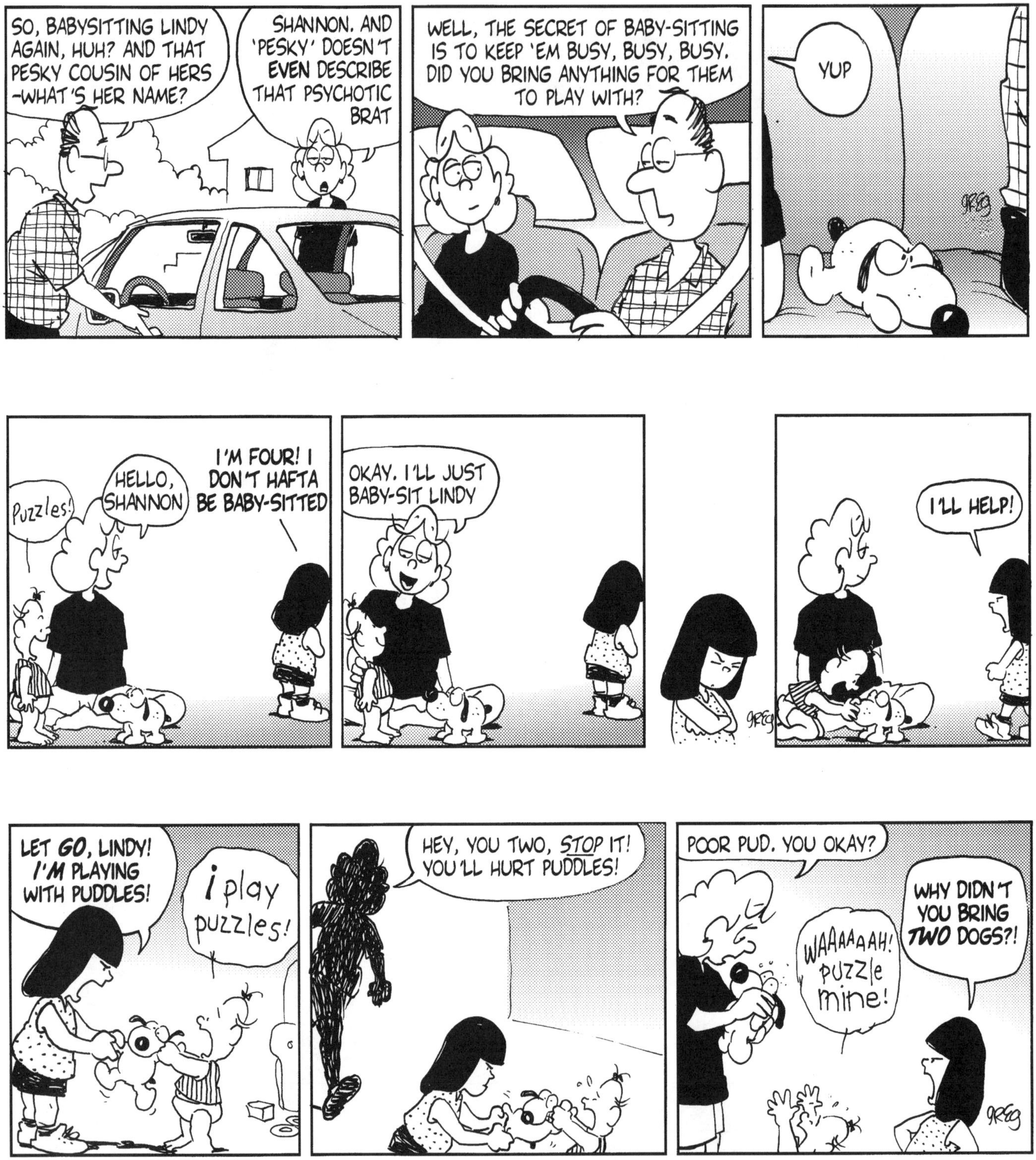
SO, BABYSITTING LINDY AGAIN, HUH? AND THAT PESKY COUSIN OF HERS -WHAT'S HER NAME?
SHANNON. AND 'PESKY' DOESN'T EVEN DESCRIBE THAT PSYCHOTIC BRAT
WELL, THE SECRET OF BABY-SITTING IS TO KEEP 'EM BUSY, BUSY, BUSY. DID YOU BRING ANYTHING FOR THEM TO PLAY WITH?
YUP
GREG
Puzzles!
HELLO, SHANNON
I'M FOUR! I DON'T HAFTA BE BABY-SITTED
OKAY. I'LL JUST BABY-SIT LINDY
GREG
I'LL HELP!
LET GO, LINDY! I'M PLAYING WITH PUDDLES!
i play puzzles!
HEY, YOU TWO, STOP IT! YOU'LL HURT PUDDLES!
POOR PUD. YOU OKAY?
WAAAAAAH! puzzle mine!
WHY DIDN'T YOU BRING TWO DOGS?!
GREG

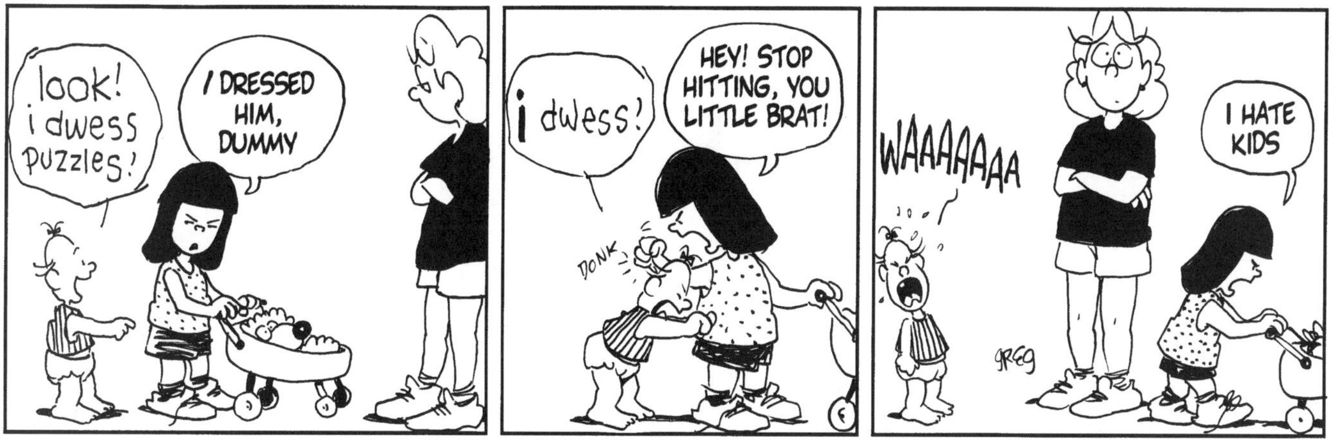
look! i dwess puzzles!
I DRESSED HIM, DUMMY
i dwess!
HEY! STOP HITTING, YOU LITTLE BRAT!
DONK
WAAAAAAA
I HATE KIDS
GREG

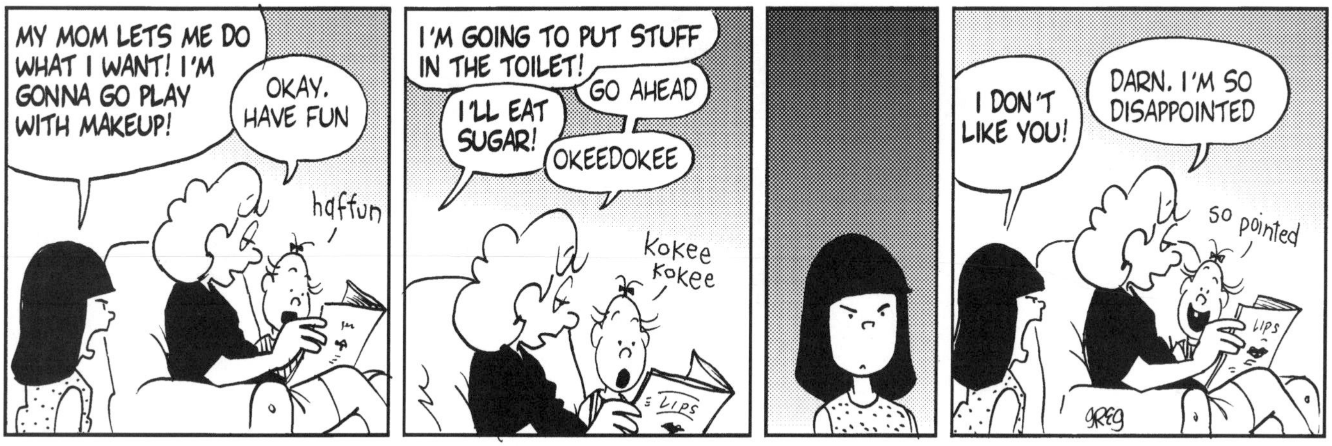
MY MOM LETS ME DO WHAT I WANT! I'M GONNA GO PLAY WITH MAKEUP!
OKAY. HAVE FUN
haffun
I'M GOING TO PUT STUFF IN THE TOILET!
GO AHEAD
I'LL EAT SUGAR!
OKEEDOKEE
kokee kokee
LIPS
I DON'T LIKE YOU!
DARN. I'M SO DISAPPOINTED
so pointed
LIPS
GREG

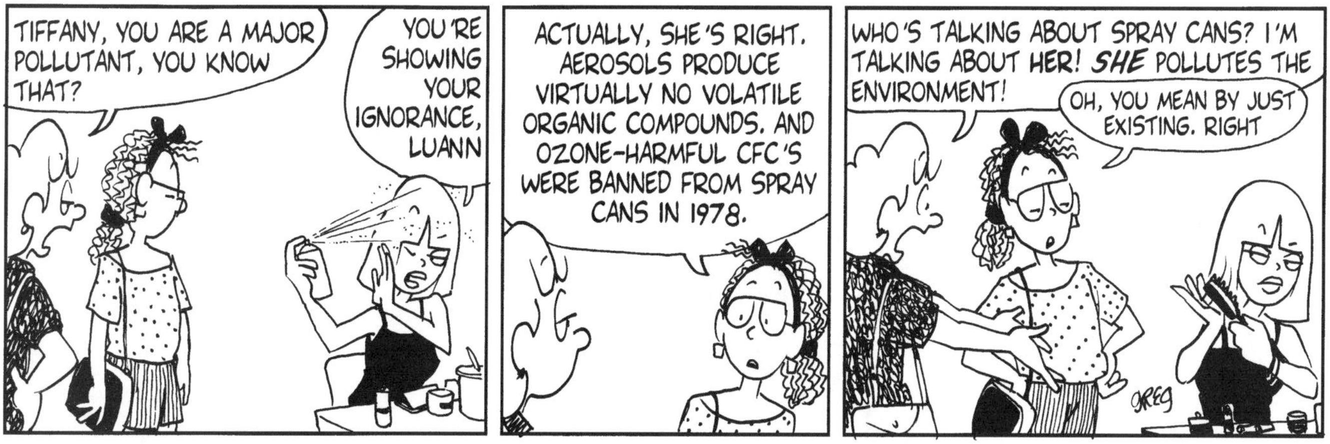
TIFFANY, YOU ARE A MAJOR POLLUTANT, YOU KNOW THAT?
YOU'RE SHOWING YOUR IGNORANCE, LUANN
ACTUALLY, SHE'S RIGHT. AEROSOLS PRODUCE VIRTUALLY NO VOLATILE ORGANIC COMPOUNDS. AND OZONE-HARMFUL CFC'S WERE BANNED FROM SPRAY CANS IN 1978.
WHO'S TALKING ABOUT SPRAY CANS? I'M TALKING ABOUT HER! SHE POLLUTES THE ENVIRONMENT!
OH, YOU MEAN BY JUST EXISTING. RIGHT
GREG

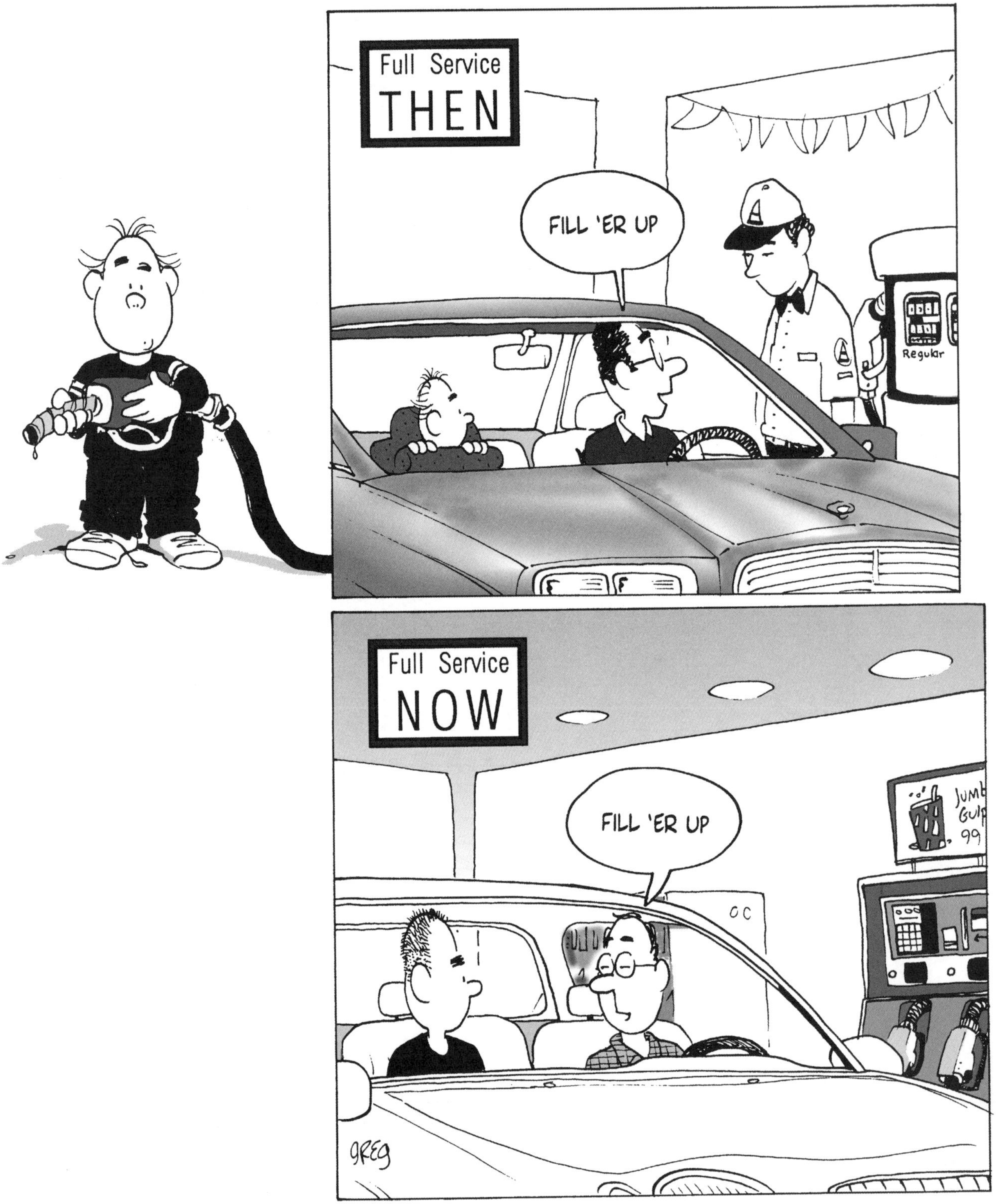
Full Service
THEN
FILL 'ER UP
Regular
Full Service
NOW
FILL 'ER UP
GREG

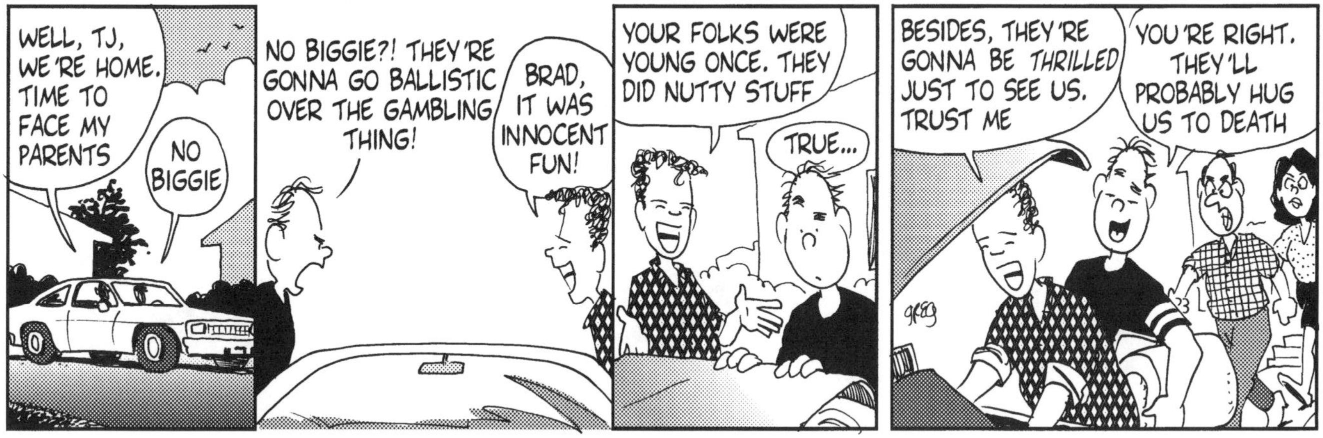
WELL, TJ, WE'RE HOME. TIME TO FACE MY PARENTS
NO BIGGIE
NO BIGGIE?! THEY'RE GONNA GO BALLISTIC OVER THE GAMBLING THING!
BRAD, IT WAS INNOCENT FUN!
YOUR FOLKS WERE YOUNG ONCE. THEY DID NUTTY STUFF
TRUE...
BESIDES, THEY'RE GONNA BE *THRILLED* JUST TO SEE US. TRUST ME
YOU'RE RIGHT. THEY'LL PROBABLY HUG US TO DEATH

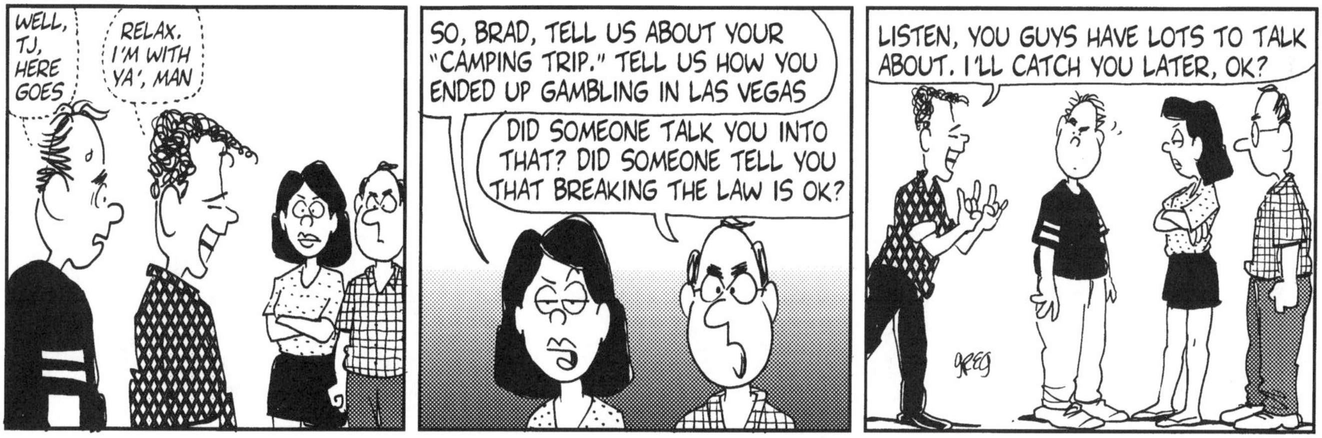
WELL, TJ, HERE GOES
RELAX. I'M WITH YA', MAN
SO, BRAD, TELL US ABOUT YOUR "CAMPING TRIP." TELL US HOW YOU ENDED UP GAMBLING IN LAS VEGAS
DID SOMEONE TALK YOU INTO THAT? DID SOMEONE TELL YOU THAT BREAKING THE LAW IS OK?
LISTEN, YOU GUYS HAVE LOTS TO TALK ABOUT. I'LL CATCH YOU LATER, OK?

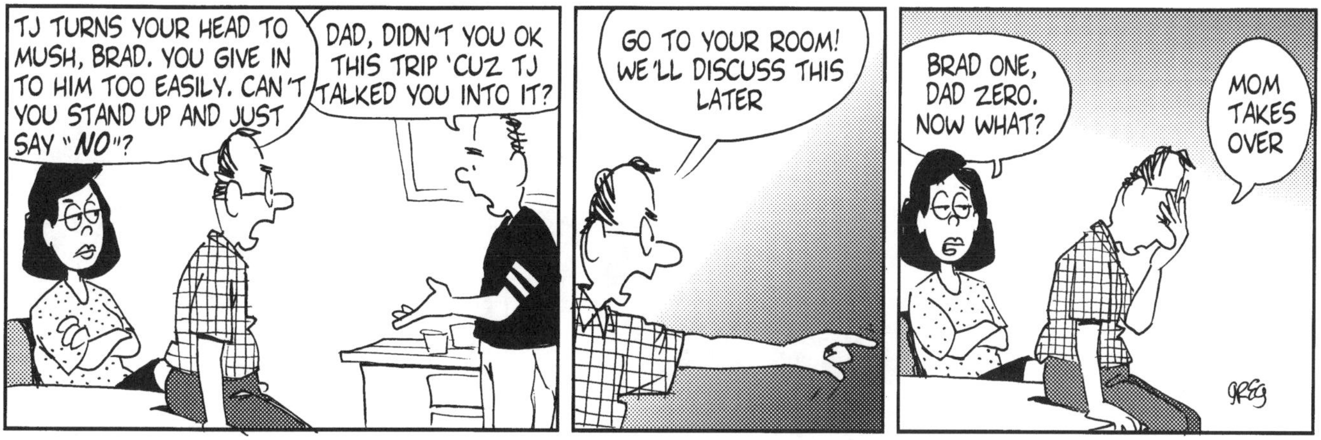
TJ TURNS YOUR HEAD TO MUSH, BRAD. YOU GIVE IN TO HIM TOO EASILY. CAN'T YOU STAND UP AND JUST SAY "***NO***"?
DAD, DIDN'T YOU OK THIS TRIP 'CUZ TJ TALKED YOU INTO IT?
GO TO YOUR ROOM! WE'LL DISCUSS THIS LATER
BRAD ONE, DAD ZERO. NOW WHAT?
MOM TAKES OVER

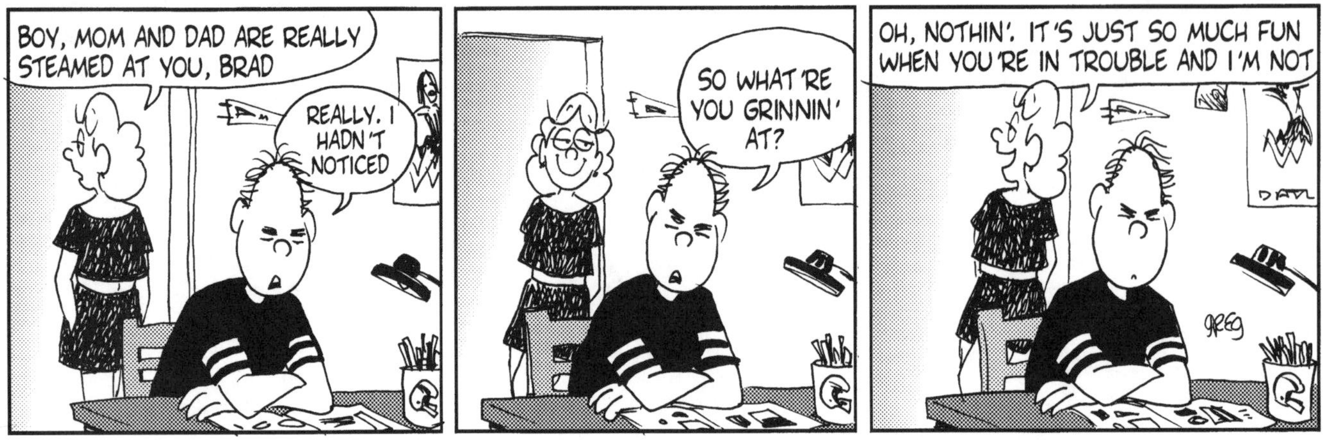
BOY, MOM AND DAD ARE REALLY STEAMED AT YOU, BRAD
REALLY. I HADN'T NOTICED
SO WHAT'RE YOU GRINNIN' AT?
OH, NOTHIN'. IT'S JUST SO MUCH FUN WHEN YOU'RE IN TROUBLE AND I'M NOT

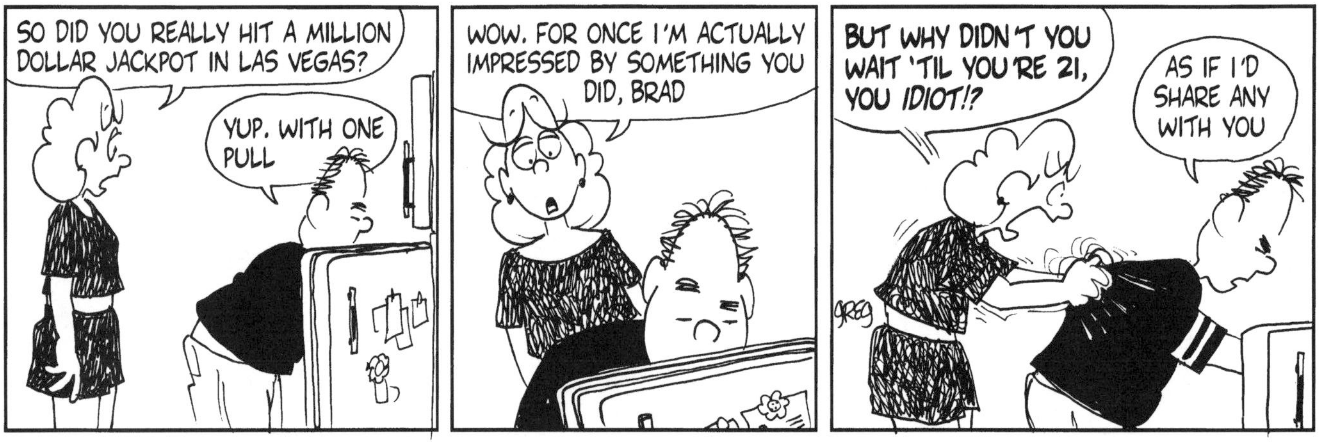
SO DID YOU REALLY HIT A MILLION DOLLAR JACKPOT IN LAS VEGAS?
YUP. WITH ONE PULL
WOW. FOR ONCE I'M ACTUALLY IMPRESSED BY SOMETHING YOU DID, BRAD
BUT WHY DIDN'T YOU WAIT 'TIL YOU'RE 21, YOU IDIOT!?
AS IF I'D SHARE ANY WITH YOU

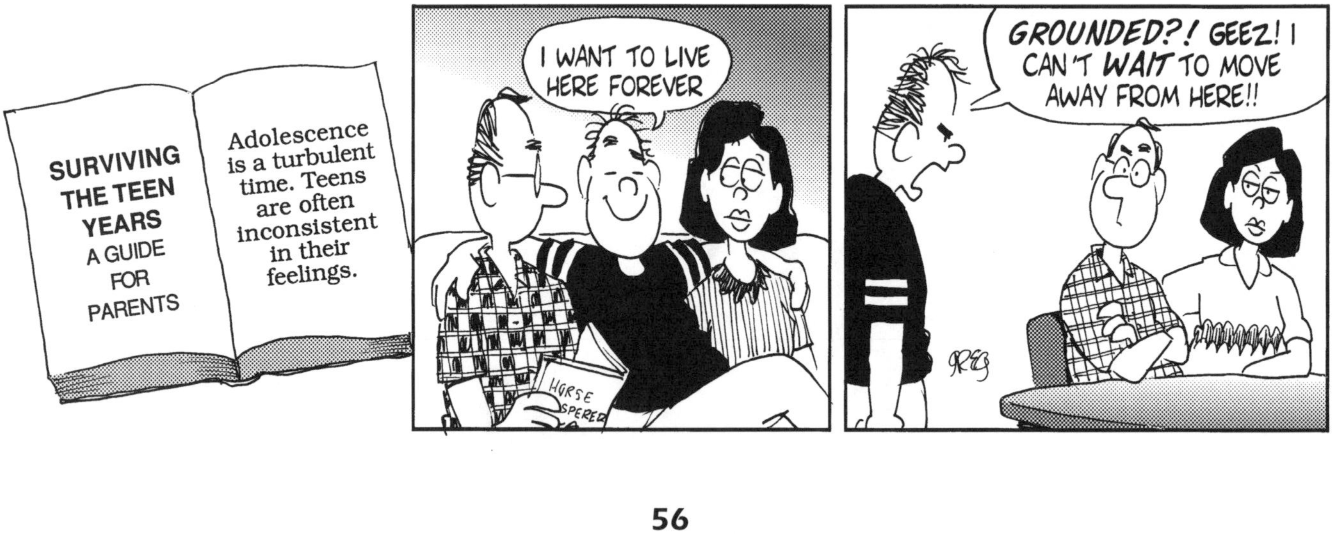
SURVIVING THE TEEN YEARS
A GUIDE FOR PARENTS
Adolescence is a turbulent time. Teens are often inconsistent in their feelings.
I WANT TO LIVE HERE FOREVER
GROUNDED?! GEEZ! I CAN'T WAIT TO MOVE AWAY FROM HERE!!

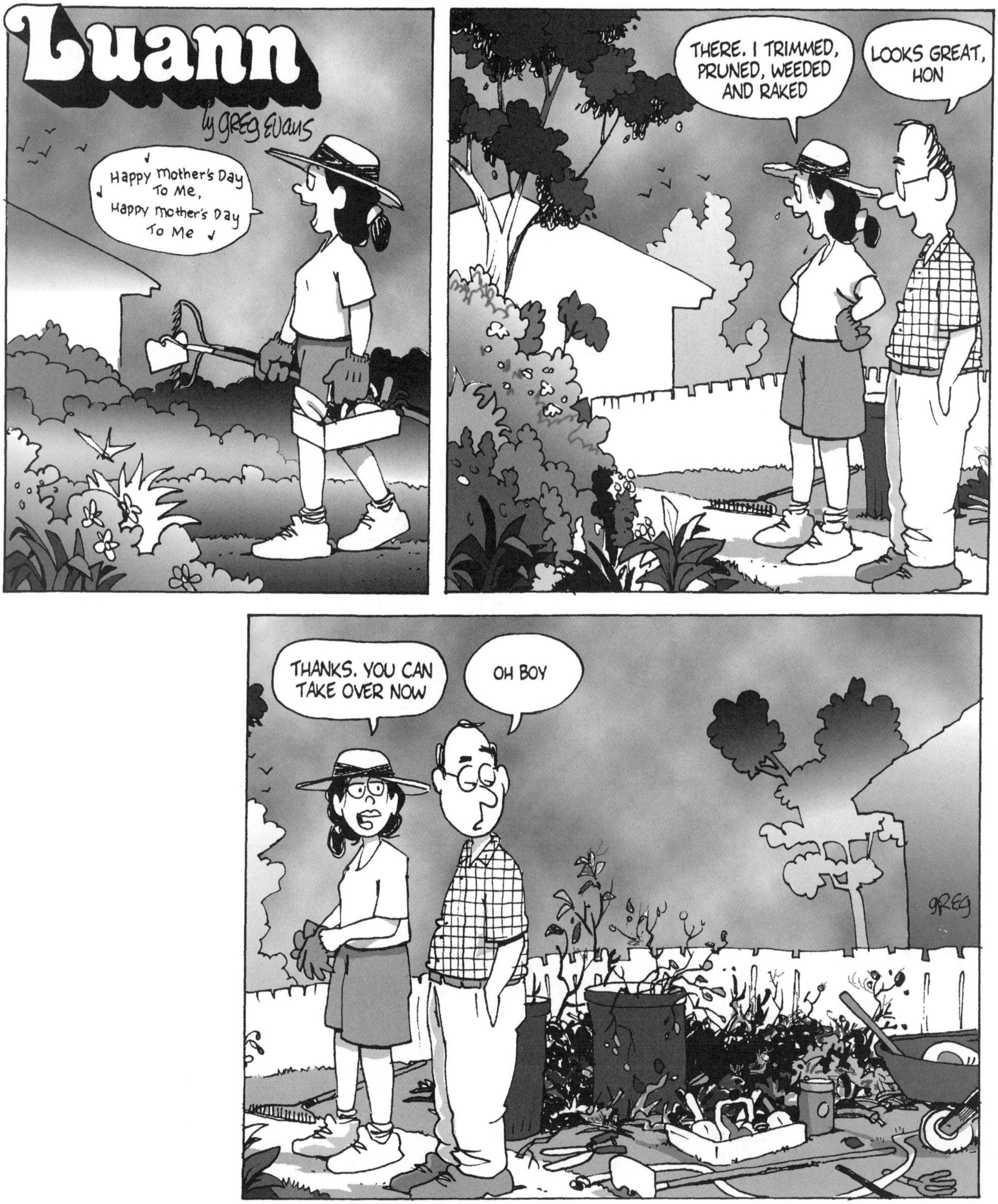
Luann
by GREG EVANS
Happy Mother's Day To Me, Happy mother's Day To Me
THERE. I TRIMMED, PRUNED, WEEDED AND RAKED
LOOKS GREAT, HON
THANKS. YOU CAN TAKE OVER NOW
OH BOY
GREG

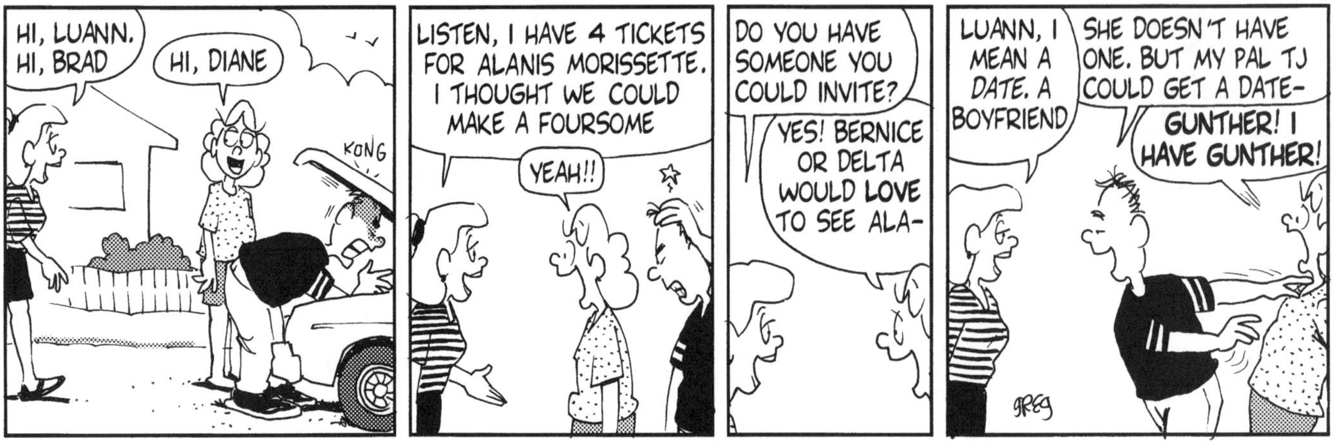
HI, LUANN. HI, BRAD
HI, DIANE
KONG
LISTEN, I HAVE 4 TICKETS FOR ALANIS MORISSETTE. I THOUGHT WE COULD MAKE A FOURSOME
YEAH!!
DO YOU HAVE SOMEONE YOU COULD INVITE?
YES! BERNICE OR DELTA WOULD LOVE TO SEE ALA-
LUANN, I MEAN A DATE. A BOYFRIEND
SHE DOESN'T HAVE ONE. BUT MY PAL TJ COULD GET A DATE-
GUNTHER! I HAVE GUNTHER!
GREG

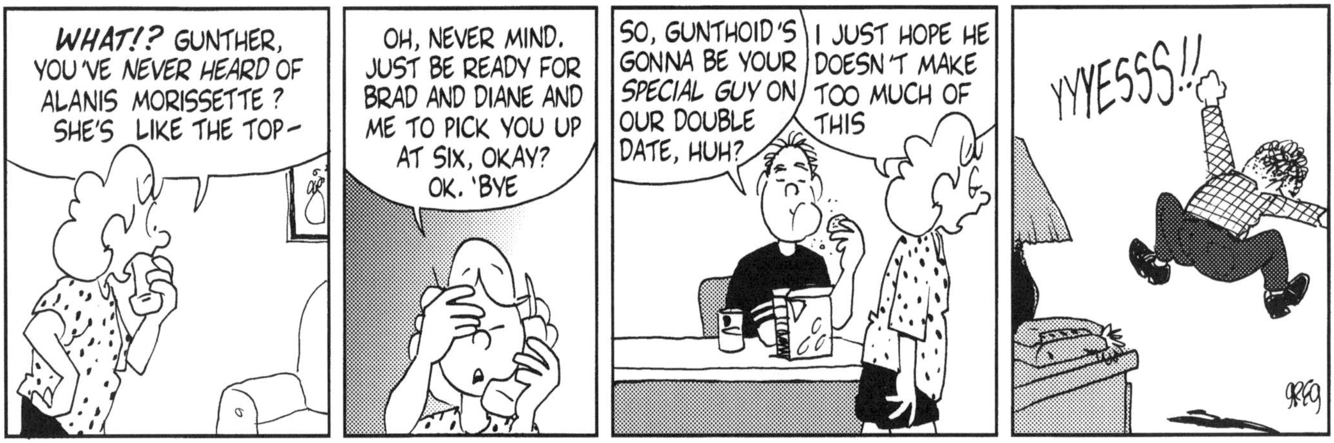
WHAT!? GUNTHER, YOU'VE NEVER HEARD OF ALANIS MORISSETTE? SHE'S LIKE THE TOP-
OH, NEVER MIND. JUST BE READY FOR BRAD AND DIANE AND ME TO PICK YOU UP AT SIX, OKAY? OK. 'BYE
SO, GUNTHOID'S GONNA BE YOUR SPECIAL GUY ON OUR DOUBLE DATE, HUH?
I JUST HOPE HE DOESN'T MAKE TOO MUCH OF THIS
YYYESSS!!
GREG

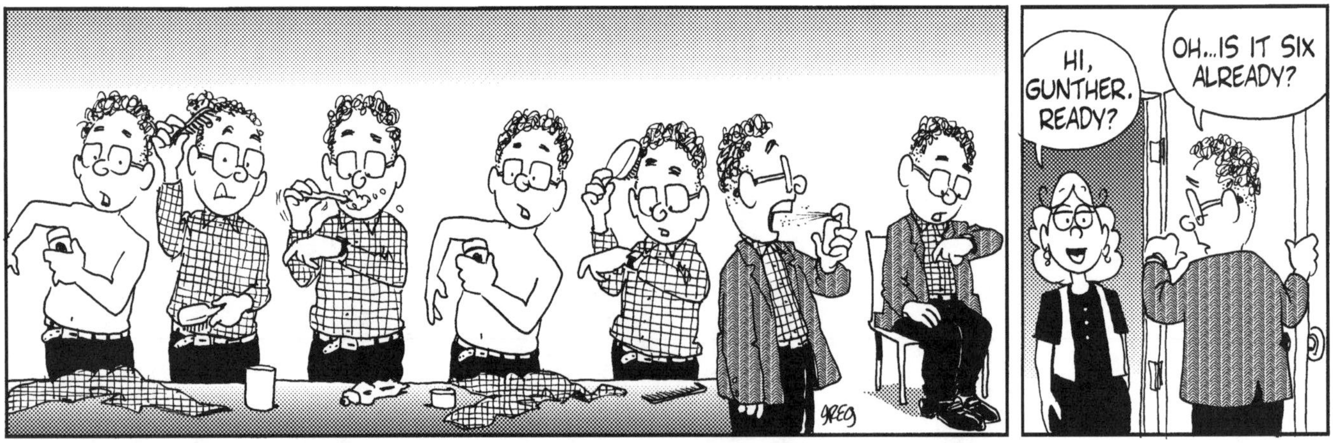
GREG
HI, GUNTHER. READY?
OH...IS IT SIX ALREADY?

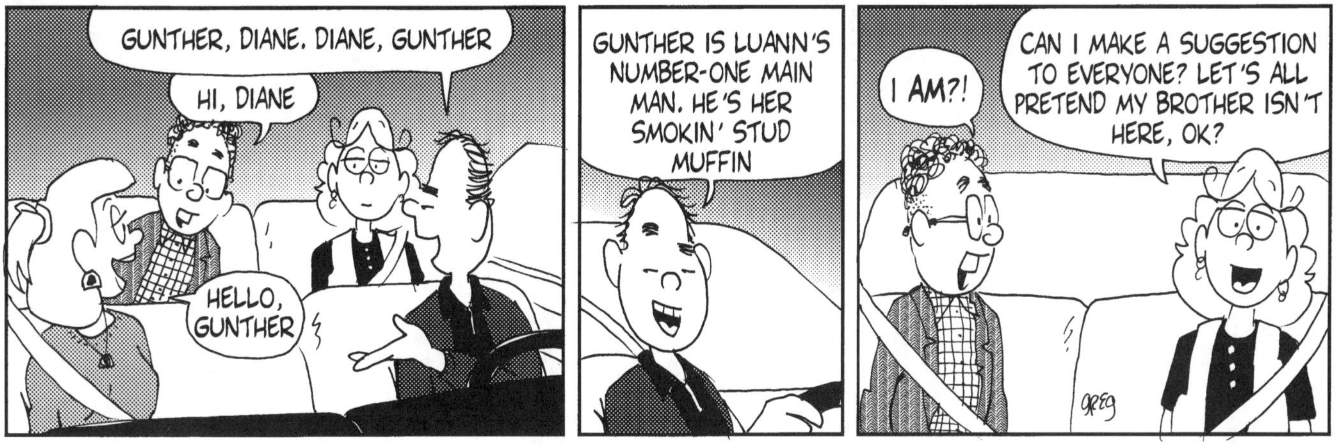
GUNTHER, DIANE. DIANE, GUNTHER
HI, DIANE
HELLO, GUNTHER
GUNTHER IS LUANN'S NUMBER-ONE MAIN MAN. HE'S HER SMOKIN' STUD MUFFIN
I AM?!
CAN I MAKE A SUGGESTION TO EVERYONE? LET'S ALL PRETEND MY BROTHER ISN'T HERE, OK?
GREG

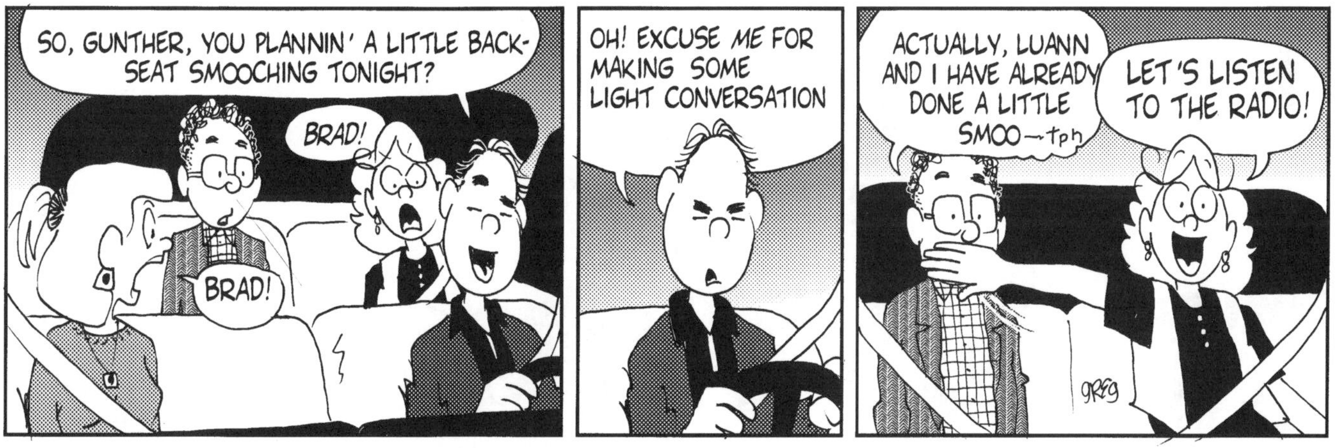
SO, GUNTHER, YOU PLANNIN' A LITTLE BACK-SEAT SMOOCHING TONIGHT?
BRAD!
BRAD!
OH! EXCUSE *ME* FOR MAKING SOME LIGHT CONVERSATION
ACTUALLY, LUANN AND I HAVE ALREADY DONE A LITTLE SMOO—tph
LET'S LISTEN TO THE RADIO!
GREG

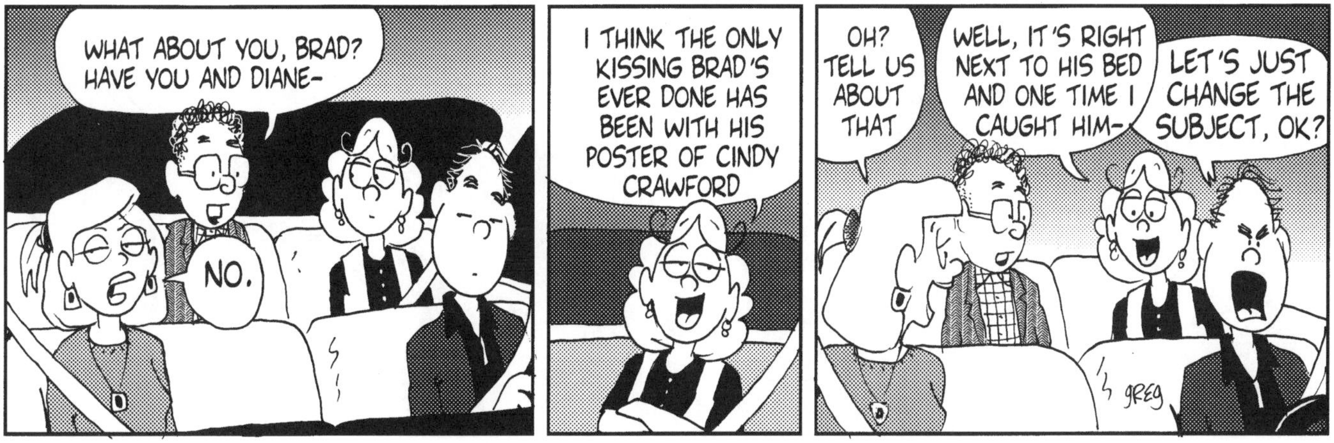
WHAT ABOUT YOU, BRAD? HAVE YOU AND DIANE-
NO.
I THINK THE ONLY KISSING BRAD'S EVER DONE HAS BEEN WITH HIS POSTER OF CINDY CRAWFORD
OH? TELL US ABOUT THAT
WELL, IT'S RIGHT NEXT TO HIS BED AND ONE TIME I CAUGHT HIM-
LET'S JUST CHANGE THE SUBJECT, OK?
GREG

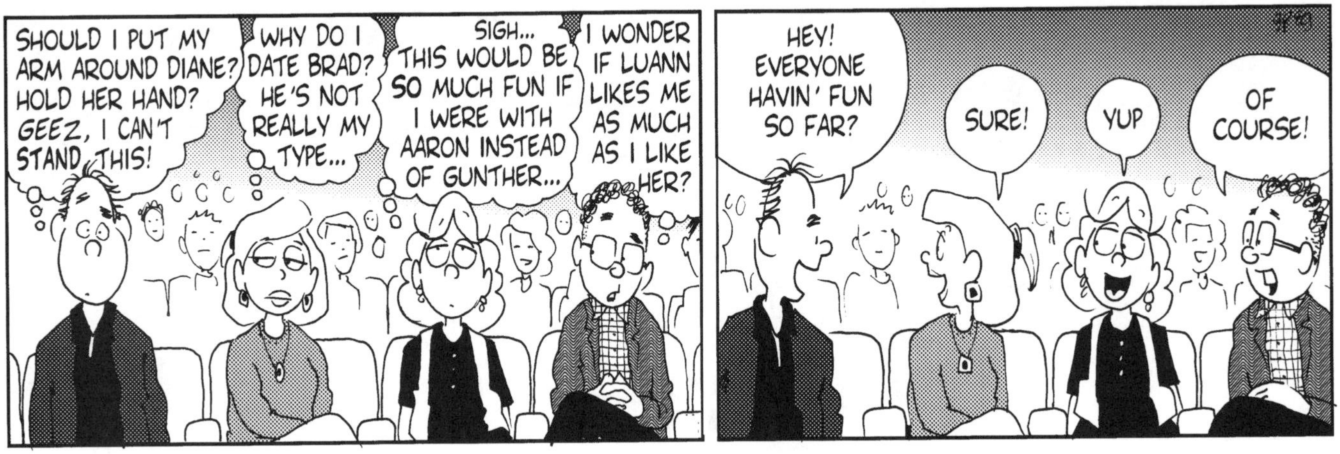
SHOULD I PUT MY ARM AROUND DIANE? HOLD HER HAND? GEEZ, I CAN'T STAND THIS!
WHY DO I DATE BRAD? HE'S NOT REALLY MY TYPE...
SIGH... THIS WOULD BE SO MUCH FUN IF I WERE WITH AARON INSTEAD OF GUNTHER...
I WONDER IF LUANN LIKES ME AS MUCH AS I LIKE HER?
HEY! EVERYONE HAVIN' FUN SO FAR?
SURE!
YUP
OF COURSE!

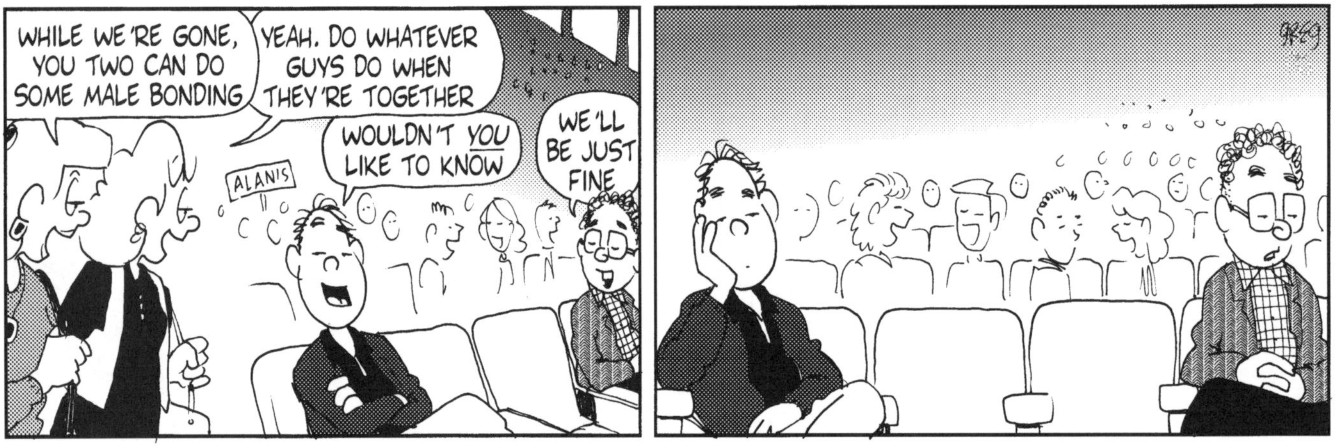
WHILE WE'RE GONE, YOU TWO CAN DO SOME MALE BONDING
YEAH. DO WHATEVER GUYS DO WHEN THEY'RE TOGETHER
ALANIS
WOULDN'T *YOU* LIKE TO KNOW
WE'LL BE JUST FINE

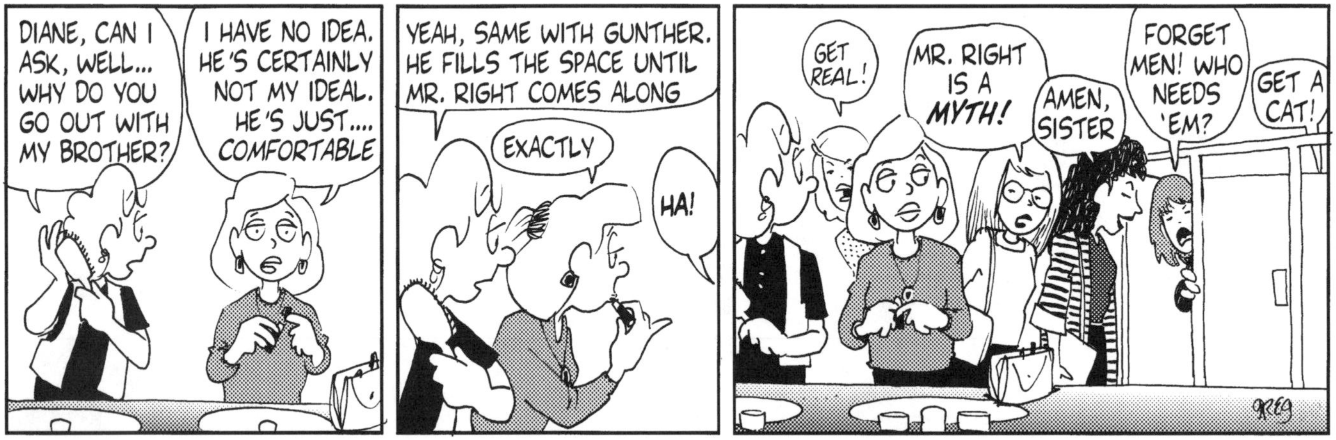
DIANE, CAN I ASK, WELL... WHY DO YOU GO OUT WITH MY BROTHER?
I HAVE NO IDEA. HE'S CERTAINLY NOT MY IDEAL. HE'S JUST.... *COMFORTABLE*
YEAH, SAME WITH GUNTHER. HE FILLS THE SPACE UNTIL MR. RIGHT COMES ALONG
EXACTLY
HA!
GET REAL!
MR. RIGHT IS A *MYTH!*
AMEN, SISTER
FORGET MEN! WHO NEEDS 'EM?
GET A CAT!
GREG

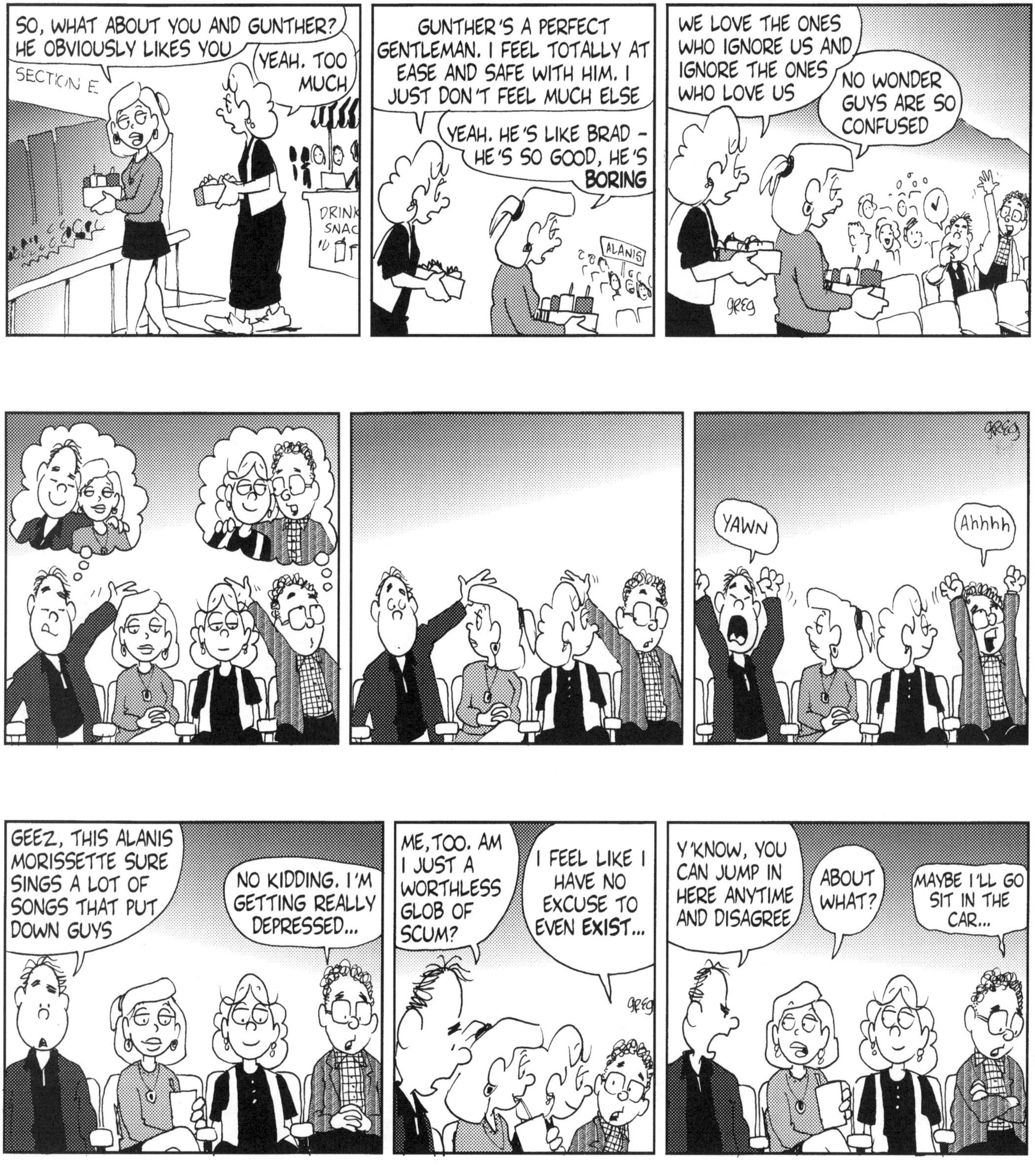
SO, WHAT ABOUT YOU AND GUNTHER? HE OBVIOUSLY LIKES YOU
YEAH. TOO MUCH
SECTION E
DRINK SNAC
GUNTHER'S A PERFECT GENTLEMAN. I FEEL TOTALLY AT EASE AND SAFE WITH HIM. I JUST DON'T FEEL MUCH ELSE
YEAH. HE'S LIKE BRAD - HE'S SO GOOD, HE'S **BORING**
ALANIS
WE LOVE THE ONES WHO IGNORE US AND IGNORE THE ONES WHO LOVE US
NO WONDER GUYS ARE SO CONFUSED
GREG
GREG
YAWN
Ahhhh
GEEZ, THIS ALANIS MORISSETTE SURE SINGS A LOT OF SONGS THAT PUT DOWN GUYS
NO KIDDING. I'M GETTING REALLY DEPRESSED...
ME, TOO. AM I JUST A WORTHLESS GLOB OF SCUM?
I FEEL LIKE I HAVE NO EXCUSE TO EVEN **EXIST**...
GREG
Y'KNOW, YOU CAN JUMP IN HERE ANYTIME AND DISAGREE
ABOUT WHAT?
MAYBE I'LL GO SIT IN THE CAR...

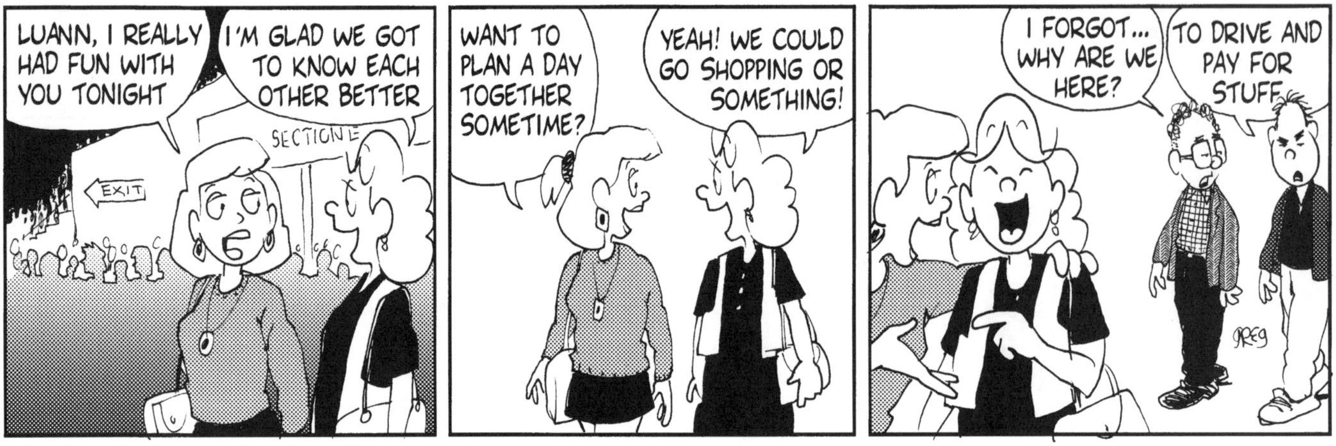
LUANN, I REALLY HAD FUN WITH YOU TONIGHT
I'M GLAD WE GOT TO KNOW EACH OTHER BETTER
SECTION E
EXIT
WANT TO PLAN A DAY TOGETHER SOMETIME?
YEAH! WE COULD GO SHOPPING OR SOMETHING!
I FORGOT... WHY ARE WE HERE?
TO DRIVE AND PAY FOR STUFF

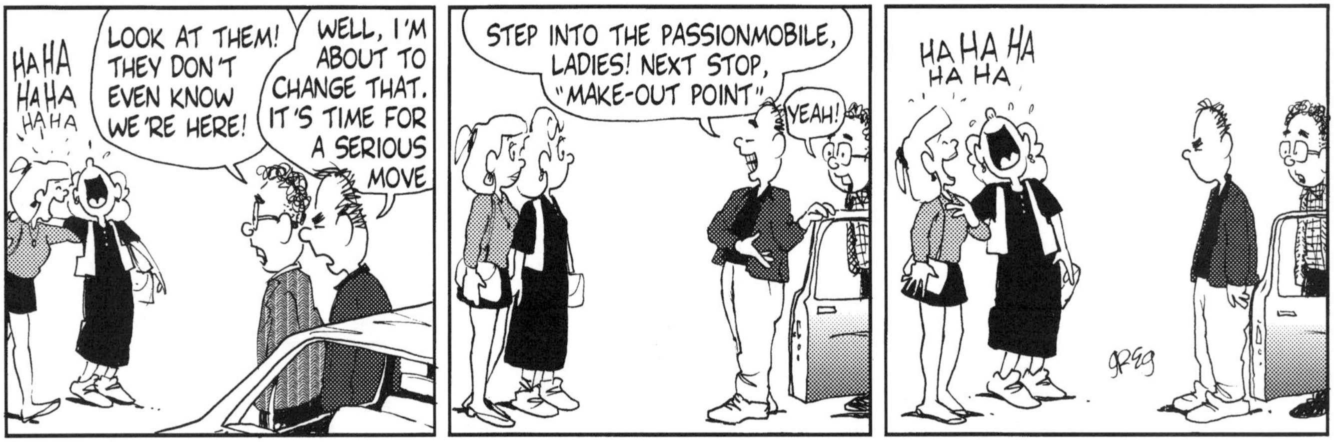
HA HA HA HA HA HA
LOOK AT THEM! THEY DON'T EVEN KNOW WE'RE HERE!
WELL, I'M ABOUT TO CHANGE THAT. IT'S TIME FOR A SERIOUS MOVE
STEP INTO THE PASSIONMOBILE, LADIES! NEXT STOP, "MAKE-OUT POINT"
YEAH!
HA HA HA HA HA

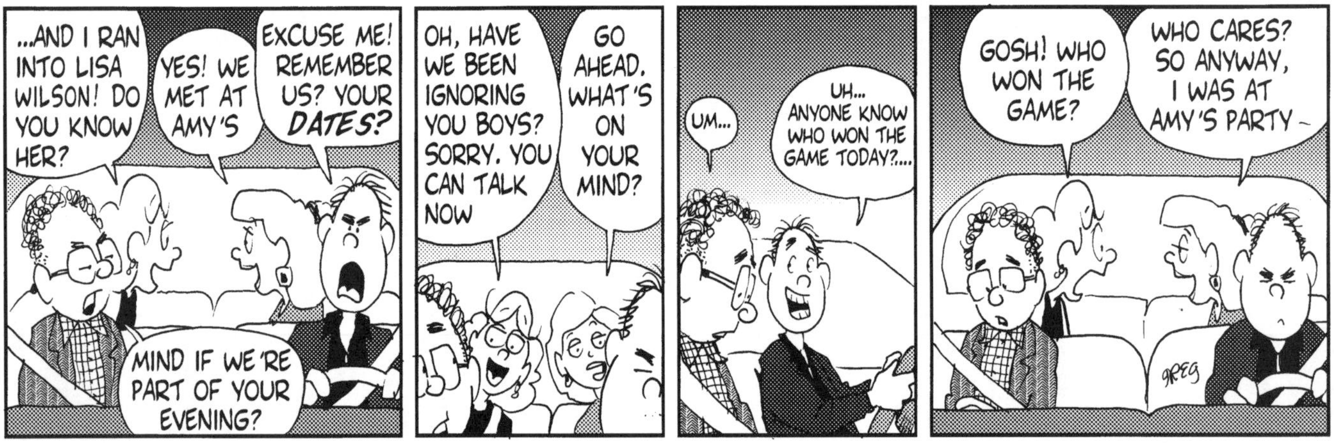
...AND I RAN INTO LISA WILSON! DO YOU KNOW HER?
YES! WE MET AT AMY'S
EXCUSE ME! REMEMBER US? YOUR DATES?
MIND IF WE'RE PART OF YOUR EVENING?
OH, HAVE WE BEEN IGNORING YOU BOYS? SORRY. YOU CAN TALK NOW
GO AHEAD. WHAT'S ON YOUR MIND?
UM...
UH... ANYONE KNOW WHO WON THE GAME TODAY?...
GOSH! WHO WON THE GAME?
WHO CARES? SO ANYWAY, I WAS AT AMY'S PARTY

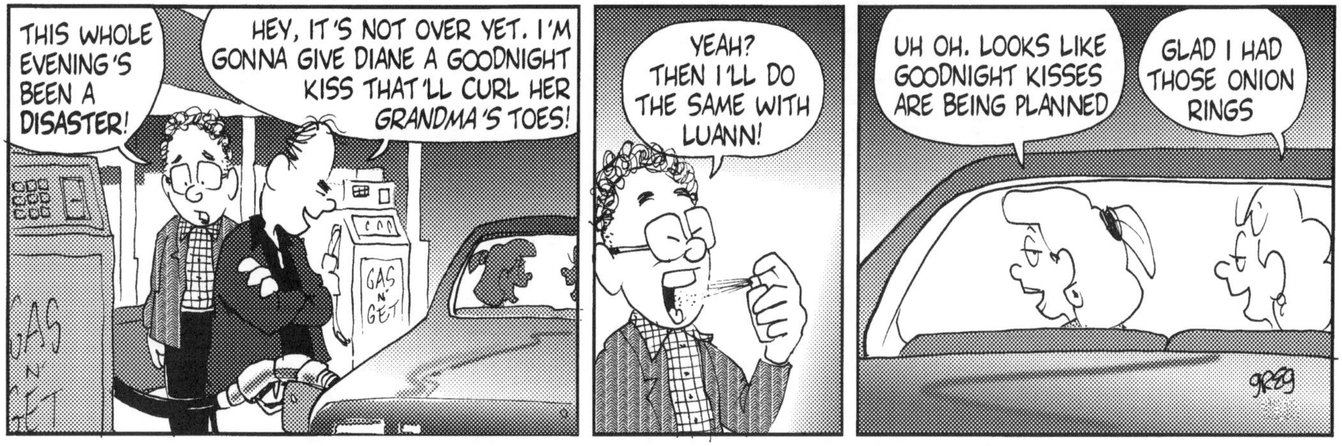
THIS WHOLE EVENING'S BEEN A DISASTER!
HEY, IT'S NOT OVER YET. I'M GONNA GIVE DIANE A GOODNIGHT KISS THAT'LL CURL HER GRANDMA'S TOES!
GAS 'N' GET
GAS 'N' GET
YEAH? THEN I'LL DO THE SAME WITH LUANN!
UH OH. LOOKS LIKE GOODNIGHT KISSES ARE BEING PLANNED
GLAD I HAD THOSE ONION RINGS
GREG

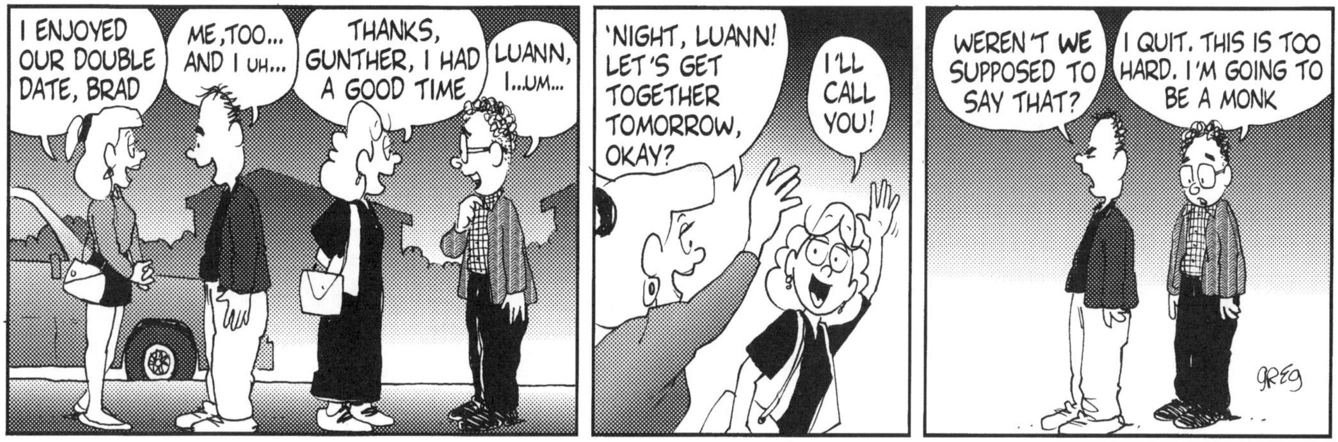
I ENJOYED OUR DOUBLE DATE, BRAD
ME, TOO... AND I UH...
THANKS, GUNTHER, I HAD A GOOD TIME
LUANN, I...UM...
'NIGHT, LUANN! LET'S GET TOGETHER TOMORROW, OKAY?
I'LL CALL YOU!
WEREN'T WE SUPPOSED TO SAY THAT?
I QUIT. THIS IS TOO HARD. I'M GOING TO BE A MONK
GREG

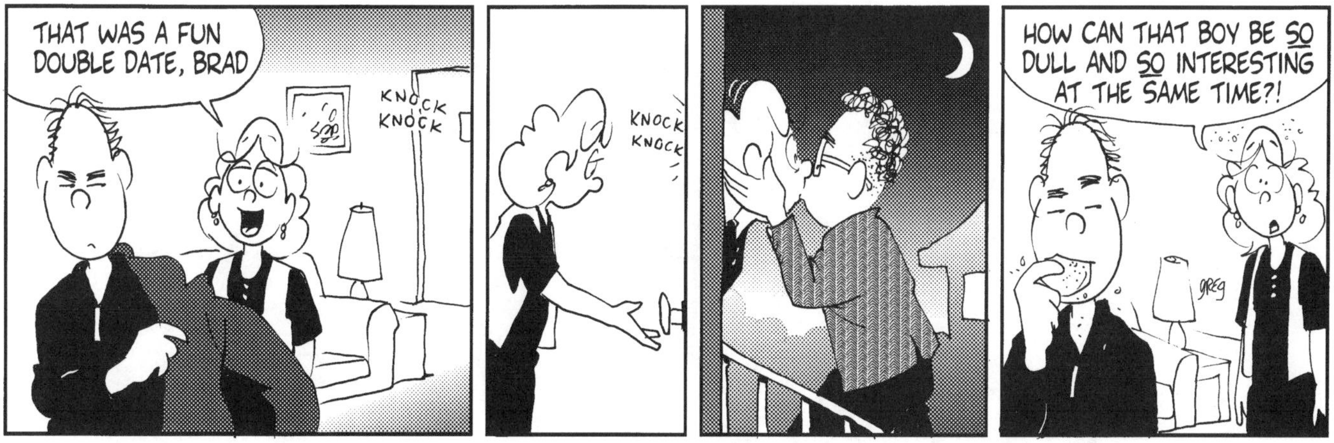
THAT WAS A FUN DOUBLE DATE, BRAD
KNOCK KNOCK
KNOCK KNOCK
HOW CAN THAT BOY BE SO DULL AND SO INTERESTING AT THE SAME TIME?!
GREG

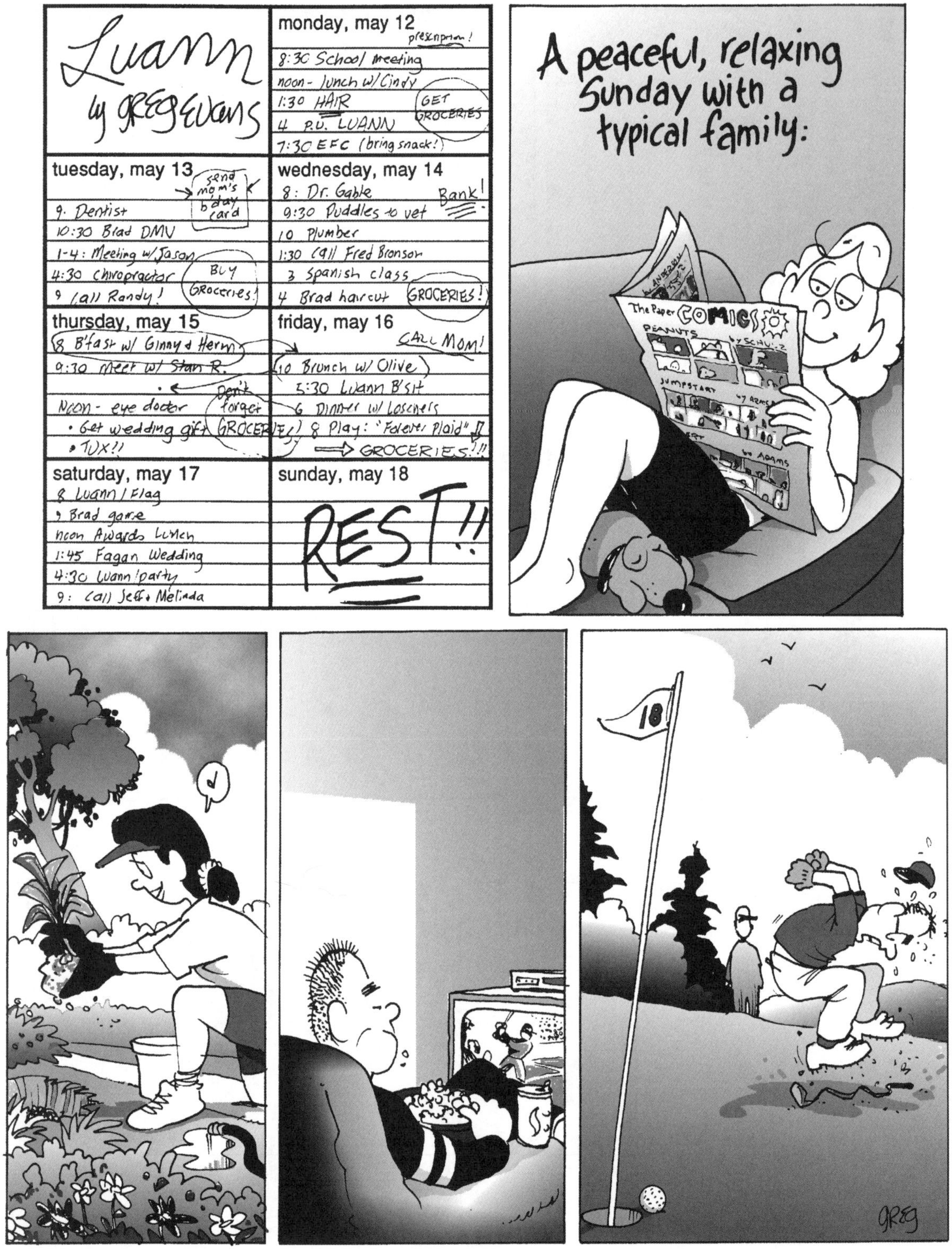
Luann
by GREG EVANS
monday, may 12
prescription!
8:30 School meeting
noon - lunch w/ Cindy
1:30 HAIR
4 P.U. LUANN
7:30 EFC (bring snack!)
GET GROCERIES
tuesday, may 13
send mom's b'day card
9. Dentist
10:30 Brad DMV
1-4: Meeting w/ Jason
4:30 chiropractor
9 Call Randy!
BUY Groceries!
wednesday, may 14
8: Dr. Gable
Bank!
9:30 Puddles to vet
10 Plumber
1:30 Call Fred Bronson
3 Spanish class
4 Brad haircut
GROCERIES!
thursday, may 15
8 B'fast w/ Ginny & Herm
9:30 Meet w/ Stan R.
Noon - eye doctor
• Get wedding gift
• TUX!!
Don't forget GROCERIES
friday, may 16
CALL MOM!
10 Brunch w/ Olive
5:30 Luann B'sit
6 Dinner w/ Loschers
8 Play: "Forever Plaid"
GROCERIES!!!
saturday, may 17
8 Luann / Flag
9 Brad game
noon Awards Lunch
1:45 Fagan Wedding
4:30 Luann party
9: Call Jeff & Melinda
sunday, may 18
REST!!
A peaceful, relaxing Sunday with a typical family:
The Paper COMICS
PEANUTS by SCHULZ
JUMPSTART by ARMSTRONG
by Adams
18
GREG

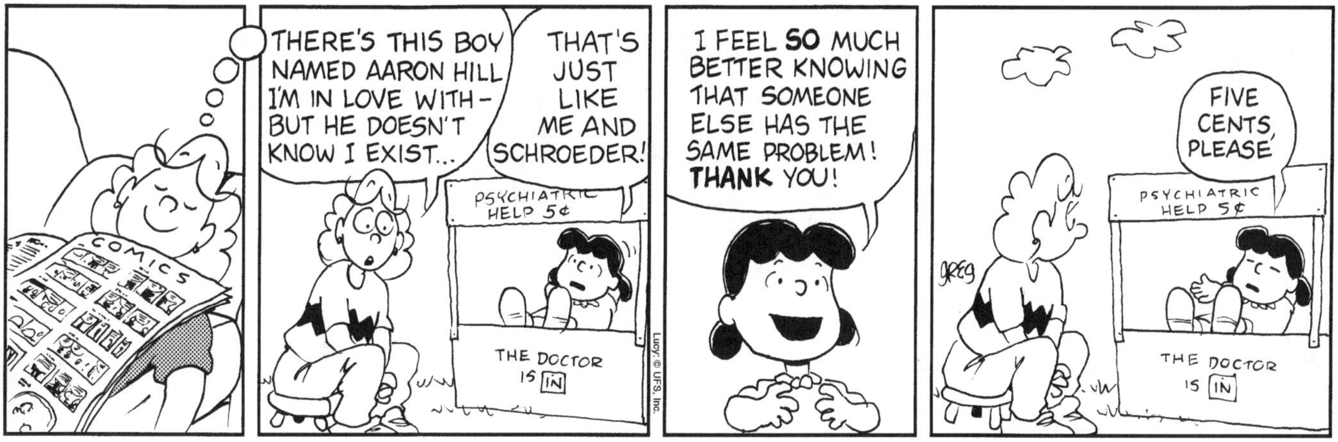
COMICS
THERE'S THIS BOY NAMED AARON HILL I'M IN LOVE WITH - BUT HE DOESN'T KNOW I EXIST...
THAT'S JUST LIKE ME AND SCHROEDER!
PSYCHIATRIC HELP 5¢
THE DOCTOR IS IN
Lucy: © UFS, Inc.
I FEEL **SO** MUCH BETTER KNOWING THAT SOMEONE ELSE HAS THE SAME PROBLEM! **THANK** YOU!
FIVE CENTS, PLEASE
PSYCHIATRIC HELP 5¢
THE DOCTOR IS IN
GREG

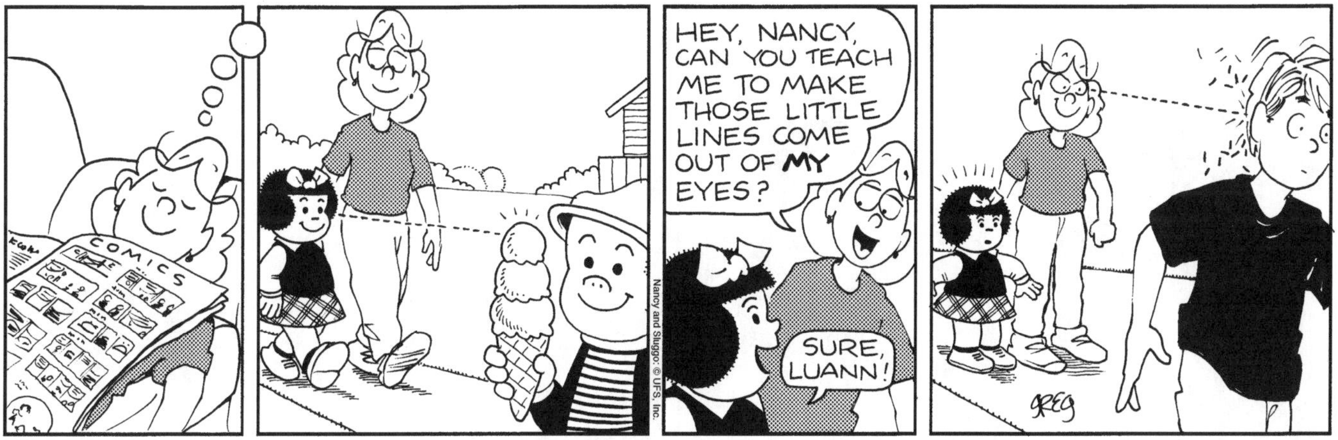
COMICS
Nancy and Sluggo: © UFS, Inc.
HEY, NANCY, CAN YOU TEACH ME TO MAKE THOSE LITTLE LINES COME OUT OF **MY** EYES?
SURE, LUANN!
GREG

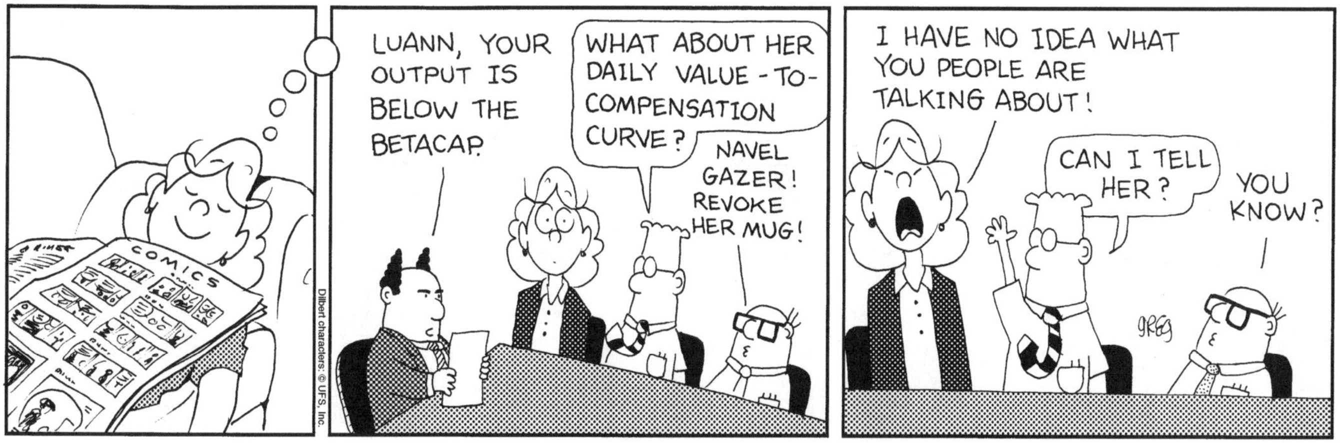
COMICS
Dilbert characters: © UFS, Inc.
LUANN, YOUR OUTPUT IS BELOW THE BETACAP.
WHAT ABOUT HER DAILY VALUE-TO-COMPENSATION CURVE?
NAVEL GAZER! REVOKE HER MUG!
I HAVE NO IDEA WHAT YOU PEOPLE ARE TALKING ABOUT!
CAN I TELL HER?
YOU KNOW?
GREG

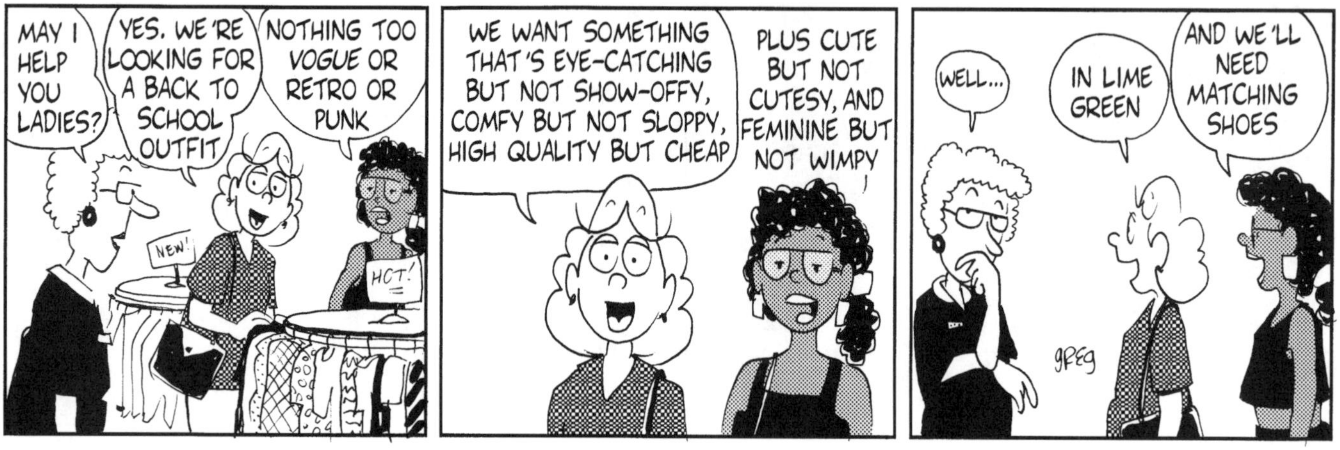
MAY I HELP YOU LADIES?
YES. WE'RE LOOKING FOR A BACK TO SCHOOL OUTFIT
NOTHING TOO *VOGUE* OR RETRO OR PUNK
NEW!
HOT!
WE WANT SOMETHING THAT'S EYE-CATCHING BUT NOT SHOW-OFFY, COMFY BUT NOT SLOPPY, HIGH QUALITY BUT CHEAP
PLUS CUTE BUT NOT CUTESY, AND FEMININE BUT NOT WIMPY
WELL...
IN LIME GREEN
AND WE'LL NEED MATCHING SHOES

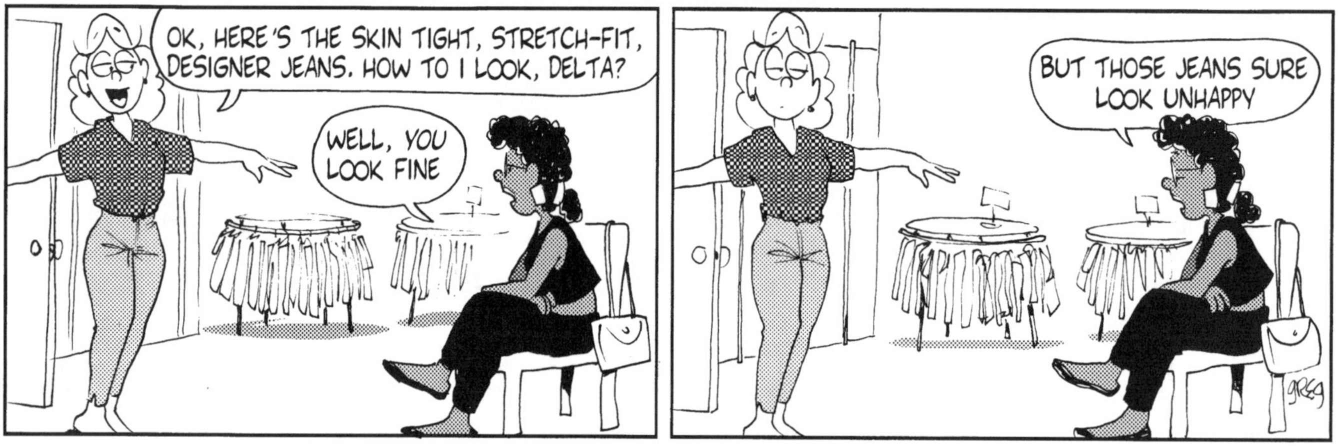
OK, HERE'S THE SKIN TIGHT, STRETCH-FIT, DESIGNER JEANS. HOW TO I LOOK, DELTA?
WELL, *YOU* LOOK FINE
BUT THOSE JEANS SURE LOOK UNHAPPY

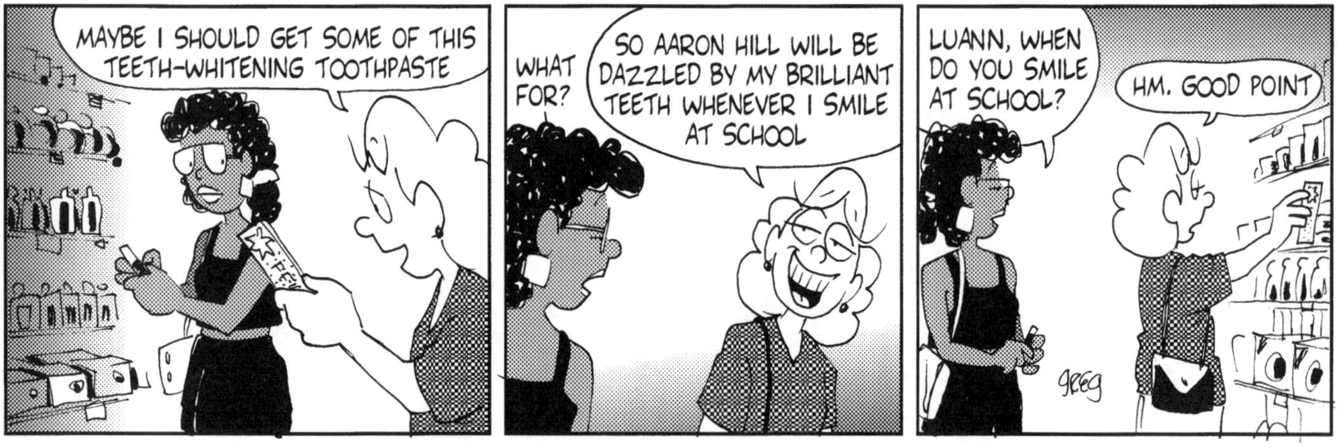
MAYBE I SHOULD GET SOME OF THIS TEETH-WHITENING TOOTHPASTE
WHAT FOR?
SO AARON HILL WILL BE DAZZLED BY MY BRILLIANT TEETH WHENEVER I SMILE AT SCHOOL
LUANN, WHEN DO YOU SMILE AT SCHOOL?
HM. GOOD POINT

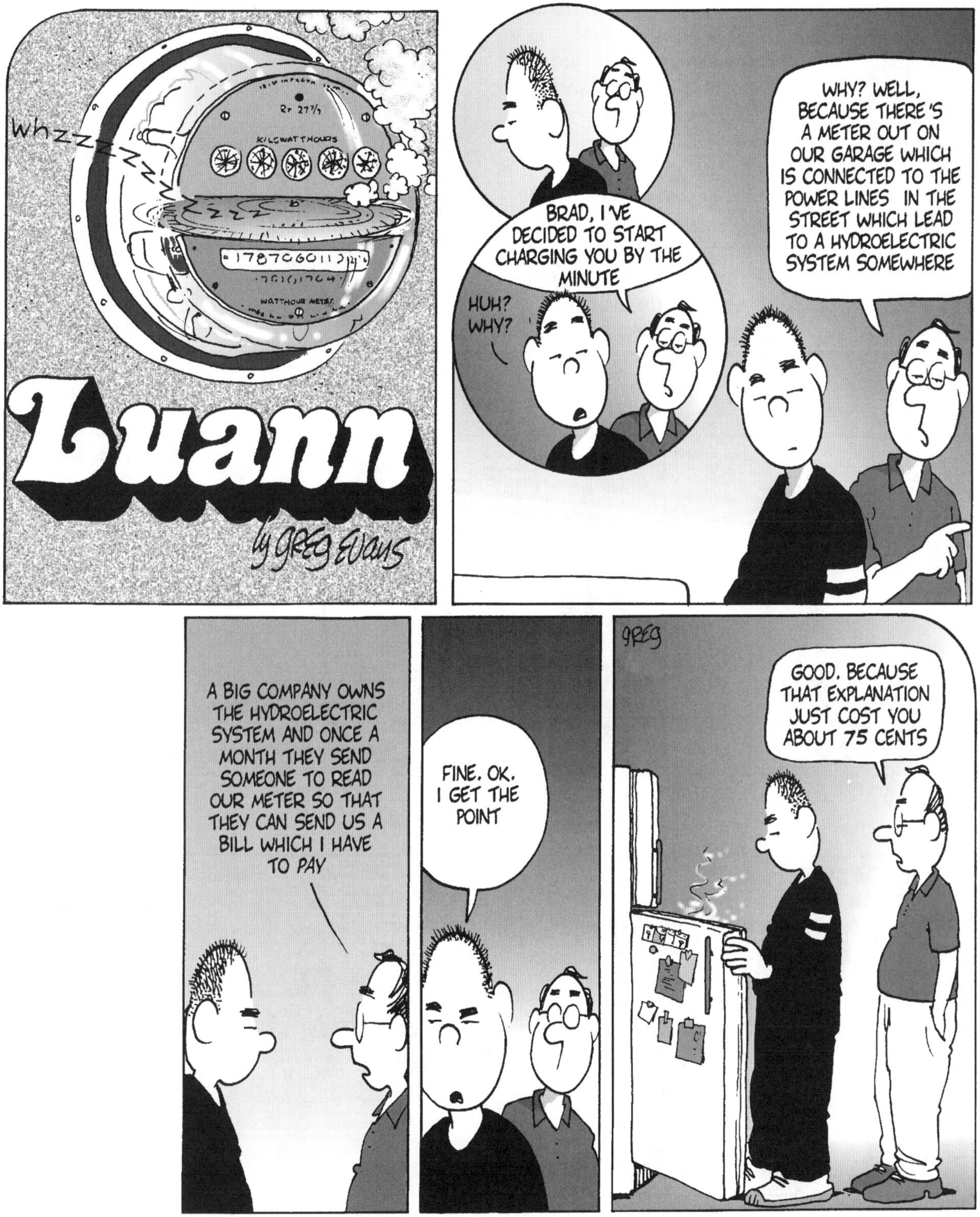
WHZZZZZZZZZ
Luann
by GREG EVANS
BRAD, I'VE DECIDED TO START CHARGING YOU BY THE MINUTE
HUH? WHY?
WHY? WELL, BECAUSE THERE'S A METER OUT ON OUR GARAGE WHICH IS CONNECTED TO THE POWER LINES IN THE STREET WHICH LEAD TO A HYDROELECTRIC SYSTEM SOMEWHERE
A BIG COMPANY OWNS THE HYDROELECTRIC SYSTEM AND ONCE A MONTH THEY SEND SOMEONE TO READ OUR METER SO THAT THEY CAN SEND US A BILL WHICH I HAVE TO *PAY*
FINE. OK. I GET THE POINT
GREG
GOOD. BECAUSE THAT EXPLANATION JUST COST YOU ABOUT 75 CENTS

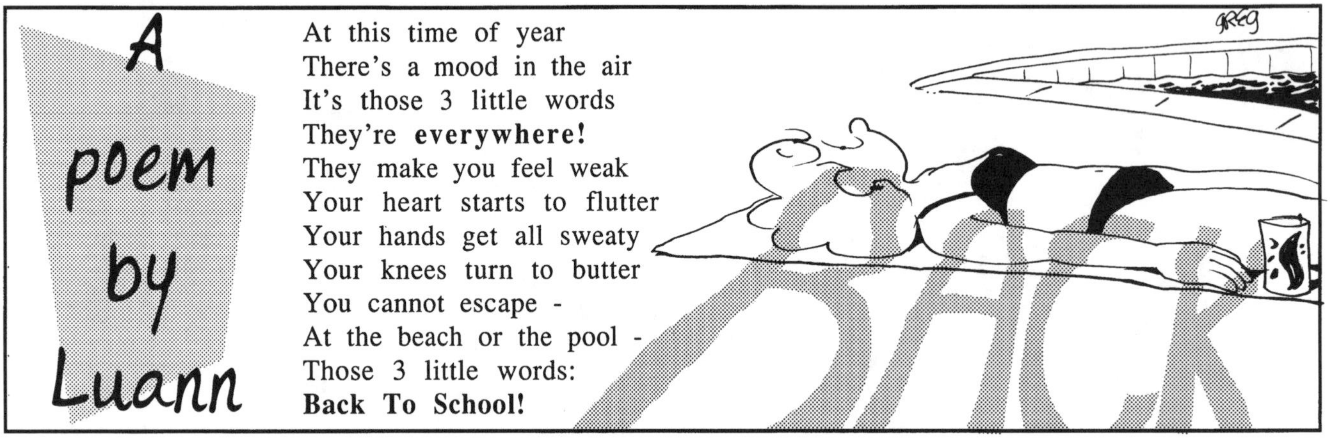
A poem by Luann
At this time of year
There's a mood in the air
It's those 3 little words
They're **everywhere!**
They make you feel weak
Your heart starts to flutter
Your hands get all sweaty
Your knees turn to butter
You cannot escape -
At the beach or the pool -
Those 3 little words:
Back To School!

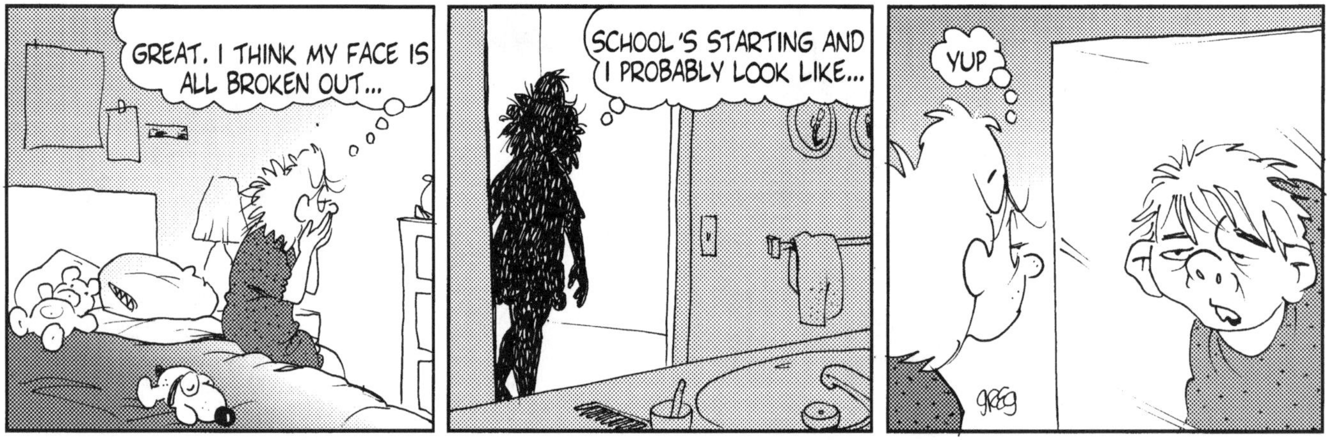
GREAT. I THINK MY FACE IS ALL BROKEN OUT...
SCHOOL'S STARTING AND I PROBABLY LOOK LIKE...
YUP

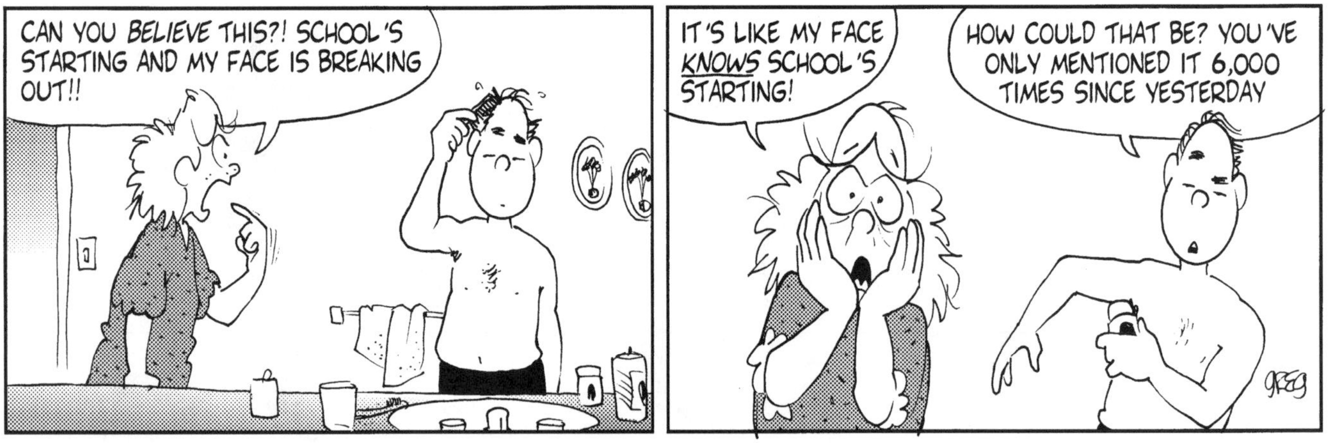
CAN YOU *BELIEVE* THIS?! SCHOOL'S STARTING AND MY FACE IS BREAKING OUT!!
IT'S LIKE MY FACE KNOWS SCHOOL'S STARTING!
HOW COULD THAT BE? YOU'VE ONLY MENTIONED IT 6,000 TIMES SINCE YESTERDAY

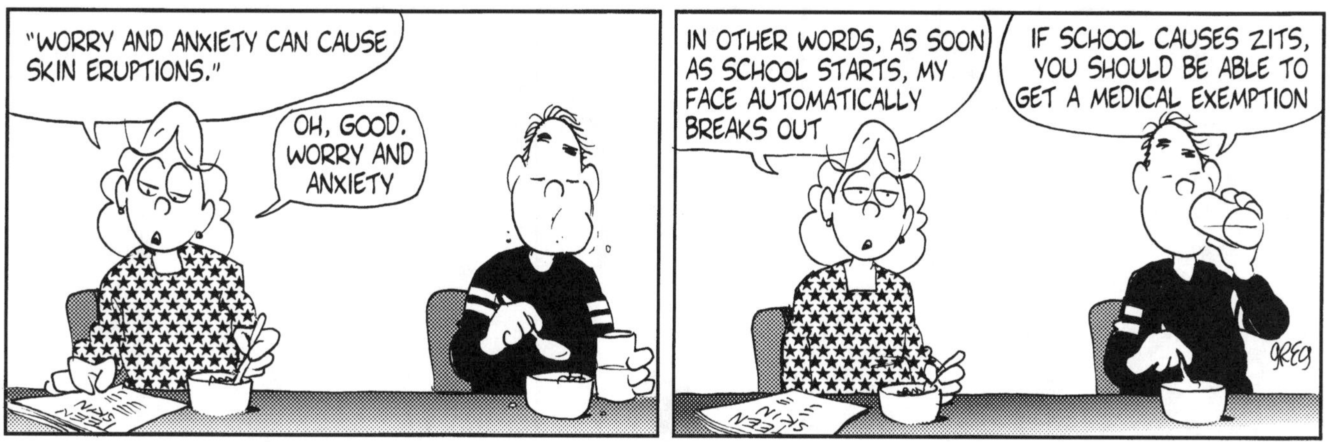
"WORRY AND ANXIETY CAN CAUSE SKIN ERUPTIONS."
OH, GOOD. WORRY AND ANXIETY
IN OTHER WORDS, AS SOON AS SCHOOL STARTS, MY FACE AUTOMATICALLY BREAKS OUT
IF SCHOOL CAUSES ZITS, YOU SHOULD BE ABLE TO GET A MEDICAL EXEMPTION

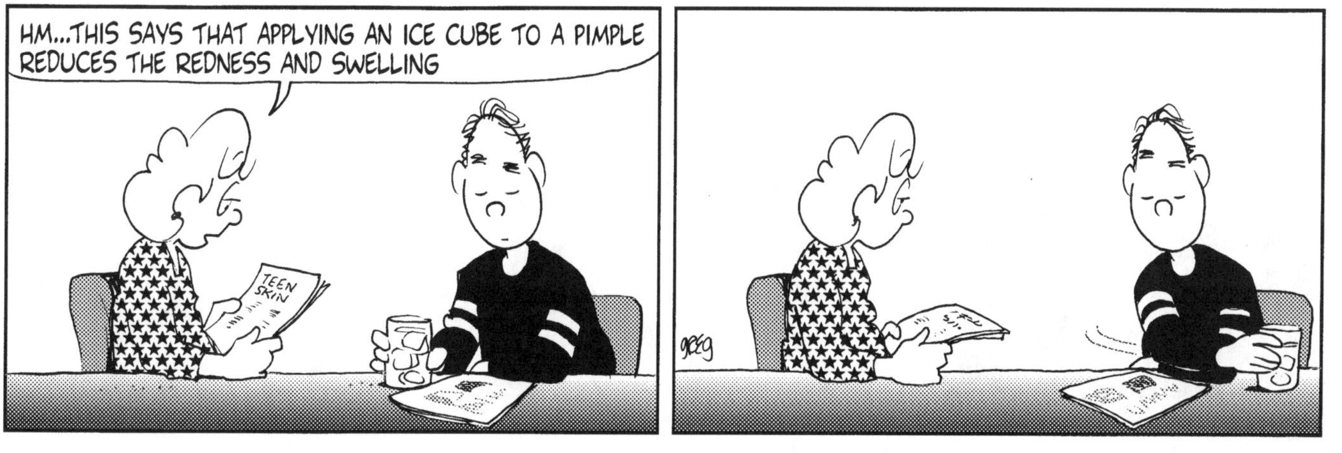
HM...THIS SAYS THAT APPLYING AN ICE CUBE TO A PIMPLE REDUCES THE REDNESS AND SWELLING
TEEN SKIN

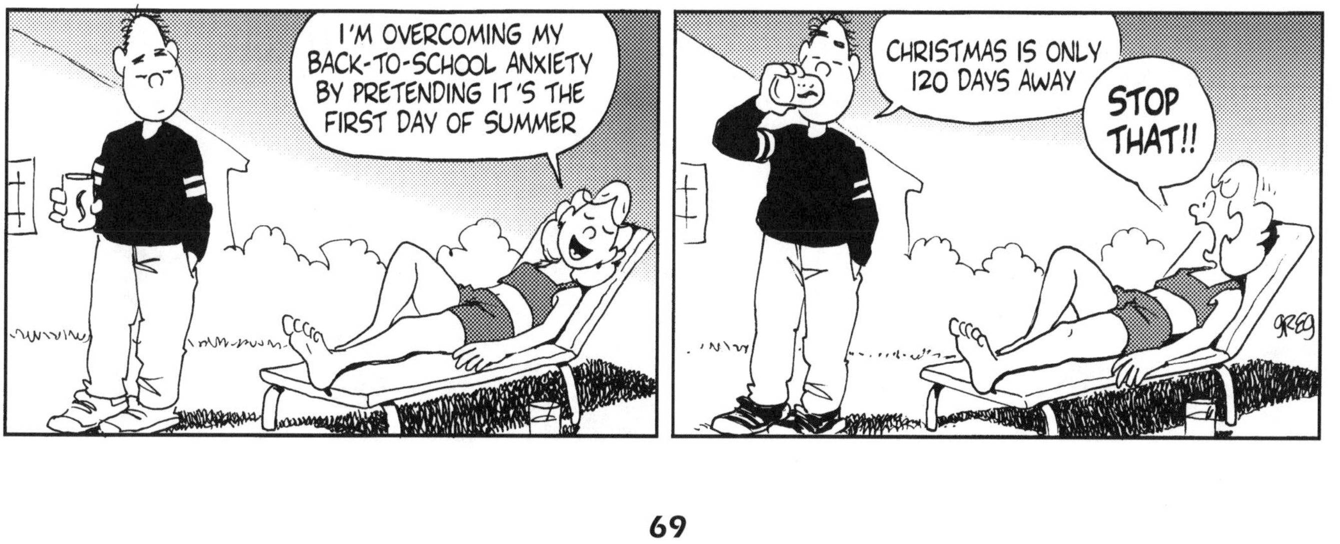
I'M OVERCOMING MY BACK-TO-SCHOOL ANXIETY BY PRETENDING IT'S THE FIRST DAY OF SUMMER
CHRISTMAS IS ONLY 120 DAYS AWAY
STOP THAT!!

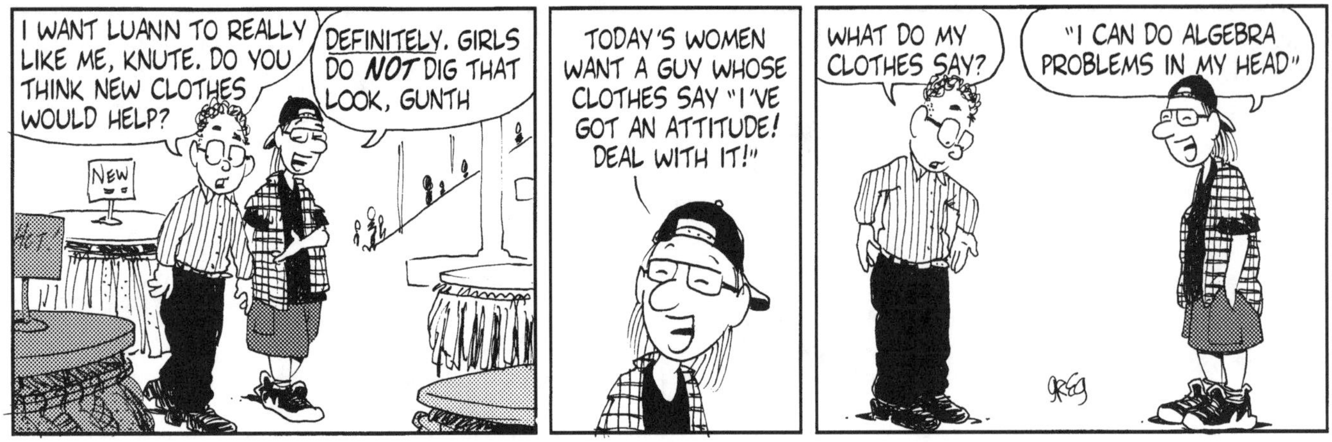
I WANT LUANN TO REALLY LIKE ME, KNUTE. DO YOU THINK NEW CLOTHES WOULD HELP?
DEFINITELY. GIRLS DO NOT DIG THAT LOOK, GUNTH
NEW
TODAY'S WOMEN WANT A GUY WHOSE CLOTHES SAY "I'VE GOT AN ATTITUDE! DEAL WITH IT!"
WHAT DO MY CLOTHES SAY?
"I CAN DO ALGEBRA PROBLEMS IN MY HEAD"

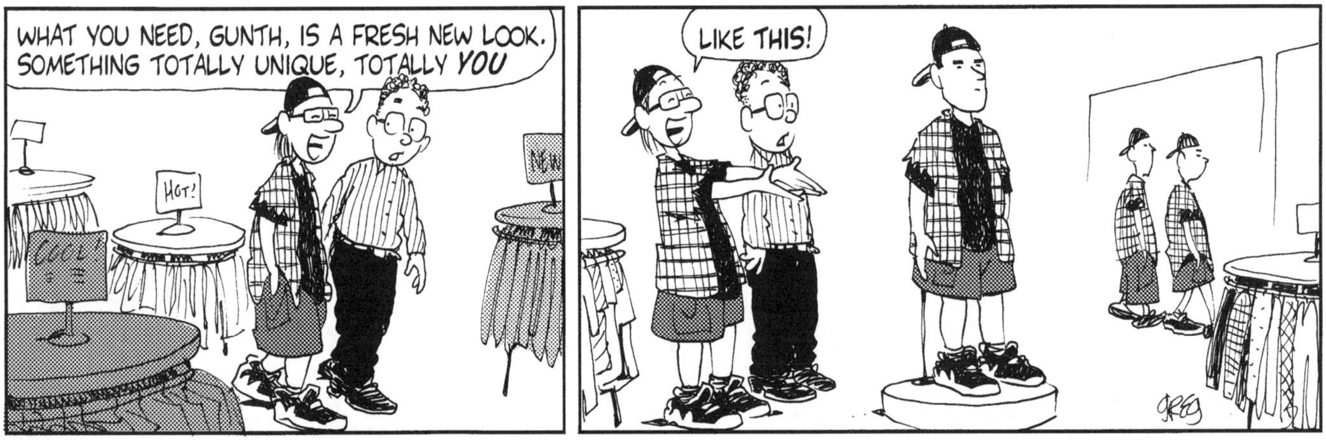
WHAT YOU NEED, GUNTH, IS A FRESH NEW LOOK. SOMETHING TOTALLY UNIQUE, TOTALLY YOU
HOT!
COOL!
LIKE THIS!

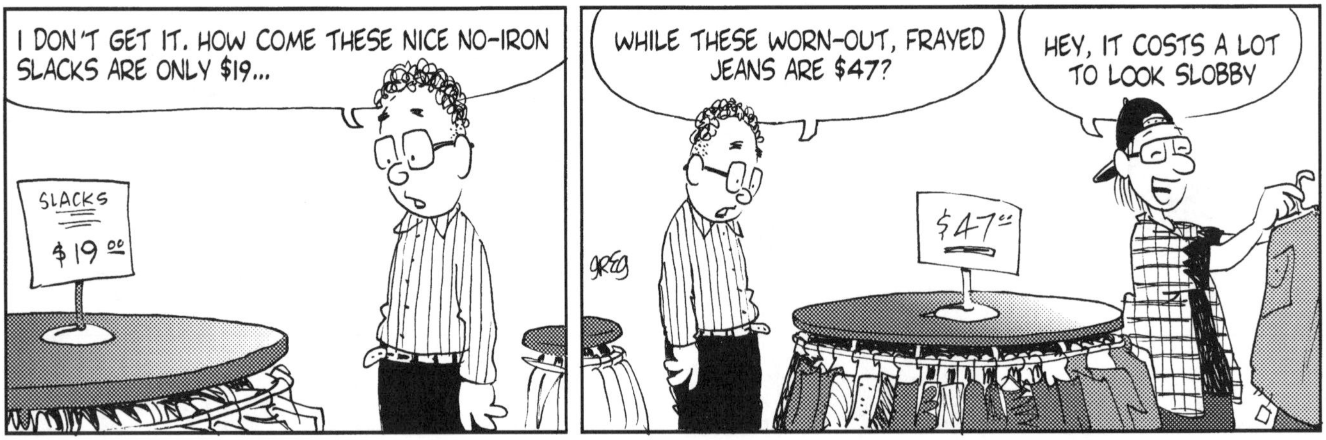
I DON'T GET IT. HOW COME THESE NICE NO-IRON SLACKS ARE ONLY $19...
SLACKS
$19.00
WHILE THESE WORN-OUT, FRAYED JEANS ARE $47?
HEY, IT COSTS A LOT TO LOOK SLOBBY
$47.00

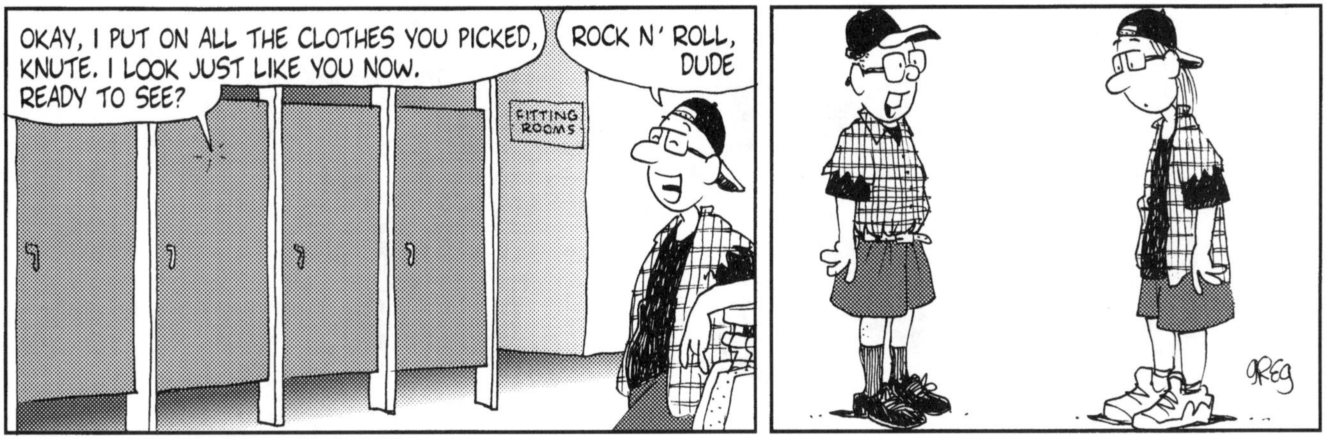
OKAY, I PUT ON ALL THE CLOTHES YOU PICKED, KNUTE. I LOOK JUST LIKE YOU NOW. READY TO SEE?
ROCK N' ROLL, DUDE
FITTING ROOMS

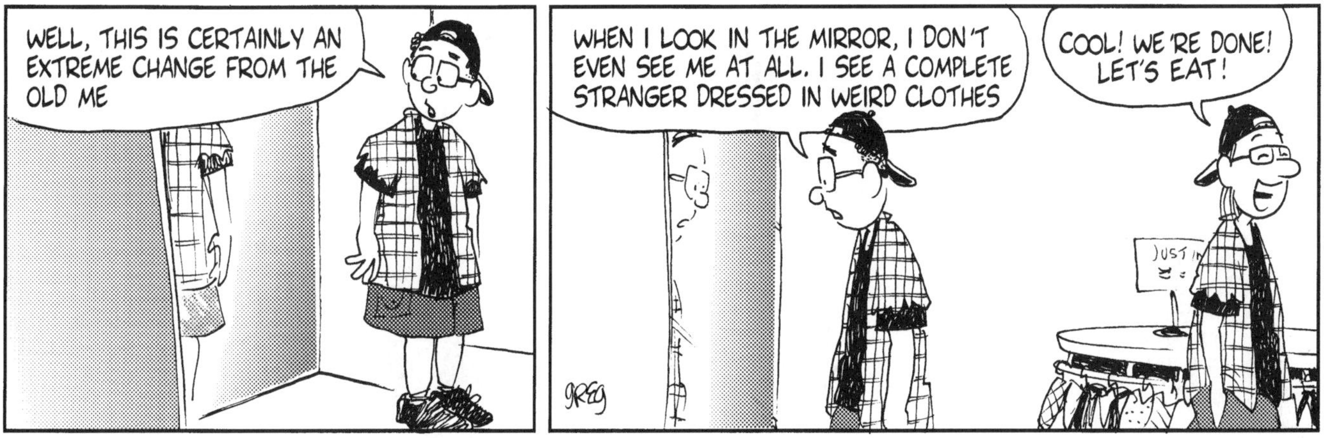
WELL, THIS IS CERTAINLY AN EXTREME CHANGE FROM THE OLD ME
WHEN I LOOK IN THE MIRROR, I DON'T EVEN SEE ME AT ALL. I SEE A COMPLETE STRANGER DRESSED IN WEIRD CLOTHES
COOL! WE'RE DONE! LET'S EAT!

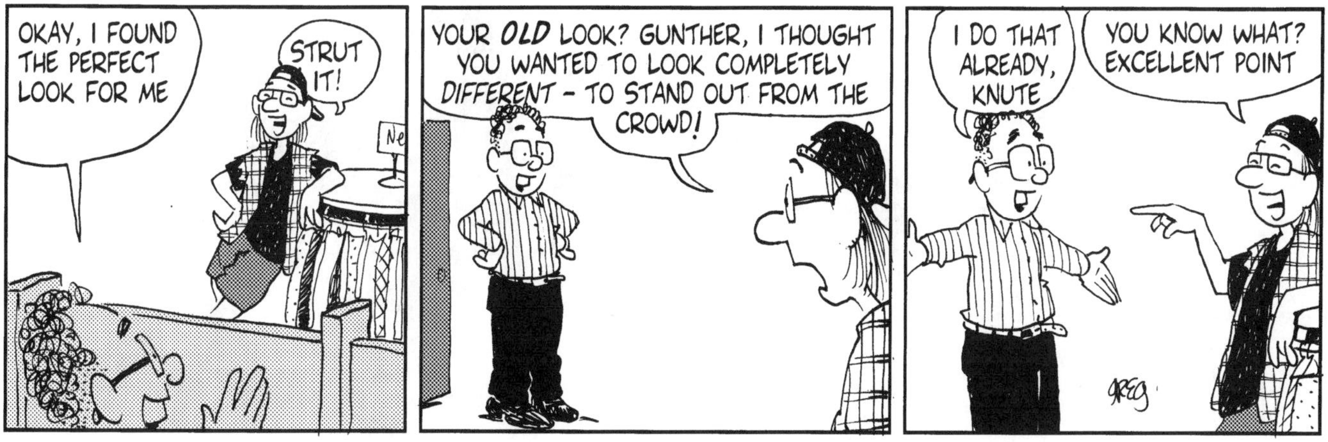
OKAY, I FOUND THE PERFECT LOOK FOR ME
STRUT IT!
YOUR *OLD* LOOK? GUNTHER, I THOUGHT YOU WANTED TO LOOK COMPLETELY *DIFFERENT* – TO STAND OUT FROM THE CROWD!
I DO THAT ALREADY, KNUTE
YOU KNOW WHAT? EXCELLENT POINT

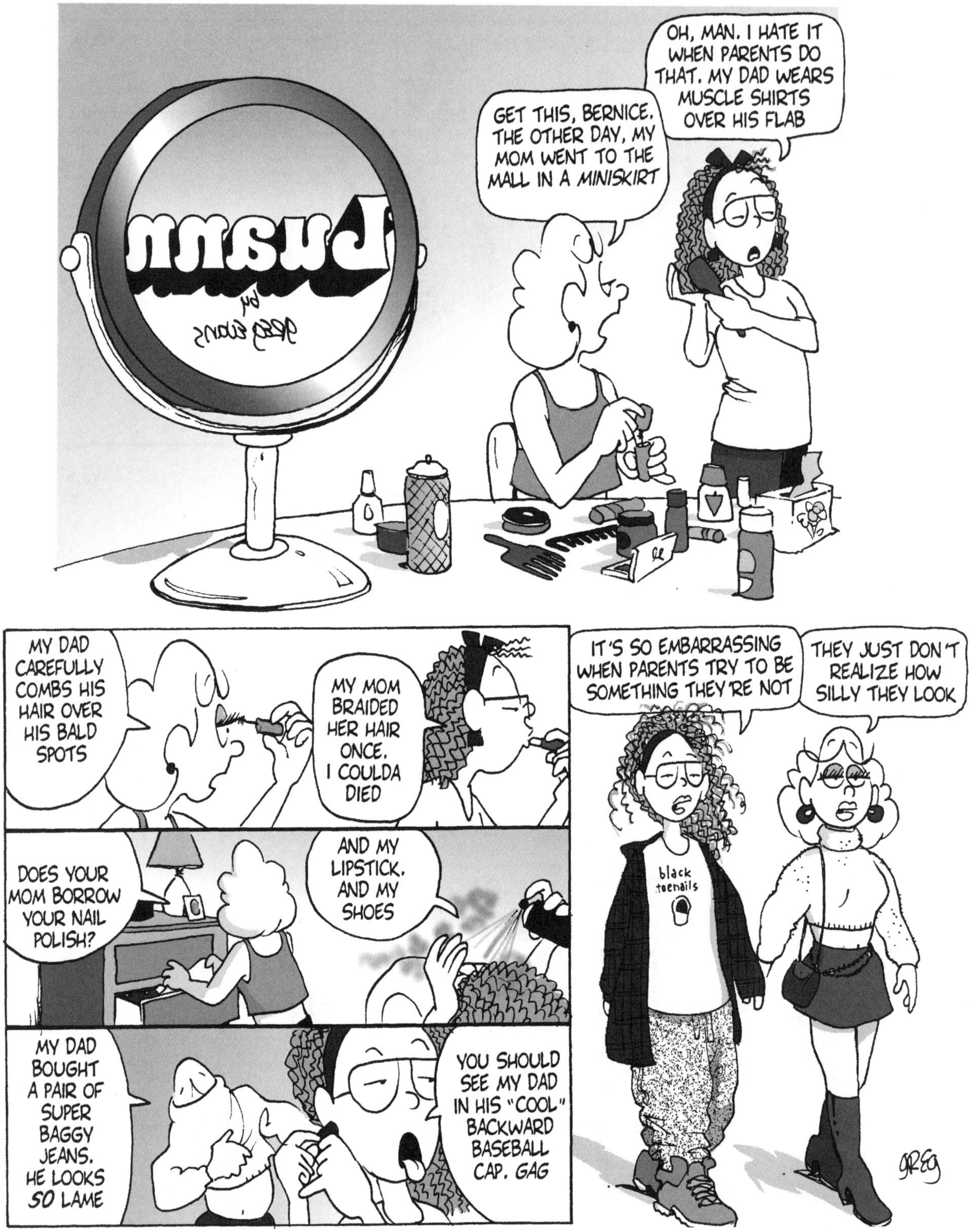
Luann
by
greg evans
GET THIS, BERNICE. THE OTHER DAY, MY MOM WENT TO THE MALL IN A *MINISKIRT*
OH, MAN. I HATE IT WHEN PARENTS DO THAT. MY DAD WEARS MUSCLE SHIRTS OVER HIS FLAB
MY DAD CAREFULLY COMBS HIS HAIR OVER HIS BALD SPOTS
MY MOM BRAIDED HER HAIR ONCE. I COULDA DIED
DOES YOUR MOM BORROW YOUR NAIL POLISH?
AND MY LIPSTICK. AND MY SHOES
MY DAD BOUGHT A PAIR OF SUPER BAGGY JEANS. HE LOOKS *SO* LAME
YOU SHOULD SEE MY DAD IN HIS "COOL" BACKWARD BASEBALL CAP. GAG
IT'S SO EMBARRASSING WHEN PARENTS TRY TO BE SOMETHING THEY'RE NOT
THEY JUST DON'T REALIZE HOW SILLY THEY LOOK
black toenails
GREG

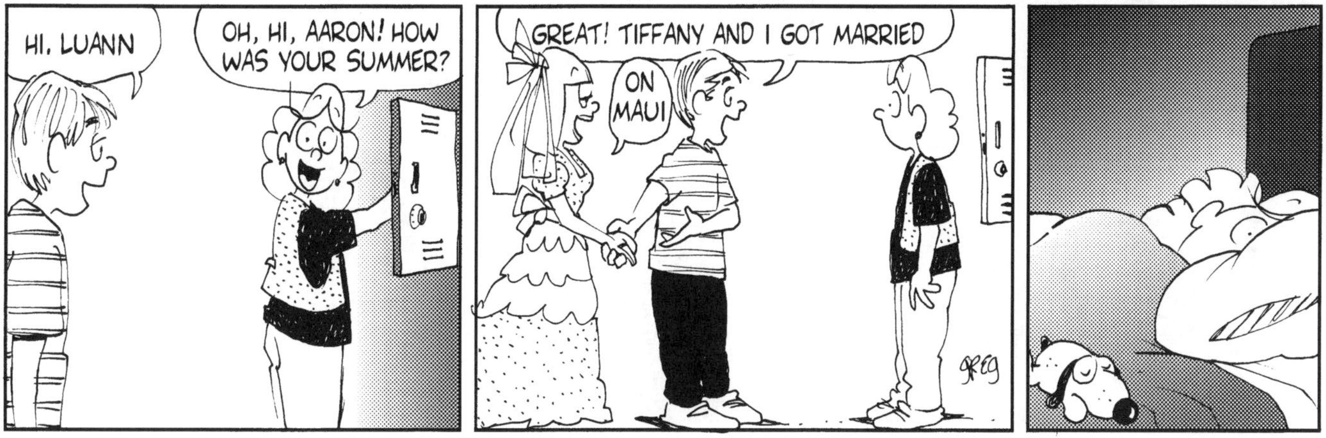
HI, LUANN
OH, HI, AARON! HOW WAS YOUR SUMMER?
GREAT! TIFFANY AND I GOT MARRIED
ON MAUI
GREG

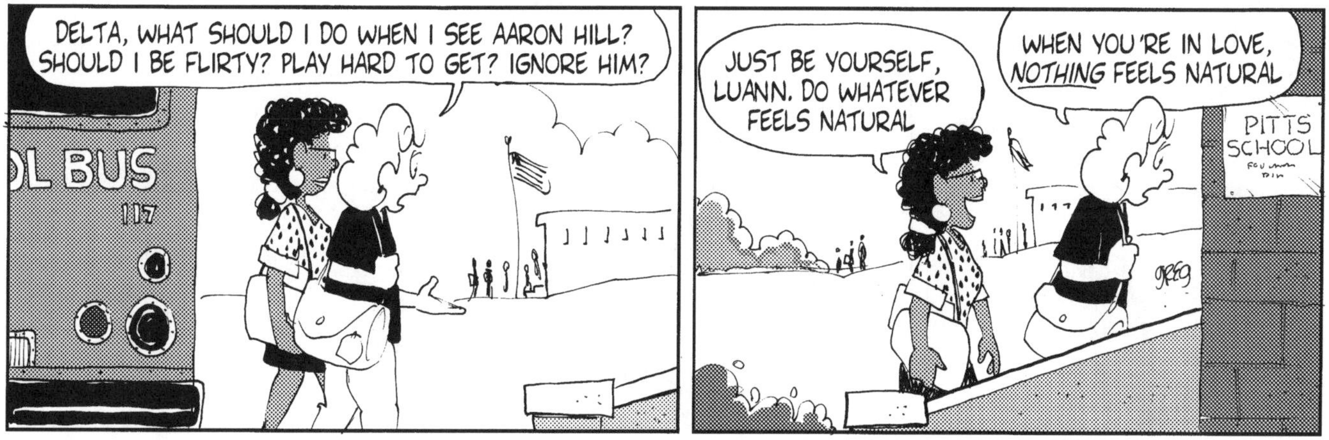
DELTA, WHAT SHOULD I DO WHEN I SEE AARON HILL? SHOULD I BE FLIRTY? PLAY HARD TO GET? IGNORE HIM?
OL BUS
117
JUST BE YOURSELF, LUANN. DO WHATEVER FEELS NATURAL
WHEN YOU'RE IN LOVE, NOTHING FEELS NATURAL
PITTS SCHOOL
GREG

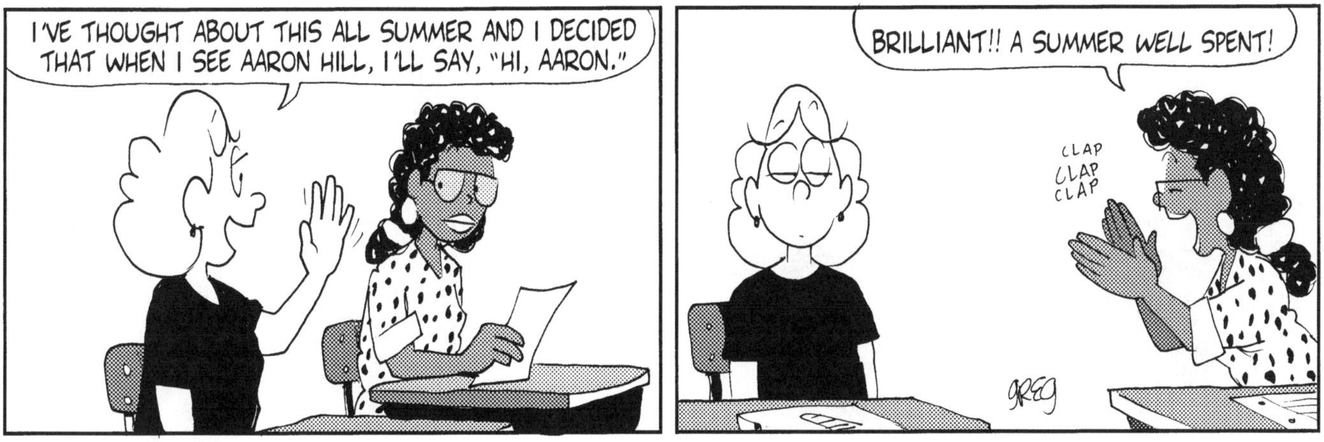
I'VE THOUGHT ABOUT THIS ALL SUMMER AND I DECIDED THAT WHEN I SEE AARON HILL, I'LL SAY, "HI, AARON."
BRILLIANT!! A SUMMER WELL SPENT!
CLAP CLAP CLAP
GREG

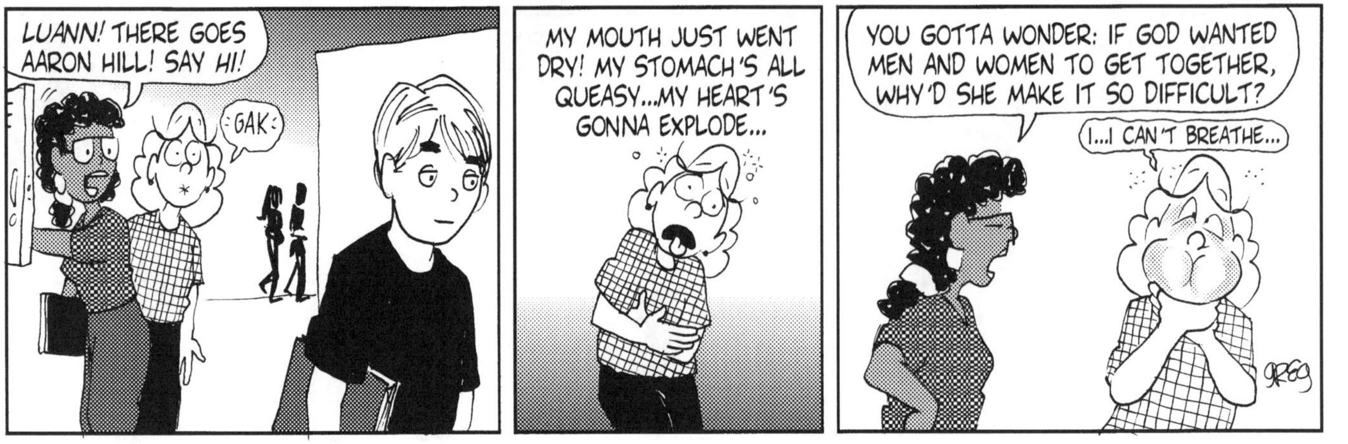
LUANN! THERE GOES AARON HILL! SAY HI!
GAK
MY MOUTH JUST WENT DRY! MY STOMACH'S ALL QUEASY...MY HEART'S GONNA EXPLODE...
YOU GOTTA WONDER: IF GOD WANTED MEN AND WOMEN TO GET TOGETHER, WHY'D SHE MAKE IT SO DIFFICULT?
I...I CAN'T BREATHE...
GREG

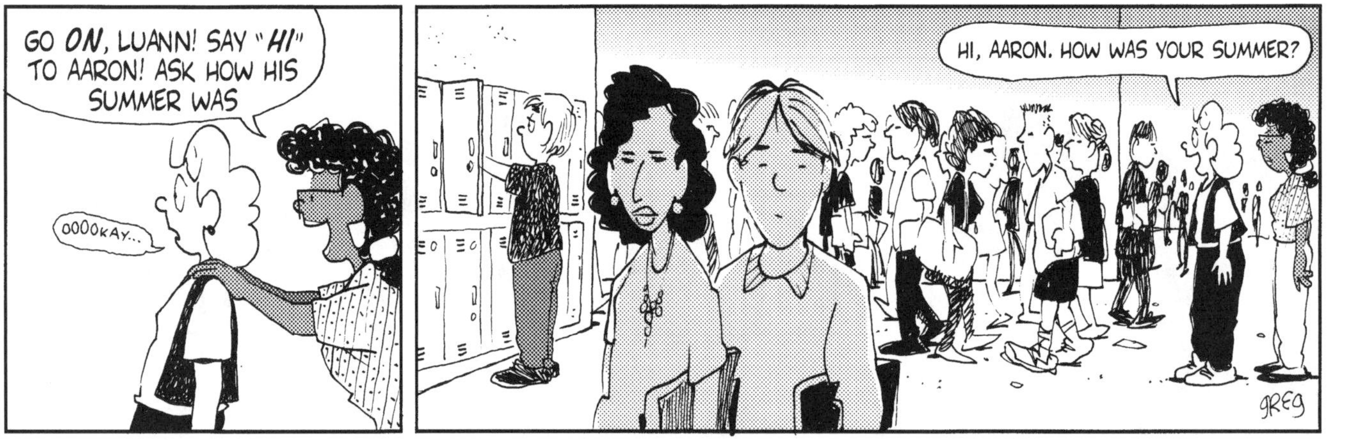
GO ON, LUANN! SAY "HI" TO AARON! ASK HOW HIS SUMMER WAS
OOOOKAY...
HI, AARON. HOW WAS YOUR SUMMER?
GREG

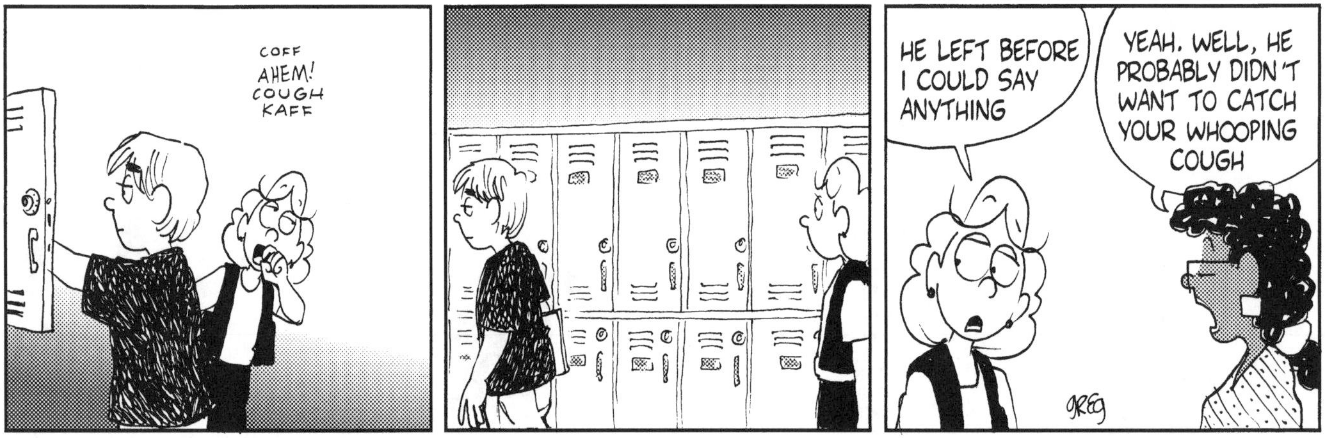
COFF
AHEM!
COUGH
KAFF
HE LEFT BEFORE I COULD SAY ANYTHING
YEAH. WELL, HE PROBABLY DIDN'T WANT TO CATCH YOUR WHOOPING COUGH
GREG

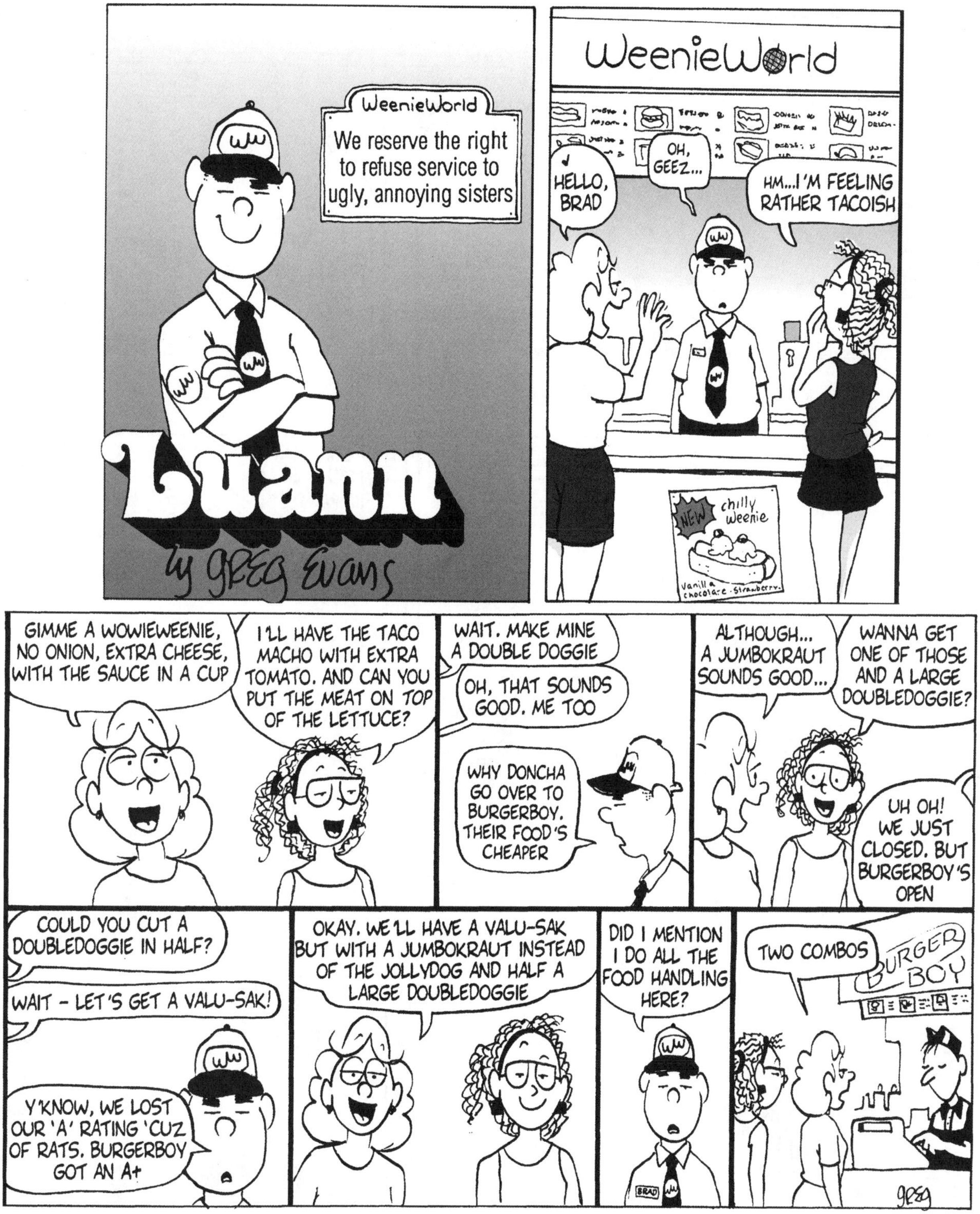
WeenieWorld
We reserve the right to refuse service to ugly, annoying sisters
Luann
by Greg Evans
WeenieWorld
HELLO, BRAD
OH, GEEZ...
HM...I'M FEELING RATHER TACOISH
NEW
chilly weenie
vanilla chocolate · strawberry
GIMME A WOWIEWEENIE, NO ONION, EXTRA CHEESE, WITH THE SAUCE IN A CUP
I'LL HAVE THE TACO MACHO WITH EXTRA TOMATO. AND CAN YOU PUT THE MEAT ON TOP OF THE LETTUCE?
WAIT. MAKE MINE A DOUBLE DOGGIE
OH, THAT SOUNDS GOOD. ME TOO
WHY DONCHA GO OVER TO BURGERBOY. THEIR FOOD'S CHEAPER
ALTHOUGH... A JUMBOKRAUT SOUNDS GOOD...
WANNA GET ONE OF THOSE AND A LARGE DOUBLEDOGGIE?
UH OH! WE JUST CLOSED. BUT BURGERBOY'S OPEN
COULD YOU CUT A DOUBLEDOGGIE IN HALF?
WAIT – LET'S GET A VALU-SAK!
Y'KNOW, WE LOST OUR 'A' RATING 'CUZ OF RATS. BURGERBOY GOT AN A+
OKAY. WE'LL HAVE A VALU-SAK BUT WITH A JUMBOKRAUT INSTEAD OF THE JOLLYDOG AND HALF A LARGE DOUBLEDOGGIE
DID I MENTION I DO ALL THE FOOD HANDLING HERE?
BRAD
TWO COMBOS
BURGER BOY
greg

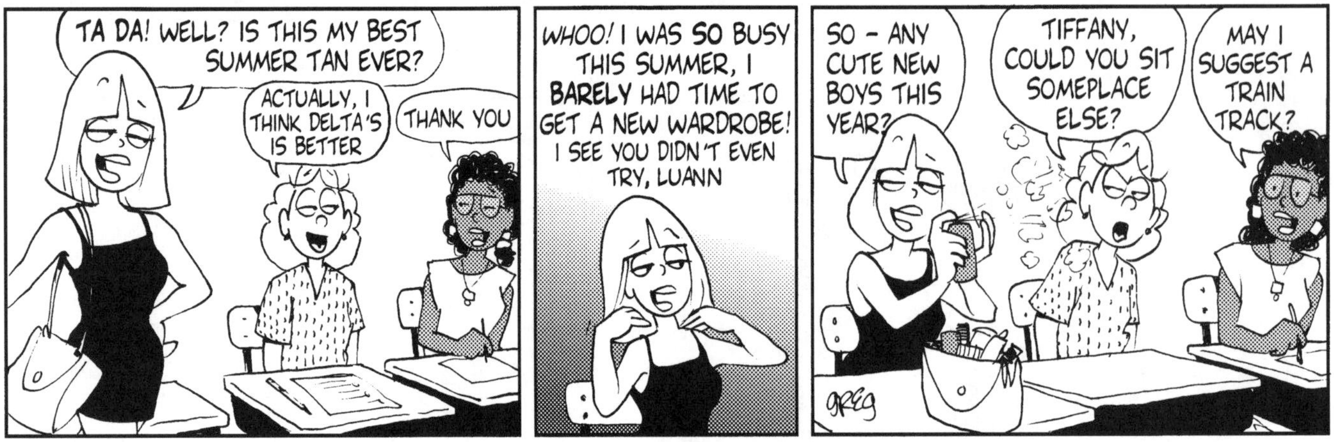
TA DA! WELL? IS THIS MY BEST SUMMER TAN EVER?
ACTUALLY, I THINK DELTA'S IS BETTER
THANK YOU
WHOO! I WAS **SO** BUSY THIS SUMMER, I **BARELY** HAD TIME TO GET A NEW WARDROBE! I SEE YOU DIDN'T EVEN TRY, LUANN
SO – ANY CUTE NEW BOYS THIS YEAR?
TIFFANY, COULD YOU SIT SOMEPLACE ELSE?
MAY I SUGGEST A TRAIN TRACK?
GREG

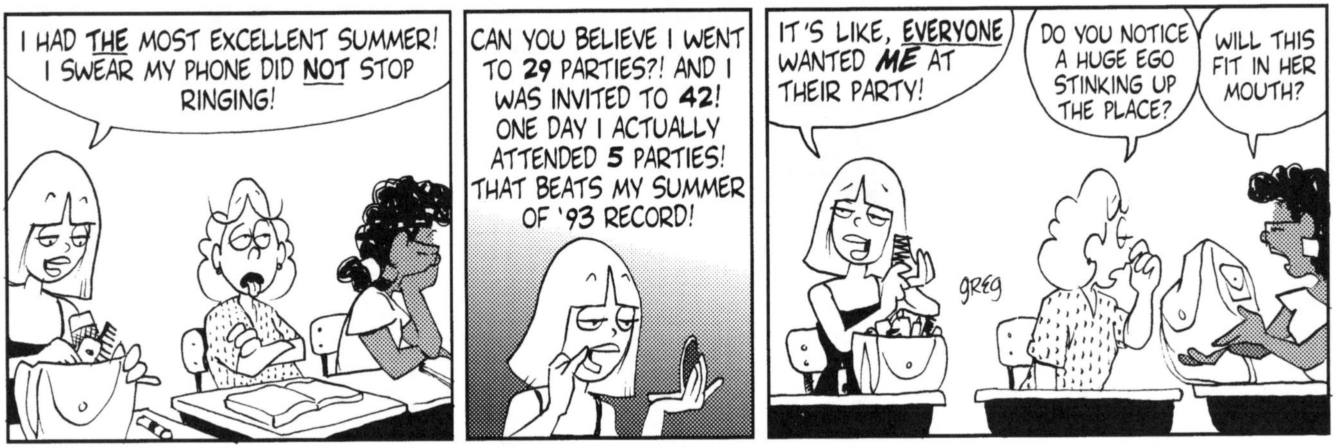
I HAD THE MOST EXCELLENT SUMMER! I SWEAR MY PHONE DID NOT STOP RINGING!
CAN YOU BELIEVE I WENT TO **29** PARTIES?! AND I WAS INVITED TO **42**! ONE DAY I ACTUALLY ATTENDED **5** PARTIES! THAT BEATS MY SUMMER OF '93 RECORD!
IT'S LIKE, EVERYONE WANTED ***ME*** AT THEIR PARTY!
DO YOU NOTICE A HUGE EGO STINKING UP THE PLACE?
WILL THIS FIT IN HER MOUTH?
GREG

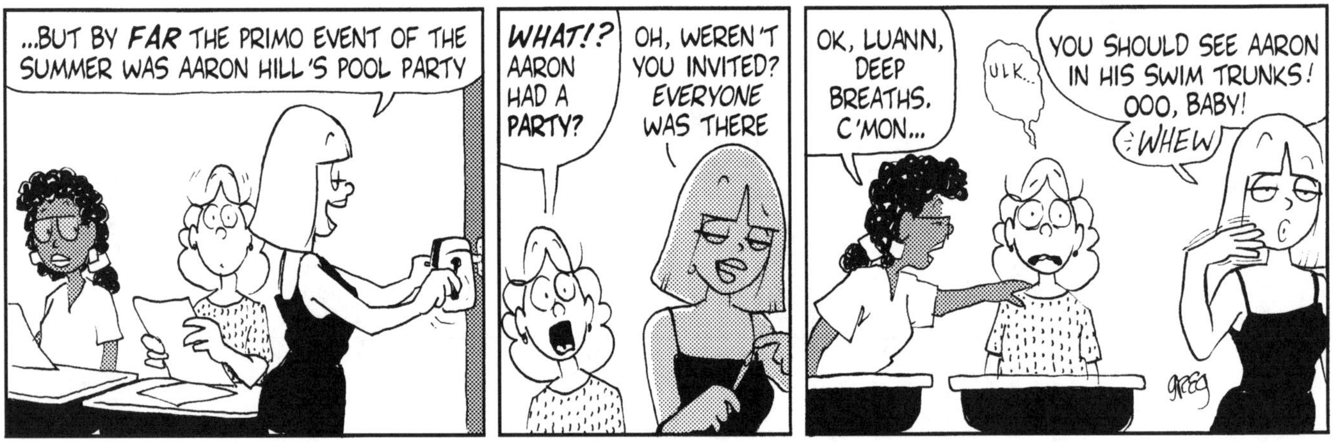
...BUT BY ***FAR*** THE PRIMO EVENT OF THE SUMMER WAS AARON HILL'S POOL PARTY
WHAT!? AARON HAD A **PARTY**?
OH, WEREN'T YOU INVITED? EVERYONE WAS THERE
OK, LUANN, DEEP BREATHS. C'MON...
ULK...
YOU SHOULD SEE AARON IN HIS SWIM TRUNKS! OOO, BABY!
WHEW
GREG

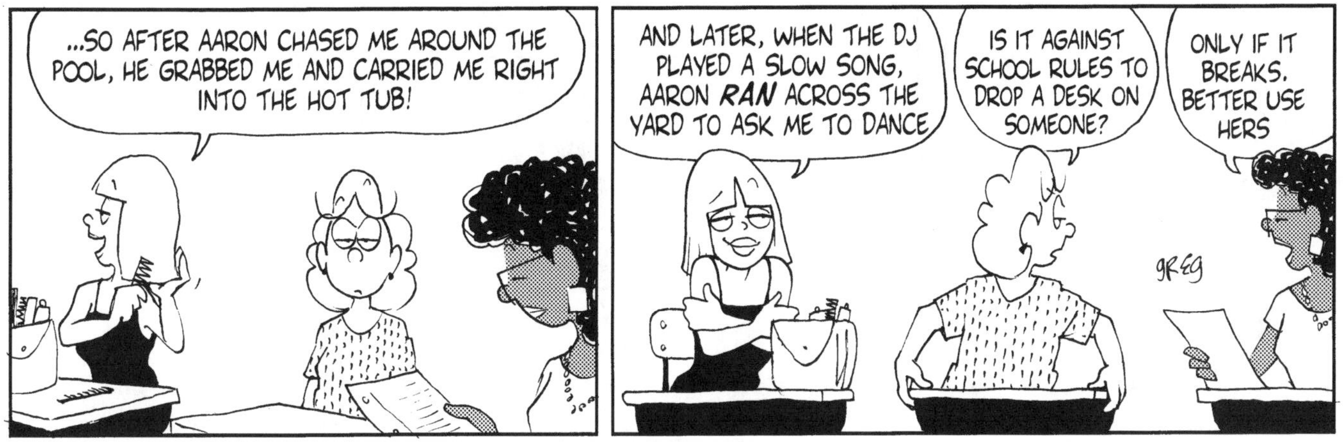
...SO AFTER AARON CHASED ME AROUND THE POOL, HE GRABBED ME AND CARRIED ME RIGHT INTO THE HOT TUB!
AND LATER, WHEN THE DJ PLAYED A SLOW SONG, AARON *RAN* ACROSS THE YARD TO ASK ME TO DANCE
IS IT AGAINST SCHOOL RULES TO DROP A DESK ON SOMEONE?
ONLY IF IT BREAKS. BETTER USE HERS
GREG

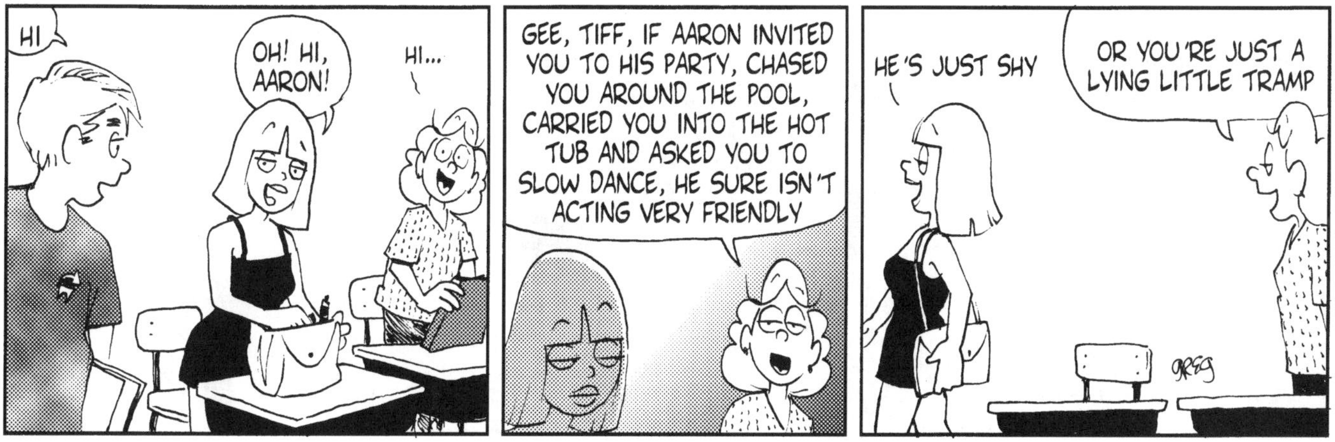
HI
OH! HI, AARON!
HI...
GEE, TIFF, IF AARON INVITED YOU TO HIS PARTY, CHASED YOU AROUND THE POOL, CARRIED YOU INTO THE HOT TUB AND ASKED YOU TO SLOW DANCE, HE SURE ISN'T ACTING VERY FRIENDLY
HE'S JUST SHY
OR YOU'RE JUST A LYING LITTLE TRAMP
GREG

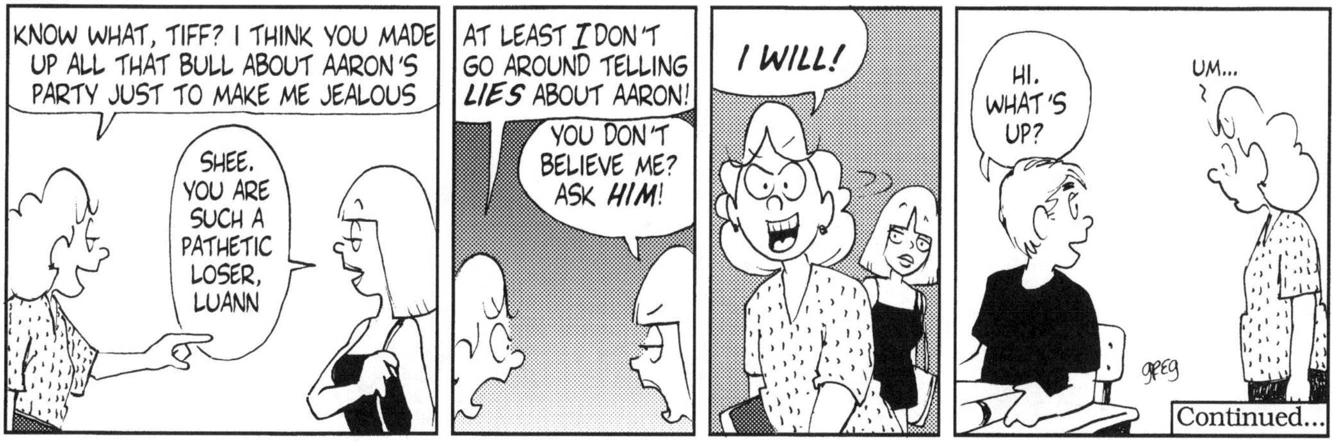
KNOW WHAT, TIFF? I THINK YOU MADE UP ALL THAT BULL ABOUT AARON'S PARTY JUST TO MAKE ME JEALOUS
SHEE. YOU ARE SUCH A PATHETIC LOSER, LUANN
AT LEAST *I* DON'T GO AROUND TELLING *LIES* ABOUT AARON!
YOU DON'T BELIEVE ME? ASK *HIM*!
I WILL!
HI. WHAT'S UP?
UM...
GREG
Continued...

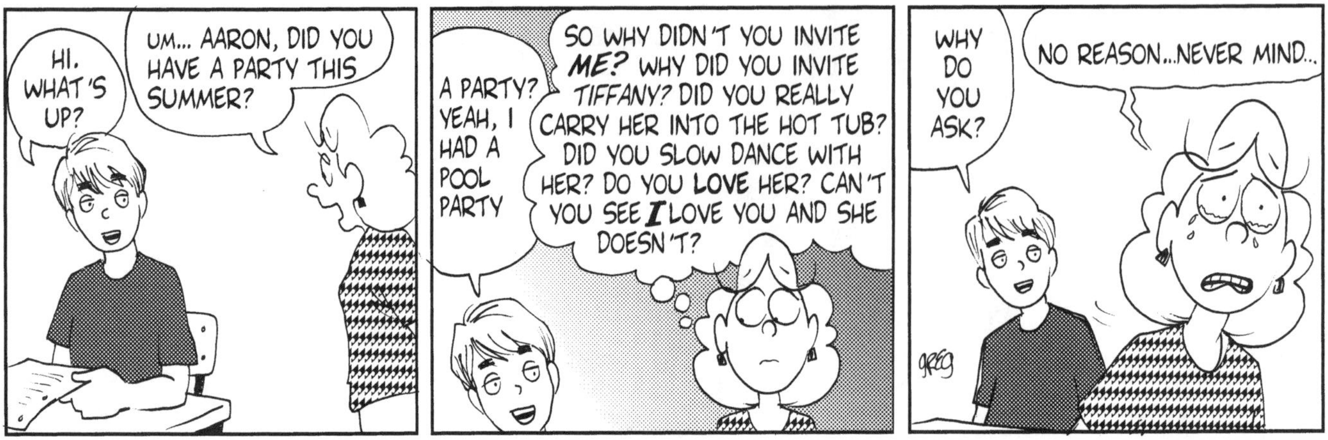
HI. WHAT'S UP?
UM... AARON, DID YOU HAVE A PARTY THIS SUMMER?
A PARTY? YEAH, I HAD A POOL PARTY
SO WHY DIDN'T YOU INVITE ME? WHY DID YOU INVITE TIFFANY? DID YOU REALLY CARRY HER INTO THE HOT TUB? DID YOU SLOW DANCE WITH HER? DO YOU LOVE HER? CAN'T YOU SEE I LOVE YOU AND SHE DOESN'T?
WHY DO YOU ASK?
NO REASON...NEVER MIND...
GREG

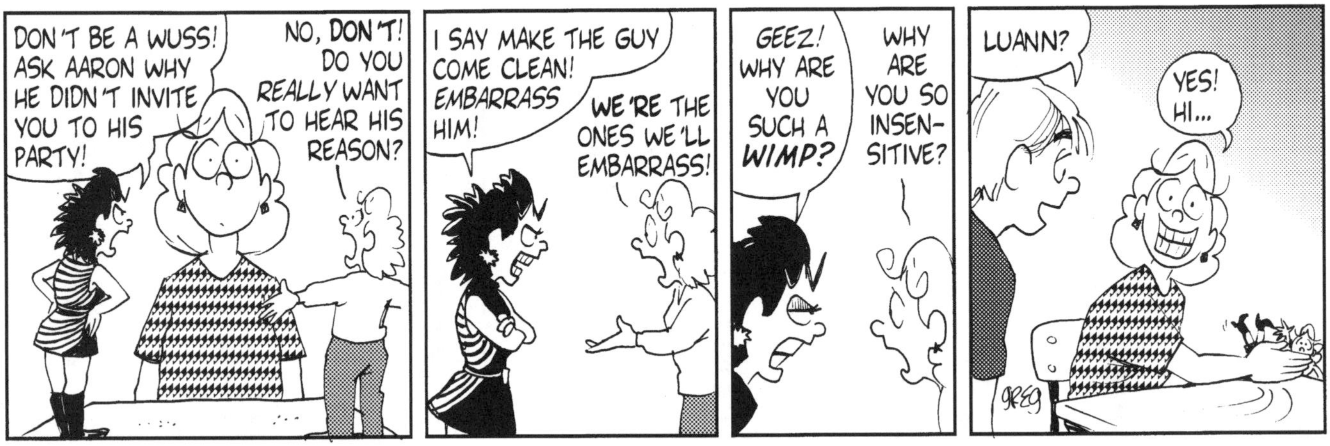
DON'T BE A WUSS! ASK AARON WHY HE DIDN'T INVITE YOU TO HIS PARTY!
NO, DON'T! DO YOU REALLY WANT TO HEAR HIS REASON?
I SAY MAKE THE GUY COME CLEAN! EMBARRASS HIM!
WE'RE THE ONES WE'LL EMBARRASS!
GEEZ! WHY ARE YOU SUCH A WIMP?
WHY ARE YOU SO INSEN-SITIVE?
LUANN?
YES! HI...
GREG

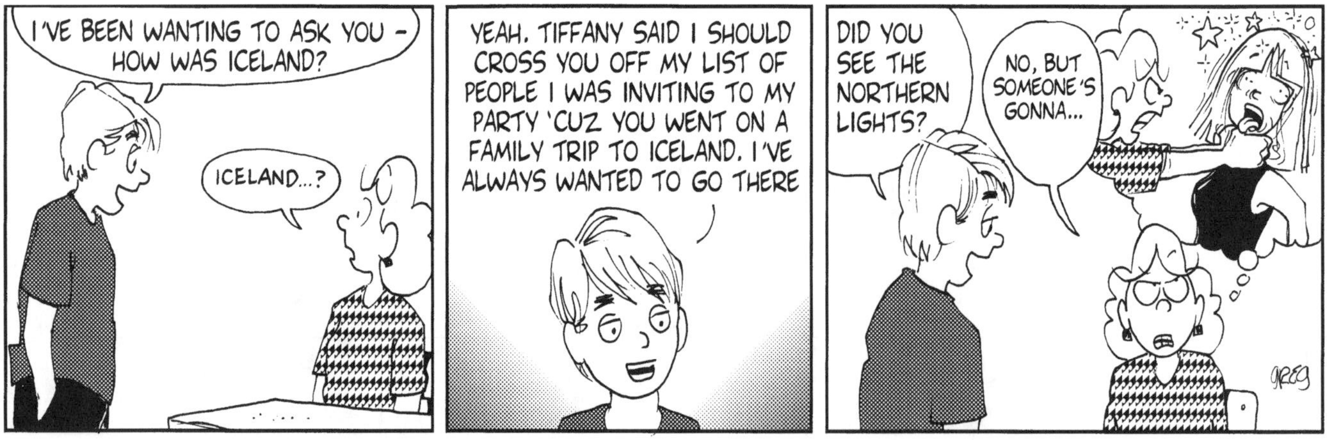
I'VE BEEN WANTING TO ASK YOU – HOW WAS ICELAND?
ICELAND...?
YEAH. TIFFANY SAID I SHOULD CROSS YOU OFF MY LIST OF PEOPLE I WAS INVITING TO MY PARTY 'CUZ YOU WENT ON A FAMILY TRIP TO ICELAND. I'VE ALWAYS WANTED TO GO THERE
DID YOU SEE THE NORTHERN LIGHTS?
NO, BUT SOMEONE'S GONNA...
GREG

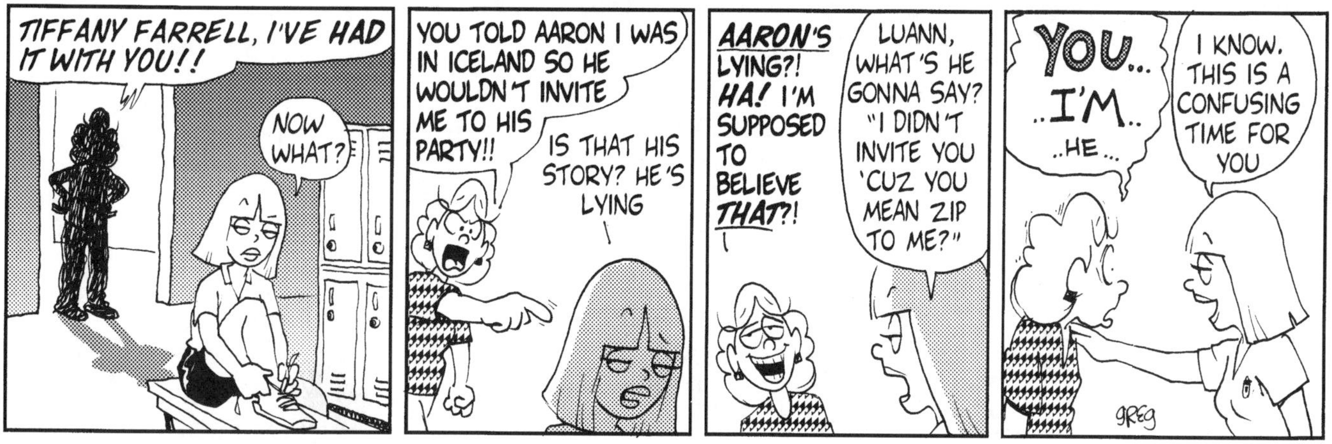
TIFFANY FARRELL, I'VE HAD IT WITH YOU!!
NOW WHAT?
YOU TOLD AARON I WAS IN ICELAND SO HE WOULDN'T INVITE ME TO HIS PARTY!!
IS THAT HIS STORY? HE'S LYING
AARON'S LYING?! HA! I'M SUPPOSED TO BELIEVE THAT?!
LUANN, WHAT'S HE GONNA SAY? "I DIDN'T INVITE YOU 'CUZ YOU MEAN ZIP TO ME?"
YOU... ..I'M.. ..HE...
I KNOW. THIS IS A CONFUSING TIME FOR YOU
GREG

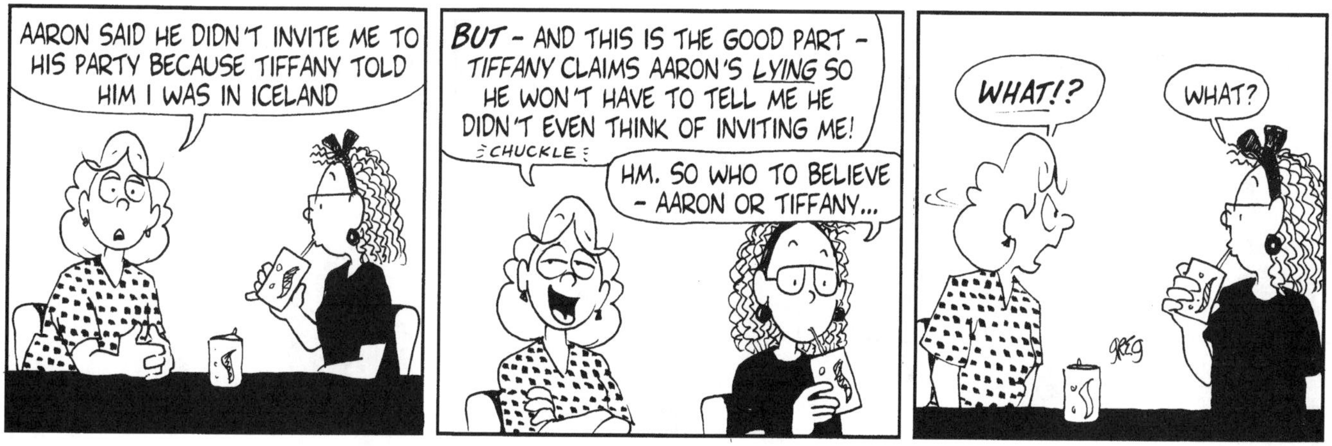
AARON SAID HE DIDN'T INVITE ME TO HIS PARTY BECAUSE TIFFANY TOLD HIM I WAS IN ICELAND
BUT - AND THIS IS THE GOOD PART - TIFFANY CLAIMS AARON'S LYING SO HE WON'T HAVE TO TELL ME HE DIDN'T EVEN THINK OF INVITING ME!
CHUCKLE
HM. SO WHO TO BELIEVE - AARON OR TIFFANY...
WHAT!?
WHAT?
GREG

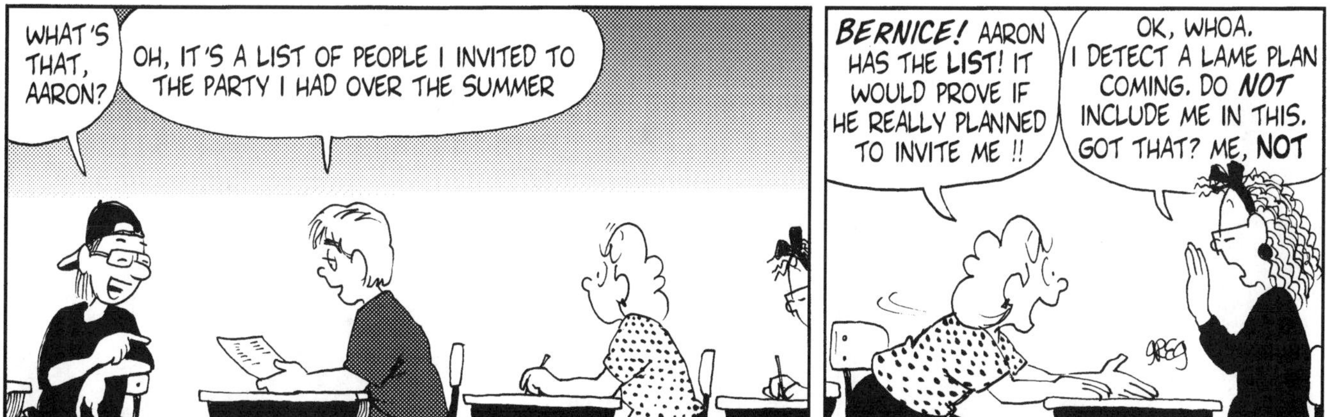
WHAT'S THAT, AARON?
OH, IT'S A LIST OF PEOPLE I INVITED TO THE PARTY I HAD OVER THE SUMMER
BERNICE! AARON HAS THE LIST! IT WOULD PROVE IF HE REALLY PLANNED TO INVITE ME !!
OK, WHOA. I DETECT A LAME PLAN COMING. DO NOT INCLUDE ME IN THIS. GOT THAT? ME, NOT
GREG

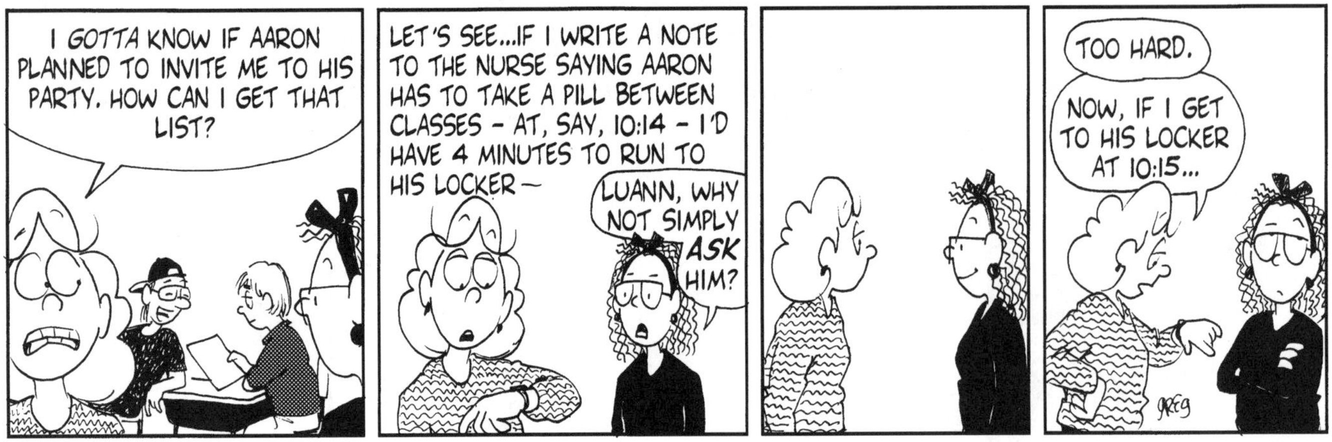
I GOTTA KNOW IF AARON PLANNED TO INVITE ME TO HIS PARTY. HOW CAN I GET THAT LIST?
LET'S SEE...IF I WRITE A NOTE TO THE NURSE SAYING AARON HAS TO TAKE A PILL BETWEEN CLASSES - AT, SAY, 10:14 - I'D HAVE 4 MINUTES TO RUN TO HIS LOCKER—
LUANN, WHY NOT SIMPLY ASK HIM?
TOO HARD.
NOW, IF I GET TO HIS LOCKER AT 10:15...
GREG

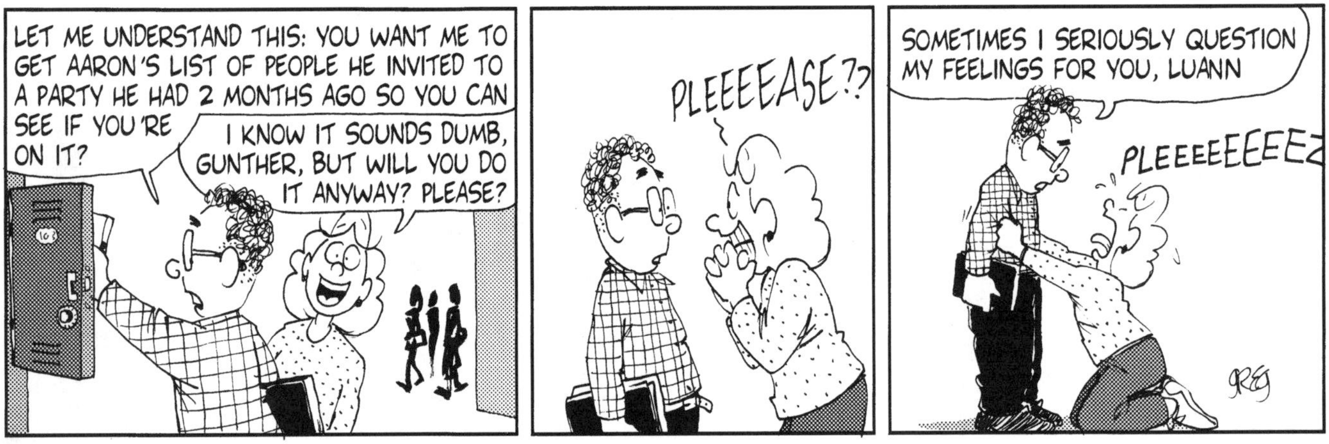
LET ME UNDERSTAND THIS: YOU WANT ME TO GET AARON'S LIST OF PEOPLE HE INVITED TO A PARTY HE HAD 2 MONTHS AGO SO YOU CAN SEE IF YOU'RE ON IT?
I KNOW IT SOUNDS DUMB, GUNTHER, BUT WILL YOU DO IT ANYWAY? PLEASE?
PLEEEEASE??
SOMETIMES I SERIOUSLY QUESTION MY FEELINGS FOR YOU, LUANN
PLEEEEEEEEZ
GREG

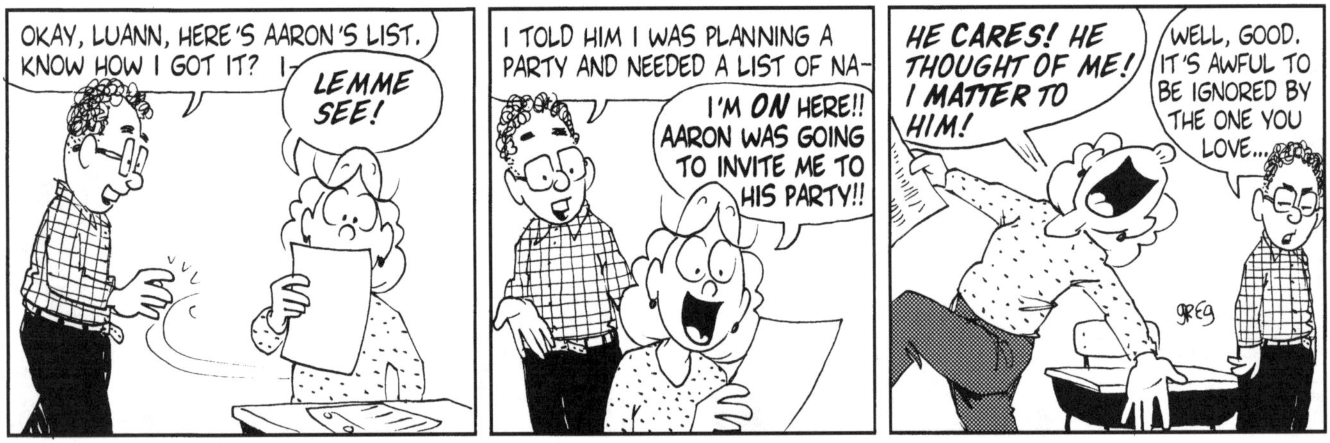
OKAY, LUANN, HERE'S AARON'S LIST. KNOW HOW I GOT IT? I—
LEMME SEE!
I TOLD HIM I WAS PLANNING A PARTY AND NEEDED A LIST OF NA—
I'M ON HERE!! AARON WAS GOING TO INVITE ME TO HIS PARTY!!
HE CARES! HE THOUGHT OF ME! I MATTER TO HIM!
WELL, GOOD. IT'S AWFUL TO BE IGNORED BY THE ONE YOU LOVE...
GREG

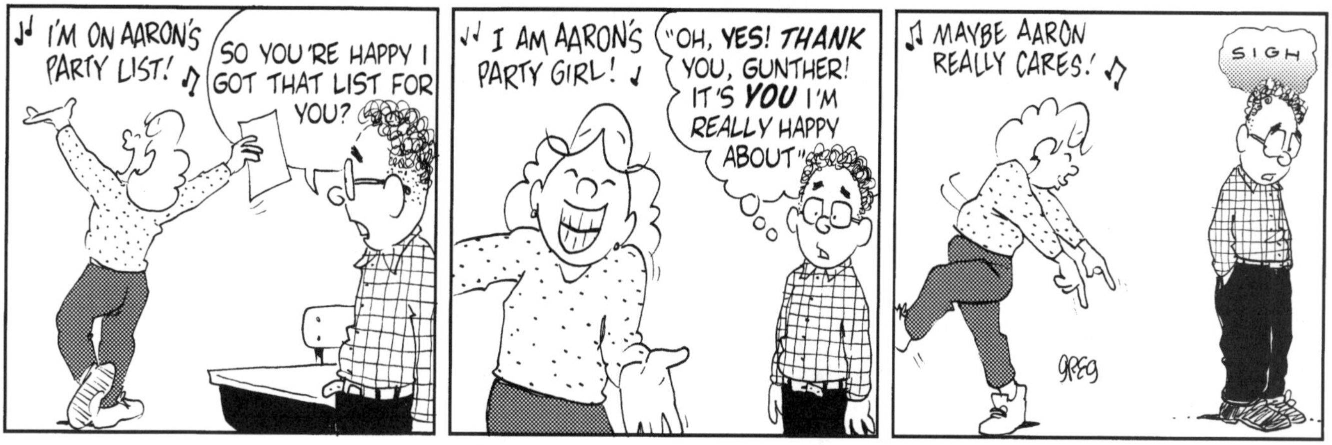
I'M ON AARON'S PARTY LIST!
SO YOU'RE HAPPY I GOT THAT LIST FOR YOU?
I AM AARON'S PARTY GIRL!
"OH, YES! THANK YOU, GUNTHER! IT'S YOU I'M REALLY HAPPY ABOUT"
MAYBE AARON REALLY CARES!
SIGH
GREG

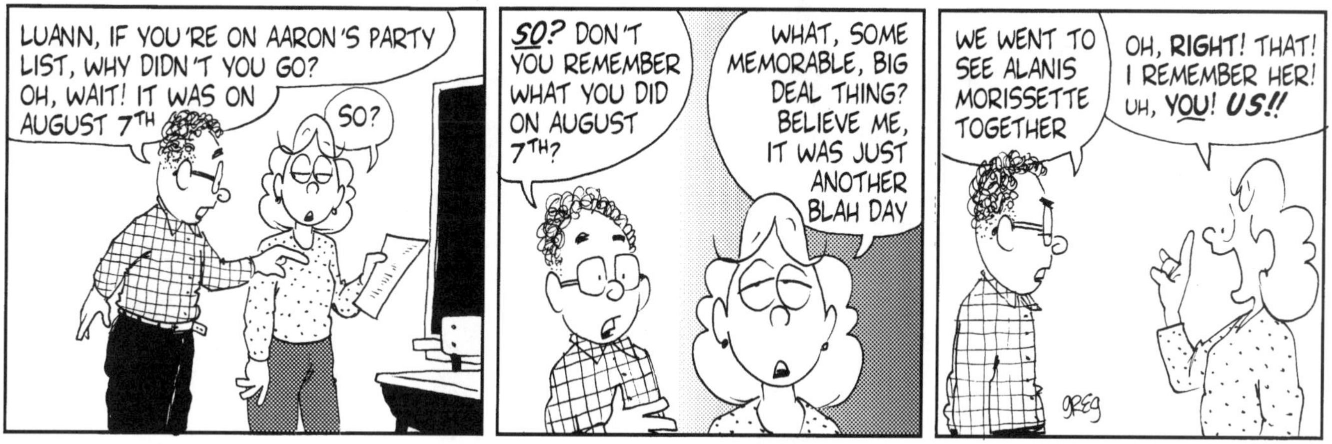
LUANN, IF YOU'RE ON AARON'S PARTY LIST, WHY DIDN'T YOU GO? OH, WAIT! IT WAS ON AUGUST 7TH
SO?
SO? DON'T YOU REMEMBER WHAT YOU DID ON AUGUST 7TH?
WHAT, SOME MEMORABLE, BIG DEAL THING? BELIEVE ME, IT WAS JUST ANOTHER BLAH DAY
WE WENT TO SEE ALANIS MORISSETTE TOGETHER
OH, RIGHT! THAT! I REMEMBER HER! UH, YOU! US!!
GREG

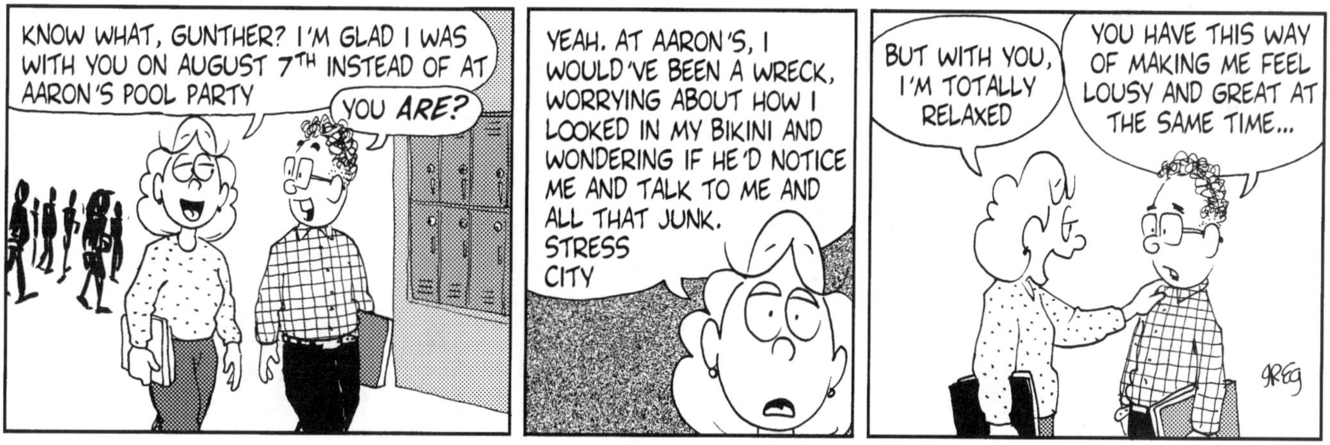
KNOW WHAT, GUNTHER? I'M GLAD I WAS WITH YOU ON AUGUST 7TH INSTEAD OF AT AARON'S POOL PARTY
YOU ARE?
YEAH. AT AARON'S, I WOULD'VE BEEN A WRECK, WORRYING ABOUT HOW I LOOKED IN MY BIKINI AND WONDERING IF HE'D NOTICE ME AND TALK TO ME AND ALL THAT JUNK. STRESS CITY
BUT WITH YOU, I'M TOTALLY RELAXED
YOU HAVE THIS WAY OF MAKING ME FEEL LOUSY AND GREAT AT THE SAME TIME...
GREG

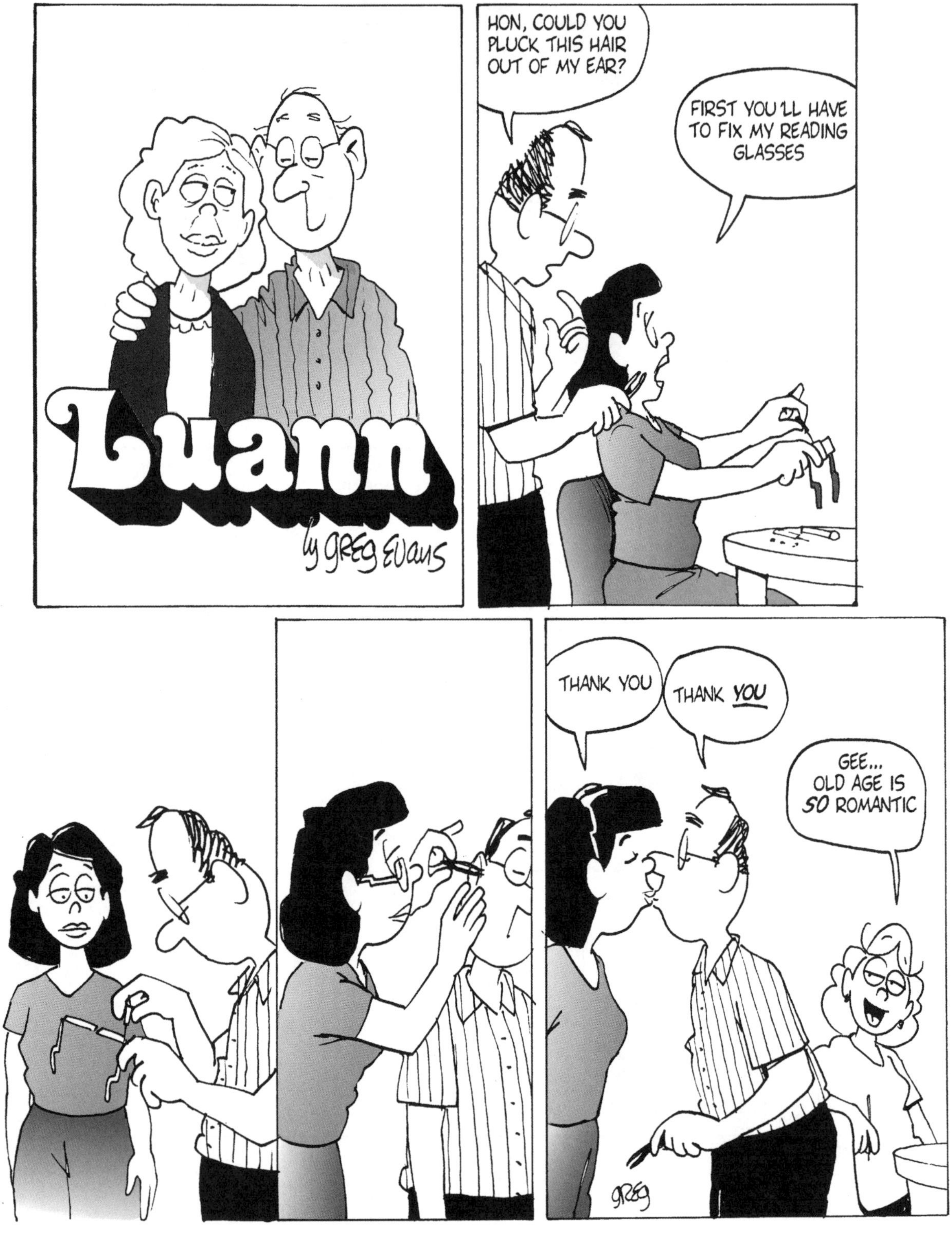
Luann
by GREG EVANS
HON, COULD YOU PLUCK THIS HAIR OUT OF MY EAR?
FIRST YOU'LL HAVE TO FIX MY READING GLASSES
THANK YOU
THANK YOU
GEE... OLD AGE IS SO ROMANTIC
GREG

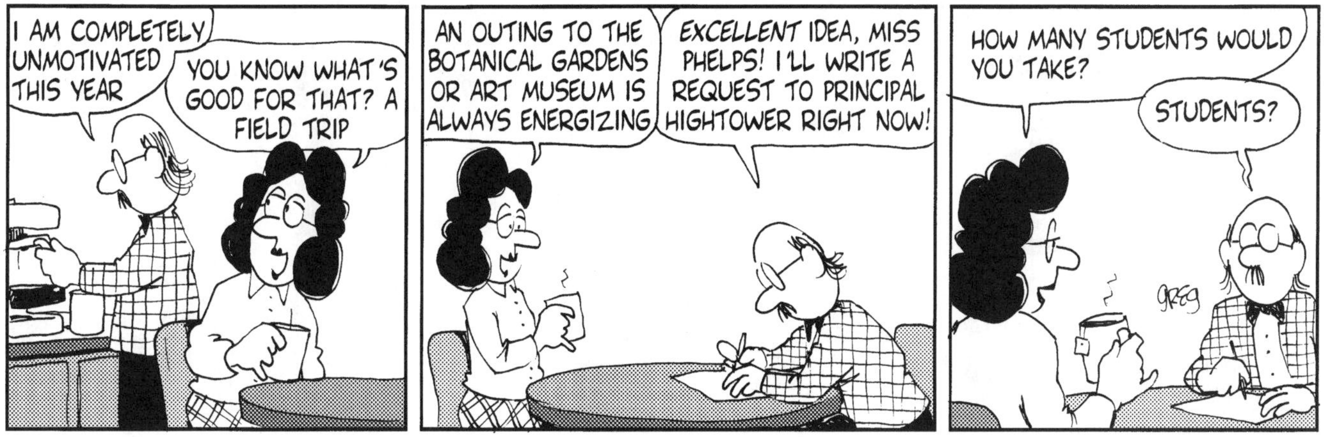
I AM COMPLETELY UNMOTIVATED THIS YEAR
YOU KNOW WHAT'S GOOD FOR THAT? A FIELD TRIP
AN OUTING TO THE BOTANICAL GARDENS OR ART MUSEUM IS ALWAYS ENERGIZING
EXCELLENT IDEA, MISS PHELPS! I'LL WRITE A REQUEST TO PRINCIPAL HIGHTOWER RIGHT NOW!
HOW MANY STUDENTS WOULD YOU TAKE?
STUDENTS?

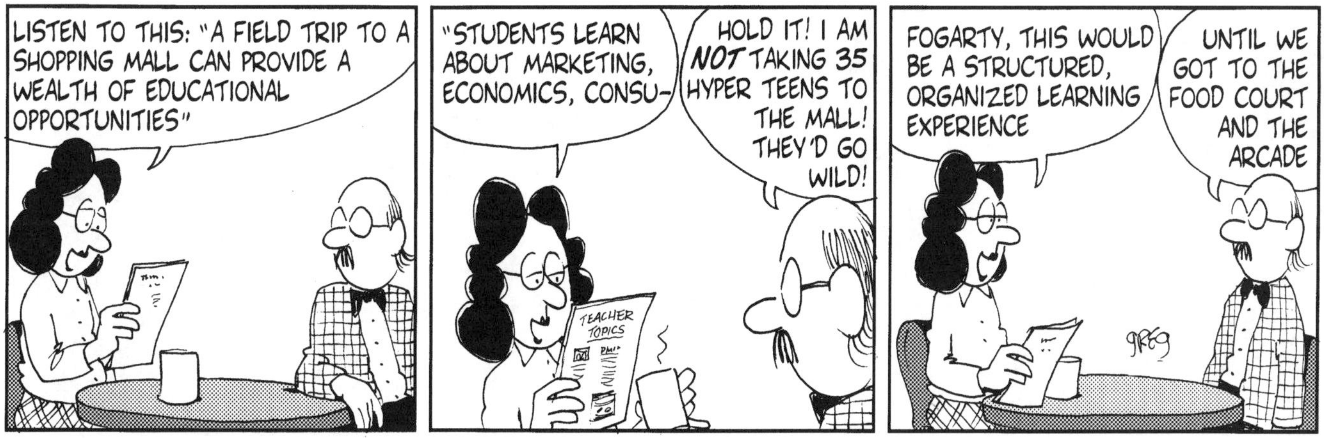
LISTEN TO THIS: "A FIELD TRIP TO A SHOPPING MALL CAN PROVIDE A WEALTH OF EDUCATIONAL OPPORTUNITIES"
"STUDENTS LEARN ABOUT MARKETING, ECONOMICS, CONSU-
HOLD IT! I AM ***NOT*** TAKING 35 HYPER TEENS TO THE MALL! THEY'D GO WILD!
TEACHER TOPICS
FOGARTY, THIS WOULD BE A STRUCTURED, ORGANIZED LEARNING EXPERIENCE
UNTIL WE GOT TO THE FOOD COURT AND THE ARCADE

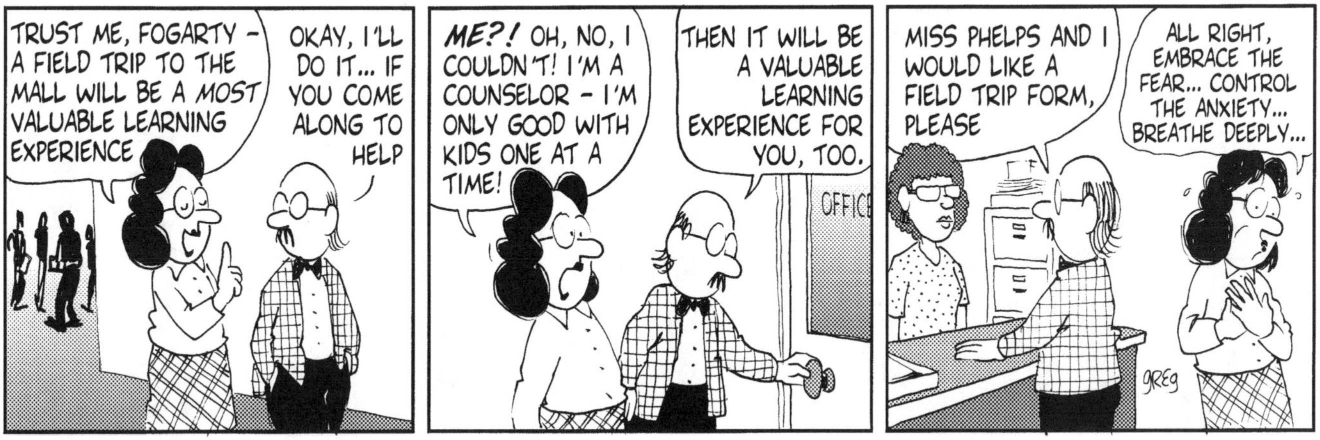
TRUST ME, FOGARTY – A FIELD TRIP TO THE MALL WILL BE A *MOST* VALUABLE LEARNING EXPERIENCE
OKAY, I'LL DO IT... IF YOU COME ALONG TO HELP
ME?! OH, NO, I COULDN'T! I'M A COUNSELOR – I'M ONLY GOOD WITH KIDS ONE AT A TIME!
THEN IT WILL BE A VALUABLE LEARNING EXPERIENCE FOR YOU, TOO.
OFFICE
MISS PHELPS AND I WOULD LIKE A FIELD TRIP FORM, PLEASE
ALL RIGHT, EMBRACE THE FEAR... CONTROL THE ANXIETY... BREATHE DEEPLY...

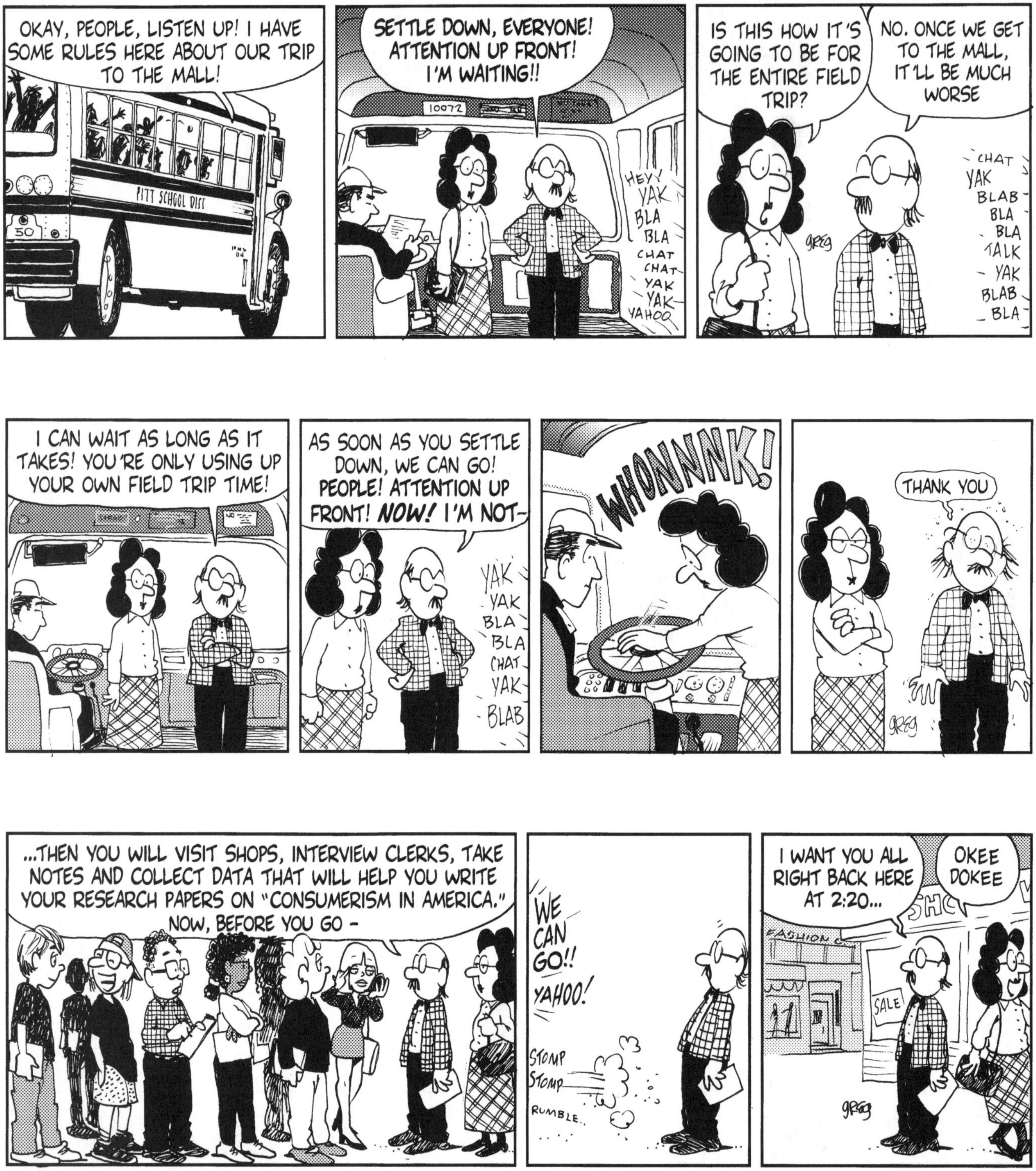
OKAY, PEOPLE, LISTEN UP! I HAVE SOME RULES HERE ABOUT OUR TRIP TO THE MALL!
PITT SCHOOL DIST
SETTLE DOWN, EVERYONE! ATTENTION UP FRONT! I'M WAITING!!
10072
HEY! YAK BLA BLA CHAT CHAT YAK YAK YAHOO
IS THIS HOW IT'S GOING TO BE FOR THE ENTIRE FIELD TRIP?
NO. ONCE WE GET TO THE MALL, IT'LL BE MUCH WORSE
CHAT YAK BLAB BLA BLA TALK YAK BLAB BLA
I CAN WAIT AS LONG AS IT TAKES! YOU'RE ONLY USING UP YOUR OWN FIELD TRIP TIME!
AS SOON AS YOU SETTLE DOWN, WE CAN GO! PEOPLE! ATTENTION UP FRONT! NOW! I'M NOT-
YAK YAK BLA BLA CHAT YAK BLAB
WHONNNK!
THANK YOU
...THEN YOU WILL VISIT SHOPS, INTERVIEW CLERKS, TAKE NOTES AND COLLECT DATA THAT WILL HELP YOU WRITE YOUR RESEARCH PAPERS ON "CONSUMERISM IN AMERICA." NOW, BEFORE YOU GO -
WE CAN GO!! YAHOO!
STOMP STOMP RUMBLE..
I WANT YOU ALL RIGHT BACK HERE AT 2:20...
OKEE DOKEE
FASHION
SALE

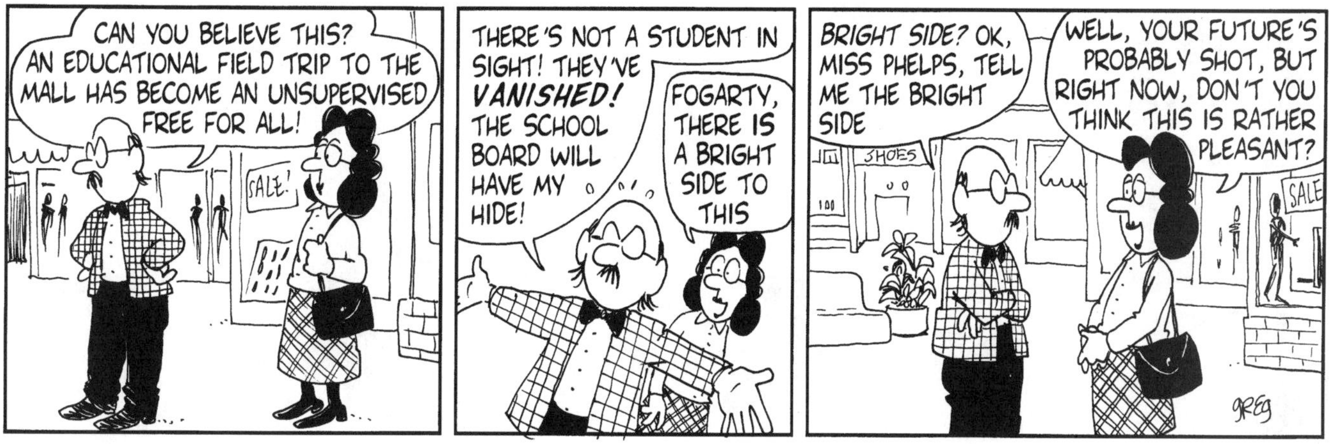
CAN YOU BELIEVE THIS? AN EDUCATIONAL FIELD TRIP TO THE MALL HAS BECOME AN UNSUPERVISED FREE FOR ALL!
THERE'S NOT A STUDENT IN SIGHT! THEY'VE *VANISHED!* THE SCHOOL BOARD WILL HAVE MY HIDE!
FOGARTY, THERE **IS** A BRIGHT SIDE TO THIS
BRIGHT SIDE? OK, MISS PHELPS, TELL ME THE BRIGHT SIDE
WELL, YOUR FUTURE'S PROBABLY SHOT, BUT RIGHT NOW, DON'T YOU THINK THIS IS RATHER PLEASANT?
GREG

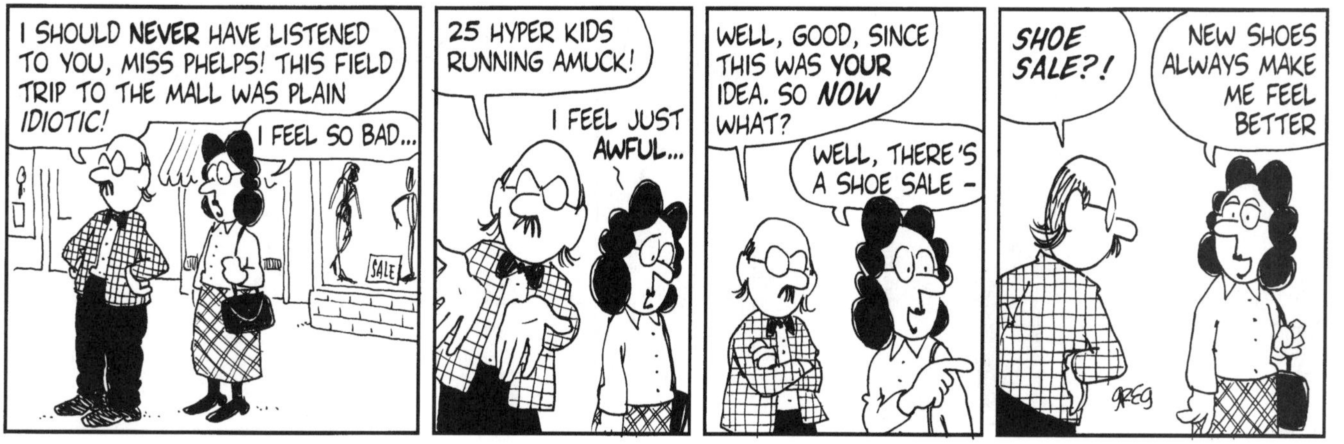
I SHOULD **NEVER** HAVE LISTENED TO YOU, MISS PHELPS! THIS FIELD TRIP TO THE MALL WAS PLAIN *IDIOTIC!*
I FEEL SO BAD...
25 HYPER KIDS RUNNING AMUCK!
I FEEL JUST **AWFUL...**
WELL, GOOD, SINCE THIS WAS **YOUR** IDEA. SO ***NOW*** WHAT?
WELL, THERE'S A SHOE SALE -
SHOE SALE?!
NEW SHOES ALWAYS MAKE ME FEEL BETTER
GREG

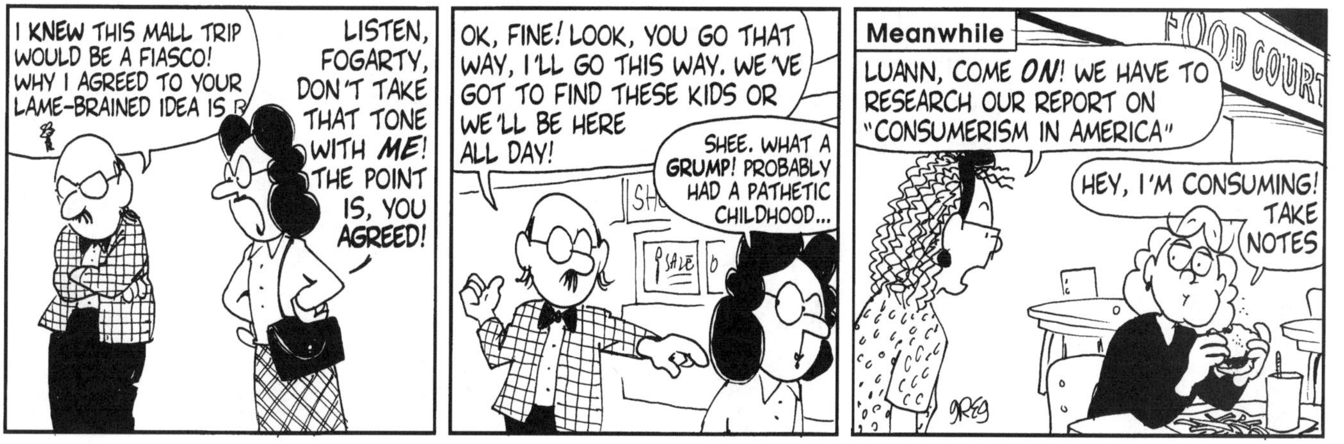
I **KNEW** THIS MALL TRIP WOULD BE A FIASCO! WHY I AGREED TO YOUR LAME-BRAINED IDEA IS
LISTEN, FOGARTY, DON'T TAKE THAT TONE WITH ***ME***! THE POINT IS, YOU **AGREED**!
OK, FINE! LOOK, YOU GO THAT WAY, I'LL GO THIS WAY. WE'VE GOT TO FIND THESE KIDS OR WE'LL BE HERE ALL DAY!
SHEE. WHAT A **GRUMP**! PROBABLY HAD A PATHETIC CHILDHOOD...
Meanwhile
LUANN, COME ***ON***! WE HAVE TO RESEARCH OUR REPORT ON "CONSUMERISM IN AMERICA"
HEY, I'M CONSUMING! TAKE NOTES
GREG

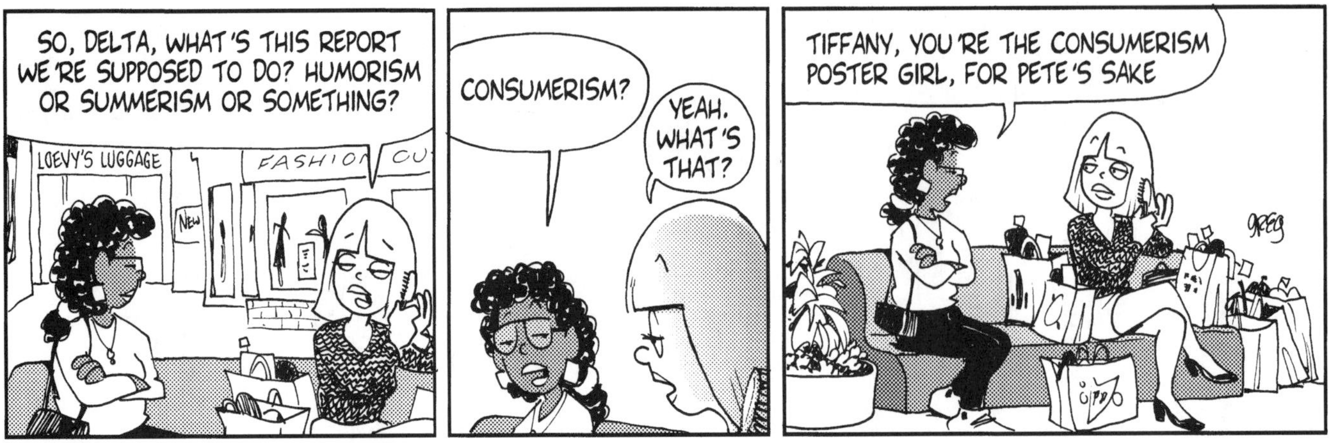
SO, DELTA, WHAT'S THIS REPORT WE'RE SUPPOSED TO DO? HUMORISM OR SUMMERISM OR SOMETHING?
LOEVY'S LUGGAGE
NEW
CONSUMERISM?
YEAH. WHAT'S THAT?
TIFFANY, YOU'RE THE CONSUMERISM POSTER GIRL, FOR PETE'S SAKE

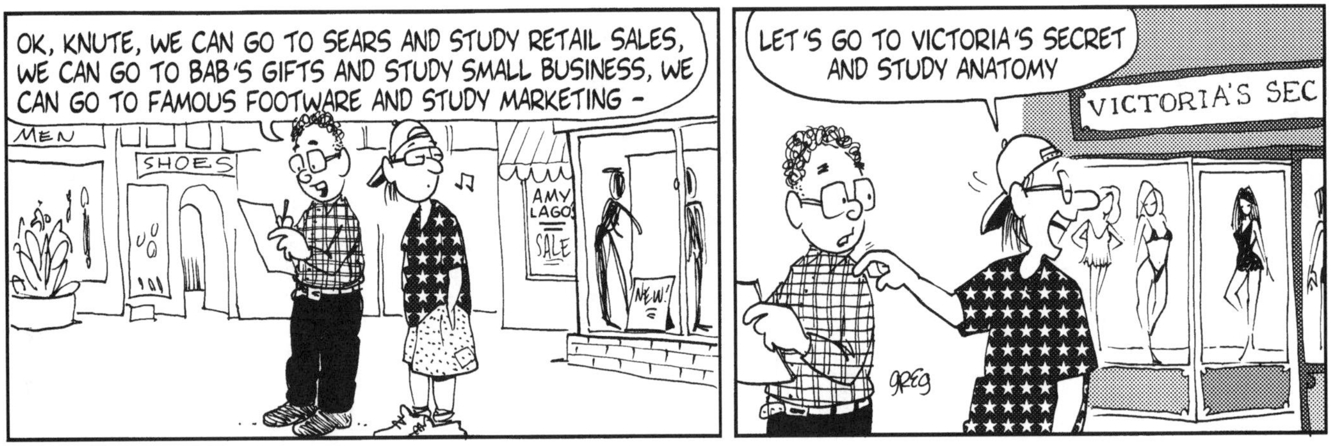
OK, KNUTE, WE CAN GO TO SEARS AND STUDY RETAIL SALES, WE CAN GO TO BAB'S GIFTS AND STUDY SMALL BUSINESS, WE CAN GO TO FAMOUS FOOTWARE AND STUDY MARKETING –
MEN
SHOES
AMY LAGO'S
SALE
NEW!
LET'S GO TO VICTORIA'S SECRET AND STUDY ANATOMY
VICTORIA'S SEC

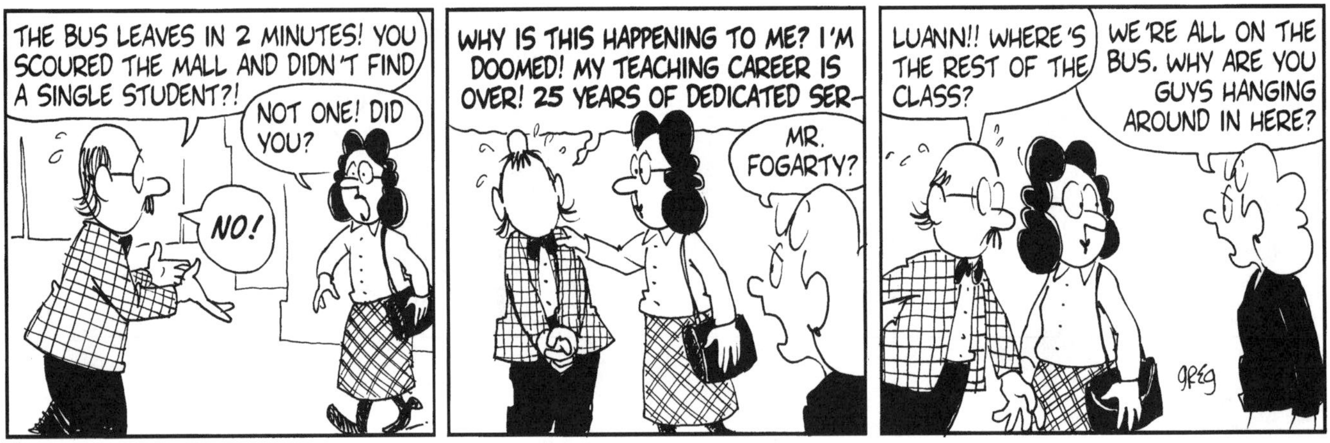
THE BUS LEAVES IN 2 MINUTES! YOU SCOURED THE MALL AND DIDN'T FIND A SINGLE STUDENT?!
NOT ONE! DID YOU?
NO!
WHY IS THIS HAPPENING TO ME? I'M DOOMED! MY TEACHING CAREER IS OVER! 25 YEARS OF DEDICATED SER-
MR. FOGARTY?
LUANN!! WHERE'S THE REST OF THE CLASS?
WE'RE ALL ON THE BUS. WHY ARE YOU GUYS HANGING AROUND IN HERE?

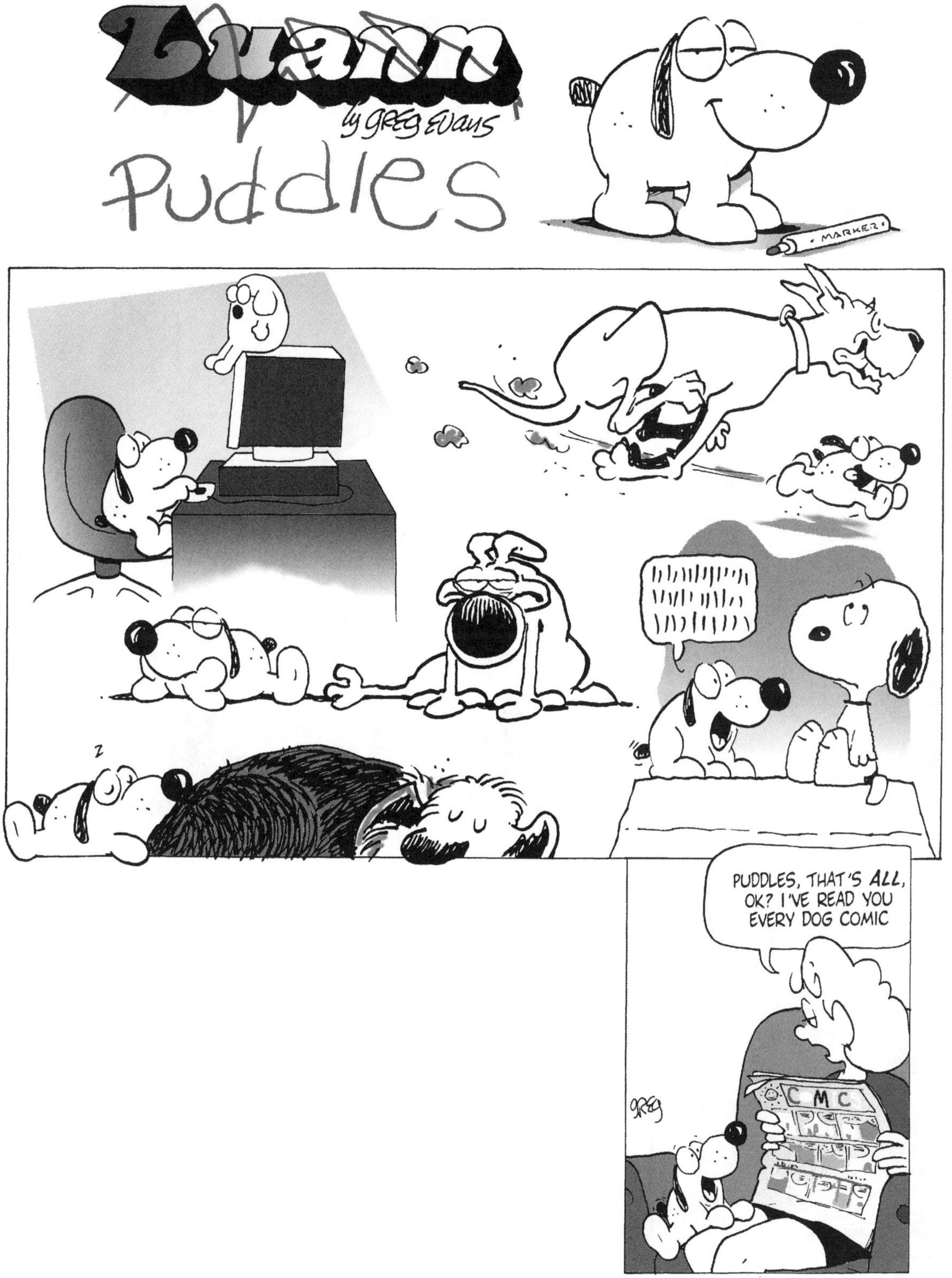
Luann
by GREG EVANS
Puddles
MARKER
PUDDLES, THAT'S ALL, OK? I'VE READ YOU EVERY DOG COMIC
GREG

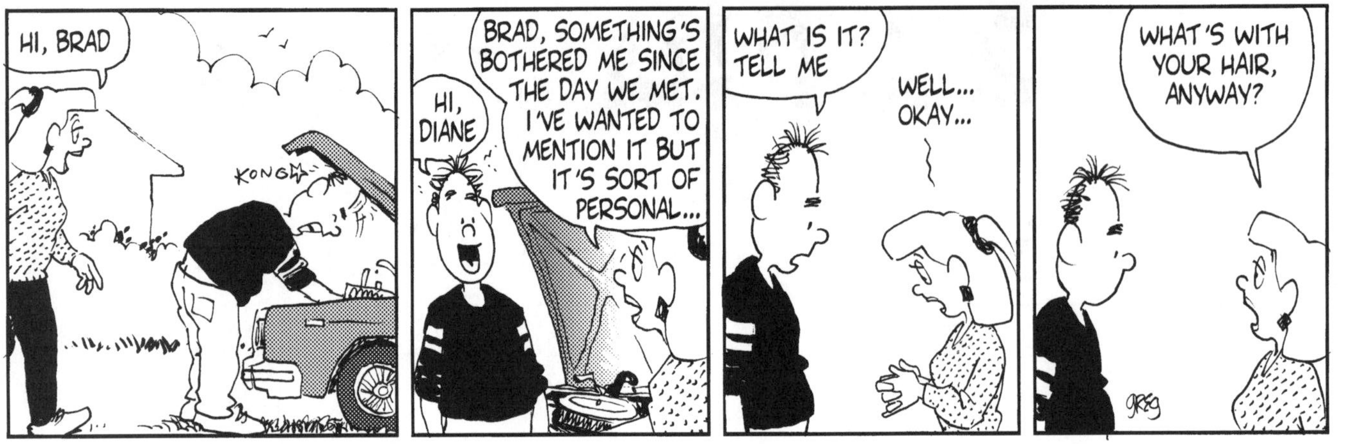
HI, BRAD
KONG
HI, DIANE
BRAD, SOMETHING'S BOTHERED ME SINCE THE DAY WE MET. I'VE WANTED TO MENTION IT BUT IT'S SORT OF PERSONAL...
WHAT IS IT? TELL ME
WELL... OKAY...
WHAT'S WITH YOUR HAIR, ANYWAY?
GREG

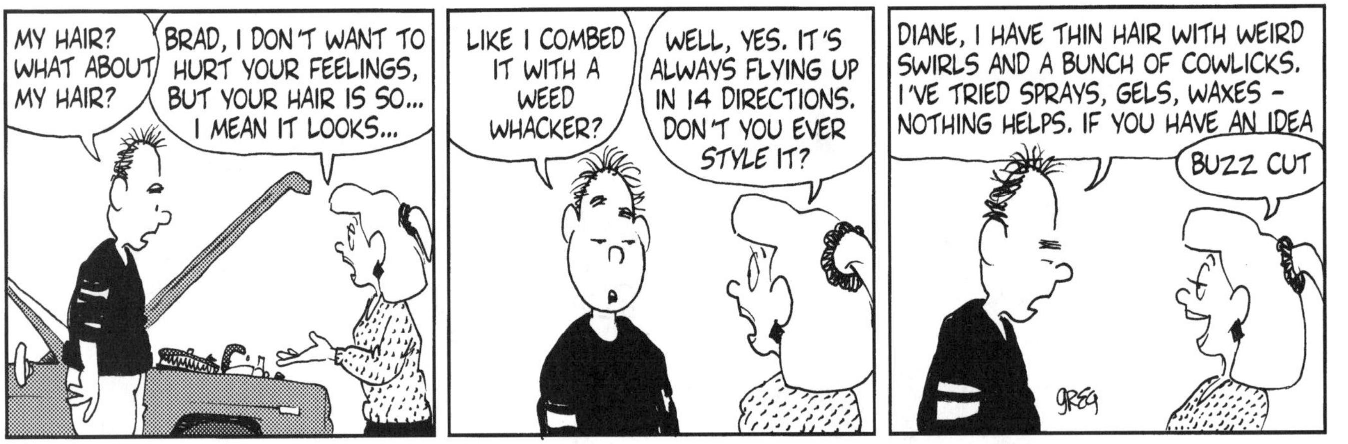
MY HAIR? WHAT ABOUT MY HAIR?
BRAD, I DON'T WANT TO HURT YOUR FEELINGS, BUT YOUR HAIR IS SO... I MEAN IT LOOKS...
LIKE I COMBED IT WITH A WEED WHACKER?
WELL, YES. IT'S ALWAYS FLYING UP IN 14 DIRECTIONS. DON'T YOU EVER STYLE IT?
DIANE, I HAVE THIN HAIR WITH WEIRD SWIRLS AND A BUNCH OF COWLICKS. I'VE TRIED SPRAYS, GELS, WAXES – NOTHING HELPS. IF YOU HAVE AN IDEA
BUZZ CUT
GREG

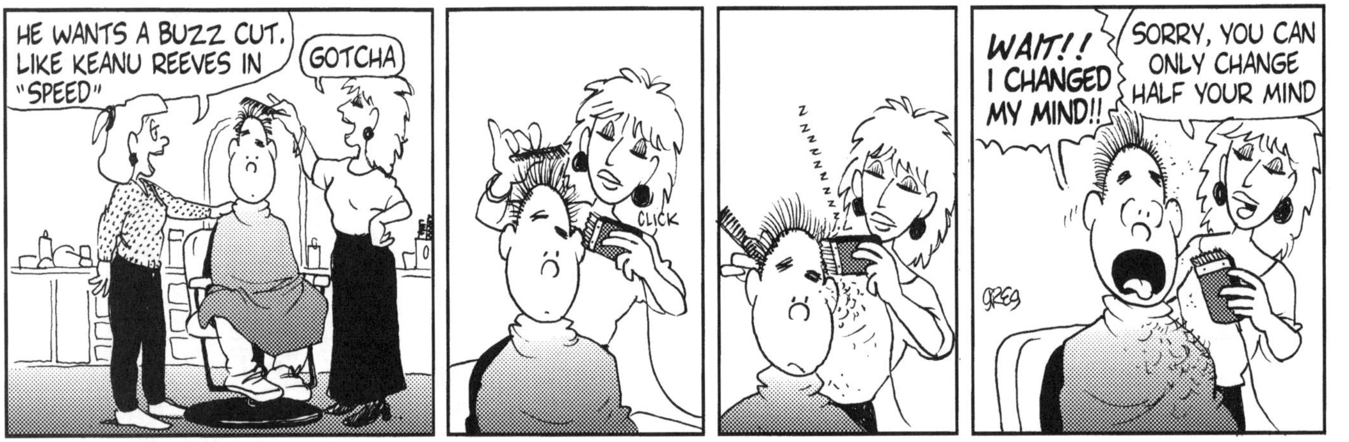
HE WANTS A BUZZ CUT. LIKE KEANU REEVES IN "SPEED"
GOTCHA
CLICK
WAIT!! I CHANGED MY MIND!!
SORRY, YOU CAN ONLY CHANGE HALF YOUR MIND
GREG

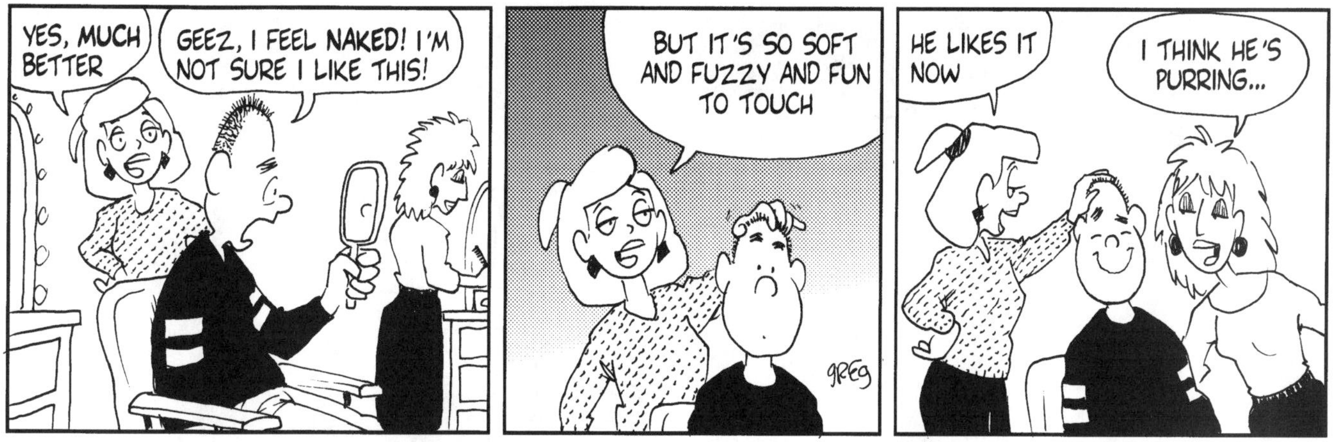
YES, MUCH BETTER
GEEZ, I FEEL NAKED! I'M NOT SURE I LIKE THIS!
BUT IT'S SO SOFT AND FUZZY AND FUN TO TOUCH
GREG
HE LIKES IT NOW
I THINK HE'S PURRING...

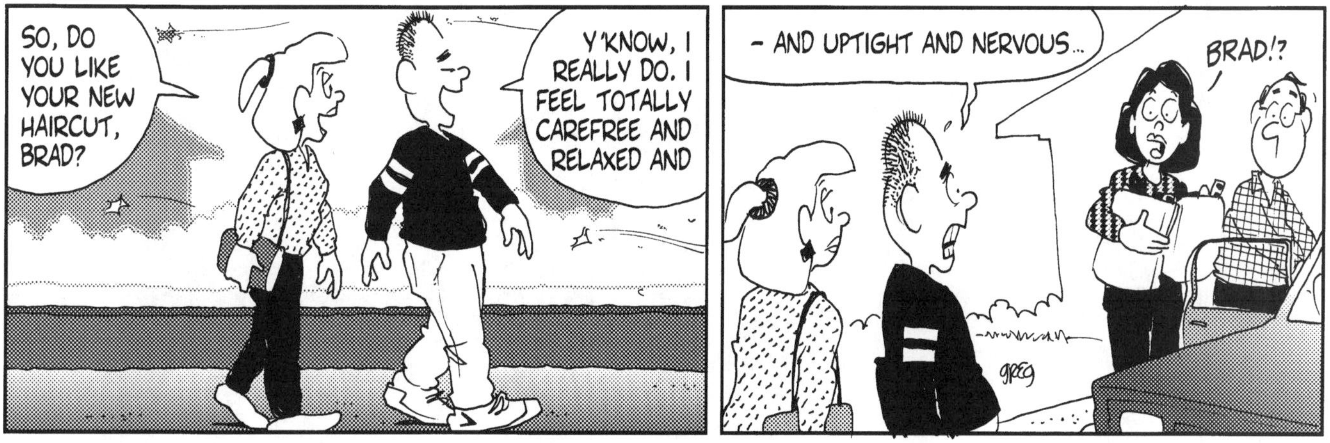
SO, DO YOU LIKE YOUR NEW HAIRCUT, BRAD?
Y'KNOW, I REALLY DO. I FEEL TOTALLY CAREFREE AND RELAXED AND
- AND UPTIGHT AND NERVOUS...
BRAD!?
GREG

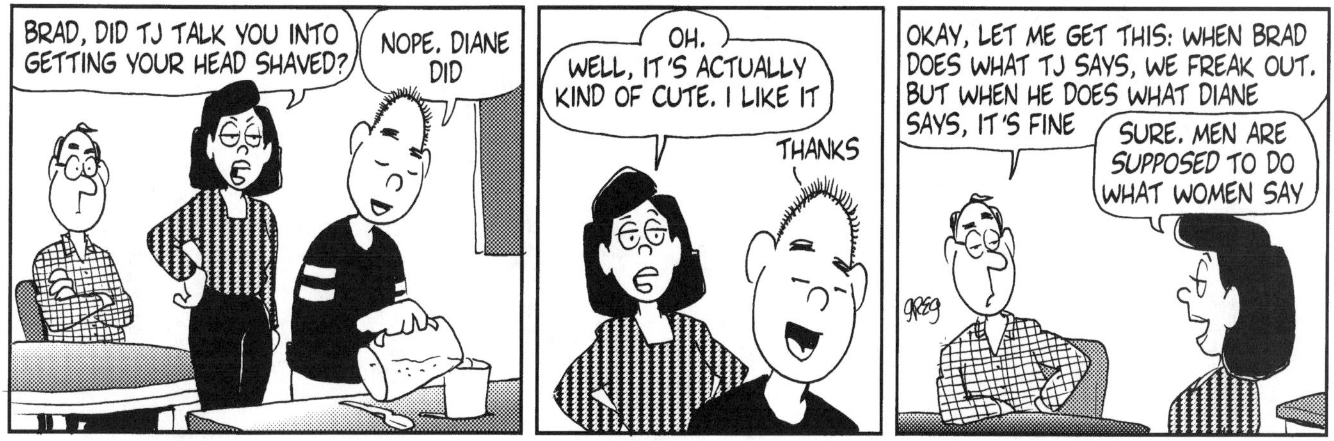
BRAD, DID TJ TALK YOU INTO GETTING YOUR HEAD SHAVED?
NOPE. DIANE DID
OH. WELL, IT'S ACTUALLY KIND OF CUTE. I LIKE IT
THANKS
OKAY, LET ME GET THIS: WHEN BRAD DOES WHAT TJ SAYS, WE FREAK OUT. BUT WHEN HE DOES WHAT DIANE SAYS, IT'S FINE
SURE. MEN ARE SUPPOSED TO DO WHAT WOMEN SAY
GREG

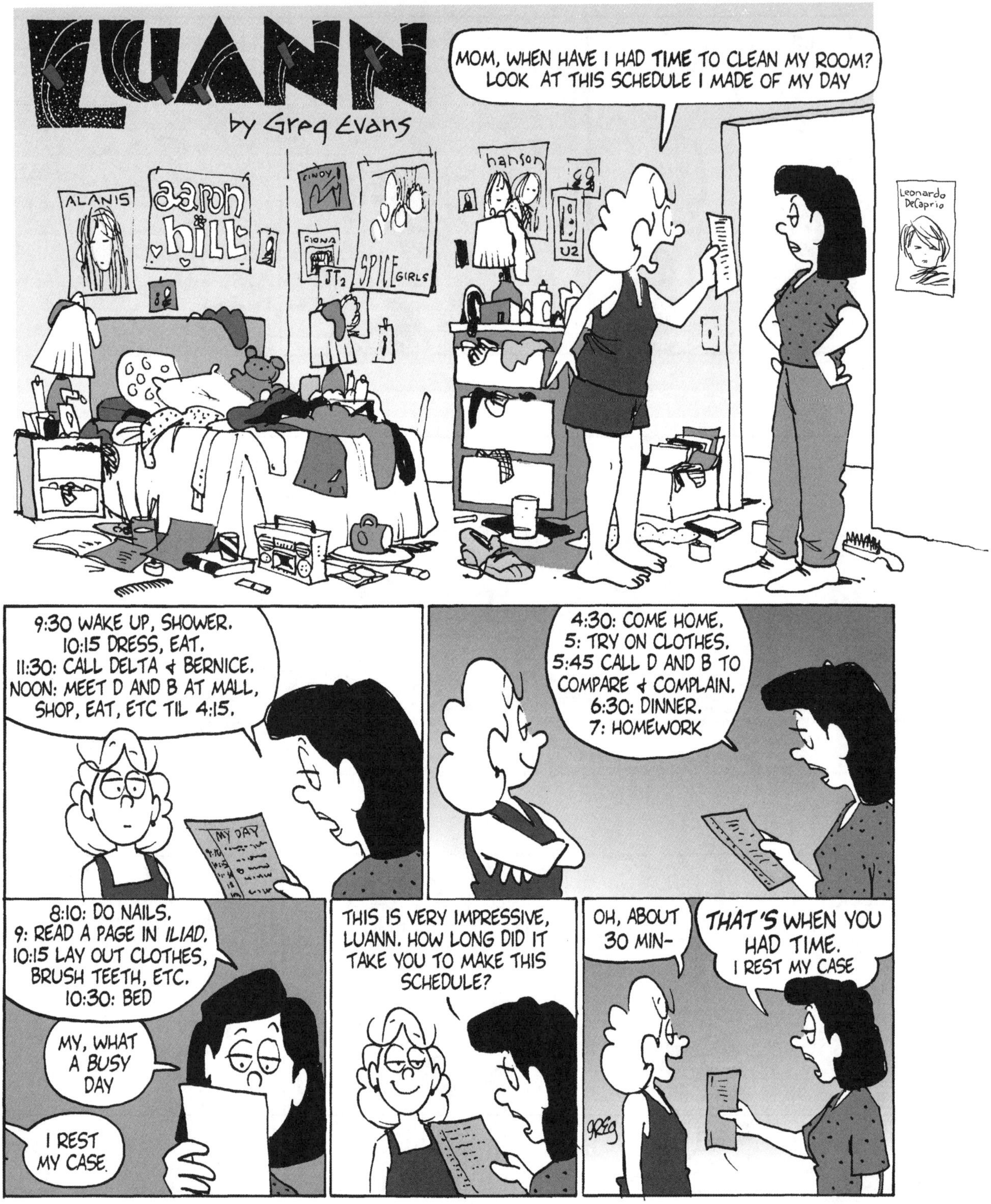
LUANN
by Greg Evans
MOM, WHEN HAVE I HAD TIME TO CLEAN MY ROOM? LOOK AT THIS SCHEDULE I MADE OF MY DAY
ALANIS
aaron hill
FIONA
SPICE GIRLS
hanson
U2
Leonardo DeCaprio
9:30 WAKE UP, SHOWER. 10:15 DRESS, EAT. 11:30: CALL DELTA & BERNICE. NOON: MEET D AND B AT MALL, SHOP, EAT, ETC TIL 4:15.
MY DAY
4:30: COME HOME. 5: TRY ON CLOTHES. 5:45 CALL D AND B TO COMPARE & COMPLAIN. 6:30: DINNER. 7: HOMEWORK
8:10: DO NAILS. 9: READ A PAGE IN ILIAD. 10:15 LAY OUT CLOTHES, BRUSH TEETH, ETC. 10:30: BED
MY, WHAT A BUSY DAY
I REST MY CASE
THIS IS VERY IMPRESSIVE, LUANN. HOW LONG DID IT TAKE YOU TO MAKE THIS SCHEDULE?
OH, ABOUT 30 MIN-
THAT'S WHEN YOU HAD TIME. I REST MY CASE
GREG

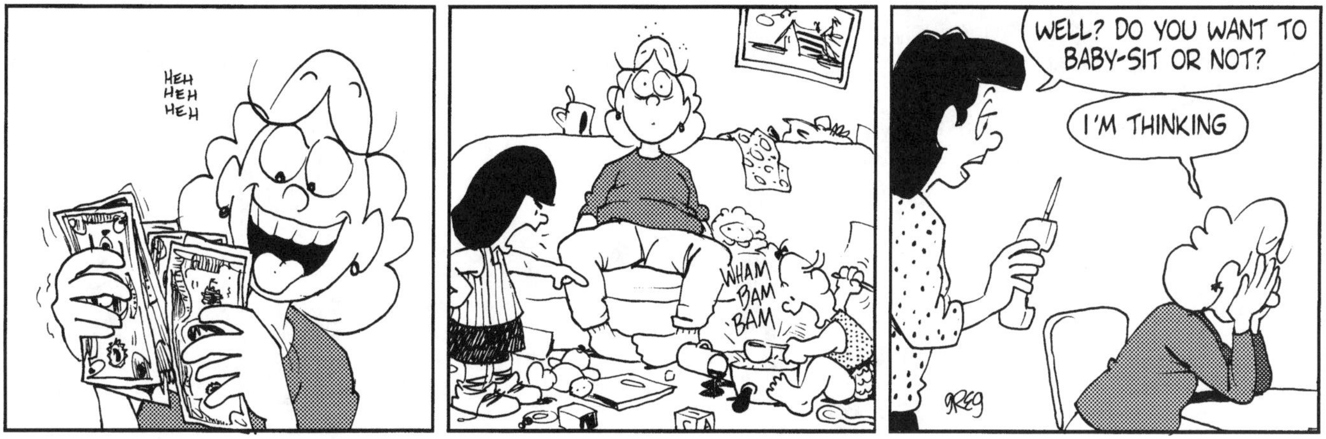
HEH
HEH
HEH
WHAM
BAM
BAM
WELL? DO YOU WANT TO BABY-SIT OR NOT?
I'M THINKING
GREG

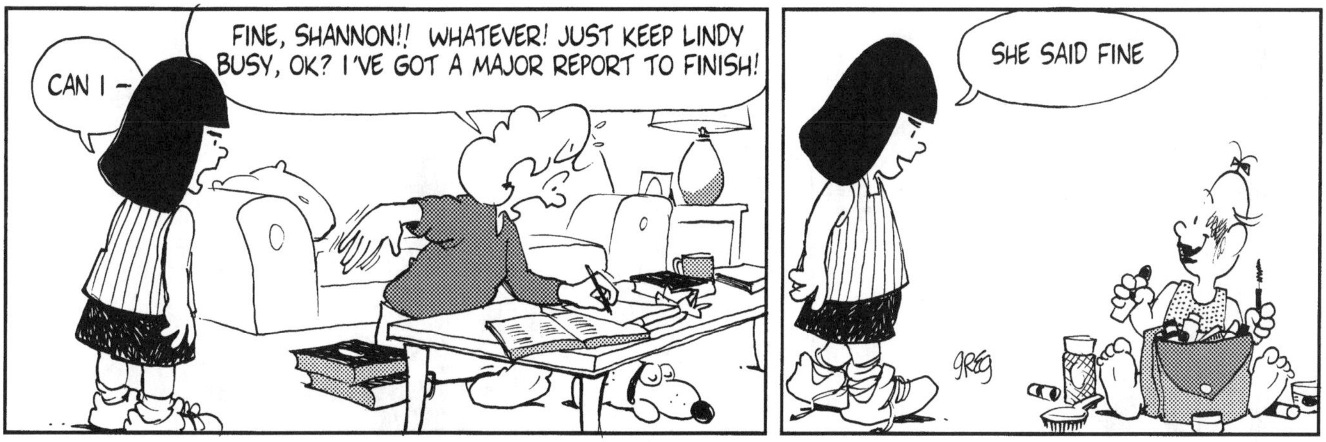
CAN I –
FINE, SHANNON!! WHATEVER! JUST KEEP LINDY BUSY, OK? I'VE GOT A MAJOR REPORT TO FINISH!
SHE SAID FINE
GREG

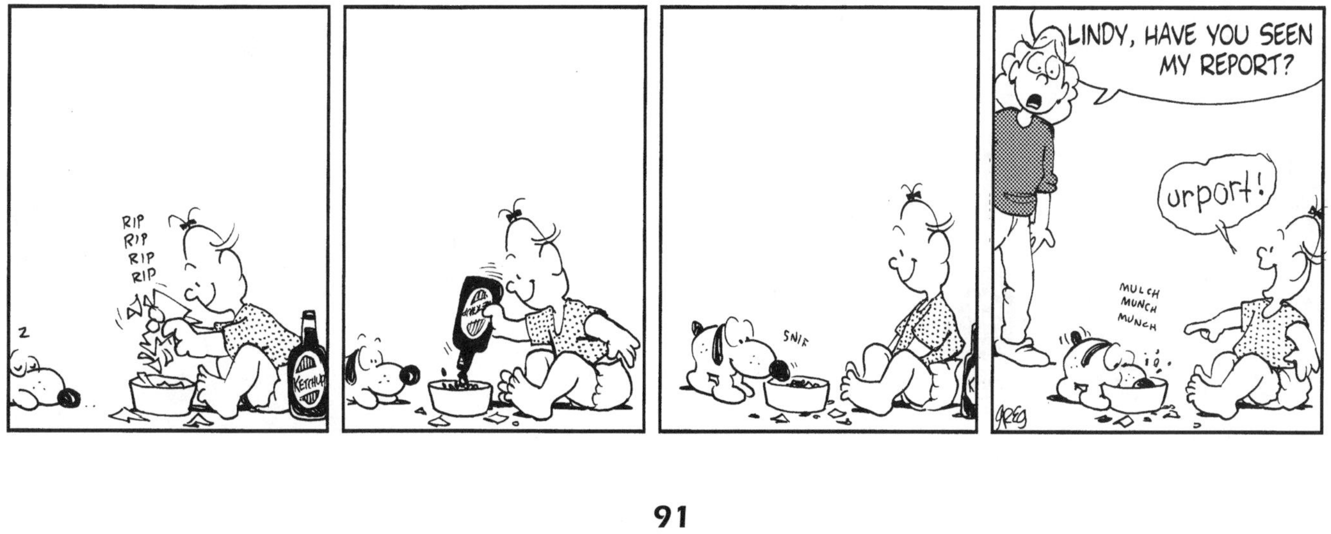
RIP
RIP
RIP
RIP
SNIF
LINDY, HAVE YOU SEEN MY REPORT?
urport!
MULCH
MUNCH
MUNCH
GREG

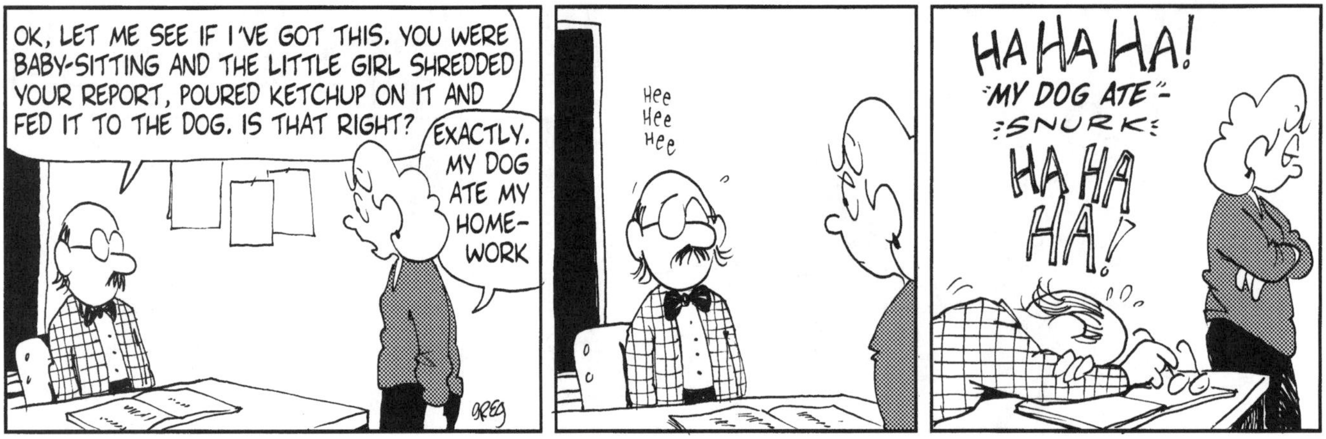
OK, LET ME SEE IF I'VE GOT THIS. YOU WERE BABY-SITTING AND THE LITTLE GIRL SHREDDED YOUR REPORT, POURED KETCHUP ON IT AND FED IT TO THE DOG. IS THAT RIGHT?
EXACTLY. MY DOG ATE MY HOMEWORK
GREG
Hee Hee Hee
HA HA HA!
MY DOG ATE
SNURK
HA HA HA!

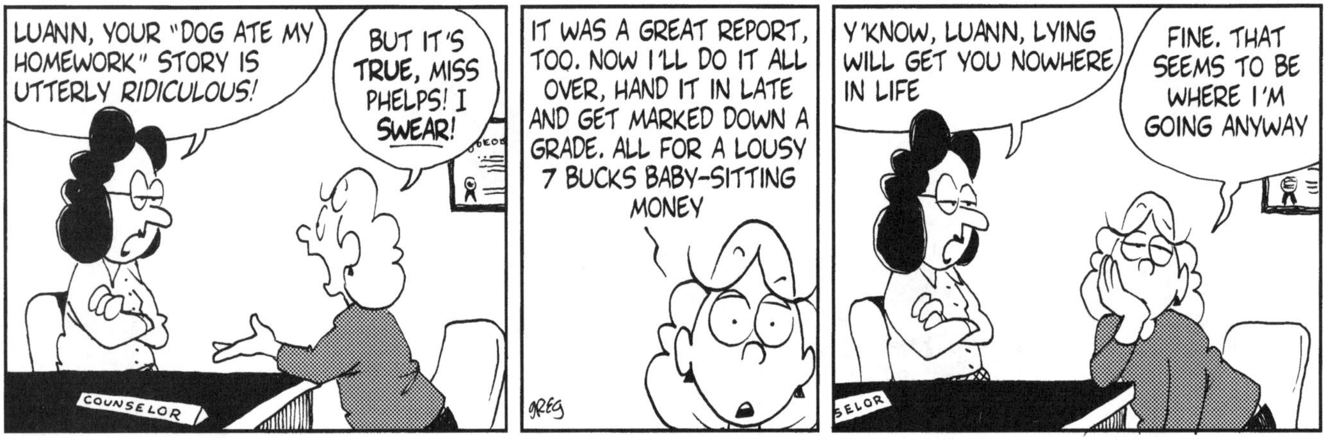
LUANN, YOUR "DOG ATE MY HOMEWORK" STORY IS UTTERLY *RIDICULOUS!*
BUT IT'S **TRUE,** MISS PHELPS! I **SWEAR!**
COUNSELOR
IT WAS A GREAT REPORT, TOO. NOW I'LL DO IT ALL OVER, HAND IT IN LATE AND GET MARKED DOWN A GRADE. ALL FOR A LOUSY 7 BUCKS BABY-SITTING MONEY
GREG
Y'KNOW, LUANN, LYING WILL GET YOU NOWHERE IN LIFE
FINE. THAT SEEMS TO BE WHERE I'M GOING ANYWAY
SELOR

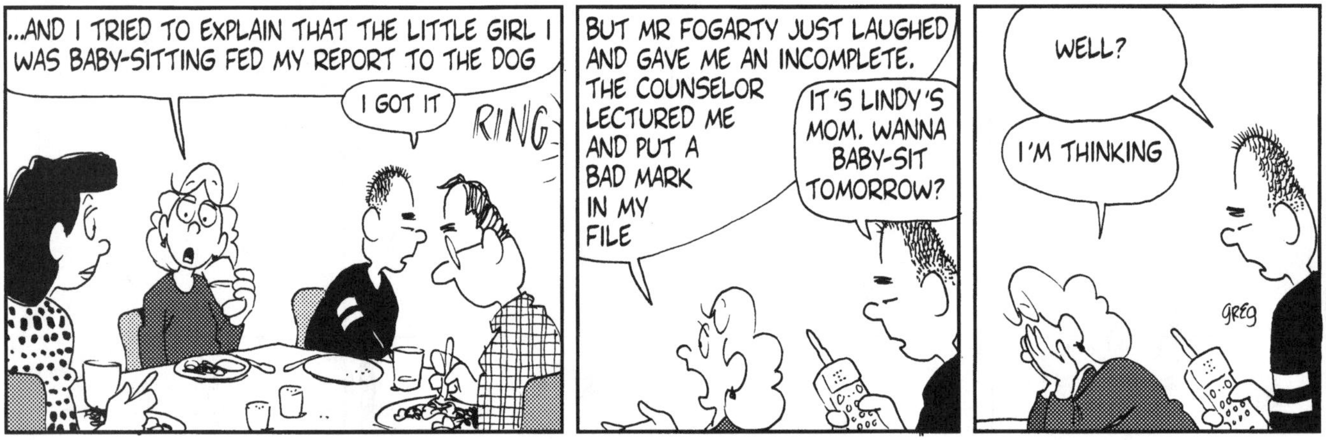
...AND I TRIED TO EXPLAIN THAT THE LITTLE GIRL I WAS BABY-SITTING FED MY REPORT TO THE DOG
I GOT IT
RING
BUT MR FOGARTY JUST LAUGHED AND GAVE ME AN INCOMPLETE.
THE COUNSELOR LECTURED ME AND PUT A BAD MARK IN MY FILE
IT'S LINDY'S MOM. WANNA BABY-SIT TOMORROW?
WELL?
I'M THINKING
GREG

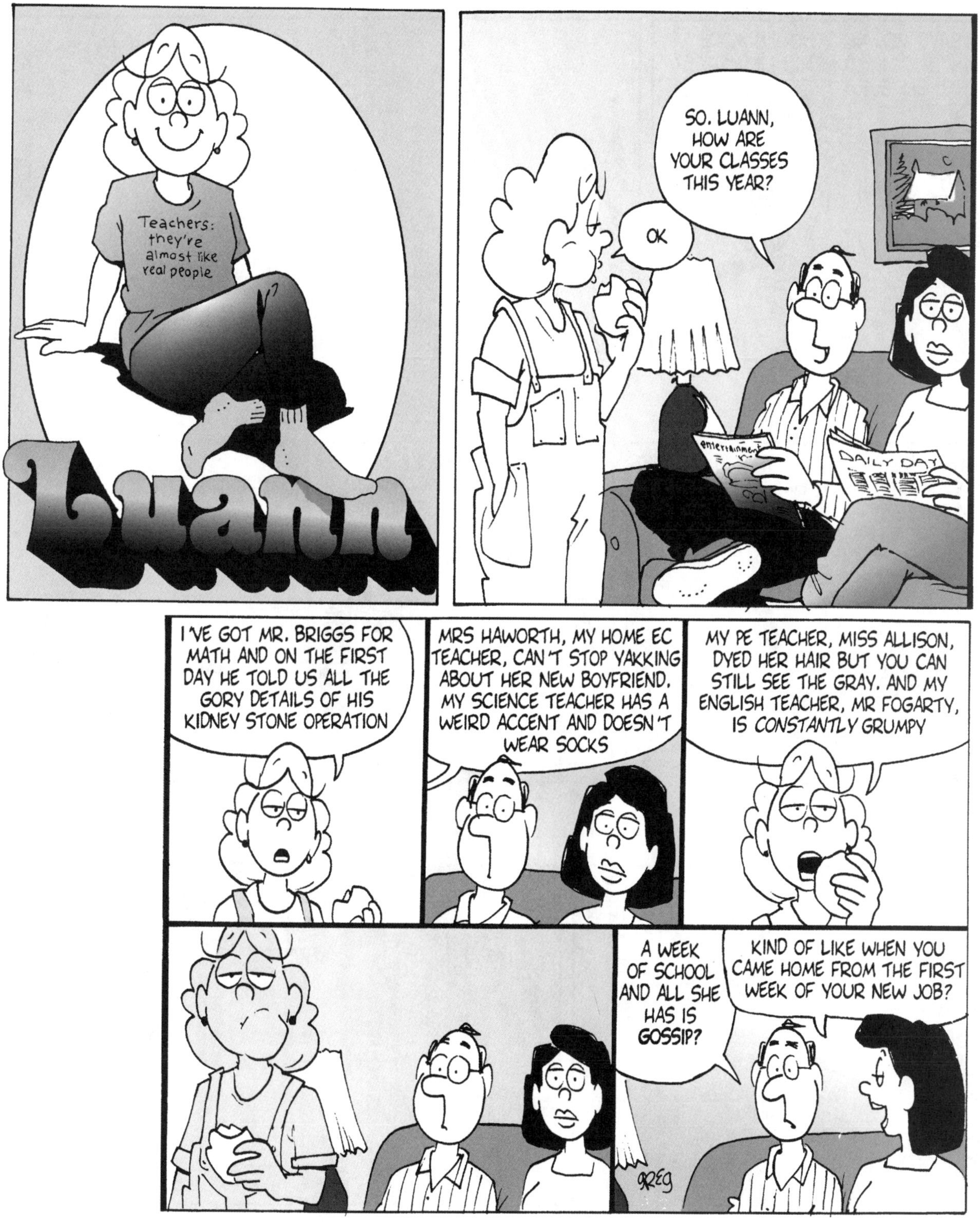
Luann
Teachers: they're almost like real people
SO. LUANN, HOW ARE YOUR CLASSES THIS YEAR?
OK
entertainment
DAILY DAY
I'VE GOT MR. BRIGGS FOR MATH AND ON THE FIRST DAY HE TOLD US ALL THE GORY DETAILS OF HIS KIDNEY STONE OPERATION
MRS HAWORTH, MY HOME EC TEACHER, CAN'T STOP YAKKING ABOUT HER NEW BOYFRIEND. MY SCIENCE TEACHER HAS A WEIRD ACCENT AND DOESN'T WEAR SOCKS
MY PE TEACHER, MISS ALLISON, DYED HER HAIR BUT YOU CAN STILL SEE THE GRAY. AND MY ENGLISH TEACHER, MR FOGARTY, IS *CONSTANTLY* GRUMPY
A WEEK OF SCHOOL AND ALL SHE HAS IS **GOSSIP**?
KIND OF LIKE WHEN YOU CAME HOME FROM THE FIRST WEEK OF YOUR NEW JOB?
GREG

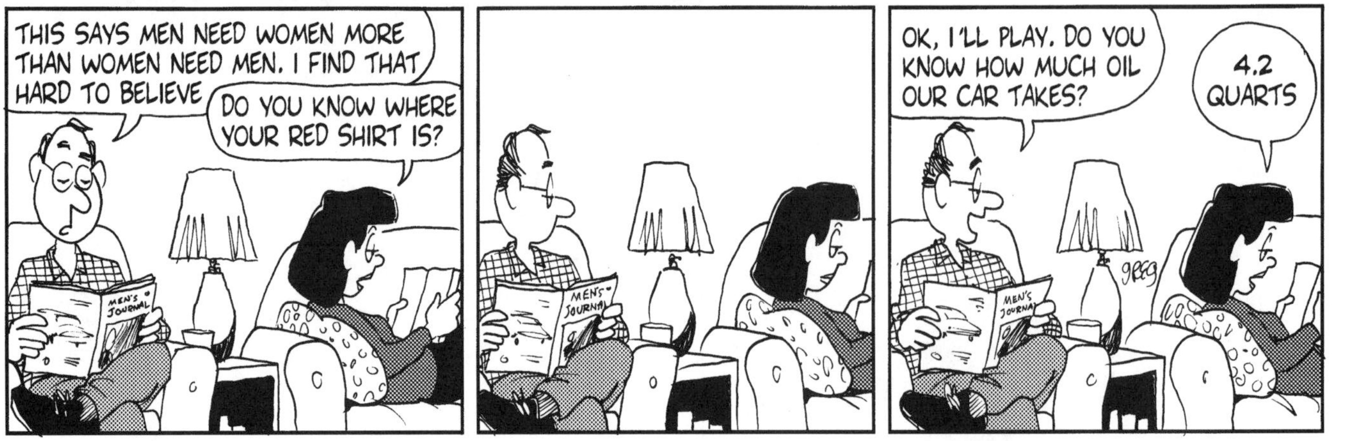
THIS SAYS MEN NEED WOMEN MORE THAN WOMEN NEED MEN. I FIND THAT HARD TO BELIEVE
DO YOU KNOW WHERE YOUR RED SHIRT IS?
OK, I'LL PLAY. DO YOU KNOW HOW MUCH OIL OUR CAR TAKES?
4.2 QUARTS

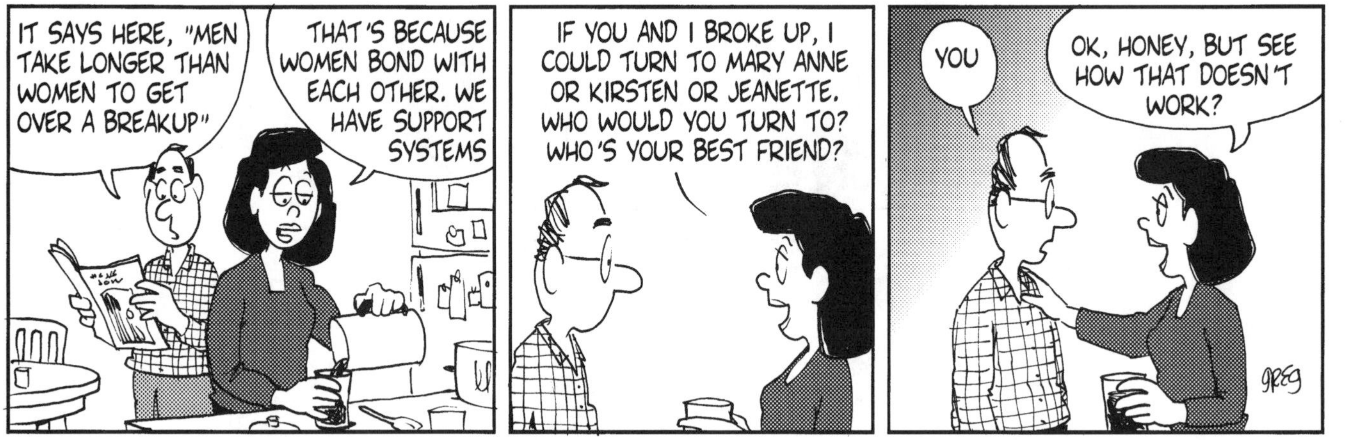
IT SAYS HERE, "MEN TAKE LONGER THAN WOMEN TO GET OVER A BREAKUP"
THAT'S BECAUSE WOMEN BOND WITH EACH OTHER. WE HAVE SUPPORT SYSTEMS
IF YOU AND I BROKE UP, I COULD TURN TO MARY ANNE OR KIRSTEN OR JEANETTE. WHO WOULD YOU TURN TO? WHO'S YOUR BEST FRIEND?
YOU
OK, HONEY, BUT SEE HOW THAT DOESN'T WORK?

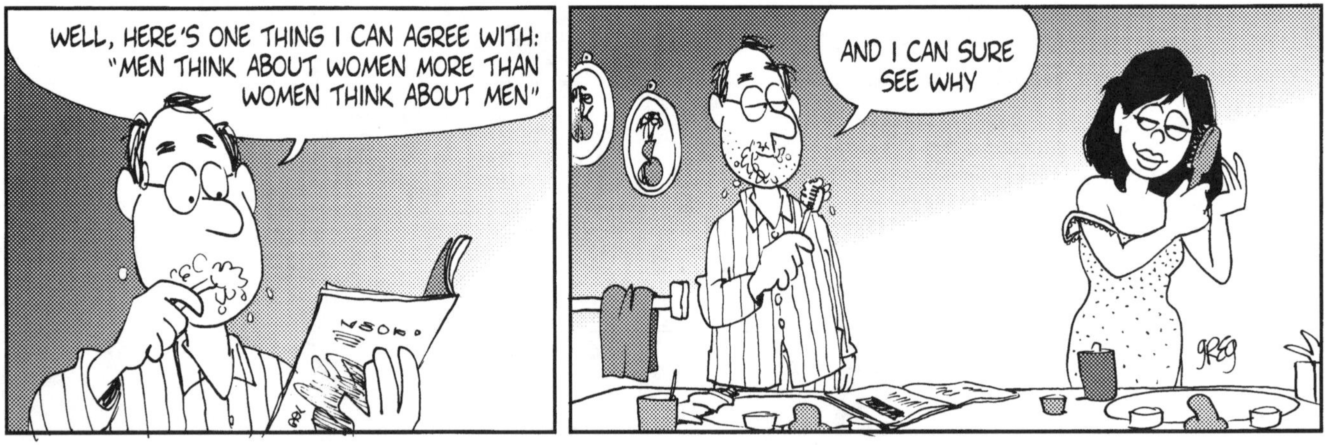
WELL, HERE'S ONE THING I CAN AGREE WITH: "MEN THINK ABOUT WOMEN MORE THAN WOMEN THINK ABOUT MEN"
AND I CAN SURE SEE WHY

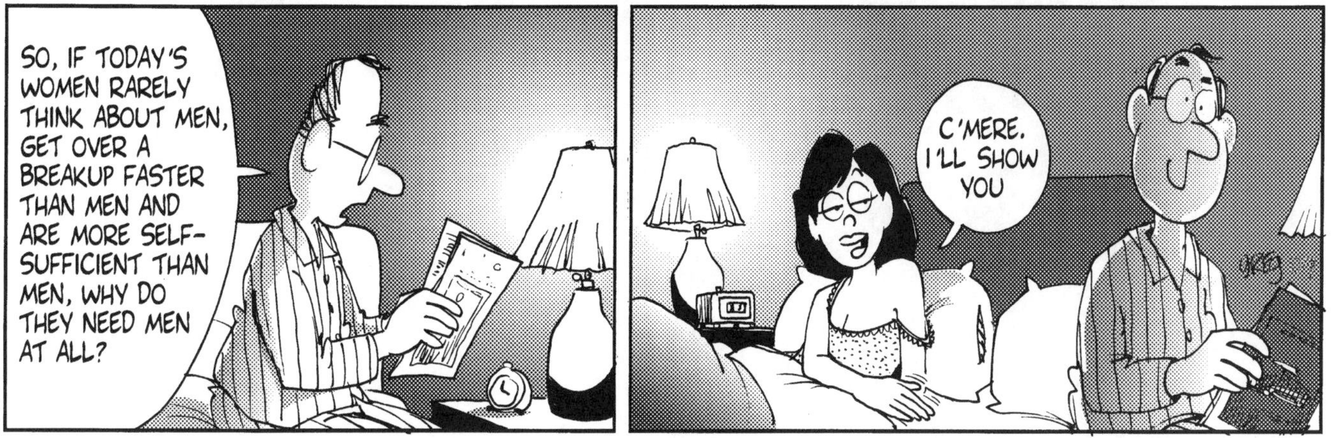
SO, IF TODAY'S WOMEN RARELY THINK ABOUT MEN, GET OVER A BREAKUP FASTER THAN MEN AND ARE MORE SELF-SUFFICIENT THAN MEN, WHY DO THEY NEED MEN AT ALL?
C'MERE. I'LL SHOW YOU

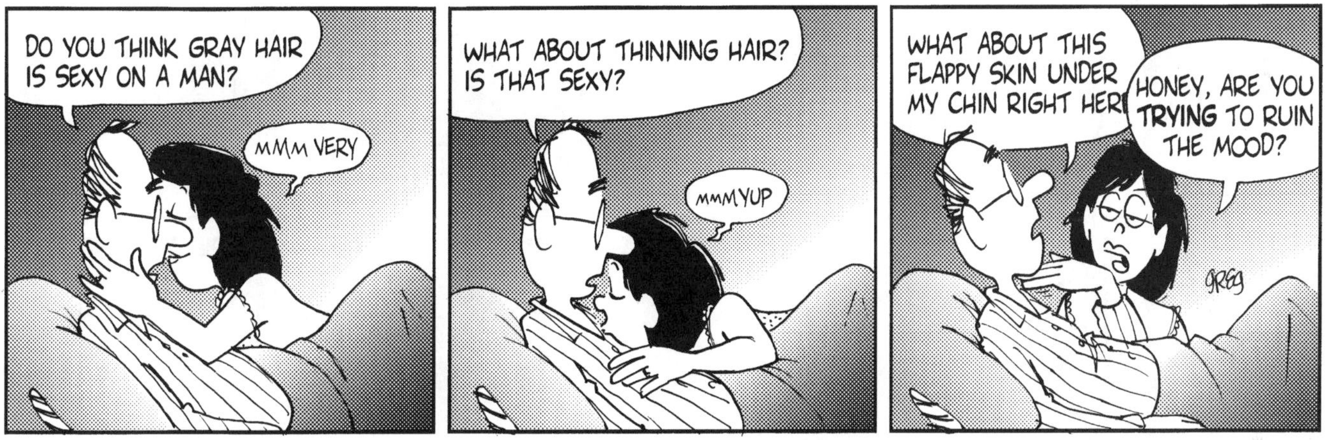
DO YOU THINK GRAY HAIR IS SEXY ON A MAN?
MMM VERY
WHAT ABOUT THINNING HAIR? IS THAT SEXY?
MMM YUP
WHAT ABOUT THIS FLAPPY SKIN UNDER MY CHIN RIGHT HER
HONEY, ARE YOU **TRYING** TO RUIN THE MOOD?

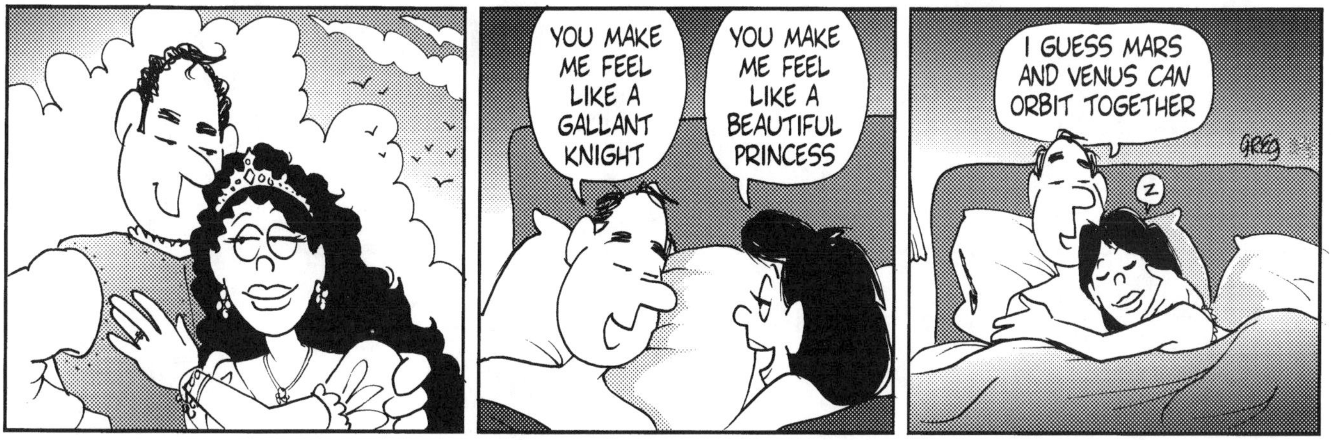
YOU MAKE ME FEEL LIKE A GALLANT KNIGHT
YOU MAKE ME FEEL LIKE A BEAUTIFUL PRINCESS
I GUESS MARS AND VENUS CAN ORBIT TOGETHER
Z

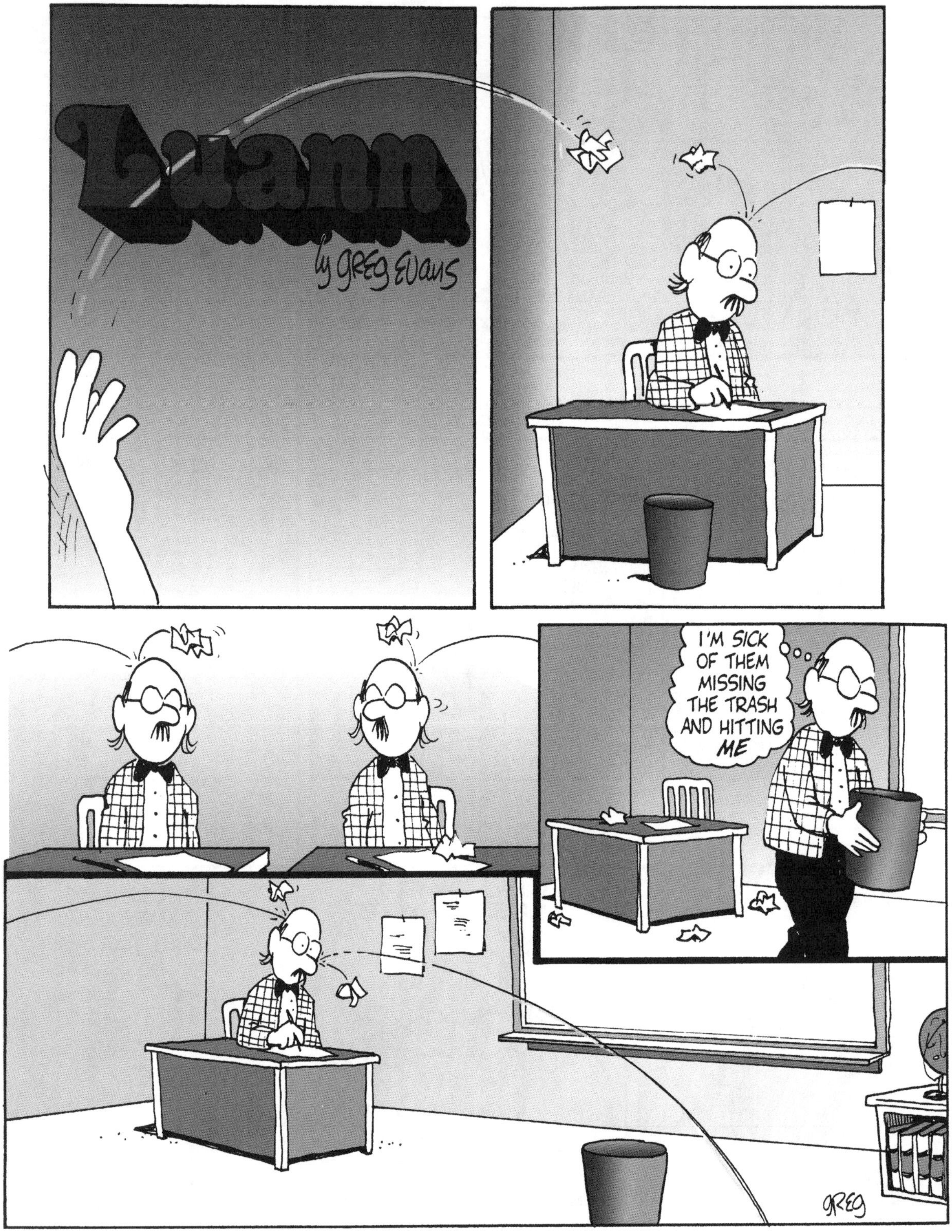
Luann
by GREG EVANS
I'M SICK OF THEM MISSING THE TRASH AND HITTING ME
GREG

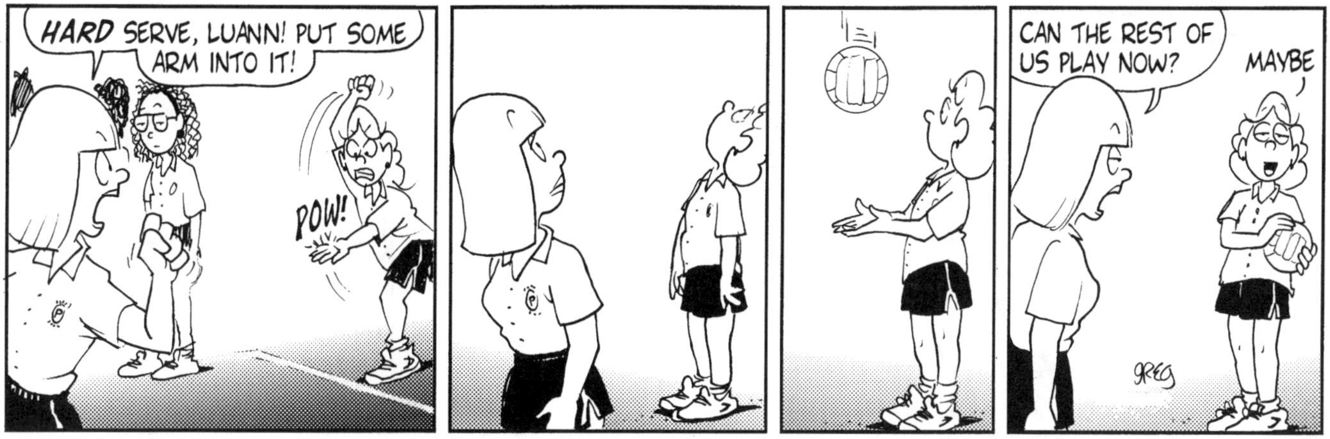
HARD SERVE, LUANN! PUT SOME ARM INTO IT!
POW!
CAN THE REST OF US PLAY NOW?
MAYBE
GREG

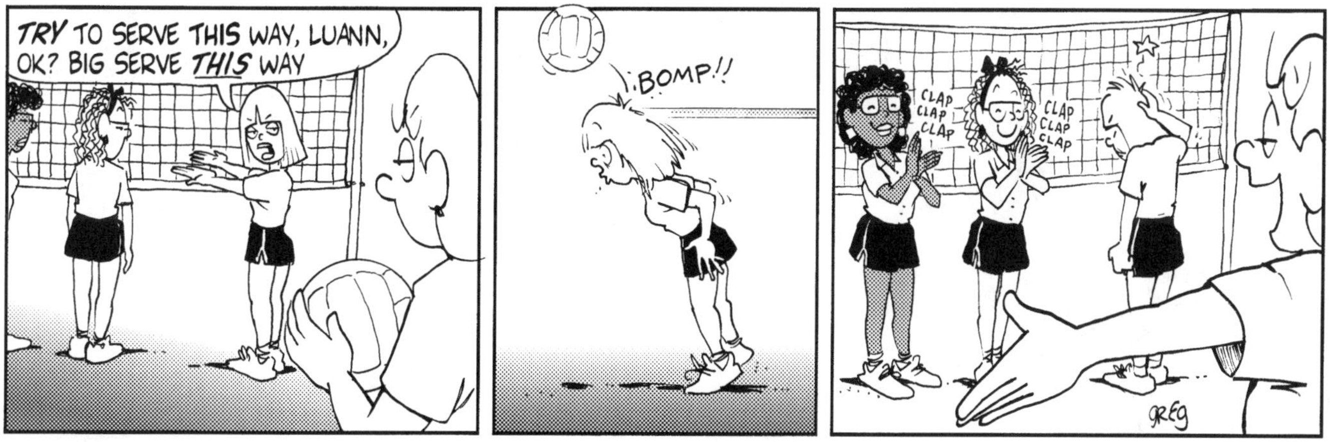
TRY TO SERVE THIS WAY, LUANN, OK? BIG SERVE THIS WAY
BOMP!!
CLAP CLAP CLAP
CLAP CLAP CLAP
GREG

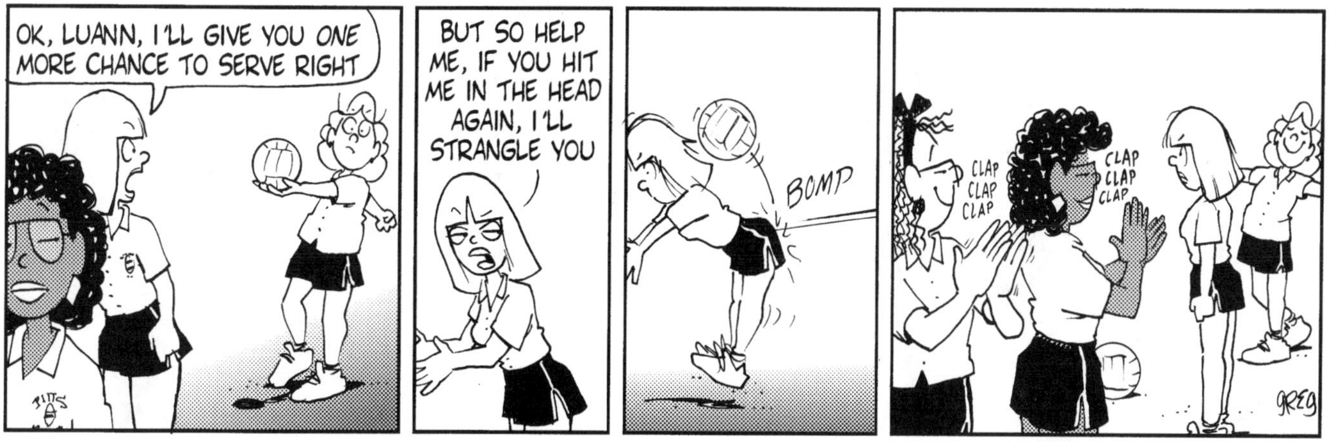
OK, LUANN, I'LL GIVE YOU ONE MORE CHANCE TO SERVE RIGHT
BUT SO HELP ME, IF YOU HIT ME IN THE HEAD AGAIN, I'LL STRANGLE YOU
BOMP
CLAP CLAP CLAP
CLAP CLAP CLAP
GREG

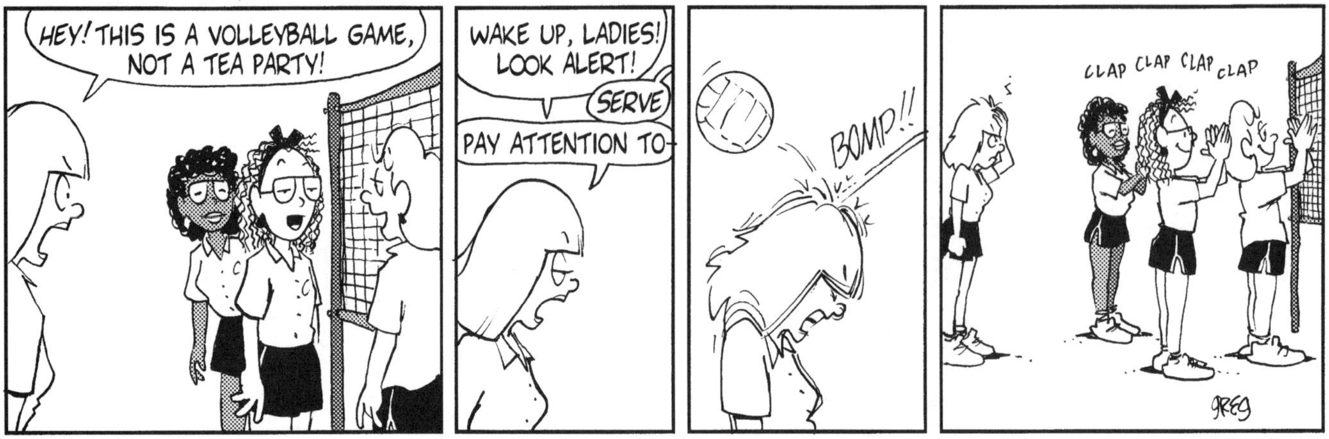
HEY! THIS IS A VOLLEYBALL GAME, NOT A TEA PARTY!
WAKE UP, LADIES! LOOK ALERT!
SERVE
PAY ATTENTION TO-
BOMP!!
CLAP CLAP CLAP CLAP
GREG

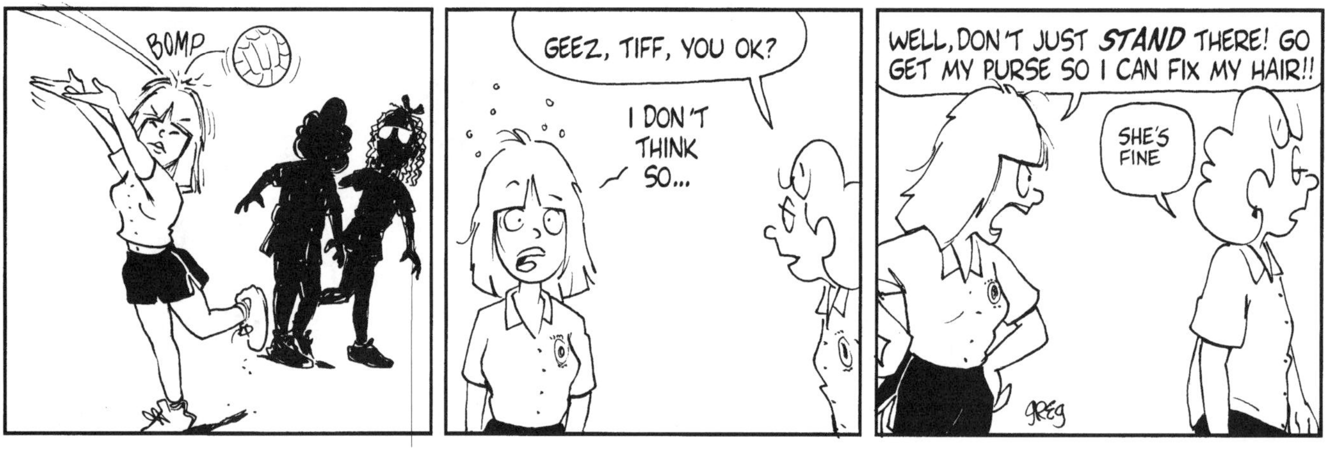
BOMP
GEEZ, TIFF, YOU OK?
I DON'T THINK SO...
WELL, DON'T JUST **STAND** THERE! GO GET MY PURSE SO I CAN FIX MY HAIR!!
SHE'S FINE
GREG

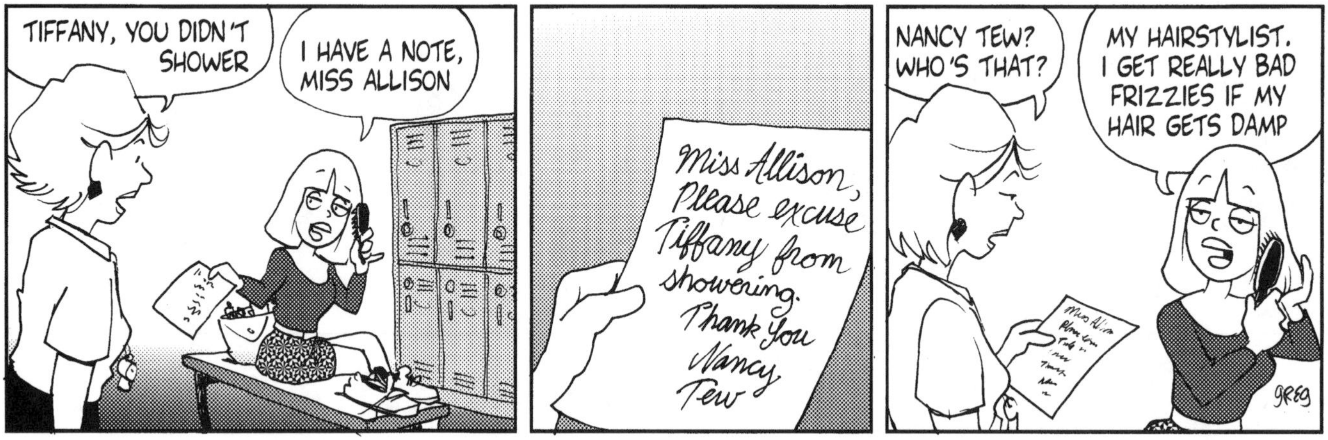
TIFFANY, YOU DIDN'T SHOWER
I HAVE A NOTE, MISS ALLISON
Miss Allison, Please excuse Tiffany from showering. Thank You Nancy Tew
NANCY TEW? WHO'S THAT?
MY HAIRSTYLIST. I GET REALLY BAD FRIZZIES IF MY HAIR GETS DAMP
GREG

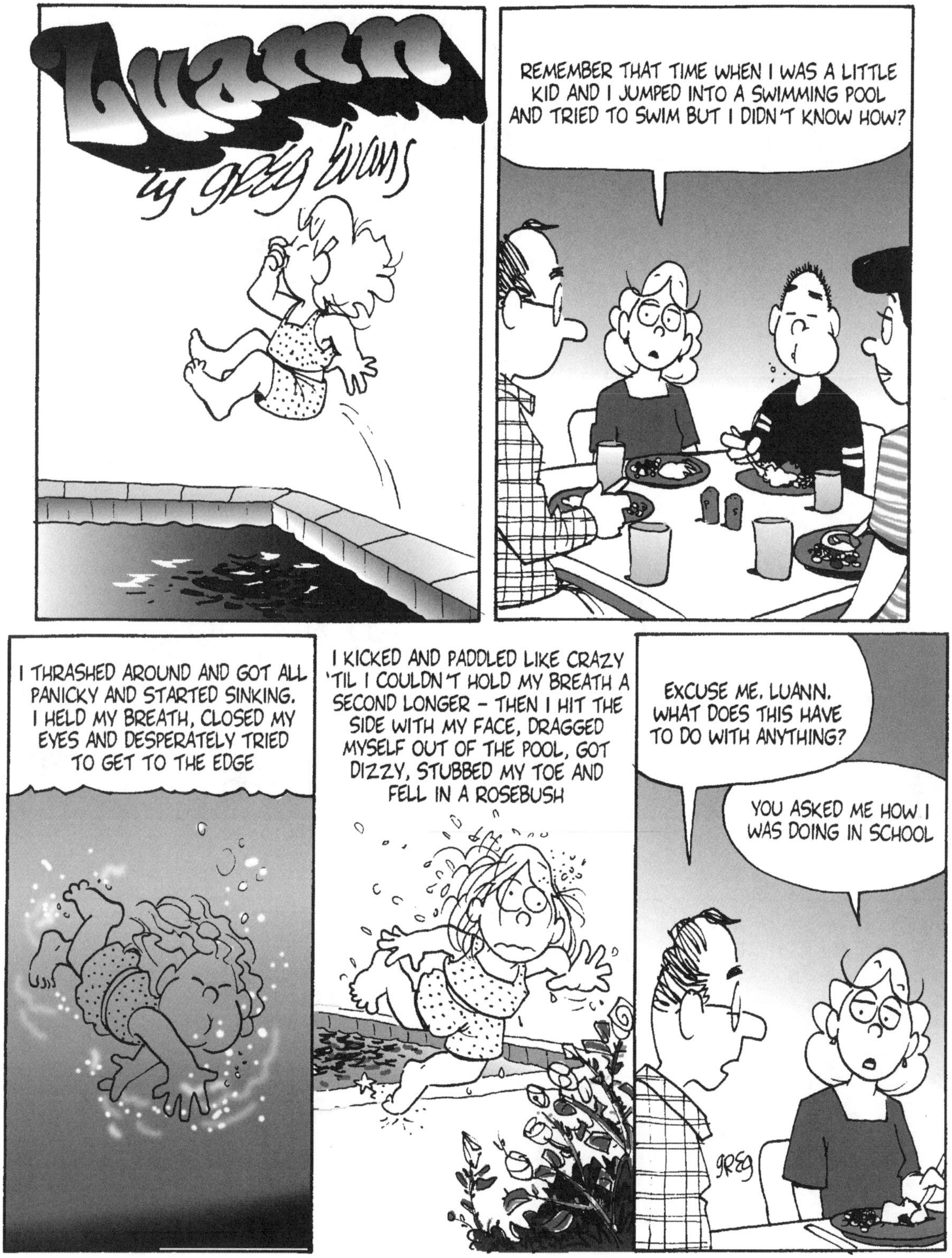
Luann
by greg evans
REMEMBER THAT TIME WHEN I WAS A LITTLE KID AND I JUMPED INTO A SWIMMING POOL AND TRIED TO SWIM BUT I DIDN'T KNOW HOW?
I THRASHED AROUND AND GOT ALL PANICKY AND STARTED SINKING. I HELD MY BREATH, CLOSED MY EYES AND DESPERATELY TRIED TO GET TO THE EDGE
I KICKED AND PADDLED LIKE CRAZY 'TIL I COULDN'T HOLD MY BREATH A SECOND LONGER – THEN I HIT THE SIDE WITH MY FACE, DRAGGED MYSELF OUT OF THE POOL, GOT DIZZY, STUBBED MY TOE AND FELL IN A ROSEBUSH
EXCUSE ME. LUANN. WHAT DOES THIS HAVE TO DO WITH ANYTHING?
YOU ASKED ME HOW I WAS DOING IN SCHOOL
GREG

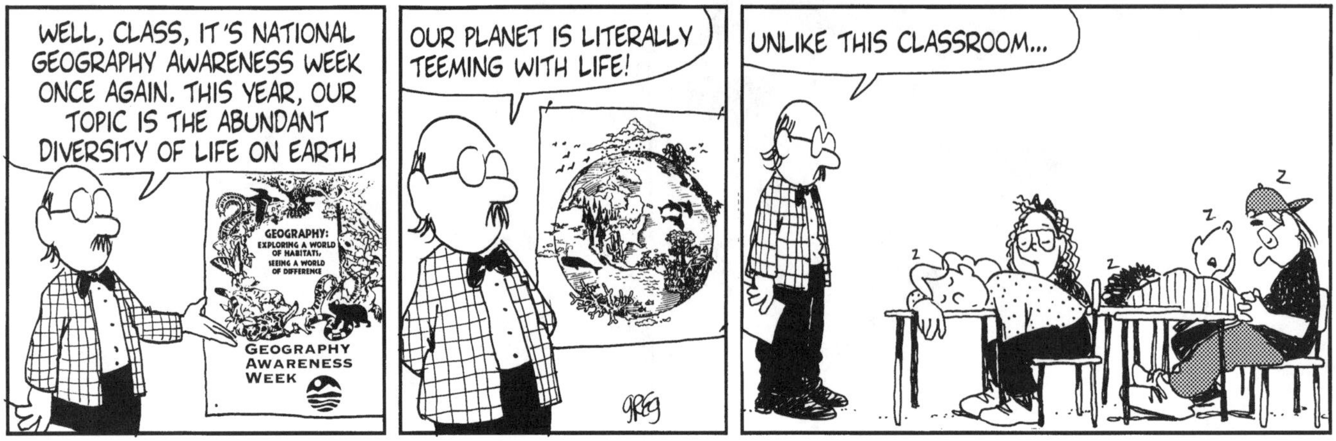
WELL, CLASS, IT'S NATIONAL GEOGRAPHY AWARENESS WEEK ONCE AGAIN. THIS YEAR, OUR TOPIC IS THE ABUNDANT DIVERSITY OF LIFE ON EARTH
GEOGRAPHY: EXPLORING A WORLD OF HABITATS, SEEING A WORLD OF DIFFERENCE
GEOGRAPHY AWARENESS WEEK
OUR PLANET IS LITERALLY TEEMING WITH LIFE!
UNLIKE THIS CLASSROOM...
Z
Z
Z
Z
GREG

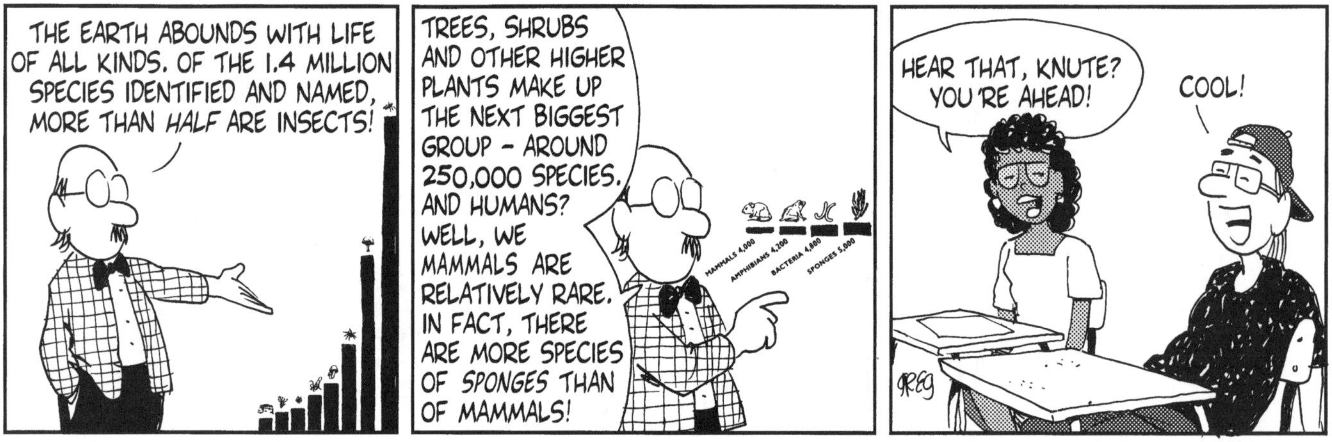
THE EARTH ABOUNDS WITH LIFE OF ALL KINDS. OF THE 1.4 MILLION SPECIES IDENTIFIED AND NAMED, MORE THAN *HALF* ARE INSECTS!
TREES, SHRUBS AND OTHER HIGHER PLANTS MAKE UP THE NEXT BIGGEST GROUP – AROUND 250,000 SPECIES. AND HUMANS? WELL, WE MAMMALS ARE RELATIVELY RARE. IN FACT, THERE ARE MORE SPECIES OF *SPONGES* THAN OF MAMMALS!
MAMMALS 4,000
AMPHIBIANS 4,200
BACTERIA 4,800
SPONGES 5,000
HEAR THAT, KNUTE? YOU'RE AHEAD!
COOL!
GREG

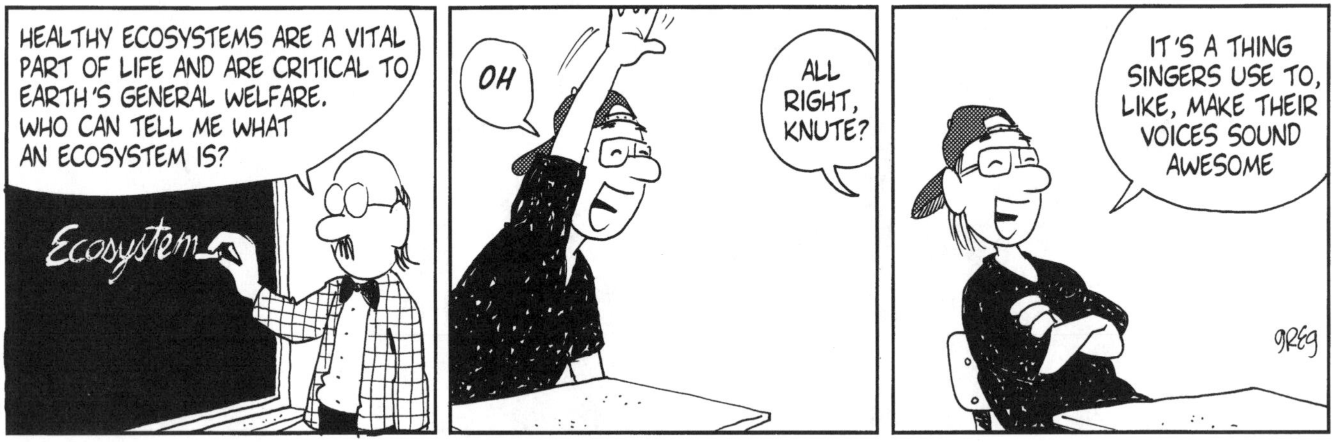
HEALTHY ECOSYSTEMS ARE A VITAL PART OF LIFE AND ARE CRITICAL TO EARTH'S GENERAL WELFARE. WHO CAN TELL ME WHAT AN ECOSYSTEM IS?
Ecosystem
OH
ALL RIGHT, KNUTE?
IT'S A THING SINGERS USE TO, LIKE, MAKE THEIR VOICES SOUND AWESOME
GREG

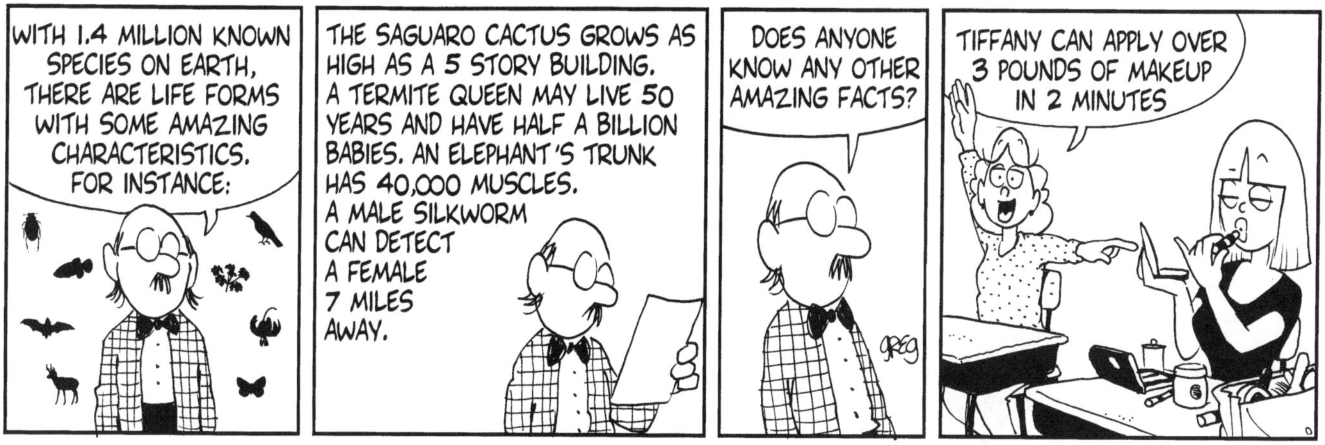
WITH 1.4 MILLION KNOWN SPECIES ON EARTH, THERE ARE LIFE FORMS WITH SOME AMAZING CHARACTERISTICS. FOR INSTANCE:
THE SAGUARO CACTUS GROWS AS HIGH AS A 5 STORY BUILDING. A TERMITE QUEEN MAY LIVE 50 YEARS AND HAVE HALF A BILLION BABIES. AN ELEPHANT'S TRUNK HAS 40,000 MUSCLES. A MALE SILKWORM CAN DETECT A FEMALE 7 MILES AWAY.
DOES ANYONE KNOW ANY OTHER AMAZING FACTS?
TIFFANY CAN APPLY OVER 3 POUNDS OF MAKEUP IN 2 MINUTES

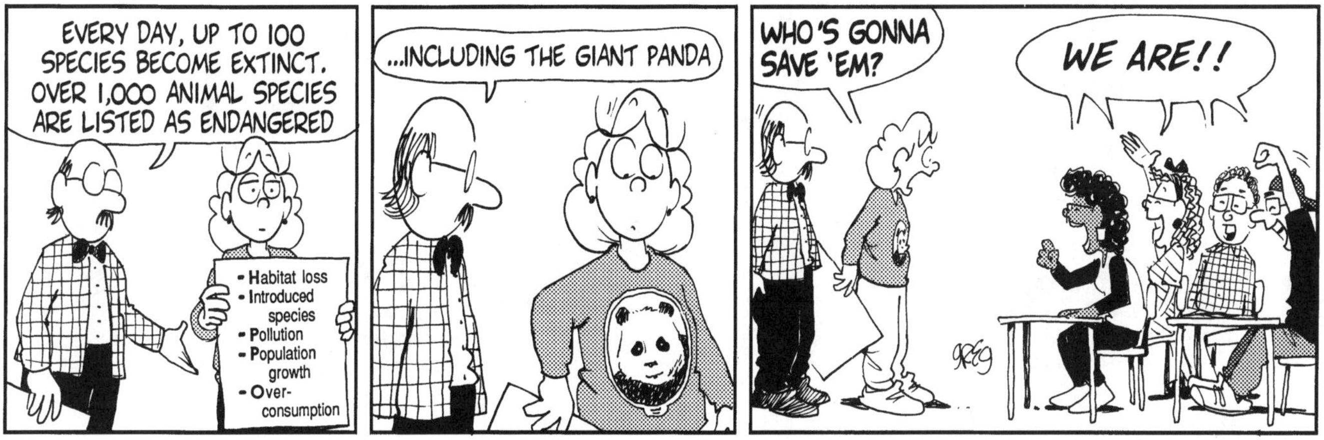
EVERY DAY, UP TO 100 SPECIES BECOME EXTINCT. OVER 1,000 ANIMAL SPECIES ARE LISTED AS ENDANGERED
- Habitat loss
- Introduced species
- Pollution
- Population growth
- Over-consumption
...INCLUDING THE GIANT PANDA
WHO'S GONNA SAVE 'EM?
WE ARE!!

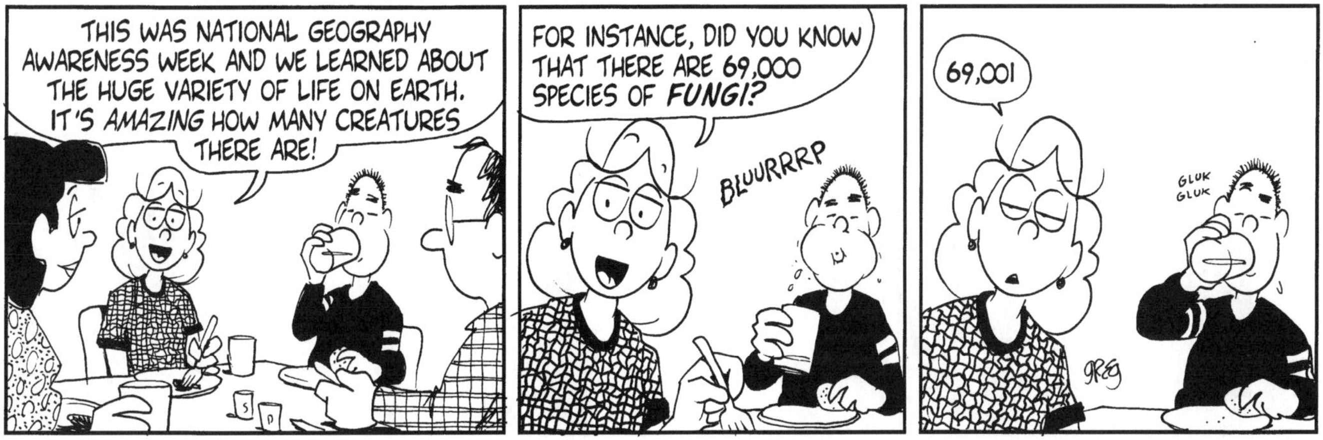
THIS WAS NATIONAL GEOGRAPHY AWARENESS WEEK AND WE LEARNED ABOUT THE HUGE VARIETY OF LIFE ON EARTH. IT'S *AMAZING* HOW MANY CREATURES THERE ARE!
FOR INSTANCE, DID YOU KNOW THAT THERE ARE 69,000 SPECIES OF *FUNGI?*
BLUURRRP
69,001
GLUK GLUK

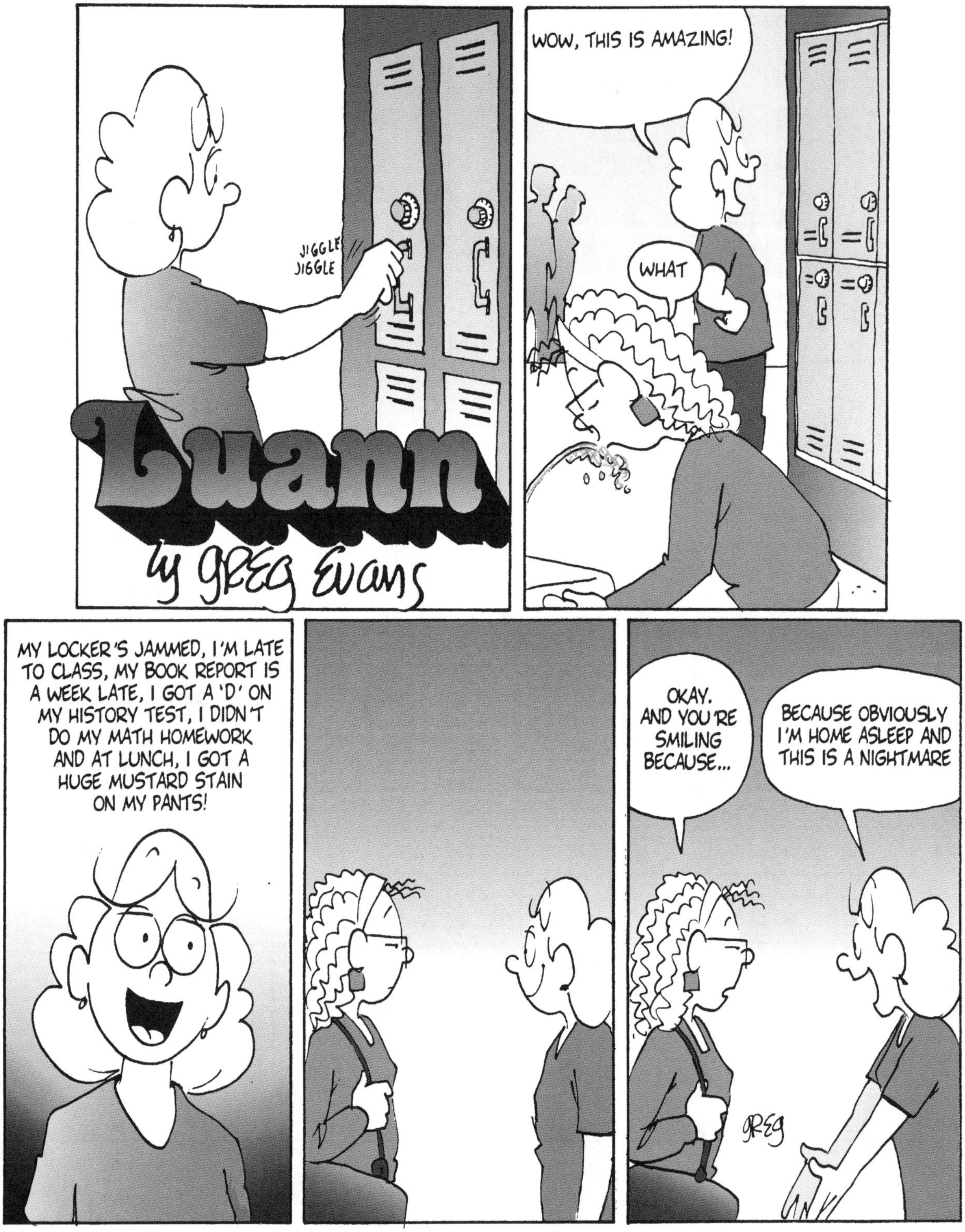
Luann
by GREG Evans
JIGGLE JIGGLE
WOW, THIS IS AMAZING!
WHAT
MY LOCKER'S JAMMED, I'M LATE TO CLASS, MY BOOK REPORT IS A WEEK LATE, I GOT A 'D' ON MY HISTORY TEST, I DIDN'T DO MY MATH HOMEWORK AND AT LUNCH, I GOT A HUGE MUSTARD STAIN ON MY PANTS!
OKAY. AND YOU'RE SMILING BECAUSE...
BECAUSE OBVIOUSLY I'M HOME ASLEEP AND THIS IS A NIGHTMARE
GREG

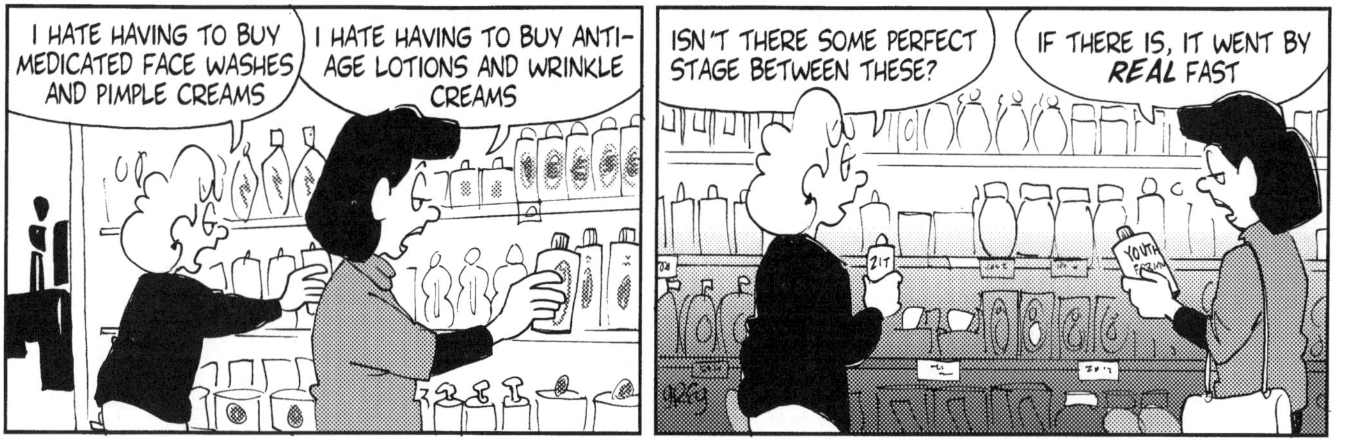
I HATE HAVING TO BUY MEDICATED FACE WASHES AND PIMPLE CREAMS
I HATE HAVING TO BUY ANTI-AGE LOTIONS AND WRINKLE CREAMS
ISN'T THERE SOME PERFECT STAGE BETWEEN THESE?
IF THERE IS, IT WENT BY **REAL** FAST

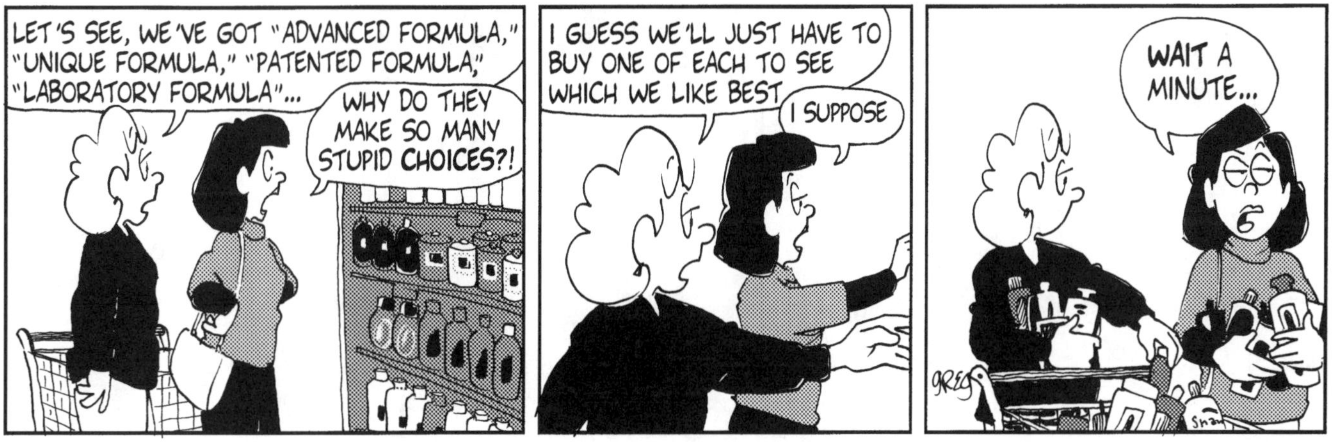
LET'S SEE, WE'VE GOT "ADVANCED FORMULA," "UNIQUE FORMULA," "PATENTED FORMULA," "LABORATORY FORMULA"...
WHY DO THEY MAKE SO MANY STUPID **CHOICES?!**
I GUESS WE'LL JUST HAVE TO BUY ONE OF EACH TO SEE WHICH WE LIKE BEST
I SUPPOSE
WAIT A MINUTE...

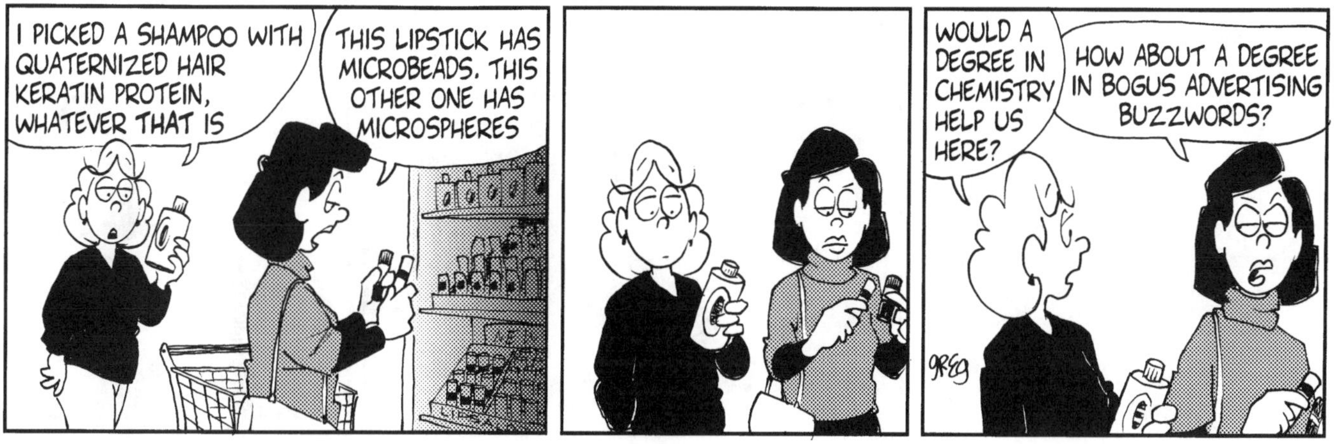
I PICKED A SHAMPOO WITH QUATERNIZED HAIR KERATIN PROTEIN, WHATEVER **THAT** IS
THIS LIPSTICK HAS MICROBEADS. THIS OTHER ONE HAS MICROSPHERES
WOULD A DEGREE IN CHEMISTRY HELP US HERE?
HOW ABOUT A DEGREE IN BOGUS ADVERTISING BUZZWORDS?

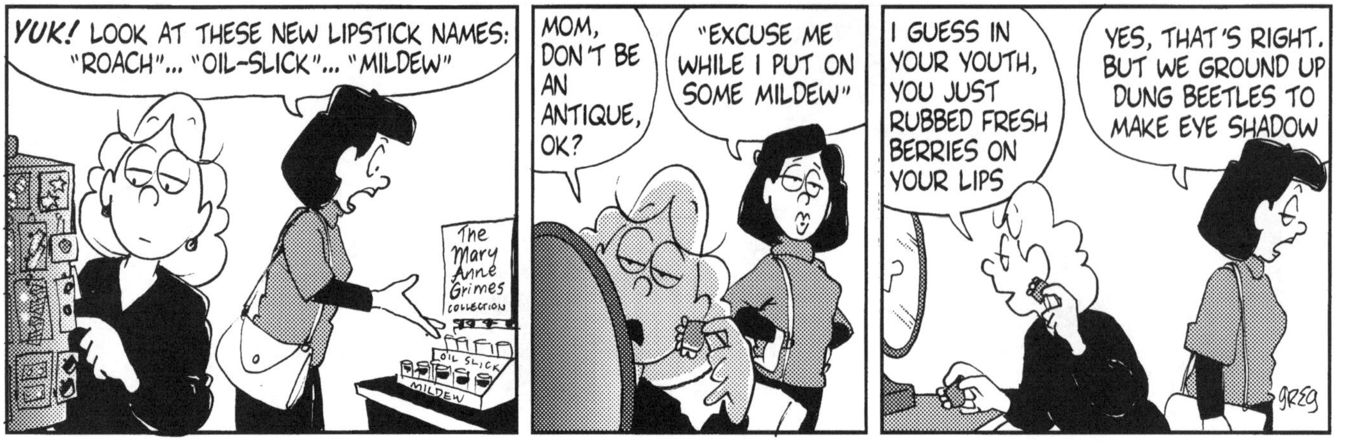
YUK! LOOK AT THESE NEW LIPSTICK NAMES: "ROACH"... "OIL-SLICK"... "MILDEW"
The Mary Anne Grimes COLLECTION
OIL SLICK
MILDEW
MOM, DON'T BE AN ANTIQUE, OK?
"EXCUSE ME WHILE I PUT ON SOME MILDEW"
I GUESS IN YOUR YOUTH, YOU JUST RUBBED FRESH BERRIES ON YOUR LIPS
YES, THAT'S RIGHT. BUT WE GROUND UP DUNG BEETLES TO MAKE EYE SHADOW

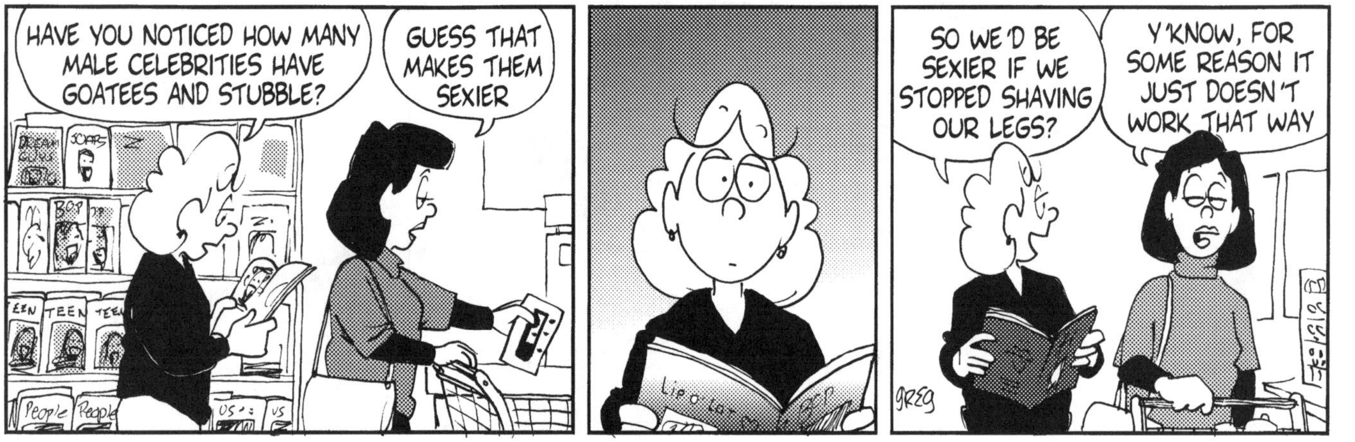
HAVE YOU NOTICED HOW MANY MALE CELEBRITIES HAVE GOATEES AND STUBBLE?
GUESS THAT MAKES THEM SEXIER
SO WE'D BE SEXIER IF WE STOPPED SHAVING OUR LEGS?
Y'KNOW, FOR SOME REASON IT JUST DOESN'T WORK THAT WAY

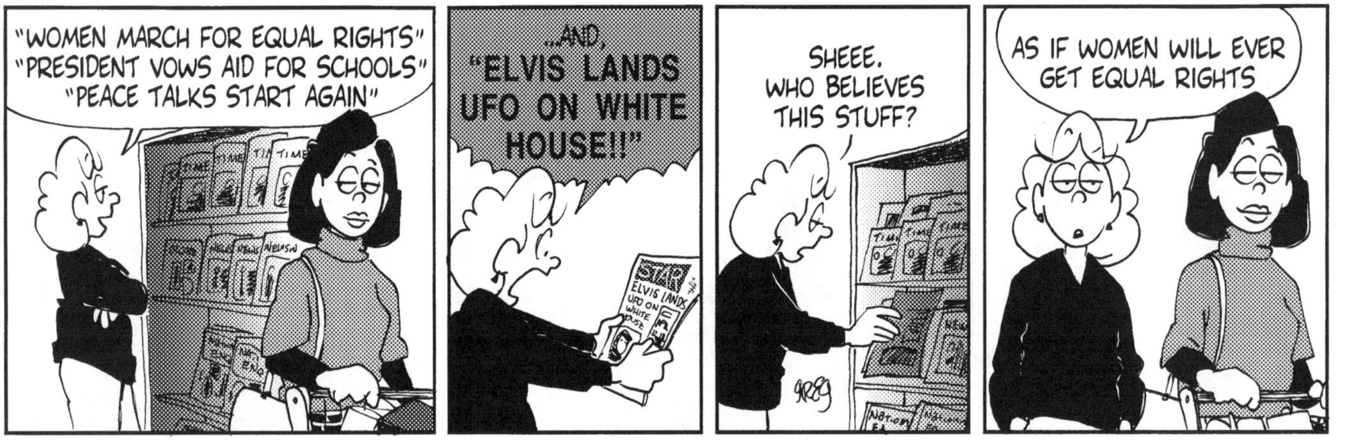
"WOMEN MARCH FOR EQUAL RIGHTS"
"PRESIDENT VOWS AID FOR SCHOOLS"
"PEACE TALKS START AGAIN"
...AND, "ELVIS LANDS UFO ON WHITE HOUSE!!"
SHEEE. WHO BELIEVES THIS STUFF?
AS IF WOMEN WILL EVER GET EQUAL RIGHTS

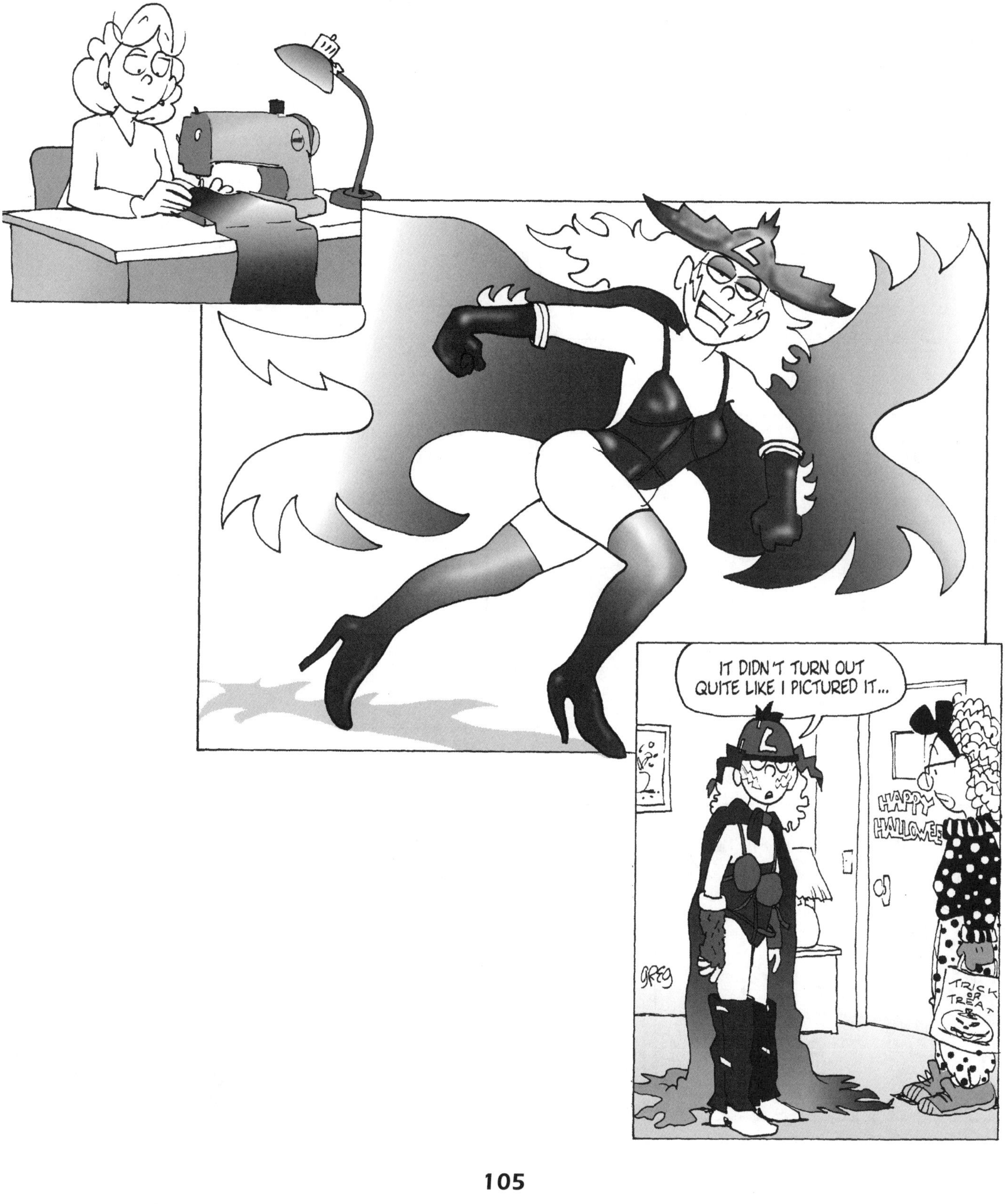
IT DIDN'T TURN OUT QUITE LIKE I PICTURED IT...
HAPPY HALLOWEE
TRICK OR TREAT
GREG

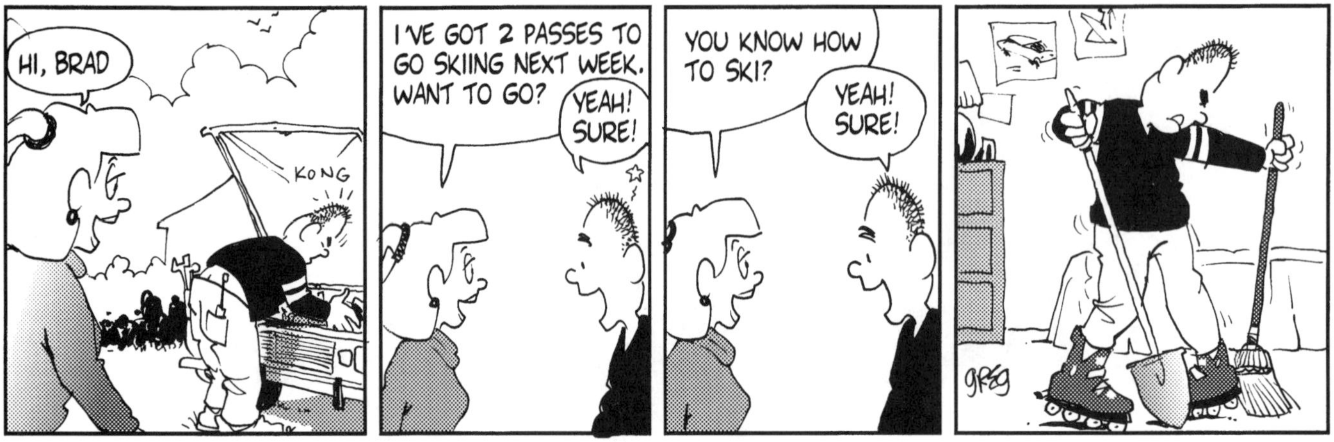
HI, BRAD
KONG
I'VE GOT 2 PASSES TO GO SKIING NEXT WEEK. WANT TO GO?
YEAH! SURE!
YOU KNOW HOW TO SKI?
YEAH! SURE!

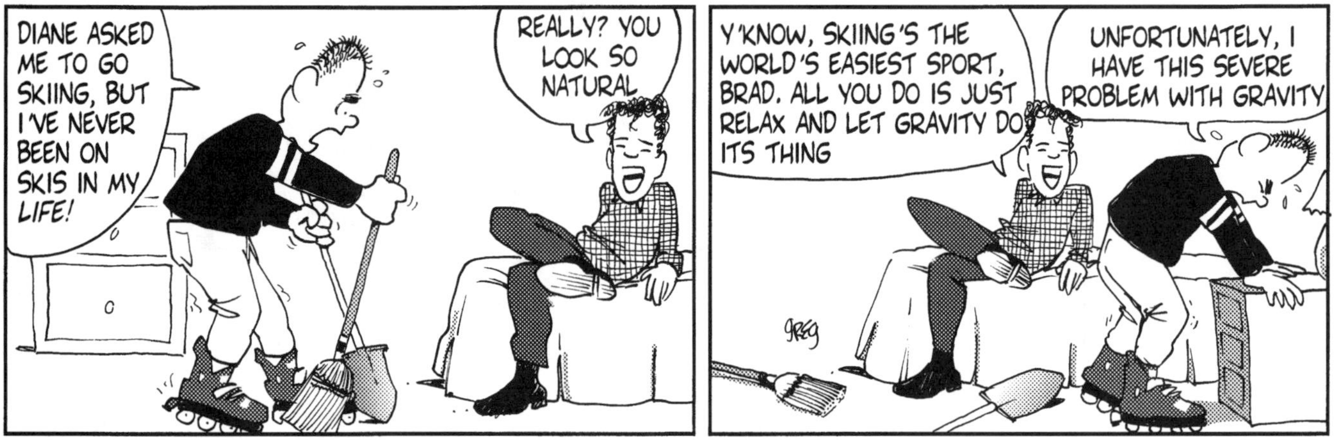
DIANE ASKED ME TO GO SKIING, BUT I'VE NEVER BEEN ON SKIS IN MY LIFE!
REALLY? YOU LOOK SO NATURAL
Y'KNOW, SKIING'S THE WORLD'S EASIEST SPORT, BRAD. ALL YOU DO IS JUST RELAX AND LET GRAVITY DO ITS THING
UNFORTUNATELY, I HAVE THIS SEVERE PROBLEM WITH GRAVITY

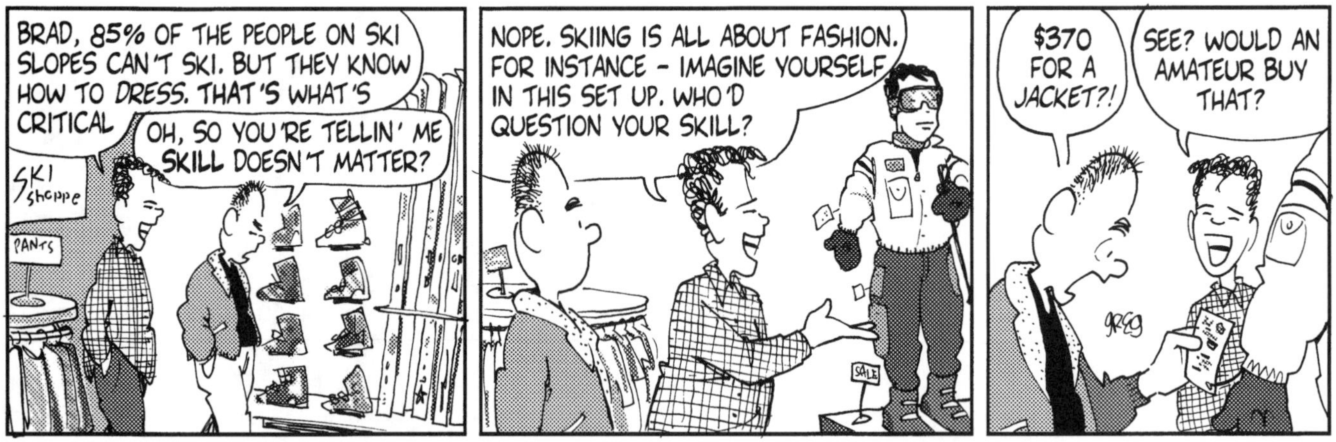
BRAD, 85% OF THE PEOPLE ON SKI SLOPES CAN'T SKI. BUT THEY KNOW HOW TO *DRESS*. THAT'S WHAT'S CRITICAL
OH, SO YOU'RE TELLIN' ME SKILL DOESN'T MATTER?
SKI SHOPPE
PANTS
NOPE. SKIING IS ALL ABOUT FASHION. FOR INSTANCE - IMAGINE YOURSELF IN THIS SET UP. WHO'D QUESTION YOUR SKILL?
SALE
$370 FOR A JACKET?!
SEE? WOULD AN AMATEUR BUY THAT?

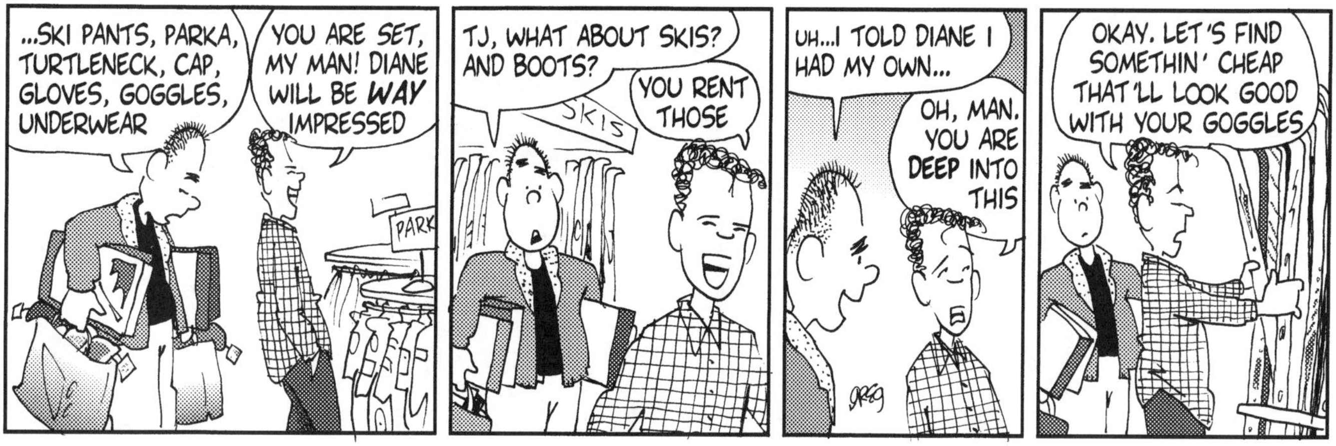
...SKI PANTS, PARKA, TURTLENECK, CAP, GLOVES, GOGGLES, UNDERWEAR
YOU ARE SET, MY MAN! DIANE WILL BE **WAY** IMPRESSED
PARK
TJ, WHAT ABOUT SKIS? AND BOOTS?
SKIS
YOU RENT THOSE
UH...I TOLD DIANE I HAD MY OWN...
OH, MAN. YOU ARE **DEEP** INTO THIS
OKAY. LET'S FIND SOMETHIN' CHEAP THAT'LL LOOK GOOD WITH YOUR GOGGLES

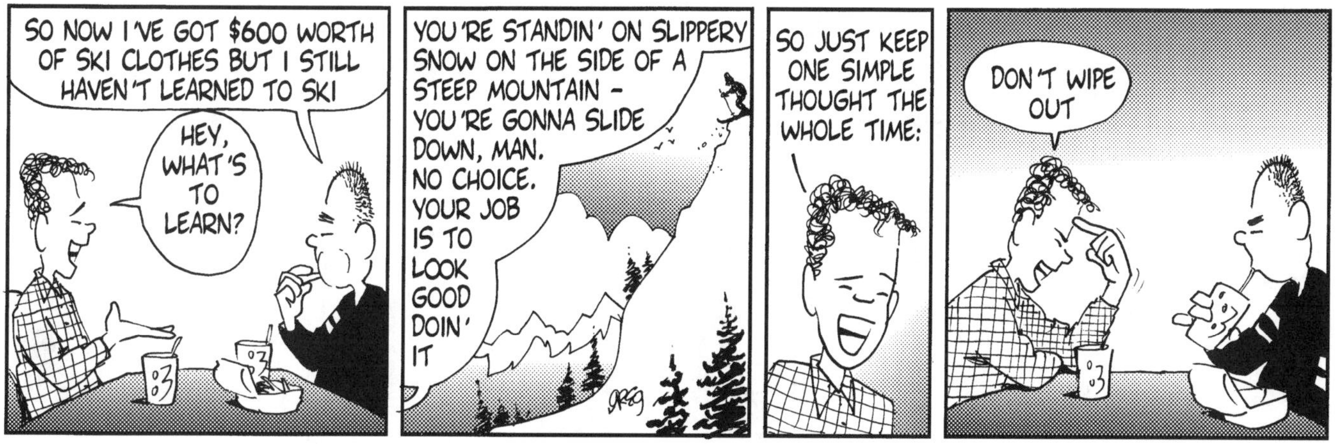
SO NOW I'VE GOT $600 WORTH OF SKI CLOTHES BUT I STILL HAVEN'T LEARNED TO SKI
HEY, WHAT'S TO LEARN?
YOU'RE STANDIN' ON SLIPPERY SNOW ON THE SIDE OF A STEEP MOUNTAIN – YOU'RE GONNA SLIDE DOWN, MAN. NO CHOICE. YOUR JOB IS TO LOOK GOOD DOIN' IT
SO JUST KEEP ONE SIMPLE THOUGHT THE WHOLE TIME:
DON'T WIPE OUT

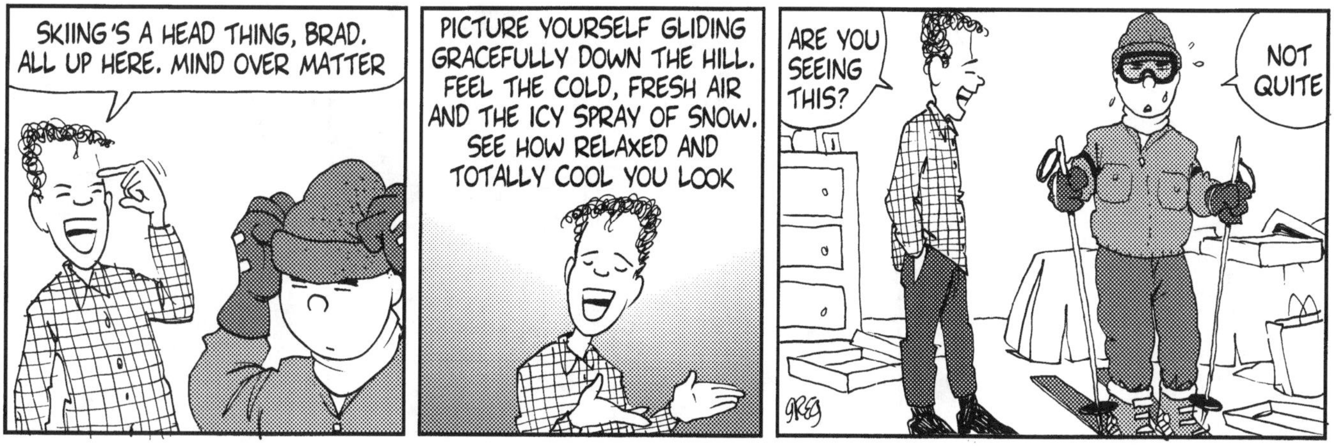
SKIING'S A HEAD THING, BRAD. ALL UP HERE. MIND OVER MATTER
PICTURE YOURSELF GLIDING GRACEFULLY DOWN THE HILL. FEEL THE COLD, FRESH AIR AND THE ICY SPRAY OF SNOW. SEE HOW RELAXED AND TOTALLY COOL YOU LOOK
ARE YOU SEEING THIS?
NOT QUITE

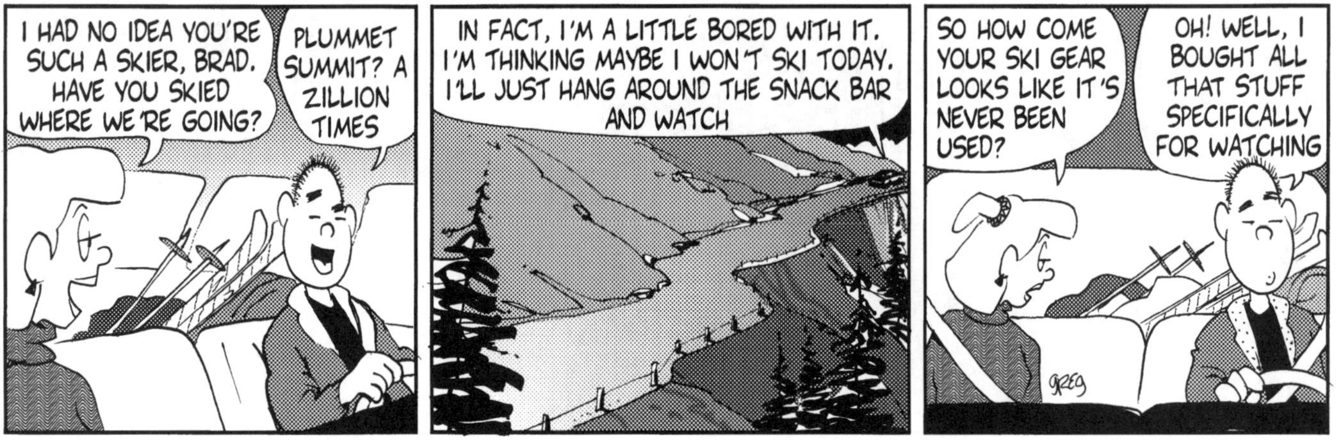
I HAD NO IDEA YOU'RE SUCH A SKIER, BRAD. HAVE YOU SKIED WHERE WE'RE GOING?
PLUMMET SUMMIT? A ZILLION TIMES
IN FACT, I'M A LITTLE BORED WITH IT. I'M THINKING MAYBE I WON'T SKI TODAY. I'LL JUST HANG AROUND THE SNACK BAR AND WATCH
SO HOW COME YOUR SKI GEAR LOOKS LIKE IT'S NEVER BEEN USED?
OH! WELL, I BOUGHT ALL THAT STUFF SPECIFICALLY FOR WATCHING
GREG

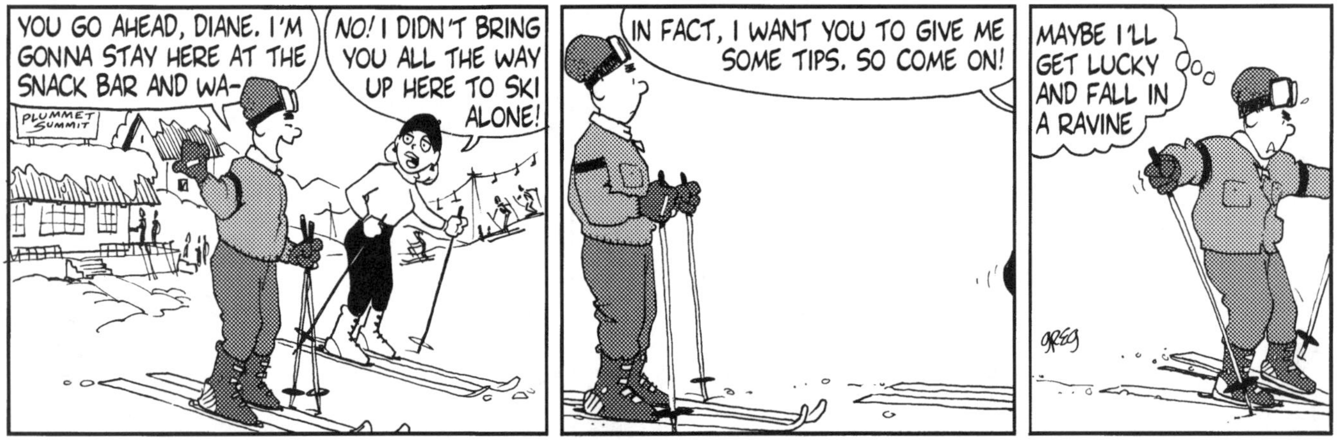
YOU GO AHEAD, DIANE. I'M GONNA STAY HERE AT THE SNACK BAR AND WA-
NO! I DIDN'T BRING YOU ALL THE WAY UP HERE TO SKI ALONE!
PLUMMET SUMMIT
IN FACT, I WANT YOU TO GIVE ME SOME TIPS. SO COME ON!
MAYBE I'LL GET LUCKY AND FALL IN A RAVINE
GREG

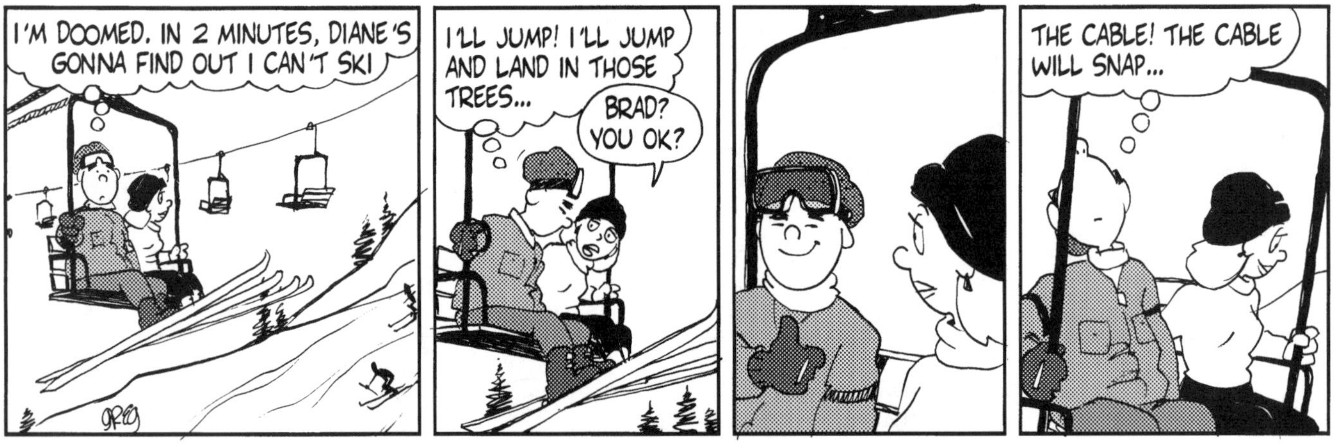
I'M DOOMED. IN 2 MINUTES, DIANE'S GONNA FIND OUT I CAN'T SKI
GREG
I'LL JUMP! I'LL JUMP AND LAND IN THOSE TREES...
BRAD? YOU OK?
THE CABLE! THE CABLE WILL SNAP...

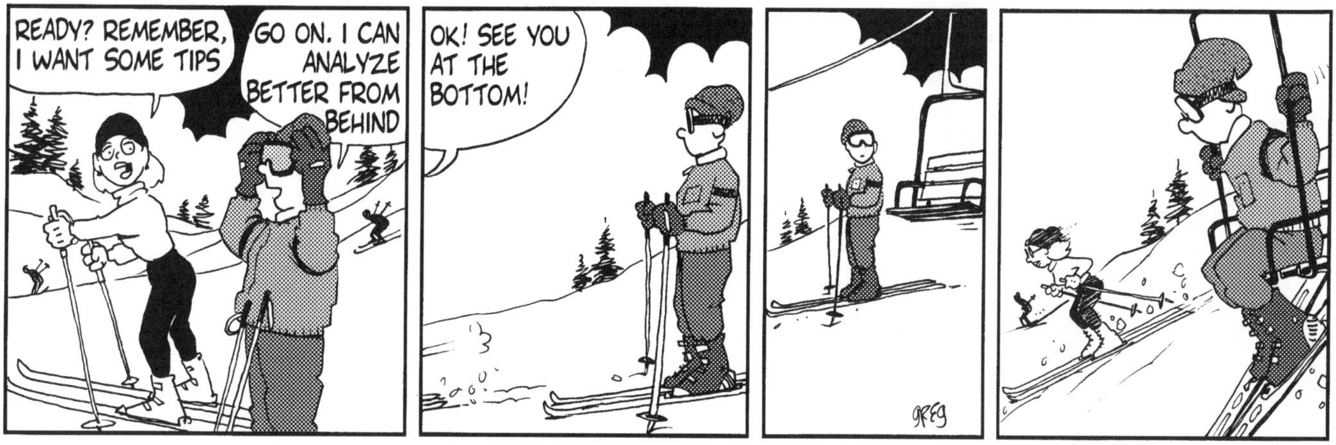
READY? REMEMBER, I WANT SOME TIPS
GO ON. I CAN ANALYZE BETTER FROM BEHIND
OK! SEE YOU AT THE BOTTOM!

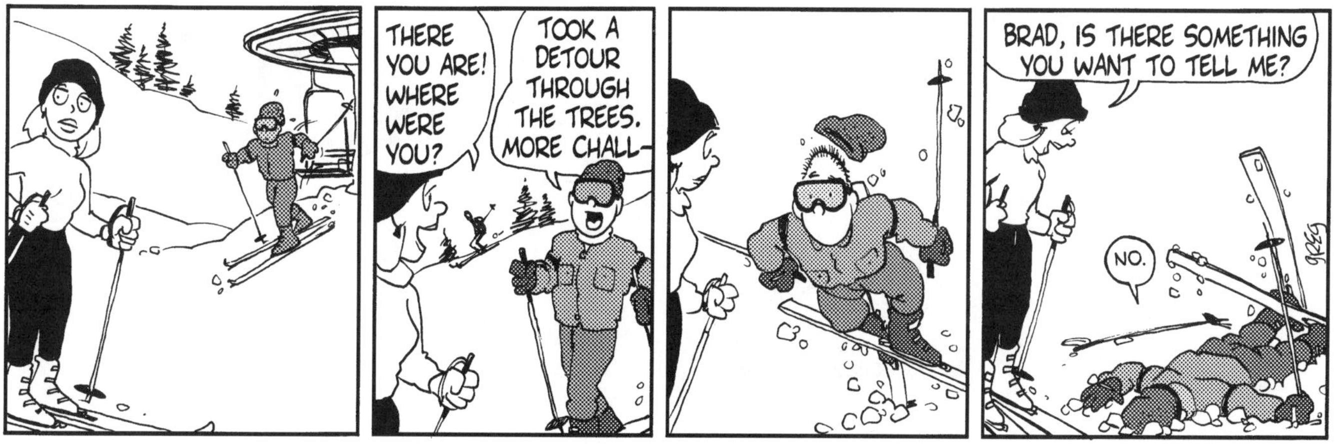
THERE YOU ARE! WHERE WERE YOU?
TOOK A DETOUR THROUGH THE TREES. MORE CHALL-
BRAD, IS THERE SOMETHING YOU WANT TO TELL ME?
NO.

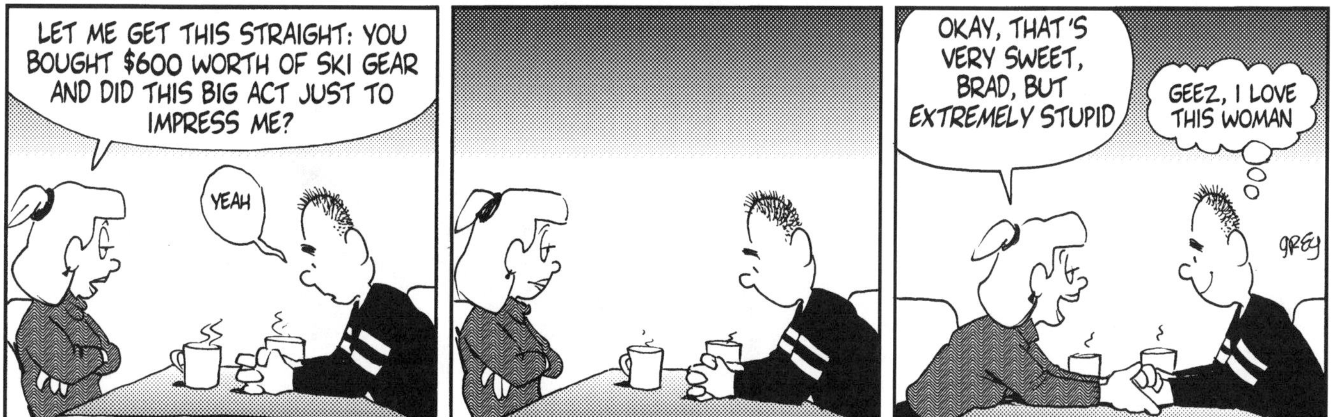
LET ME GET THIS STRAIGHT: YOU BOUGHT $600 WORTH OF SKI GEAR AND DID THIS BIG ACT JUST TO IMPRESS ME?
YEAH
OKAY, THAT'S VERY SWEET, BRAD, BUT EXTREMELY STUPID
GEEZ, I LOVE THIS WOMAN

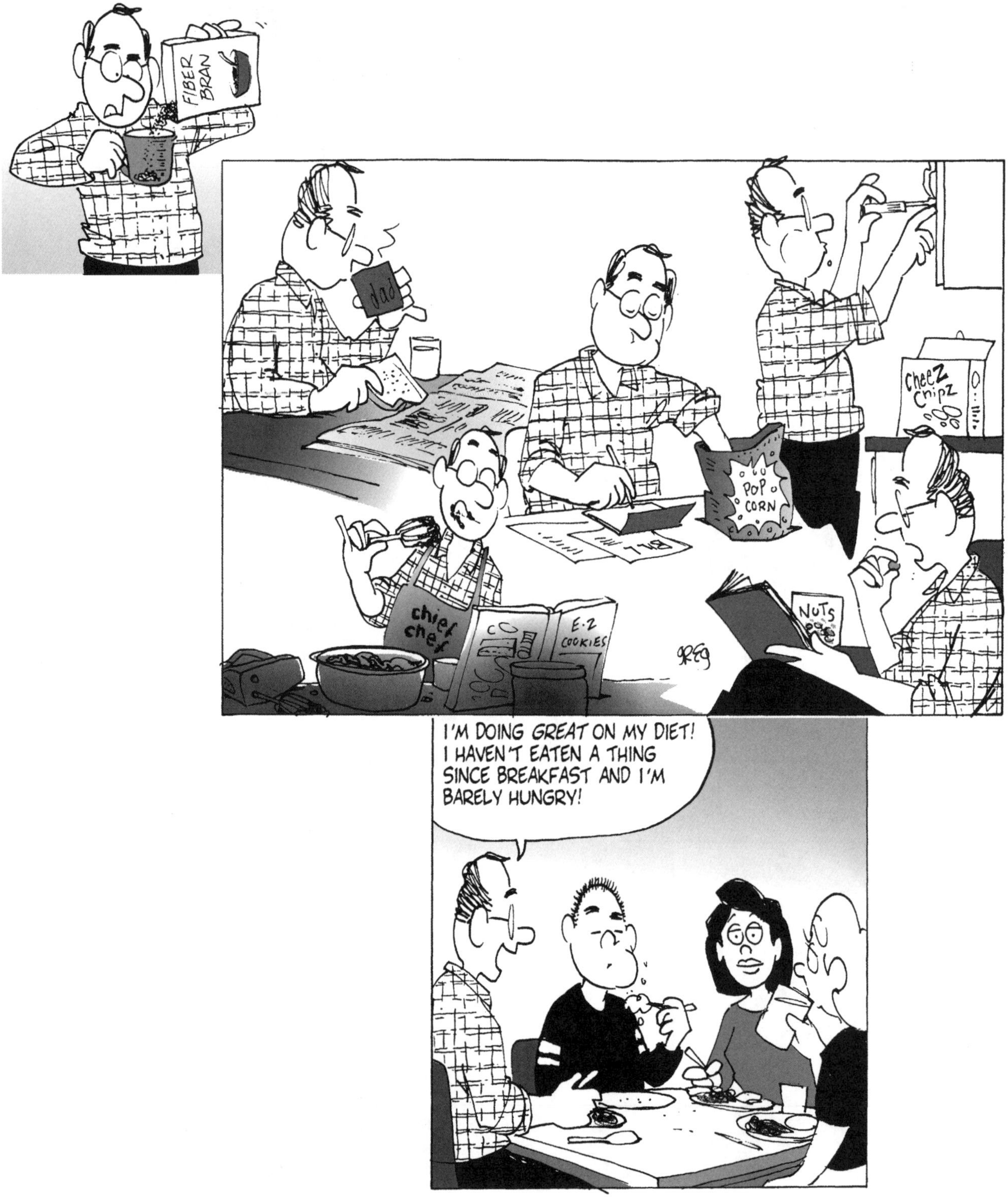
FIBER BRAN
dad
CheeZ Chipz
POP CORN
chief chef
E-Z COOKIES
NUTS
I'M DOING GREAT ON MY DIET! I HAVEN'T EATEN A THING SINCE BREAKFAST AND I'M BARELY HUNGRY!

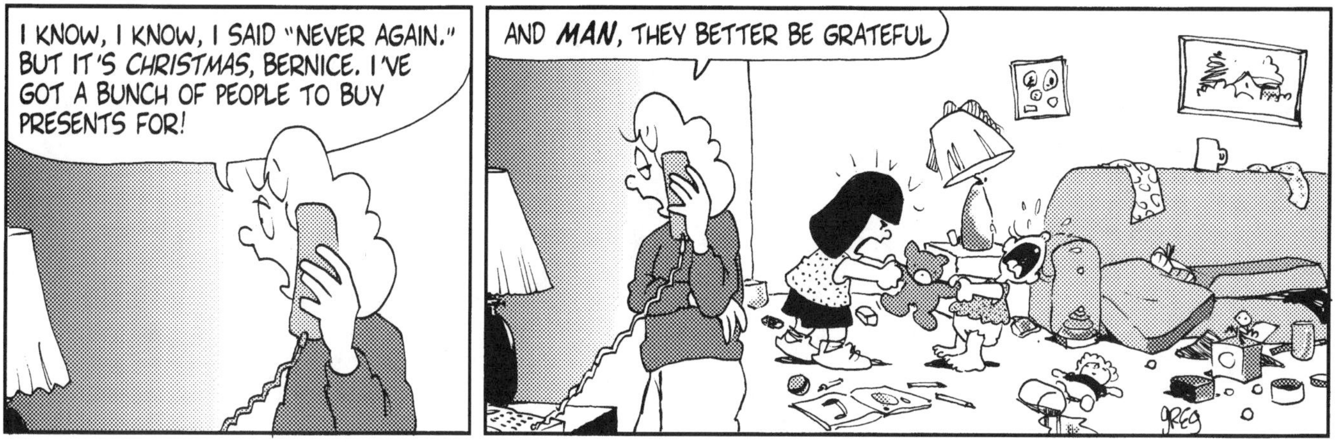
I KNOW, I KNOW, I SAID "NEVER AGAIN." BUT IT'S *CHRISTMAS*, BERNICE. I'VE GOT A BUNCH OF PEOPLE TO BUY PRESENTS FOR!
AND ***MAN***, THEY BETTER BE GRATEFUL
GREG

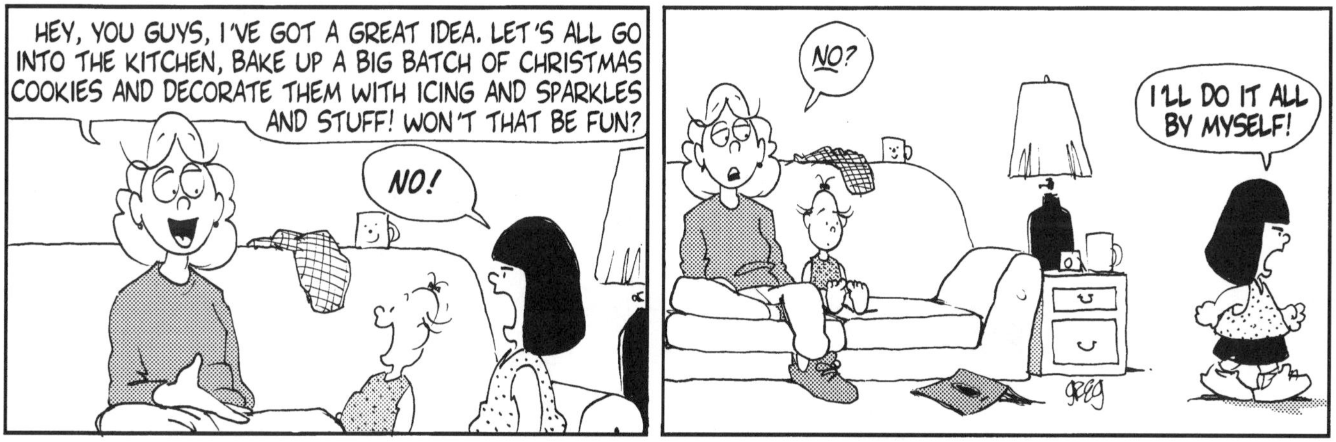
HEY, YOU GUYS, I'VE GOT A GREAT IDEA. LET'S ALL GO INTO THE KITCHEN, BAKE UP A BIG BATCH OF CHRISTMAS COOKIES AND DECORATE THEM WITH ICING AND SPARKLES AND STUFF! WON'T THAT BE FUN?
NO!
NO?
I'LL DO IT ALL BY MYSELF!
GREG

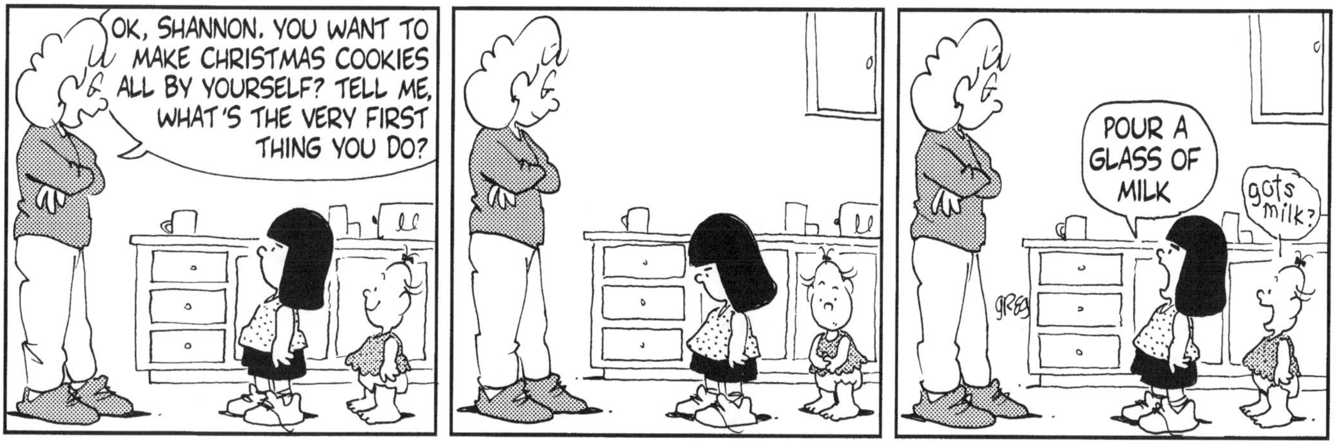
OK, SHANNON. YOU WANT TO MAKE CHRISTMAS COOKIES ALL BY YOURSELF? TELL ME, WHAT'S THE VERY FIRST THING YOU DO?
POUR A GLASS OF MILK
gots milk?
GREG

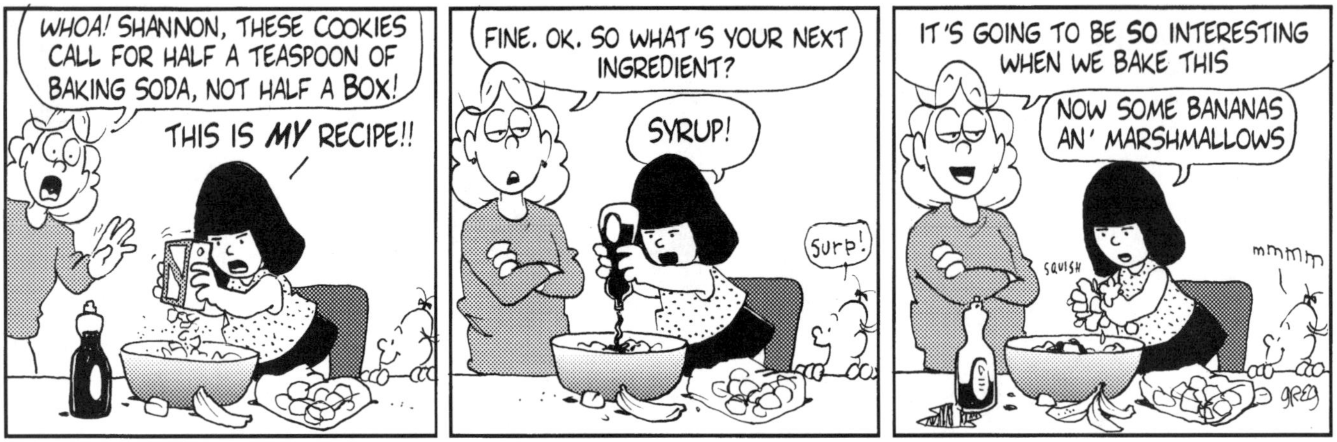
WHOA! SHANNON, THESE COOKIES CALL FOR HALF A TEASPOON OF BAKING SODA, NOT HALF A BOX!
THIS IS MY RECIPE!!
FINE. OK. SO WHAT'S YOUR NEXT INGREDIENT?
SYRUP!
Surp!
IT'S GOING TO BE SO INTERESTING WHEN WE BAKE THIS
NOW SOME BANANAS AN' MARSHMALLOWS
SQUISH
mmmm

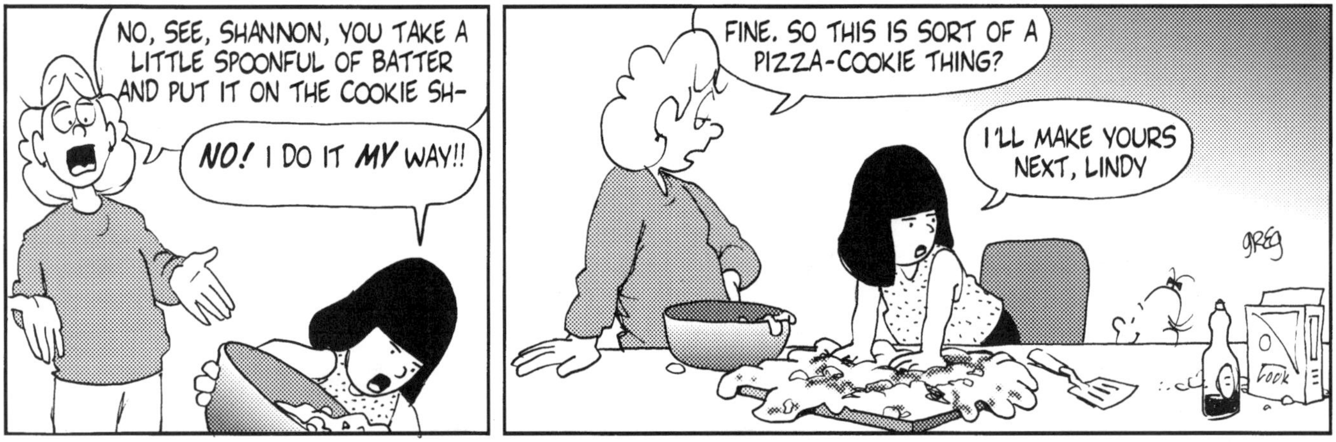
NO, SEE, SHANNON, YOU TAKE A LITTLE SPOONFUL OF BATTER AND PUT IT ON THE COOKIE SH-
NO! I DO IT MY WAY!!
FINE. SO THIS IS SORT OF A PIZZA-COOKIE THING?
I'LL MAKE YOURS NEXT, LINDY

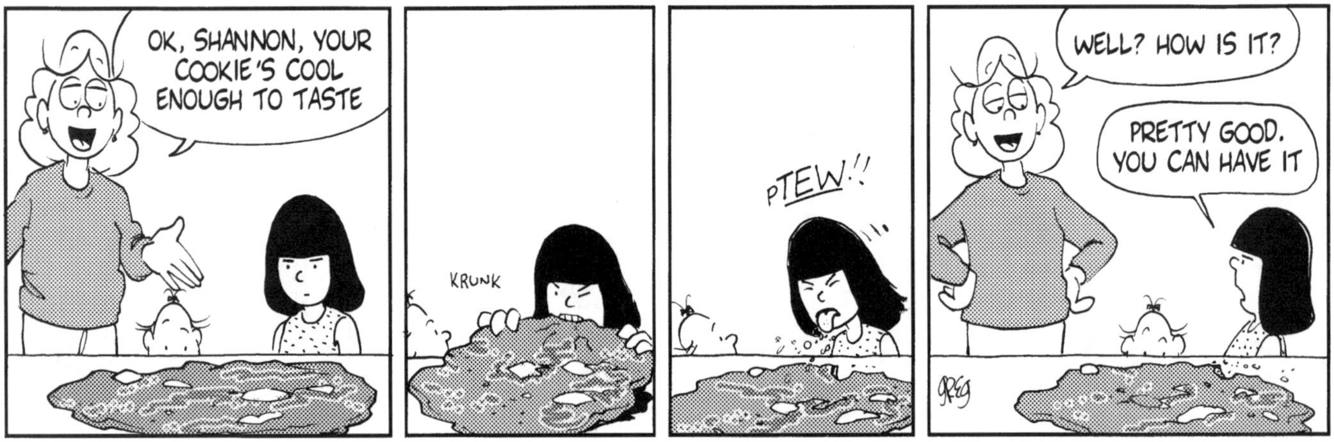
OK, SHANNON, YOUR COOKIE'S COOL ENOUGH TO TASTE
KRUNK
PTEW!!
WELL? HOW IS IT?
PRETTY GOOD. YOU CAN HAVE IT

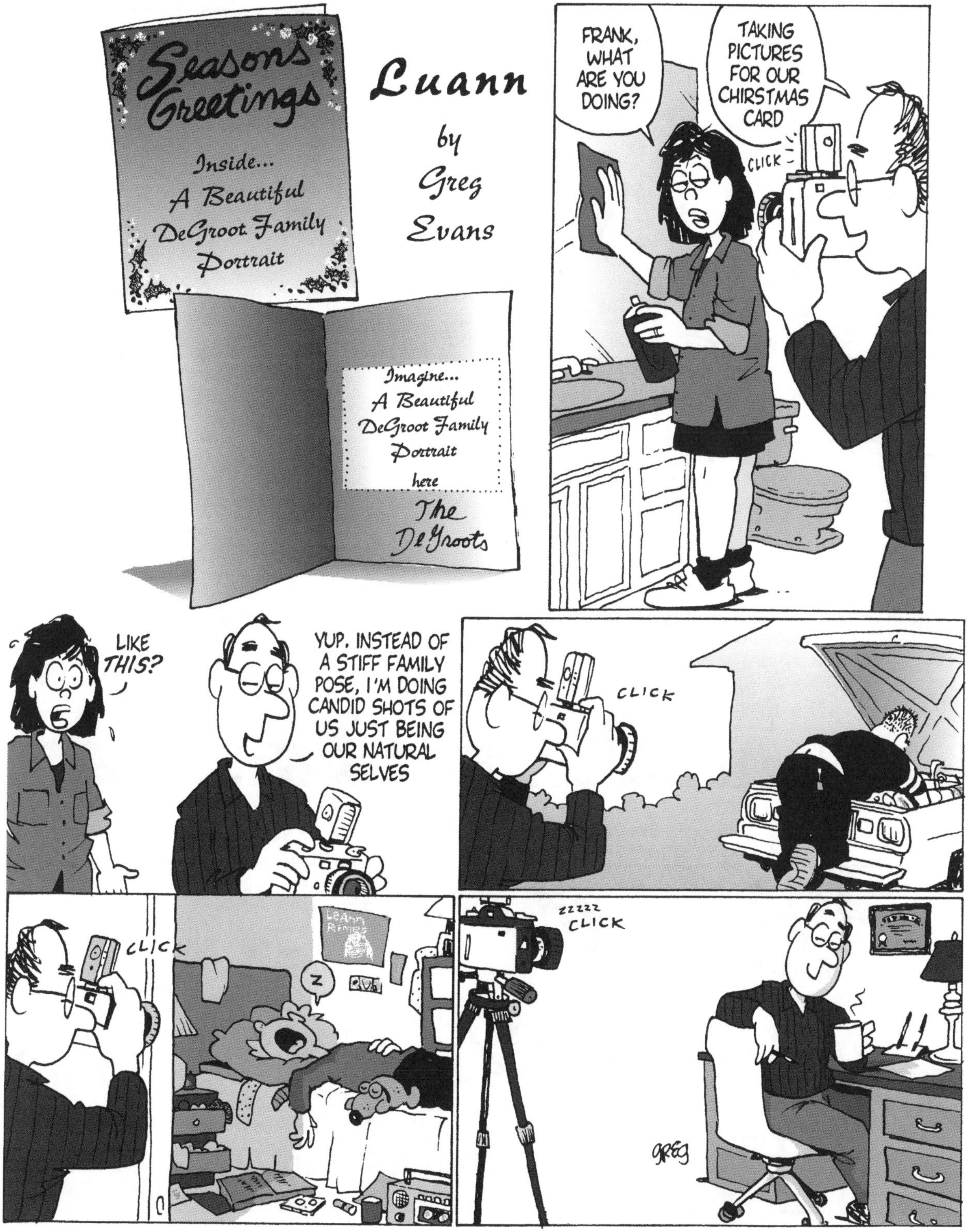
Seasons Greetings
Inside... A Beautiful DeGroot Family Portrait
Luann
by Greg Evans
Imagine... A Beautiful DeGroot Family Portrait here
The DeGroots
FRANK, WHAT ARE YOU DOING?
TAKING PICTURES FOR OUR CHIRSTMAS CARD
CLICK
LIKE THIS?
YUP. INSTEAD OF A STIFF FAMILY POSE, I'M DOING CANDID SHOTS OF US JUST BEING OUR NATURAL SELVES
CLICK
CLICK
Z
ZZZZZ CLICK
GREG

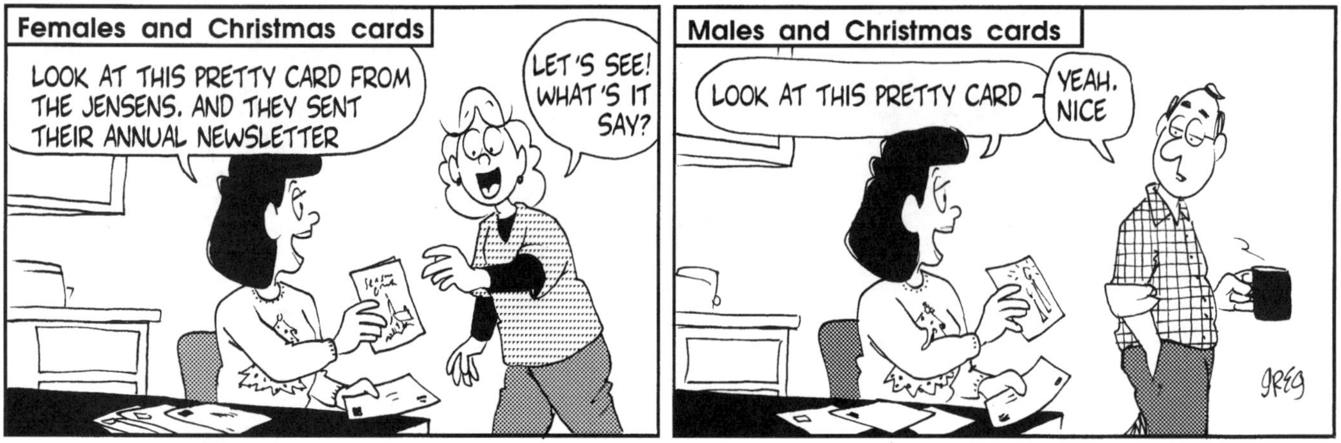
Females and Christmas cards
LOOK AT THIS PRETTY CARD FROM THE JENSENS. AND THEY SENT THEIR ANNUAL NEWSLETTER
LET'S SEE! WHAT'S IT SAY?
Males and Christmas cards
LOOK AT THIS PRETTY CARD
YEAH. NICE
GREG

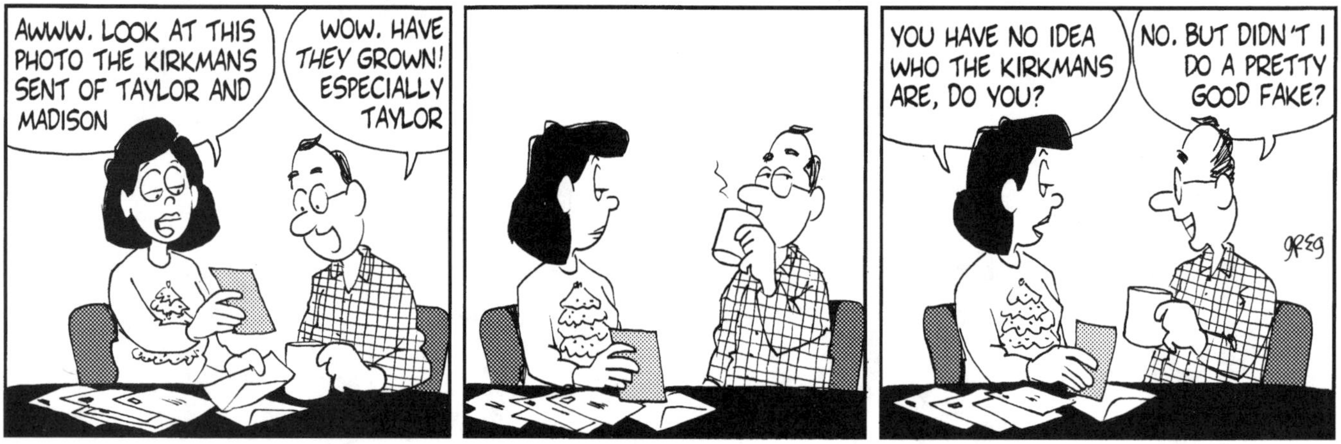
AWWW. LOOK AT THIS PHOTO THE KIRKMANS SENT OF TAYLOR AND MADISON
WOW. HAVE THEY GROWN! ESPECIALLY TAYLOR
YOU HAVE NO IDEA WHO THE KIRKMANS ARE, DO YOU?
NO. BUT DIDN'T I DO A PRETTY GOOD FAKE?
GREG

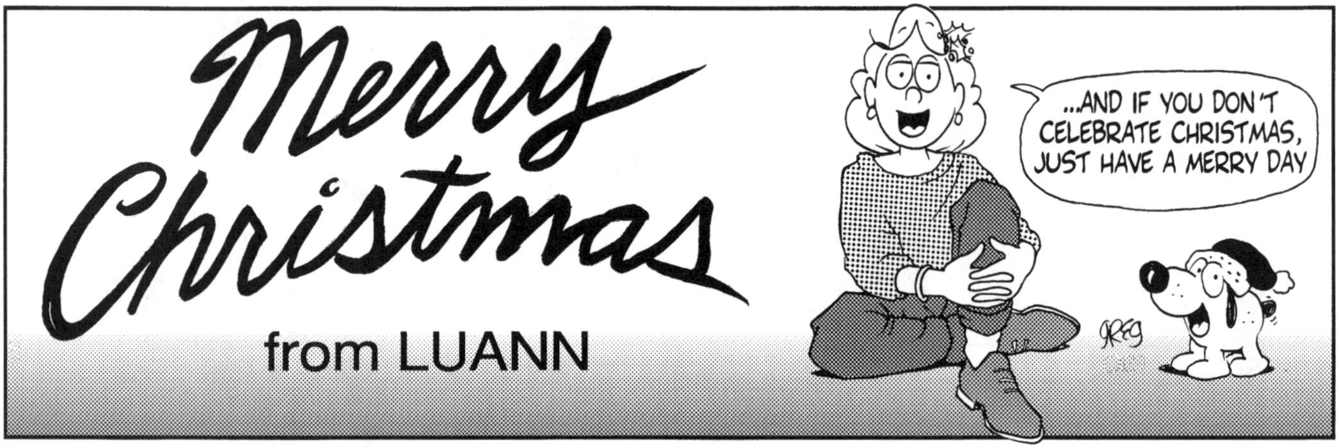
Merry Christmas
from LUANN
...AND IF YOU DON'T CELEBRATE CHRISTMAS, JUST HAVE A MERRY DAY
GREG

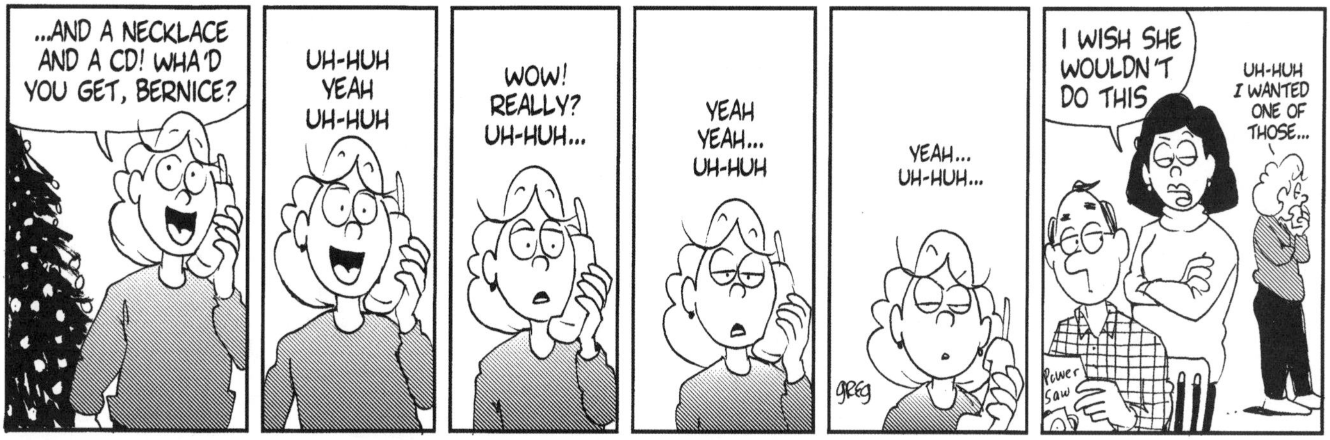
...AND A NECKLACE AND A CD! WHA'D YOU GET, BERNICE?
UH-HUH YEAH UH-HUH
WOW! REALLY? UH-HUH...
YEAH YEAH... UH-HUH
YEAH... UH-HUH...
I WISH SHE WOULDN'T DO THIS
UH-HUH I WANTED ONE OF THOSE...
Power Saw

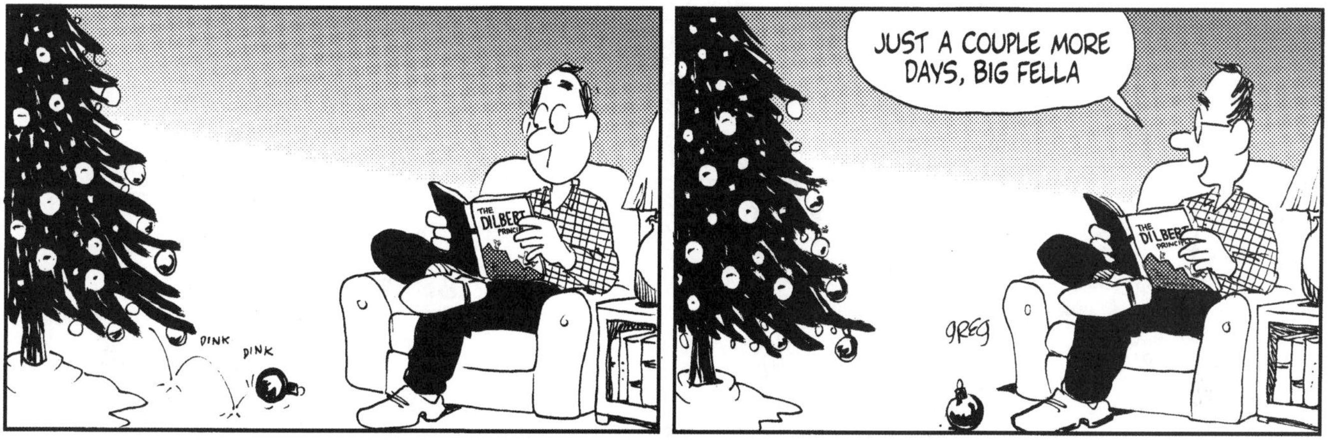
DINK
DINK
JUST A COUPLE MORE DAYS, BIG FELLA

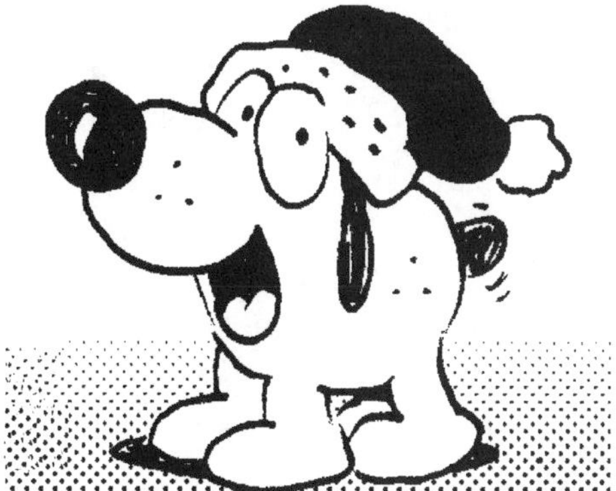

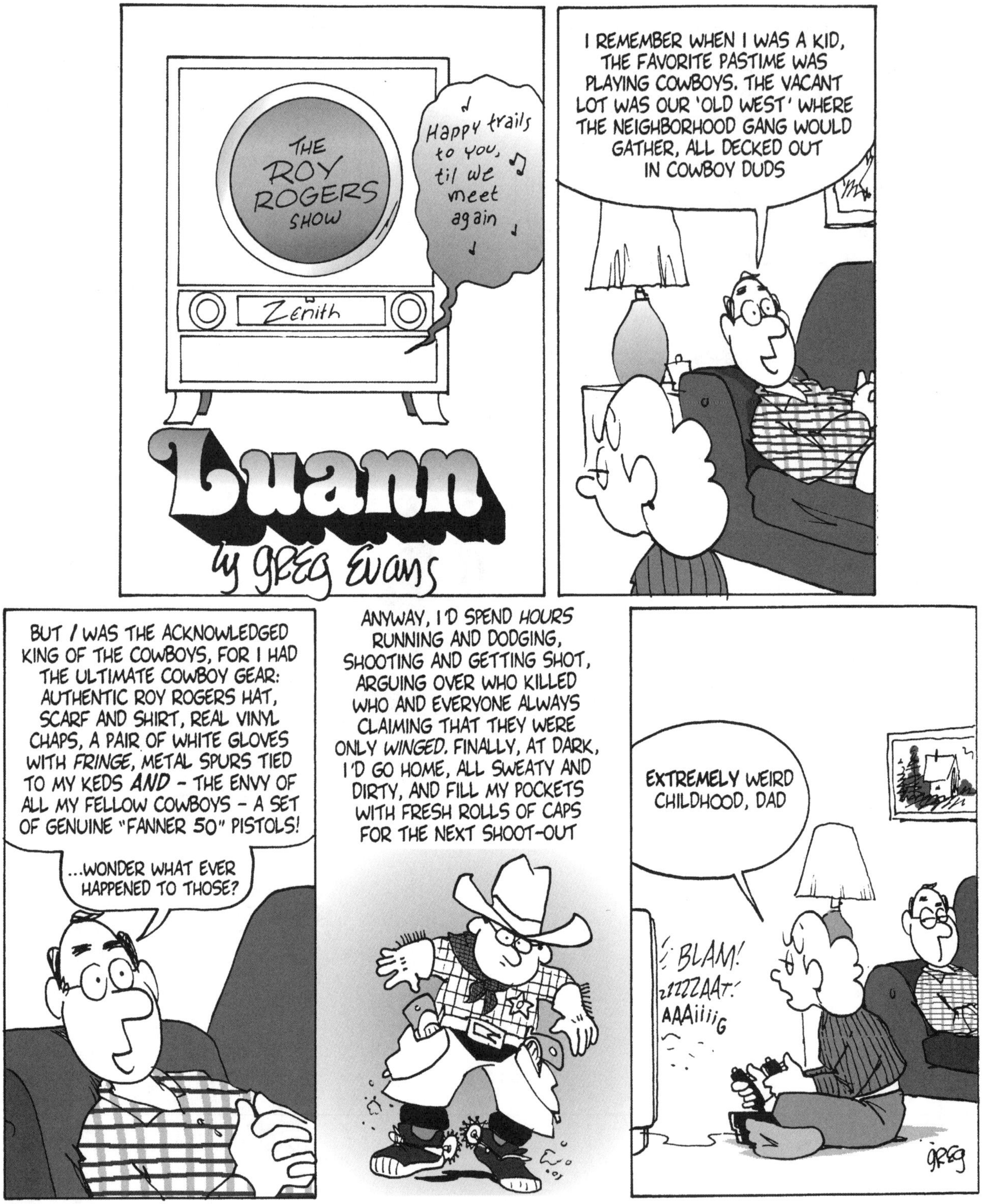
THE ROY ROGERS SHOW
Zenith
Happy trails to you, til we meet again
Luann
by GREG EVANS
I REMEMBER WHEN I WAS A KID, THE FAVORITE PASTIME WAS PLAYING COWBOYS. THE VACANT LOT WAS OUR 'OLD WEST' WHERE THE NEIGHBORHOOD GANG WOULD GATHER, ALL DECKED OUT IN COWBOY DUDS
BUT I WAS THE ACKNOWLEDGED KING OF THE COWBOYS, FOR I HAD THE ULTIMATE COWBOY GEAR: AUTHENTIC ROY ROGERS HAT, SCARF AND SHIRT, REAL VINYL CHAPS, A PAIR OF WHITE GLOVES WITH FRINGE, METAL SPURS TIED TO MY KEDS AND - THE ENVY OF ALL MY FELLOW COWBOYS - A SET OF GENUINE "FANNER 50" PISTOLS!
...WONDER WHAT EVER HAPPENED TO THOSE?
ANYWAY, I'D SPEND HOURS RUNNING AND DODGING, SHOOTING AND GETTING SHOT, ARGUING OVER WHO KILLED WHO AND EVERYONE ALWAYS CLAIMING THAT THEY WERE ONLY WINGED. FINALLY, AT DARK, I'D GO HOME, ALL SWEATY AND DIRTY, AND FILL MY POCKETS WITH FRESH ROLLS OF CAPS FOR THE NEXT SHOOT-OUT
EXTREMELY WEIRD CHILDHOOD, DAD
BLAM!
ZZZZZAAT!
AAAiiiiG
GREG

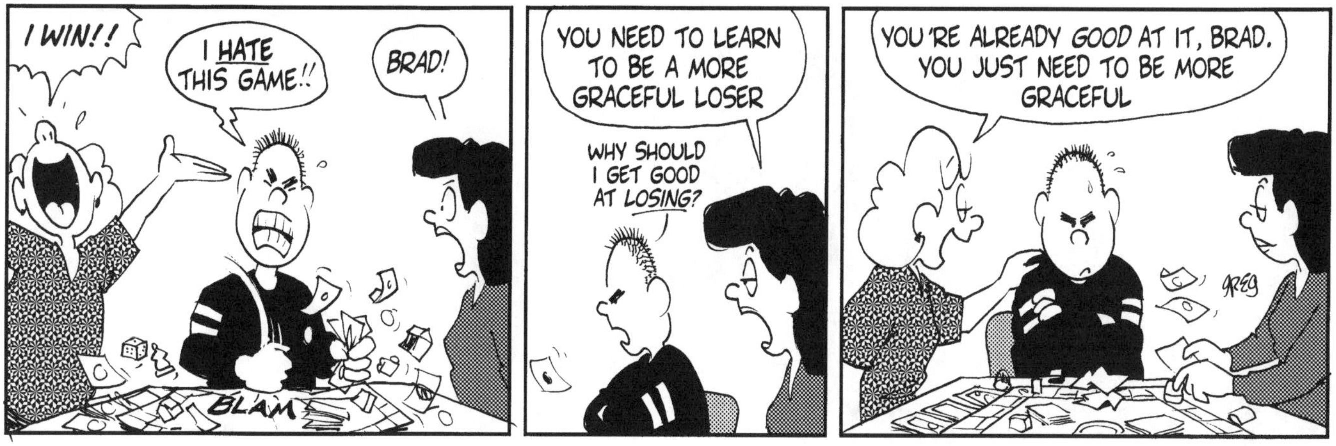
I WIN!!
I HATE THIS GAME!!
BLAM
BRAD!
YOU NEED TO LEARN TO BE A MORE GRACEFUL LOSER
WHY SHOULD I GET GOOD AT LOSING?
YOU'RE ALREADY GOOD AT IT, BRAD. YOU JUST NEED TO BE MORE GRACEFUL
GREG

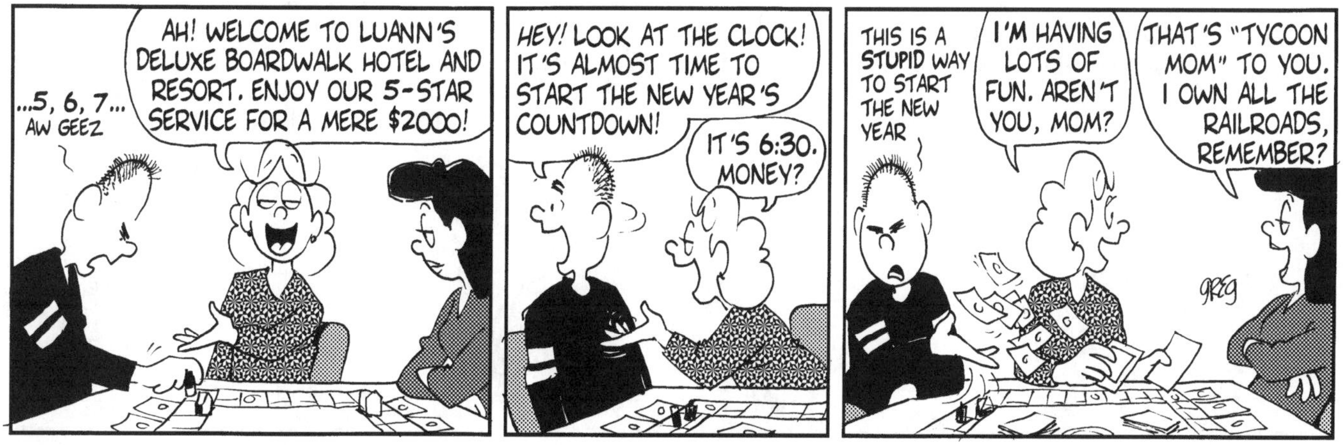
...5, 6, 7... AW GEEZ
AH! WELCOME TO LUANN'S DELUXE BOARDWALK HOTEL AND RESORT. ENJOY OUR 5-STAR SERVICE FOR A MERE $2000!
HEY! LOOK AT THE CLOCK! IT'S ALMOST TIME TO START THE NEW YEAR'S COUNTDOWN!
IT'S 6:30. MONEY?
THIS IS A STUPID WAY TO START THE NEW YEAR
I'M HAVING LOTS OF FUN. AREN'T YOU, MOM?
THAT'S "TYCOON MOM" TO YOU. I OWN ALL THE RAILROADS, REMEMBER?
GREG

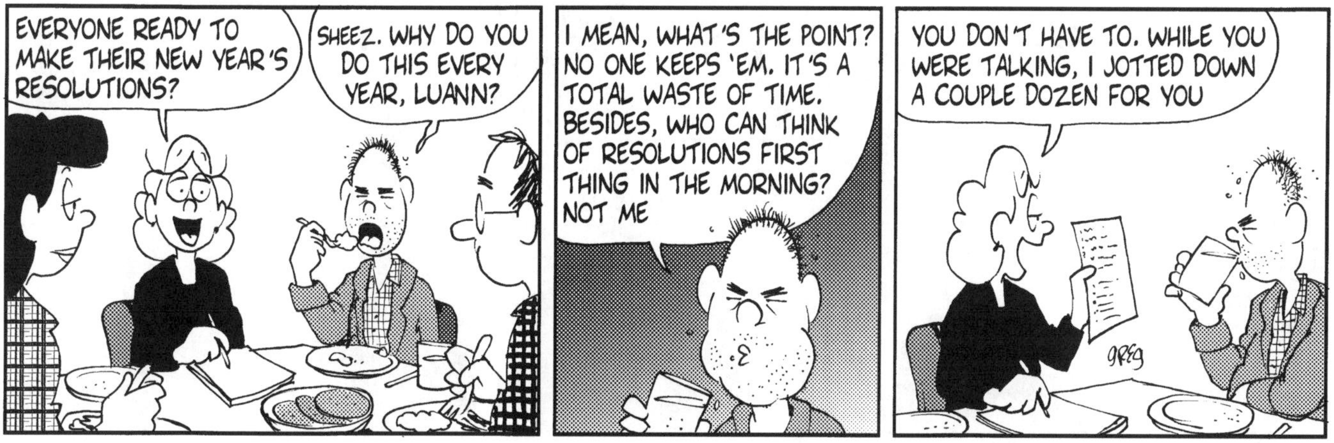
EVERYONE READY TO MAKE THEIR NEW YEAR'S RESOLUTIONS?
SHEEZ. WHY DO YOU DO THIS EVERY YEAR, LUANN?
I MEAN, WHAT'S THE POINT? NO ONE KEEPS 'EM. IT'S A TOTAL WASTE OF TIME. BESIDES, WHO CAN THINK OF RESOLUTIONS FIRST THING IN THE MORNING? NOT ME
YOU DON'T HAVE TO. WHILE YOU WERE TALKING, I JOTTED DOWN A COUPLE DOZEN FOR YOU
GREG

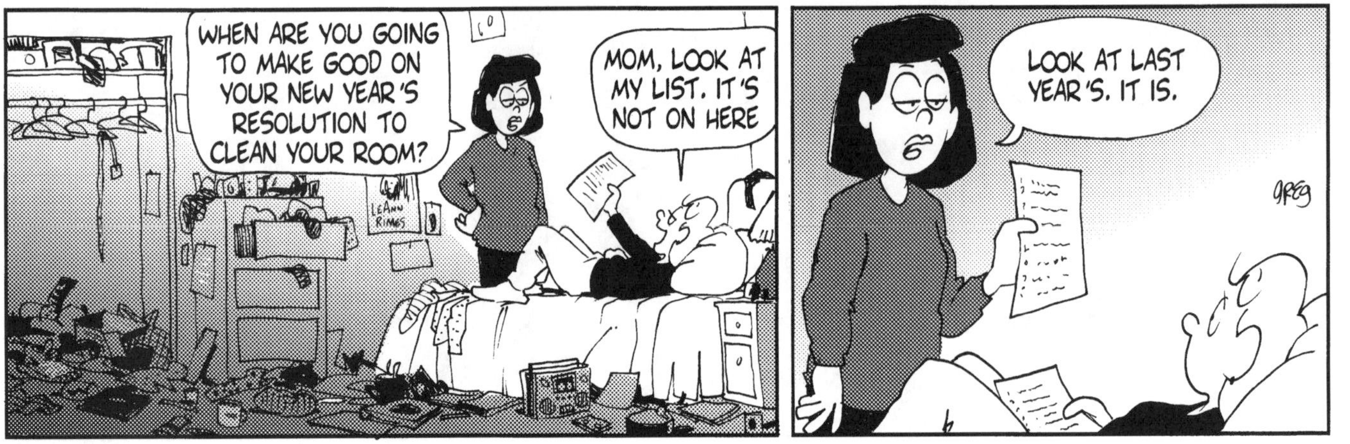
WHEN ARE YOU GOING TO MAKE GOOD ON YOUR NEW YEAR'S RESOLUTION TO CLEAN YOUR ROOM?
MOM, LOOK AT MY LIST. IT'S NOT ON HERE
LOOK AT LAST YEAR'S. IT IS.
GREG

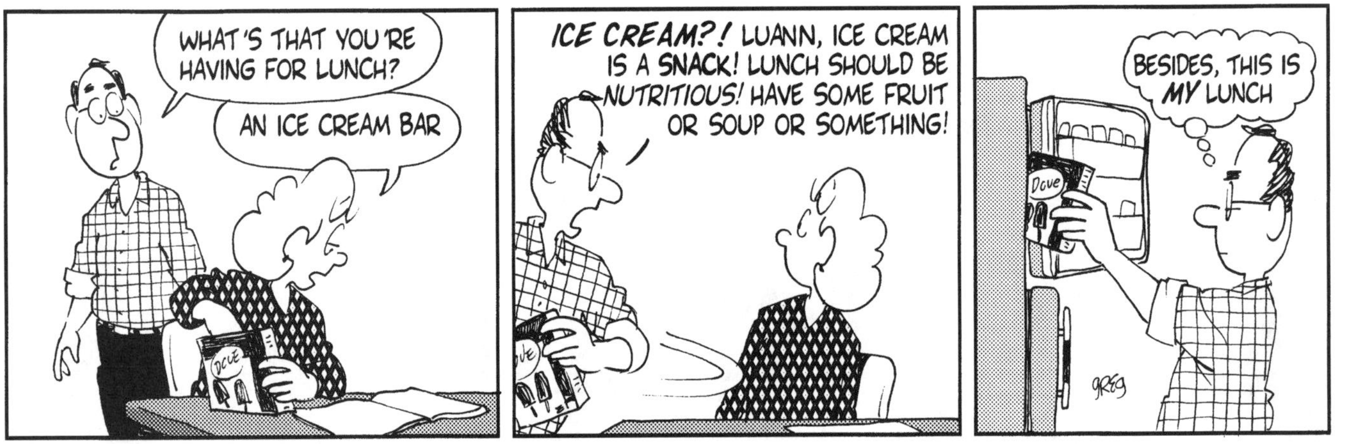
WHAT'S THAT YOU'RE HAVING FOR LUNCH?
AN ICE CREAM BAR
ICE CREAM?! LUANN, ICE CREAM IS A SNACK! LUNCH SHOULD BE NUTRITIOUS! HAVE SOME FRUIT OR SOUP OR SOMETHING!
BESIDES, THIS IS MY LUNCH
DOVE
GREG

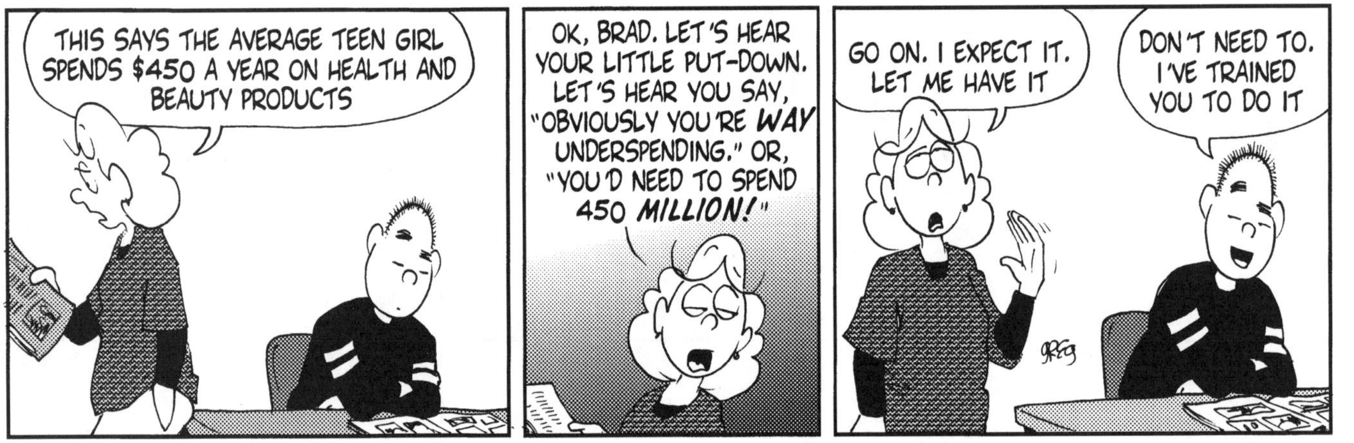
THIS SAYS THE AVERAGE TEEN GIRL SPENDS $450 A YEAR ON HEALTH AND BEAUTY PRODUCTS
OK, BRAD. LET'S HEAR YOUR LITTLE PUT-DOWN. LET'S HEAR YOU SAY, "OBVIOUSLY YOU'RE WAY UNDERSPENDING." OR, "YOU'D NEED TO SPEND 450 MILLION!"
GO ON. I EXPECT IT. LET ME HAVE IT
DON'T NEED TO. I'VE TRAINED YOU TO DO IT
GREG

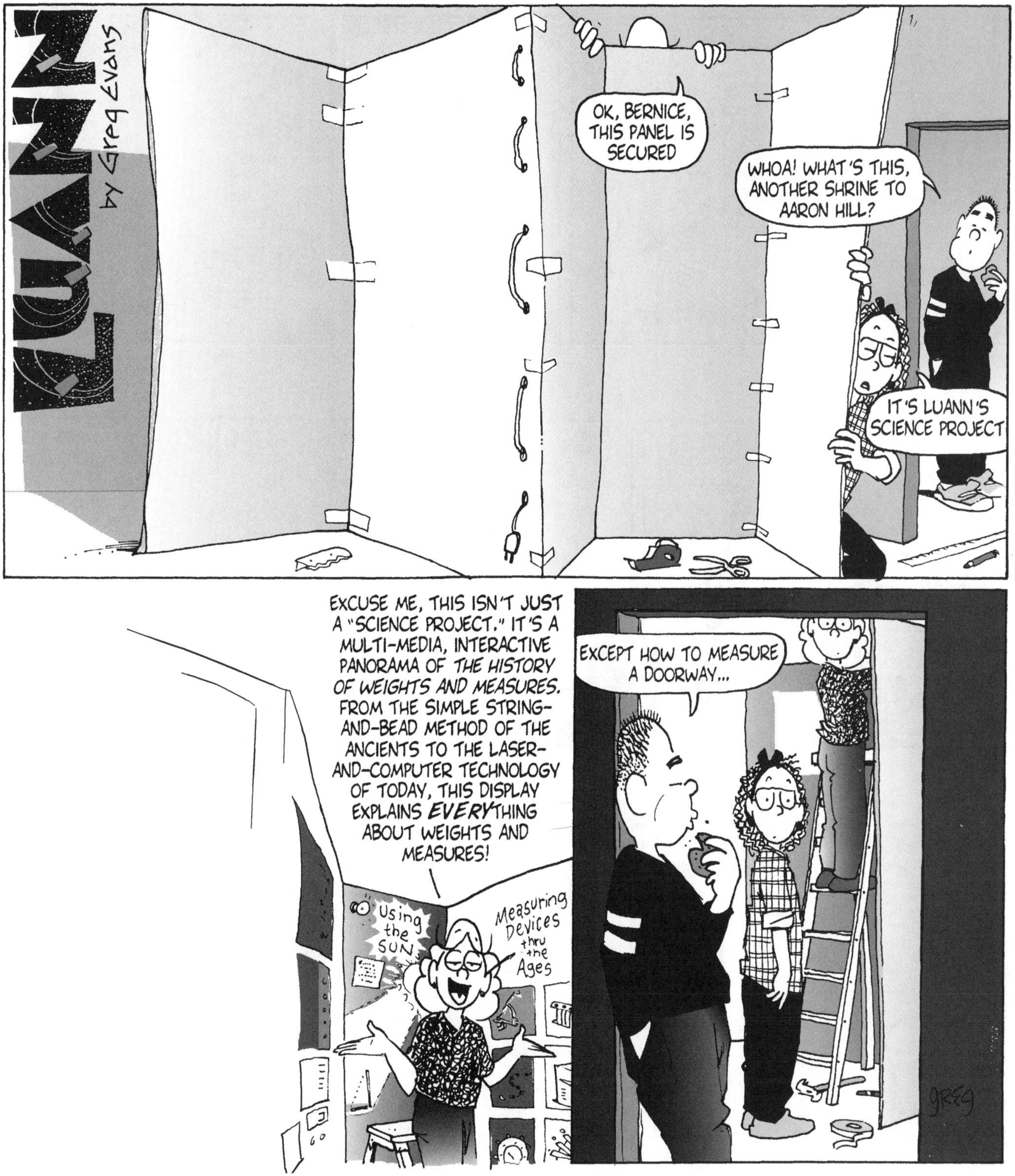
LUANN
by Greg Evans
OK, BERNICE, THIS PANEL IS SECURED
WHOA! WHAT'S THIS, ANOTHER SHRINE TO AARON HILL?
IT'S LUANN'S SCIENCE PROJECT
EXCUSE ME, THIS ISN'T JUST A "SCIENCE PROJECT." IT'S A MULTI-MEDIA, INTERACTIVE PANORAMA OF *THE HISTORY OF WEIGHTS AND MEASURES.* FROM THE SIMPLE STRING-AND-BEAD METHOD OF THE ANCIENTS TO THE LASER-AND-COMPUTER TECHNOLOGY OF TODAY, THIS DISPLAY EXPLAINS *EVERY*THING ABOUT WEIGHTS AND MEASURES!
Using the SUN
Measuring Devices thru the Ages
EXCEPT HOW TO MEASURE A DOORWAY...
GREG

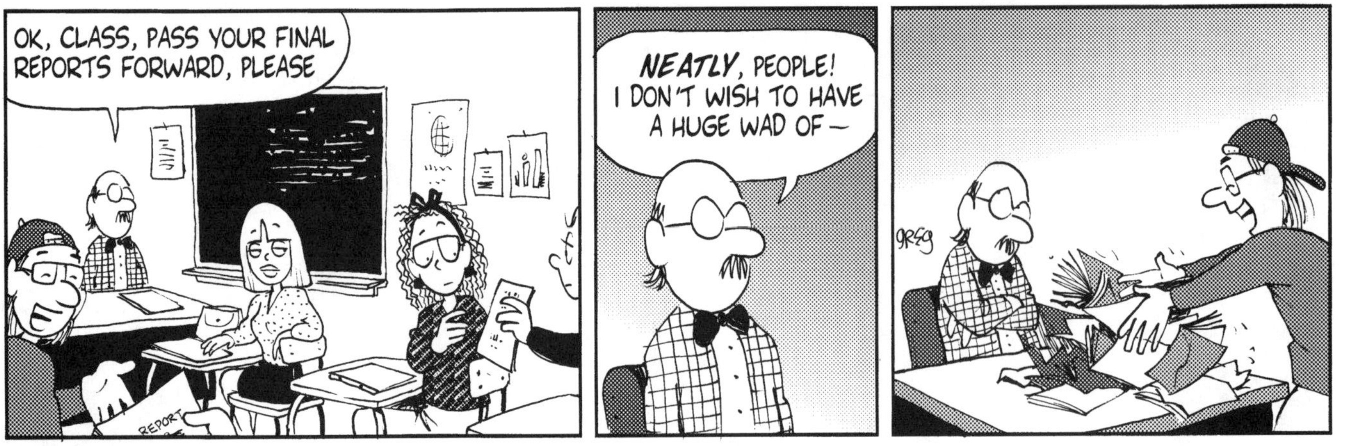
OK, CLASS, PASS YOUR FINAL REPORTS FORWARD, PLEASE
REPORT
NEATLY, PEOPLE! I DON'T WISH TO HAVE A HUGE WAD OF—

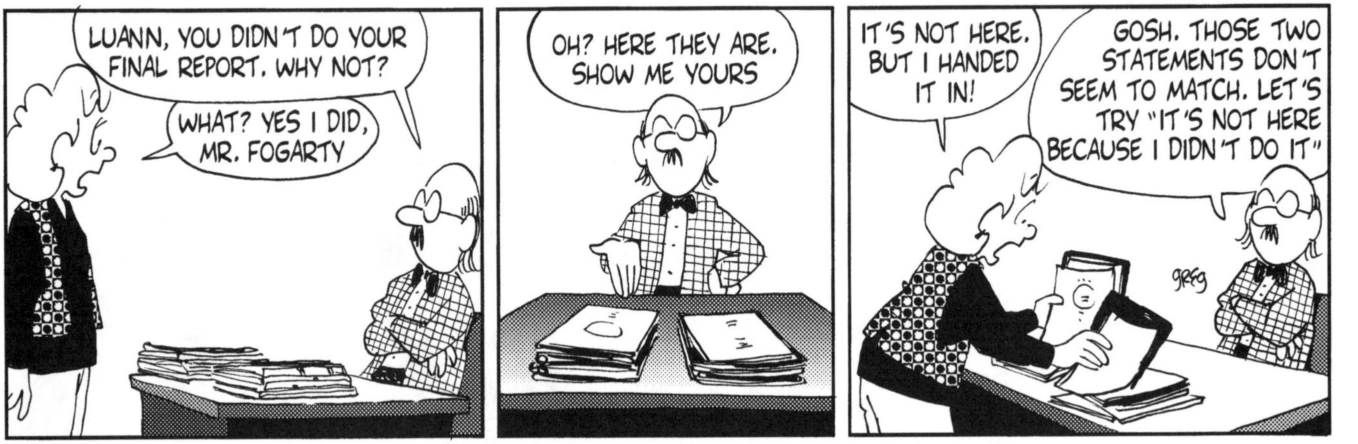
LUANN, YOU DIDN'T DO YOUR FINAL REPORT. WHY NOT?
WHAT? YES I DID, MR. FOGARTY
OH? HERE THEY ARE. SHOW ME YOURS
IT'S NOT HERE. BUT I HANDED IT IN!
GOSH. THOSE TWO STATEMENTS DON'T SEEM TO MATCH. LET'S TRY "IT'S NOT HERE BECAUSE I DIDN'T DO IT"

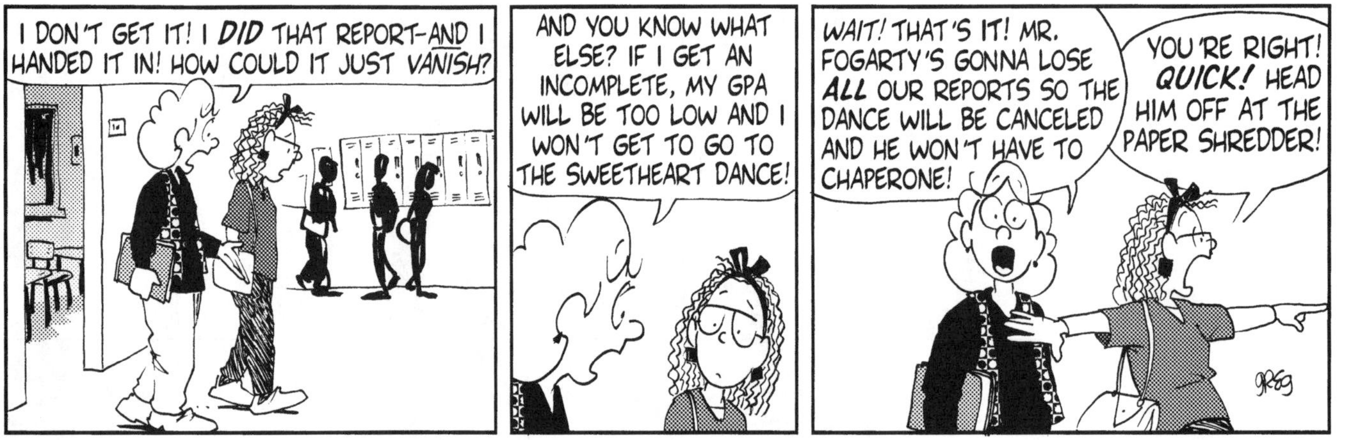
I DON'T GET IT! I *DID* THAT REPORT—AND I HANDED IT IN! HOW COULD IT JUST VANISH?
AND YOU KNOW WHAT ELSE? IF I GET AN INCOMPLETE, MY GPA WILL BE TOO LOW AND I WON'T GET TO GO TO THE SWEETHEART DANCE!
WAIT! THAT'S IT! MR. FOGARTY'S GONNA LOSE ***ALL*** OUR REPORTS SO THE DANCE WILL BE CANCELED AND HE WON'T HAVE TO CHAPERONE!
YOU'RE RIGHT! ***QUICK!*** HEAD HIM OFF AT THE PAPER SHREDDER!

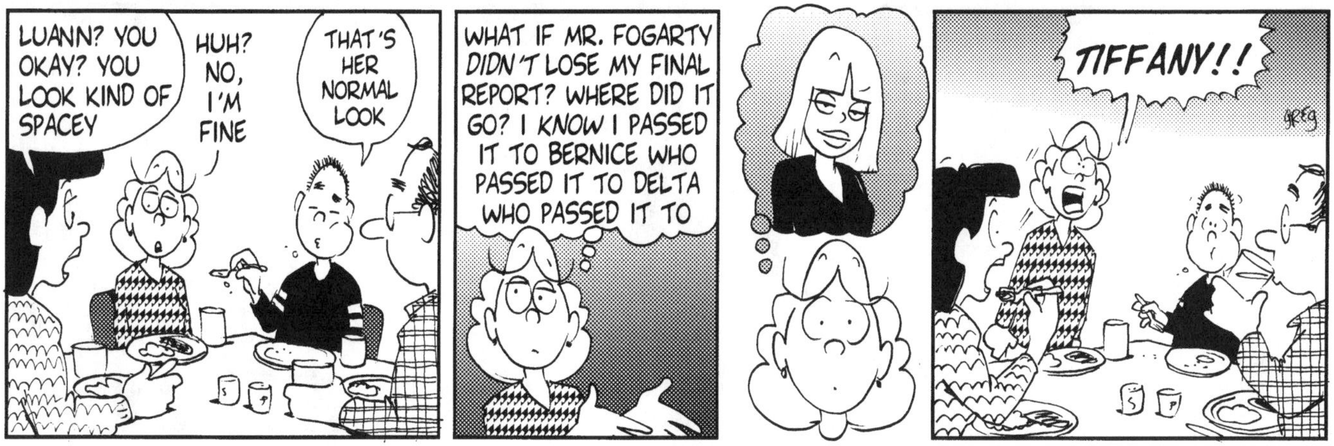
LUANN? YOU OKAY? YOU LOOK KIND OF SPACEY
HUH? NO, I'M FINE
THAT'S HER NORMAL LOOK
WHAT IF MR. FOGARTY *DIDN'T* LOSE MY FINAL REPORT? WHERE DID IT GO? I KNOW I PASSED IT TO BERNICE WHO PASSED IT TO DELTA WHO PASSED IT TO
TIFFANY!!
GREG

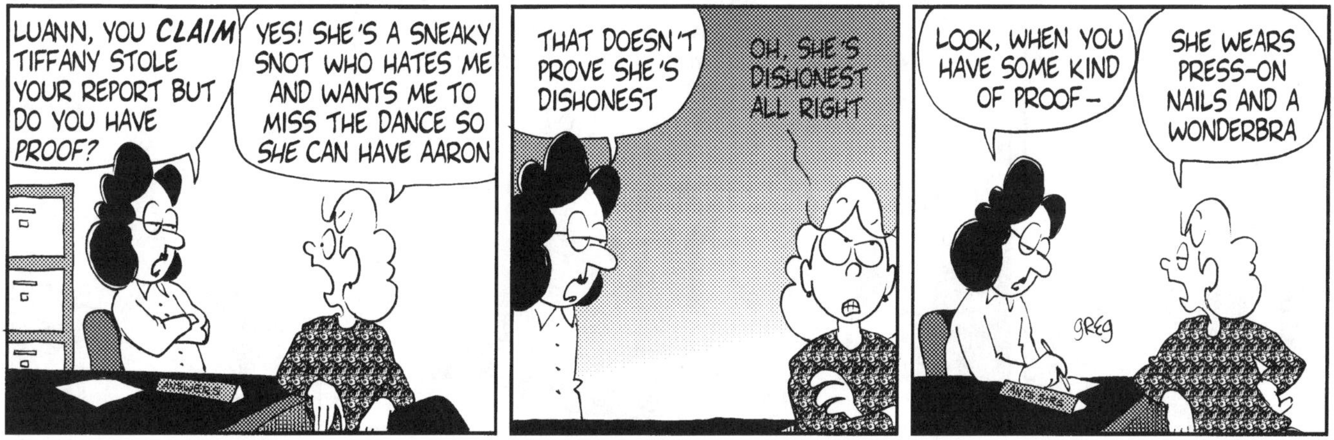
LUANN, YOU **CLAIM** TIFFANY STOLE YOUR REPORT BUT DO YOU HAVE *PROOF?*
YES! SHE'S A SNEAKY SNOT WHO HATES ME AND WANTS ME TO MISS THE DANCE SO *SHE* CAN HAVE AARON
ANSWERS
THAT DOESN'T PROVE SHE'S DISHONEST
OH, SHE'S DISHONEST ALL RIGHT
LOOK, WHEN YOU HAVE SOME KIND OF PROOF–
SHE WEARS PRESS-ON NAILS AND A WONDERBRA
GREG

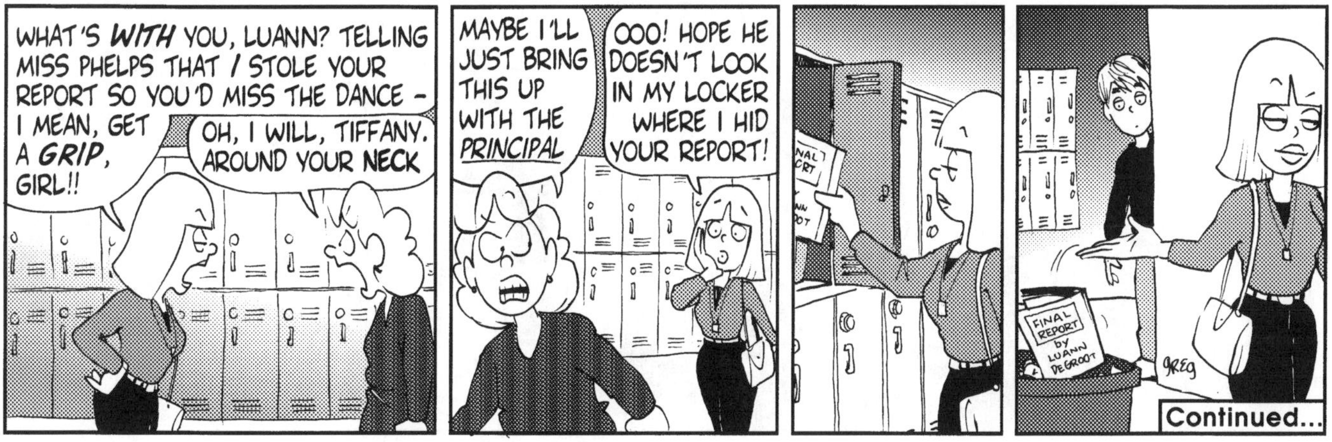
WHAT'S **WITH** YOU, LUANN? TELLING MISS PHELPS THAT *I* STOLE YOUR REPORT SO YOU'D MISS THE DANCE – I MEAN, GET A **GRIP**, GIRL!!
OH, I WILL, TIFFANY. AROUND YOUR **NECK**
MAYBE I'LL JUST BRING THIS UP WITH THE PRINCIPAL
OOO! HOPE HE DOESN'T LOOK IN MY LOCKER WHERE I HID YOUR REPORT!
FINAL REPORT by LUANN DEGROOT
GREG
Continued...

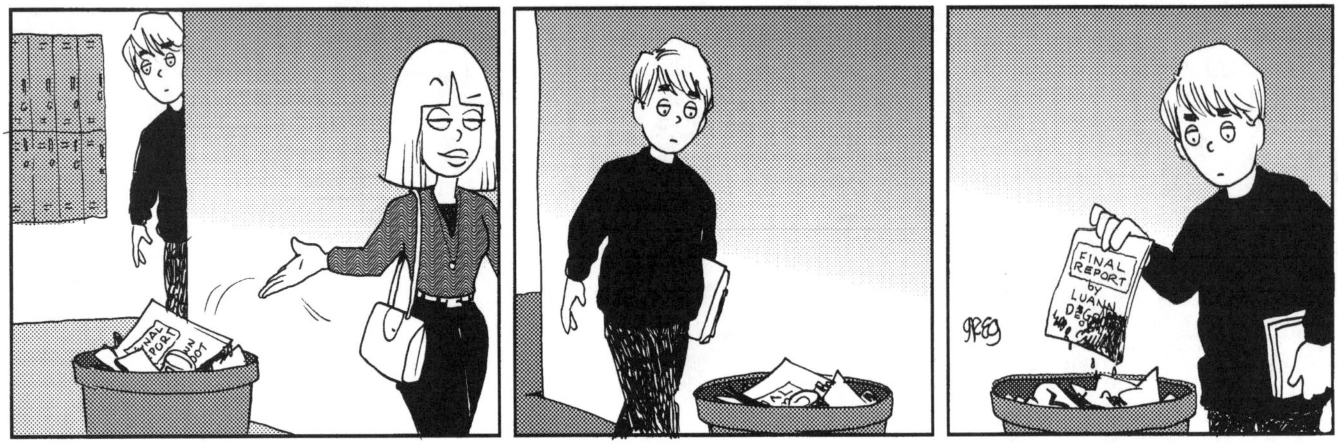
FINAL REPORT
by
LUANN

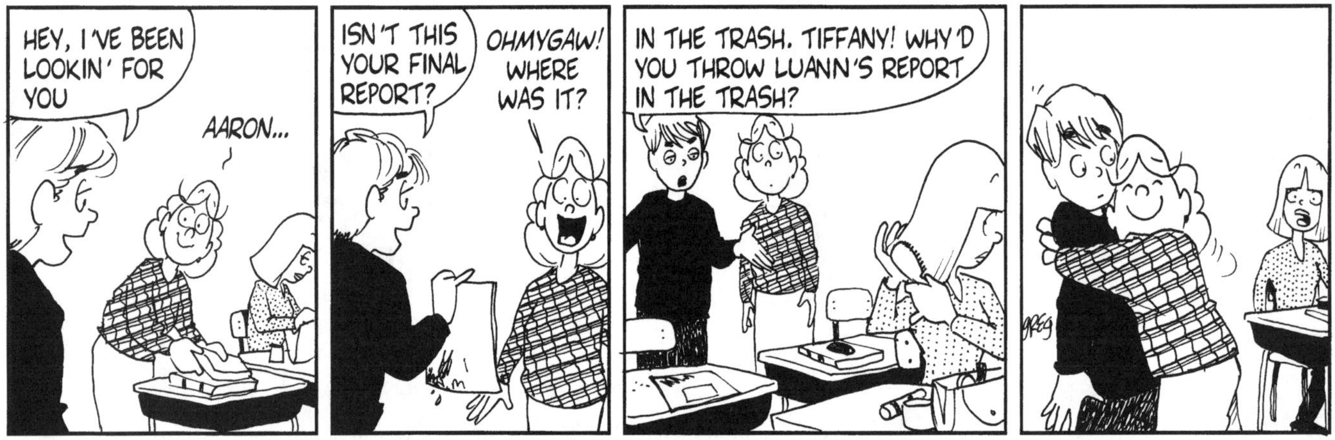
HEY, I'VE BEEN LOOKIN' FOR YOU
AARON...
ISN'T THIS YOUR FINAL REPORT?
OHMYGAW! WHERE WAS IT?
IN THE TRASH. TIFFANY! WHY'D YOU THROW LUANN'S REPORT IN THE TRASH?

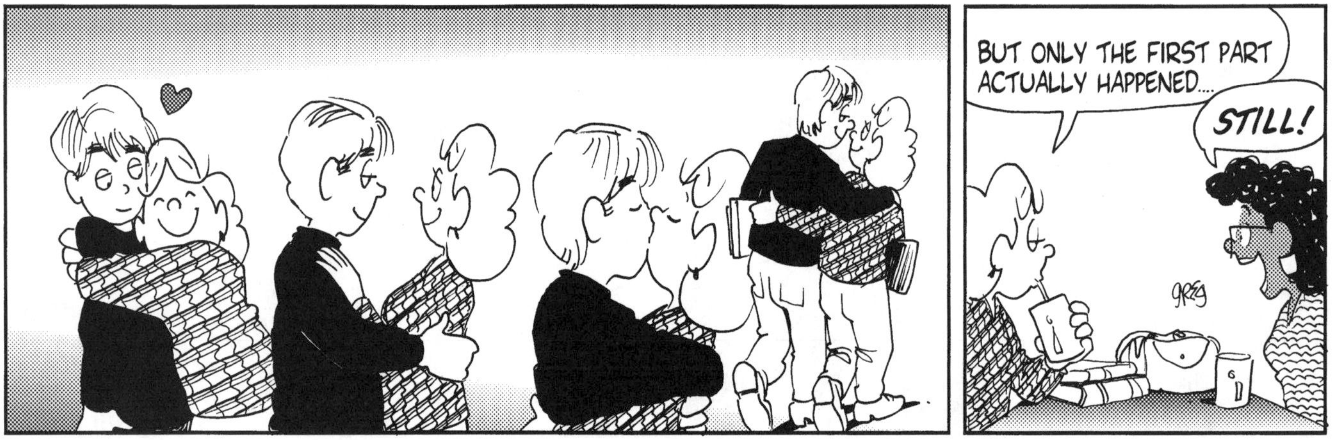
BUT ONLY THE FIRST PART ACTUALLY HAPPENED....
STILL!

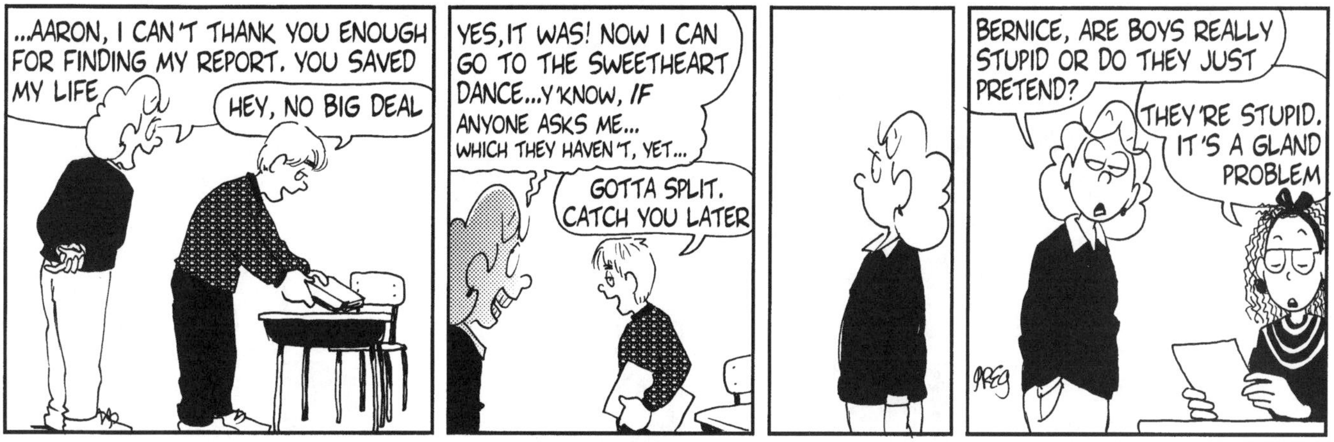
...AARON, I CAN'T THANK YOU ENOUGH FOR FINDING MY REPORT. YOU SAVED MY LIFE
HEY, NO BIG DEAL
YES, IT WAS! NOW I CAN GO TO THE SWEETHEART DANCE...Y'KNOW, *IF* ANYONE ASKS ME... WHICH THEY HAVEN'T, YET...
GOTTA SPLIT. CATCH YOU LATER
BERNICE, ARE BOYS REALLY STUPID OR DO THEY JUST PRETEND?
THEY'RE STUPID. IT'S A GLAND PROBLEM

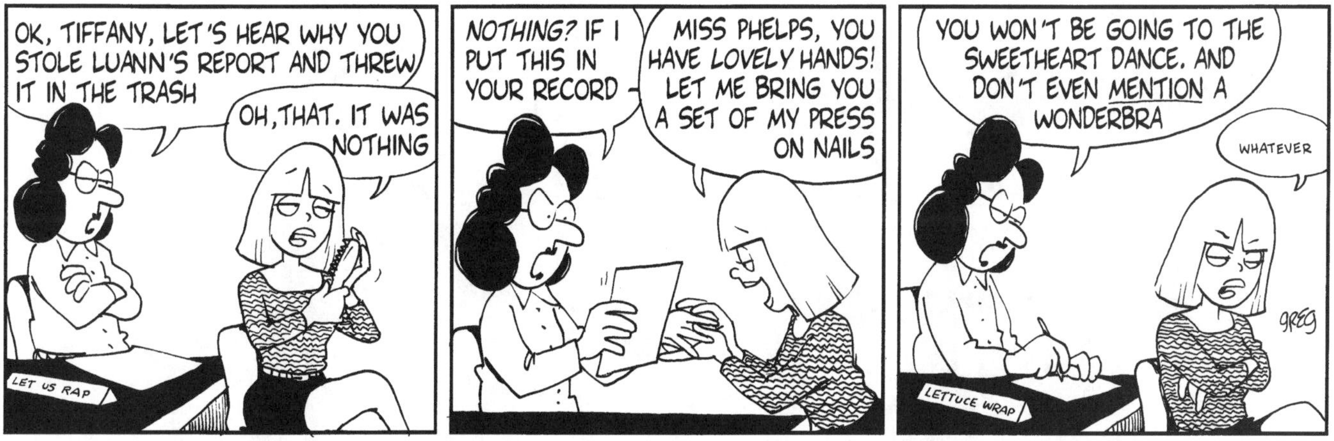
OK, TIFFANY, LET'S HEAR WHY YOU STOLE LUANN'S REPORT AND THREW IT IN THE TRASH
OH, THAT. IT WAS NOTHING
LET US RAP
NOTHING? IF I PUT THIS IN YOUR RECORD -
MISS PHELPS, YOU HAVE *LOVELY* HANDS! LET ME BRING YOU A SET OF MY PRESS ON NAILS
YOU WON'T BE GOING TO THE SWEETHEART DANCE. AND DON'T EVEN MENTION A WONDERBRA
WHATEVER
LETTUCE WRAP

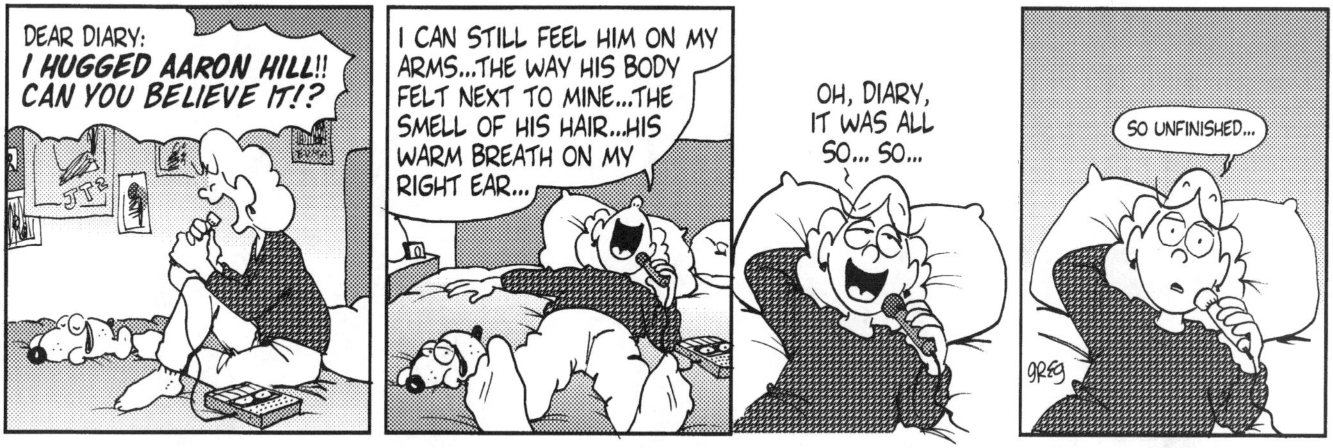
DEAR DIARY:
I HUGGED AARON HILL!! CAN YOU BELIEVE IT!?
I CAN STILL FEEL HIM ON MY ARMS...THE WAY HIS BODY FELT NEXT TO MINE...THE SMELL OF HIS HAIR...HIS WARM BREATH ON MY RIGHT EAR...
OH, DIARY, IT WAS ALL SO... SO...
SO UNFINISHED...

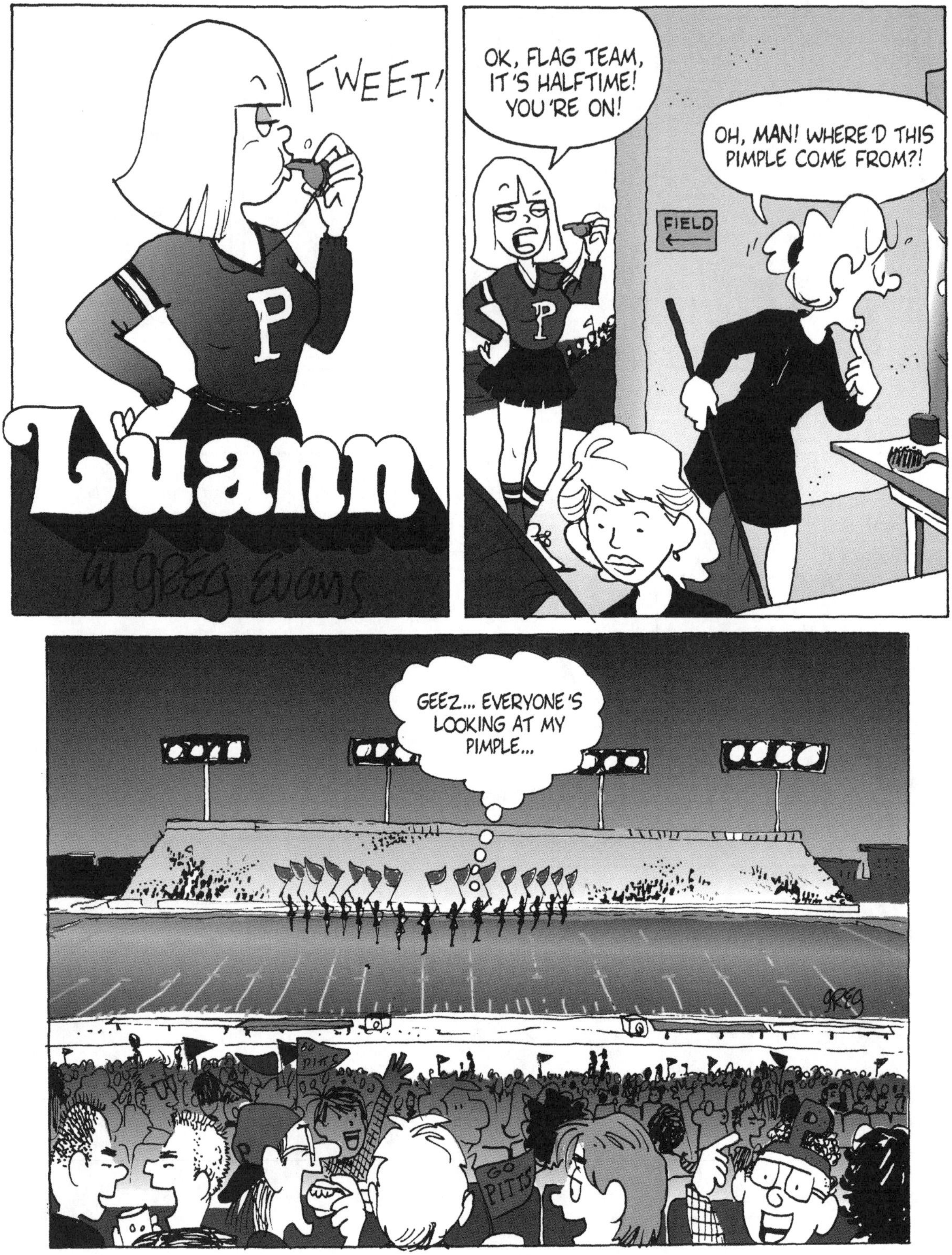

Luann
by Greg Evans
FWEET!
OK, FLAG TEAM, IT'S HALFTIME! YOU'RE ON!
FIELD
OH, MAN! WHERE'D THIS PIMPLE COME FROM?!
GEEZ... EVERYONE'S LOOKING AT MY PIMPLE...
GREG

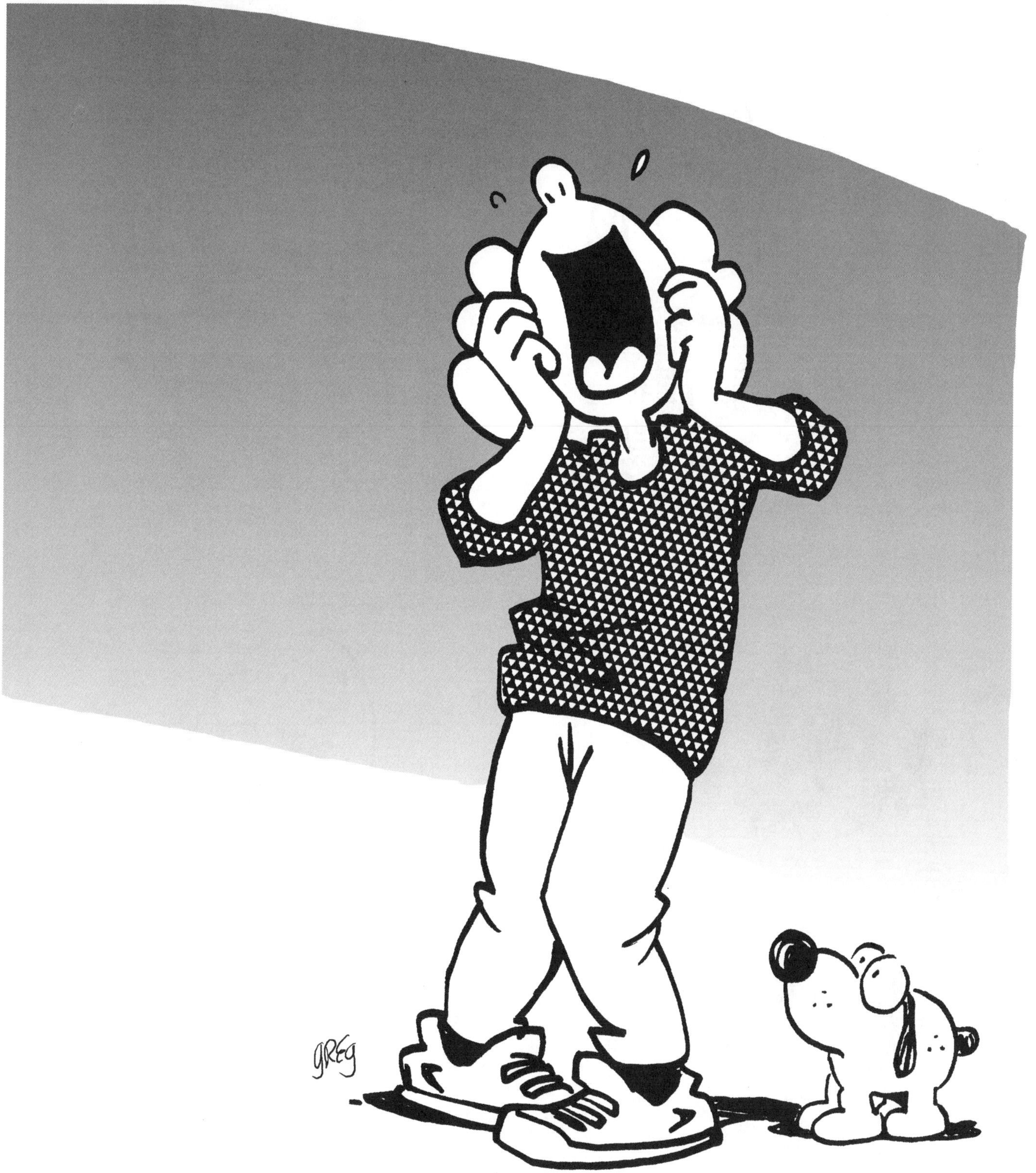
gREg

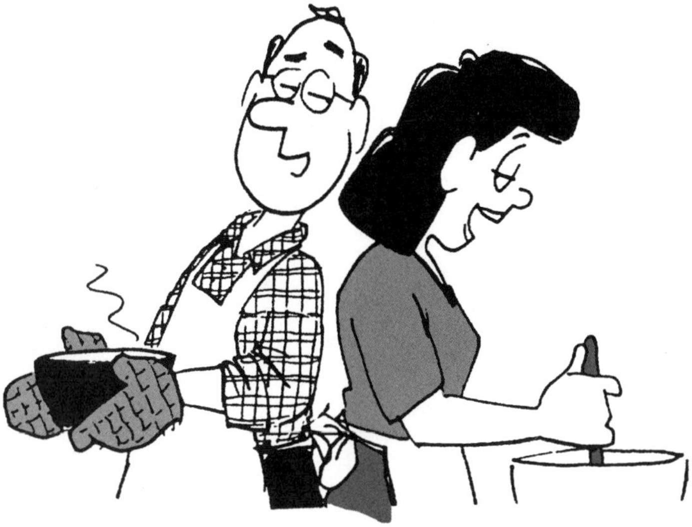

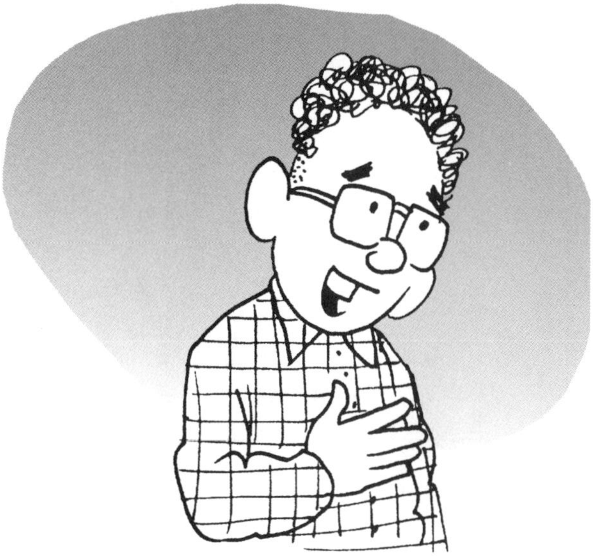

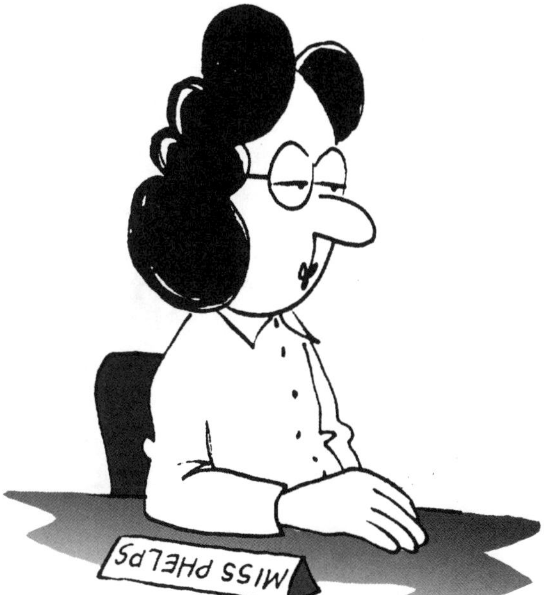
MISS PHELPS

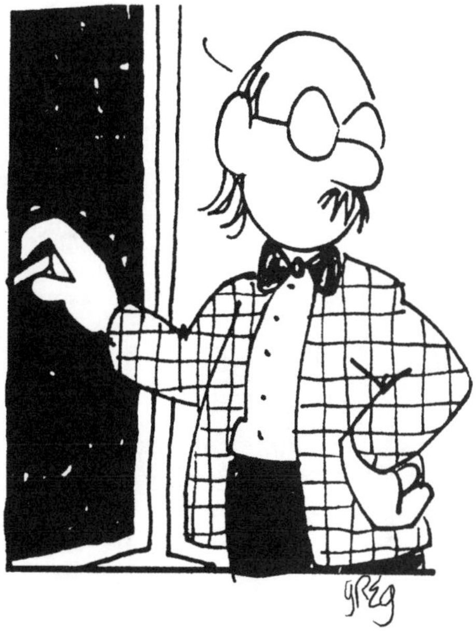